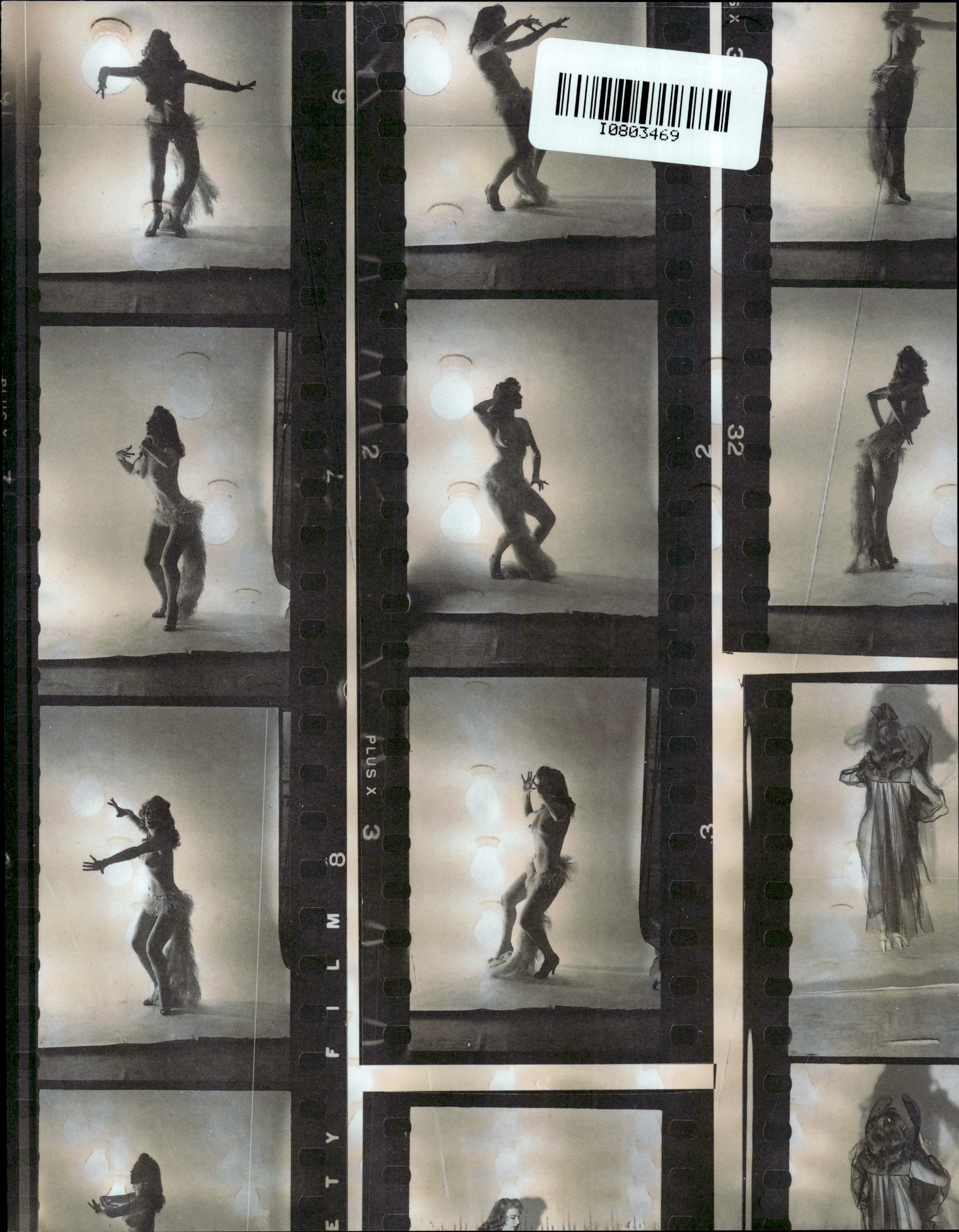

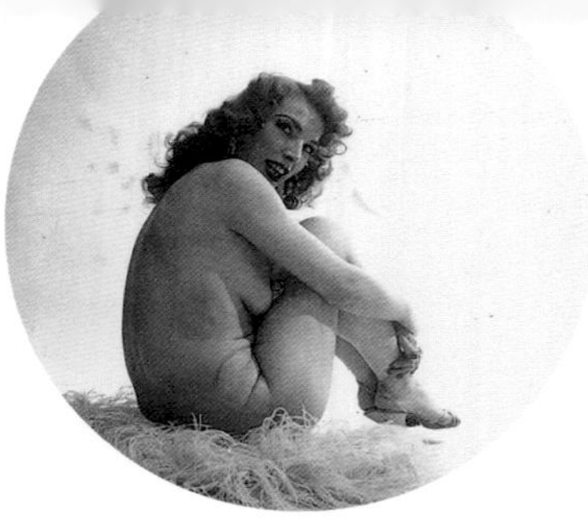

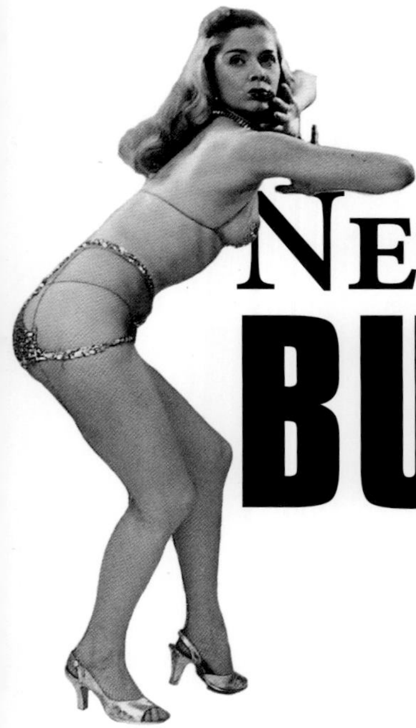

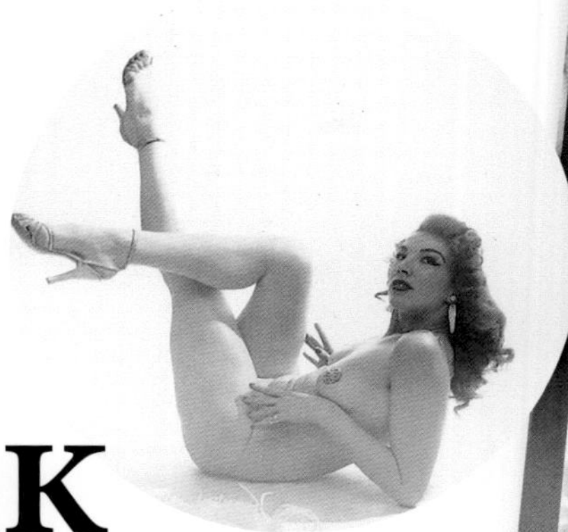

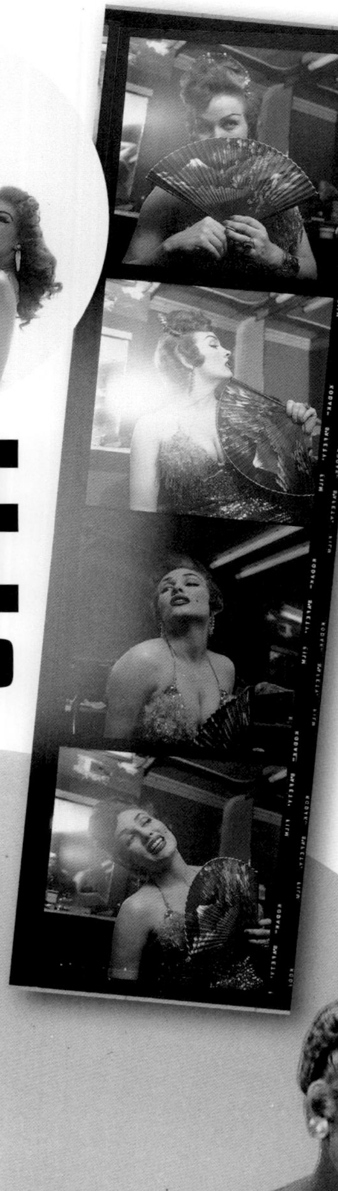

New York BURLESQUE

Photographs By **ROY KEMP**

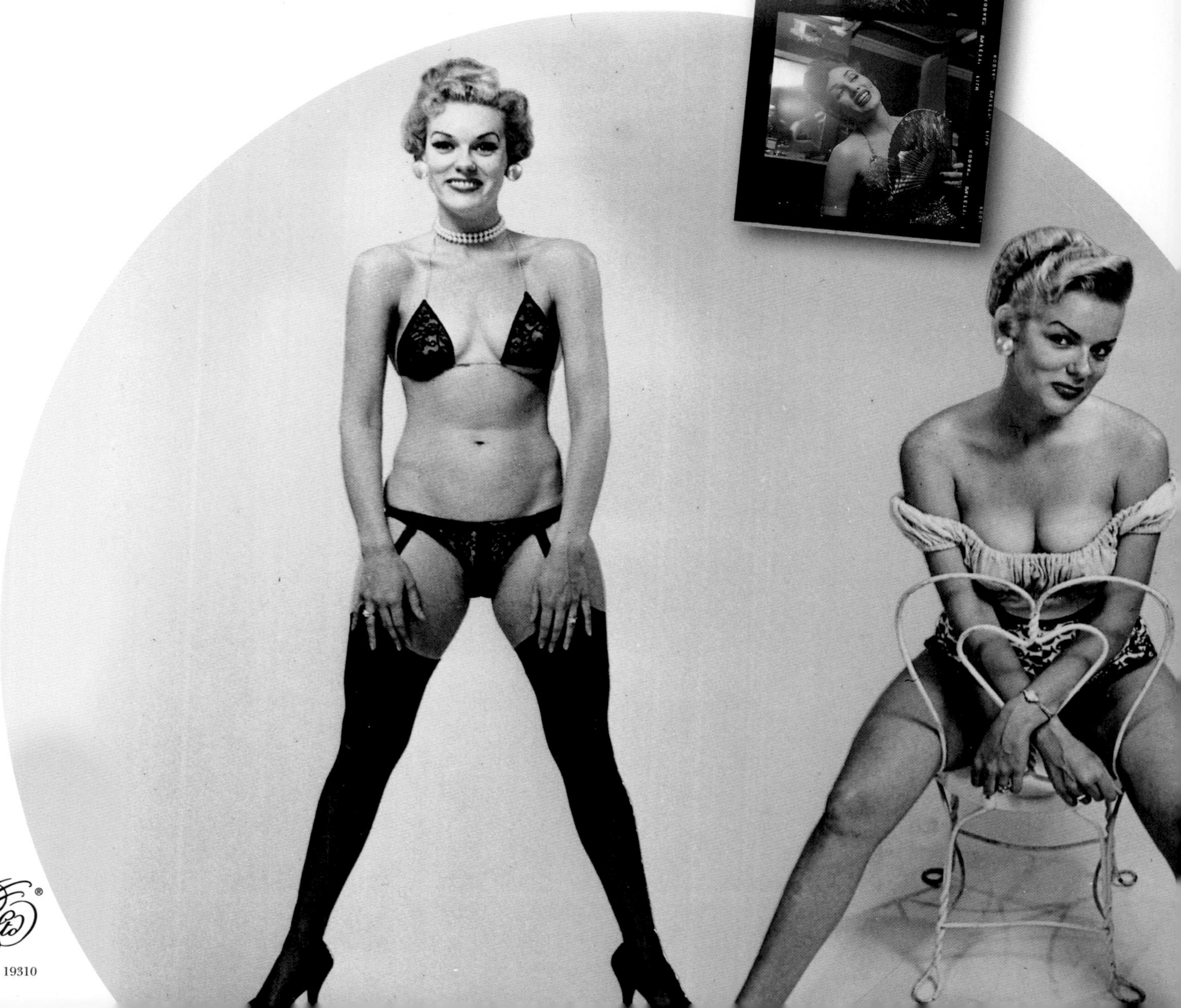

Schiffer Publishing Ltd

80 Lower Valley Road • Atglen, PA 19310

For Susan Kemp, 1950-2013

Other Schiffer Books on Related Subjects:
Burlesque: Exotic Dancers of the 50s & 60s, $24.99
ISBN: 978-0-7643-3667-6
The Queens of Burlesque: Vintage Photographs from the 1940s and 1950s, $19.99
ISBN: 978-0-7643-0449-1
Striptease Artists of the 1950s, $24.95
ISBN: 978-0-7643-2800-8

Library of Congress Control Number: 2014947254

Designed by John P. Cheek
Cover design by Danielle D. Farmer
Type set in LamplighterScript/Minion Pro

ISBN: 978-0-7643-4687-3
Printed in China

Published by Schiffer Publishing, Ltd.
4880 Lower Valley Road
Atglen, PA 19310
Phone: (610) 593-1777; Fax: (610) 593-2002
E-mail: Info@schifferbooks.com

For our complete selection of fine books on this and related subjects, please visit our website at www.schifferbooks.com. You may also write for a free catalog.

This book may be purchased from the publisher. Please try your bookstore first.

We are always looking for people to write books on new and related subjects. If you have an idea for a book, please contact us at proposals@ schifferbooks.com.

Schiffer Publishing's titles are available at special discounts for bulk purchases for sales promotions or premiums. Special editions, including personalized covers, corporate imprints, and excerpts can be created in large quantities for special needs. For more information, contact the publisher.

Contents

About the photographer

Franklin Roy Kemp was a photojournalist who loved black and white photography. He was born in Toronto, Canada, and attended the University of Toronto. Before WWII, he was a staff photographer at the *Toronto Star*, where he met his future wife, Mary Hyrchenuk, a staff illustrator. Seeing that the *Star* paid more for work purchased from the United States, the couple decided to move to New York City and work as freelancers. During the war, Kemp served as a photographer for the Royal Canadian Navy overseas, while Mary stayed in New York illustrating books. After the war, he continued to freelance and, in the 1960s, became associated with Bernsen's International Press Service (BIPS), which had offices on five continents. In New York, Kemp would find or develop stories (often human interest stories), photograph and write them up, do the darkroom work, and send them to the main office in Holland for international sale and distribution.

Due to international demand for stories about the United States and American products, Kemp became interested in America's image abroad. At the time of his death in 1978, he was preparing a grant proposal to submit to the State Department that showed images that negatively portrayed the U.S. in the international news. His hope was to counteract this trend by garnering support to produce positive news images and stories. He died on October 7, 1978, of pancreatic cancer.

Other facts about Roy Kemp:

- He was a boxer in college.
- He played the violin.
- His sister was the wife of H. Northrop Frye, the famous Canadian literary critic.
- His father founded the Canadian Society for the Deaf.
- His mother was an advocate for birth control in Canada.
- His daughter became a public advocacy lawyer in New York City.
- His son was a social worker with Child Protective Services in New York City.

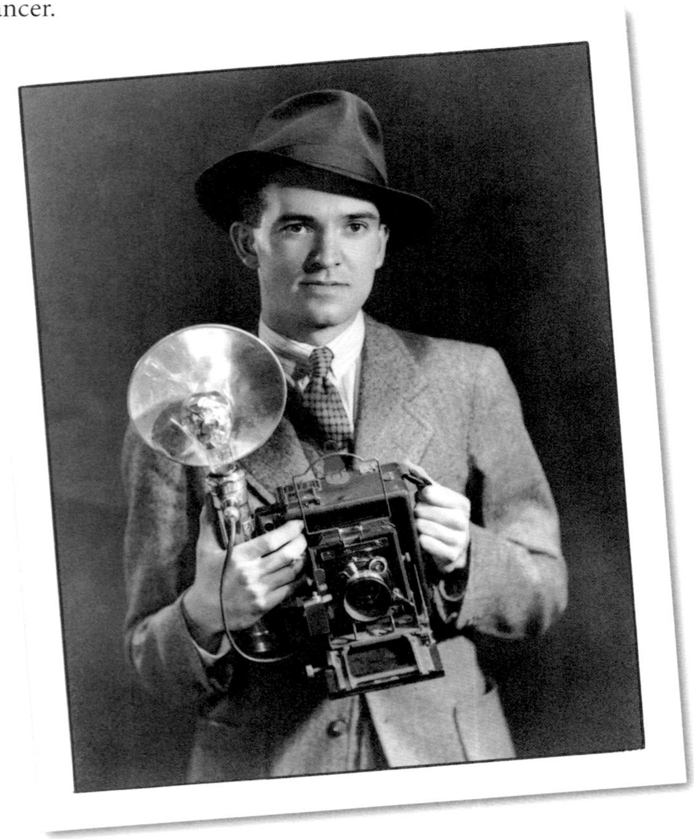

Foreword

I never met F. Roy Kemp, my maternal grandfather. He died of cancer two weeks before my parents married, so I have only known him through his photography. Over the years, my mother would occasionally show us some of the large prints of his work we had stored in our basement covering Operation Sail (the 1976 international boating display that occurred in New York for the U.S. bicentennial) or headshots he took of my mother while she was pursuing an acting career in her 20s. But, I got to really know his work when, as an adult with a library science degree and part-time cataloguing job, my mother convinced me to begin cataloguing the entire twenty-box collection of photographic prints and negatives that made up his life's work. In addition to thousands of prints of my mother and her brother, news stories, portraits of New Yorkers in the 1960s, Manhattan street scenes, children playing in Central Park, and weird inventions my grandfather was writing up for magazines, I discovered the gritty photographs of the New York burlesque scene of the 1950s that are contained in this book.

What first struck me about this portion of his work was how he brought a photojournalist's eye to the subject; he catches the seedy backstage areas of clubs, the dancers' disorganized vanities strewn with half-used lipstick, as well as the blank, awkward looks of club-going couples with pasties twirling in their peripheral vision. Unlike the soft-focus, artfully staged pin-up images that we associate with this genre, my grandfather's work offers a partial ethnography of the scene. Despite many being posed, his images incorporate context and, when viewed in sequence, they also provide an abridged, yet rich, narrative.

What I enjoy so much about these photographs is that they capture moments that break through the audacious, tenacious façade of burlesque culture. Genuine levity, mirth, and sweetness shine through on many of the dancers' faces.

At the same time, the awkward engineering that facilitates a performance of sexiness is also visible. For example, see the images in Carmela's chapter, where, against a completely white background, the leg of a wheeled lamp that is holding down the backdrop is visible in every single shot. Or Betty Howard's pin-ups that are staged in what is obviously someone's living room. The viewer can't jump entirely into the fantasy of the performance with these indicators of the dancer's real life in the way. My grandfather's intention in framing images in this way is entirely unclear, even to someone who has seen virtually all his work on a number of topics. Was context explicitly important to him, or was he simply out of his element with burlesque? His files include burlesque photographs taken by other professional photographers, so he was certainly aware of the dominant aesthetic.

This collection is also valuable, as is all documentation of historical burlesque, because it shows how much has changed for women in the entertainment business, in terms of how they are expected to look. Seeing natural figures on stage is gratifying for contemporary women. Going through these pictures, I was filled with nostalgia for an era before my time when a woman with a large bust was also expected to have thick legs and a belly. Though these photographs have their share of demure smiles and come-hither looks, it's also pleasing to see the dancers use a wide emotional vocabulary in their expressions as they pose and dance. Intensity and power went along with the kitten and the kitsch.

As I've gone through these prints and come to know each dancer, I've developed some favorites, many of whom I appreciate for their inventive style. For instance, what is up with Bubbles Darlene's big, fringed hat? Same with Jessica Rogers—are those plastic, breast-shaped, bird cages she has attached to her chest? Would Irma the Body be able to make it as a dancer these days? And Arlene Stevens' Pearl Dance looks simply mesmerizing as a photo montage—I wish I could have seen it in real life.

Tana Louise knocks your socks off with her Betty Page look-alike hairdo and futuristic leather outfit (with a strange little beret with a pompom on top!). Or Paula Uhsan, whose entire shtick is that she plays the violin—and boy it is weird when she's posing with it in a suggestive manner. And in the final chapter, the Fabulous Zorita seems like a tragic figure. We see photos of her looking young and beautiful, followed by some that look like they were taken a few years later, in which she looks older, more tired, performing a tawdry act where she simulates sex with the shadow of a man. I wonder what personal triumphs and failures dotted the path leading to her transformation.

In the chapters ahead, I have included a reproduction of original biographic material, written by my grandfather, as an introduction to each dancer. Where no introduction remains that he may have written, I've left the space blank. All montages seen in the book were created by my grandfather, and I've included contact sheets for many of the dancers, rather than single images, to create a similar effect of movement and dance as your eye scans the page. I hope you enjoy!

Katherine Sydenham
December 2013

Alice Paul

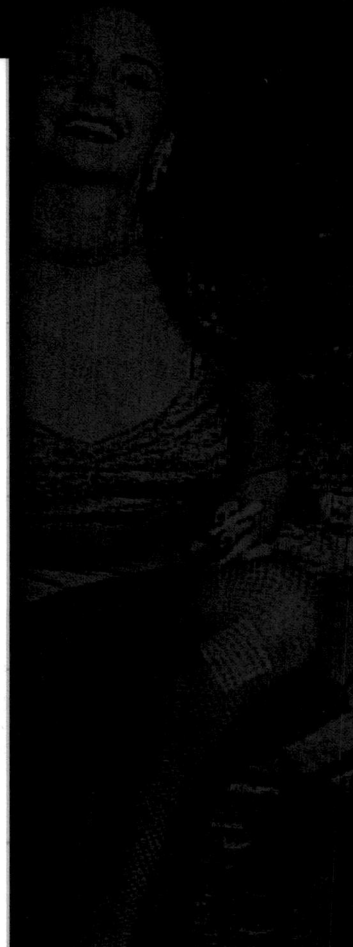

ALICE PAUL

Twenty-two-year-old Alice Paul hails from Maine where she once held the title "Potato Queen". She knows a lot about nutrition and is strong on the use of milk, both internally and externally, as a beauty aid. "It adds tone to the skin," she says. Where did she get this idea ? Well, Cleopatra and other famous ladies used milk baths, so why shouldn't she ? It works fine, so soothing and relaxing, especially after an active dance performance."Nature's way is best,"says Alice.

Alice is an interpretive dancer, calls herself " a musical comedy and performing actress." She's half French, half English, looks very Spanish without losing that fresh country look. She uses the stage name of Mimi Maiselle. Mimi's act is seductive, dramatic and tantalizing. She has bright red hair, adds a long black hair-piece when she dances.

She recently returned from Montreal and made her first New York appearance at the Village Nut Club. Favorite model among artists and photographers, Alice, "Mimi", whatever you like to call her, is a very busy gal. Her measurements are 35,22, 34½. She is 5'4" tall.

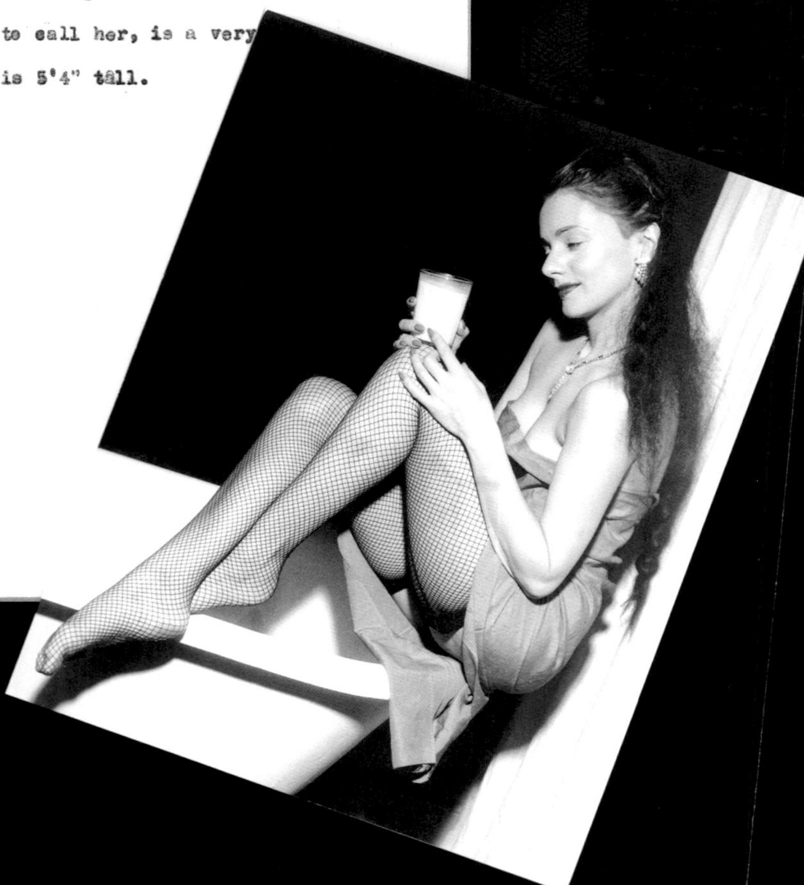

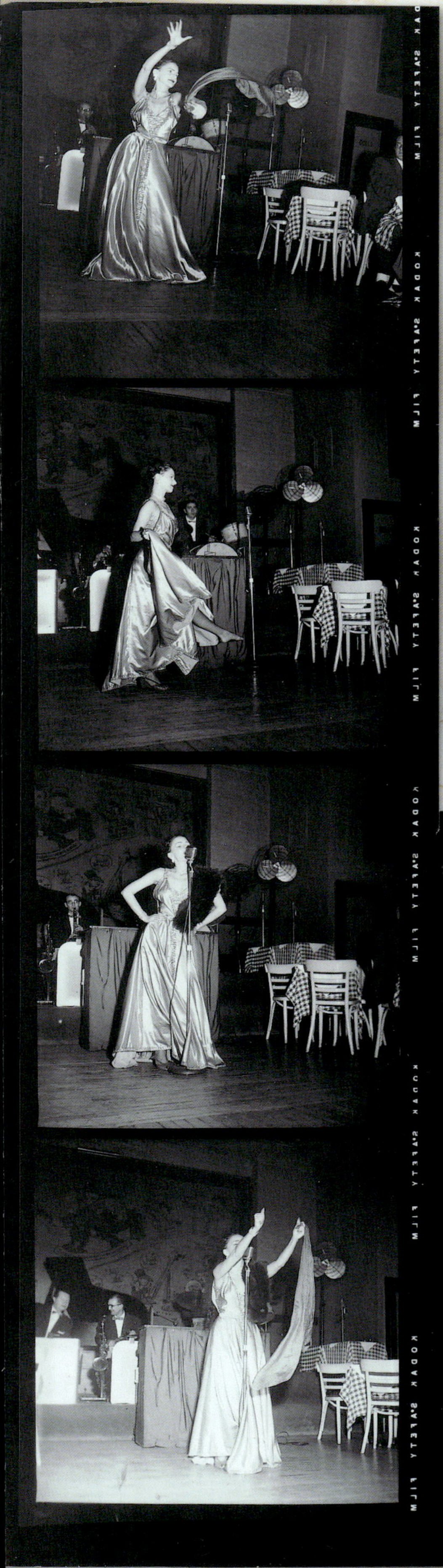

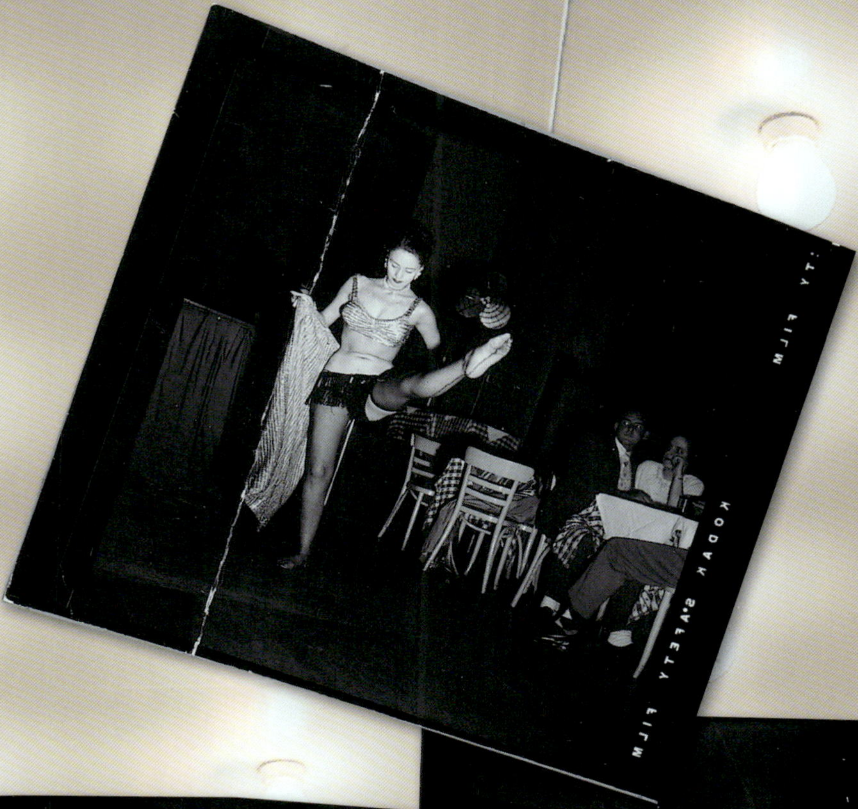

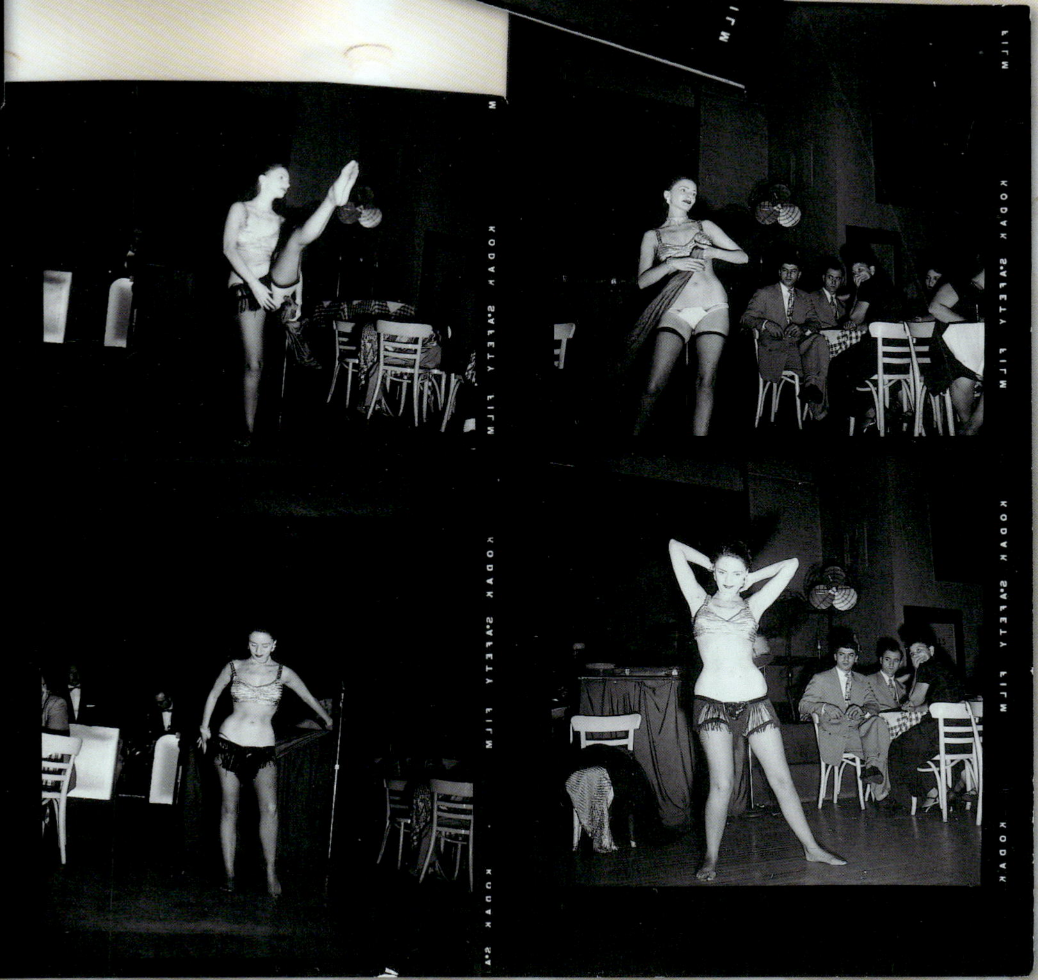

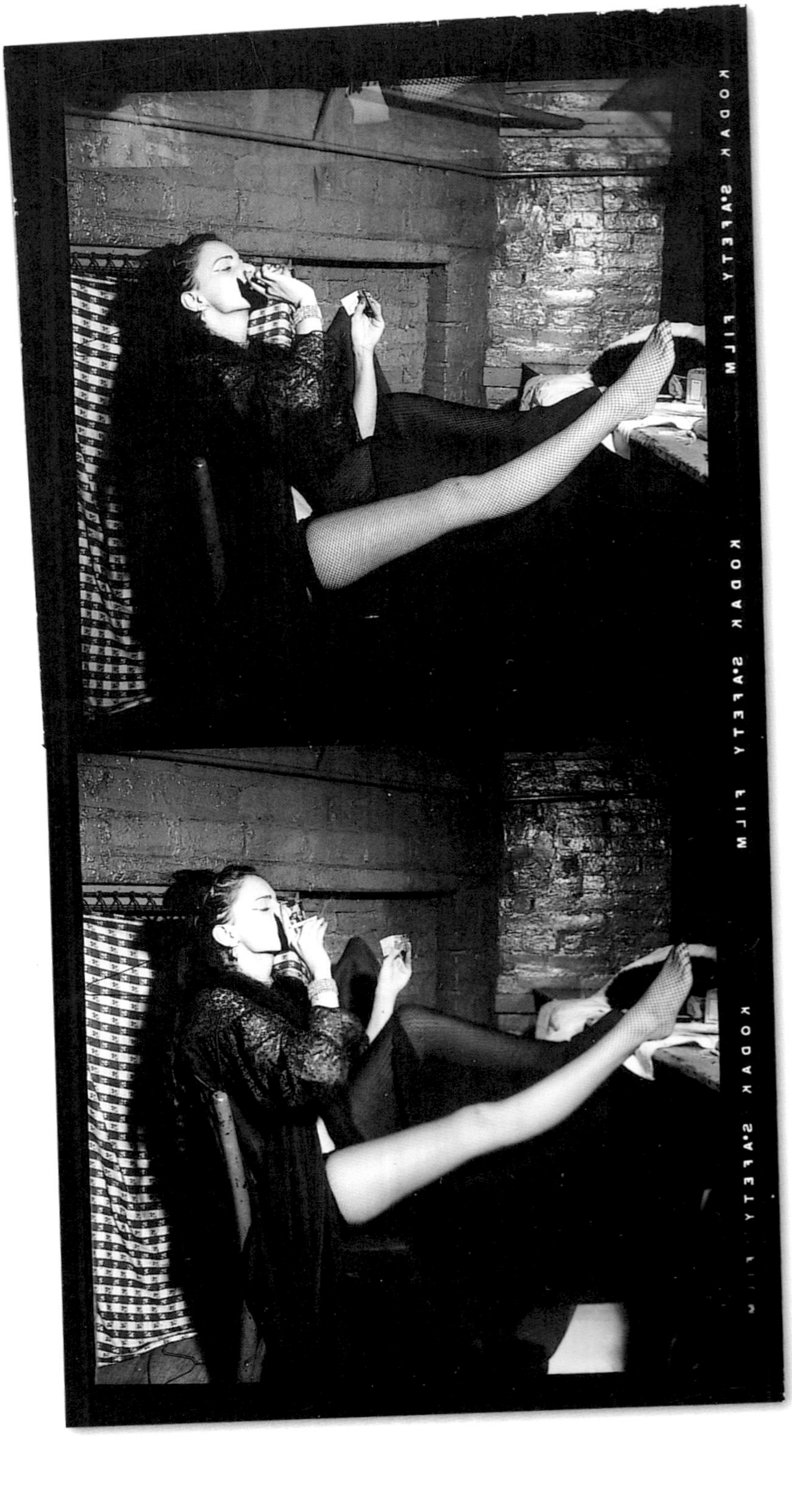

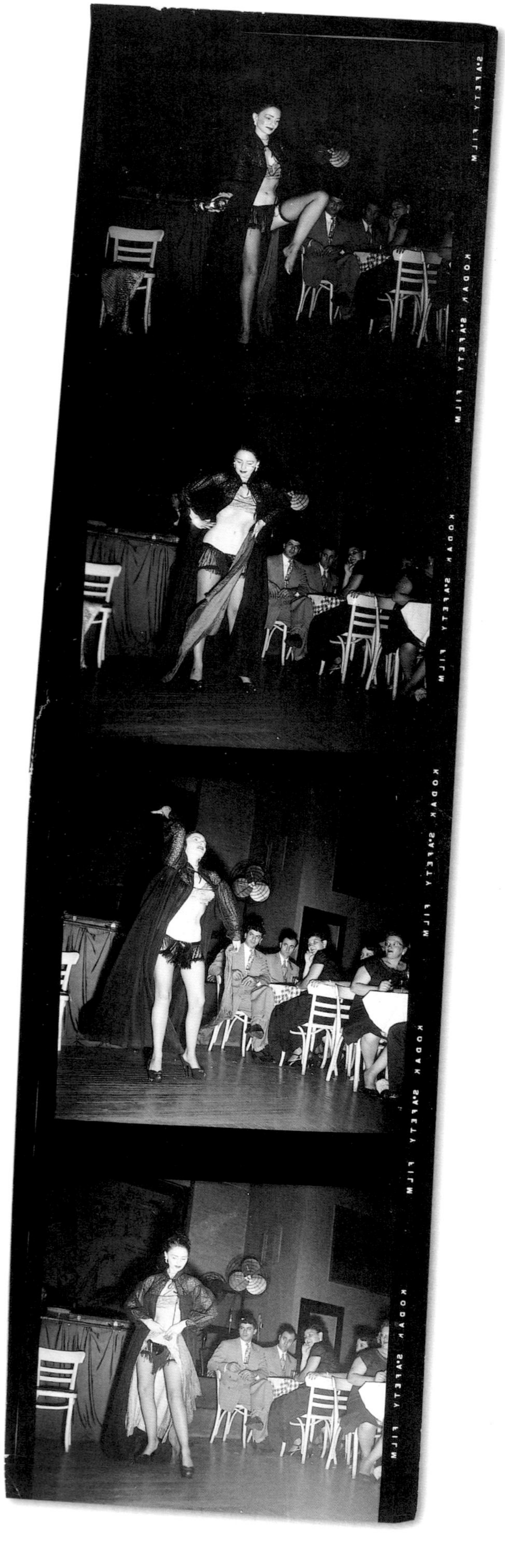

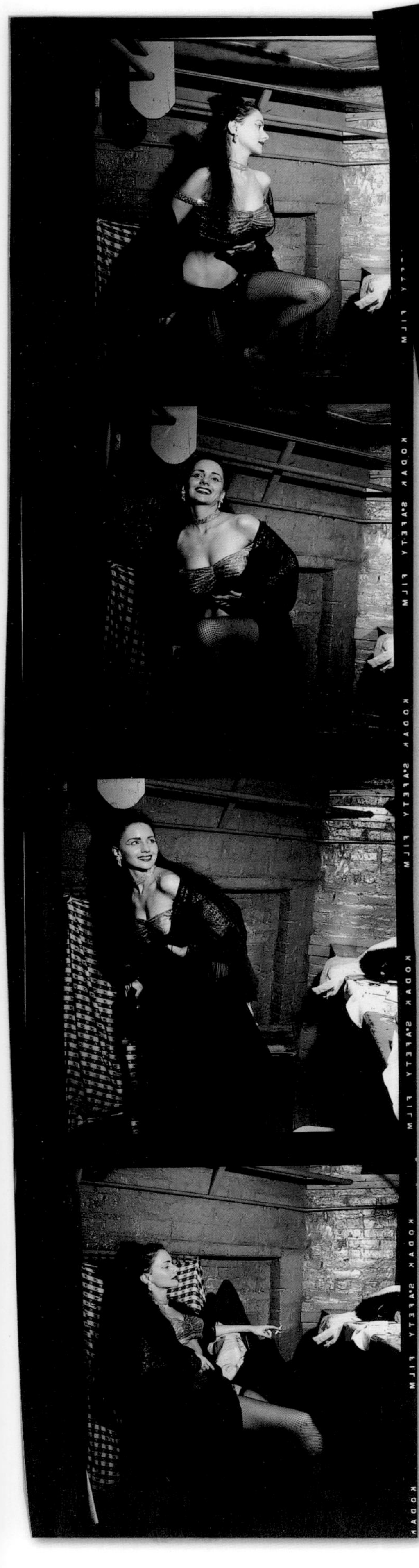
KODAK SAFETY FILM

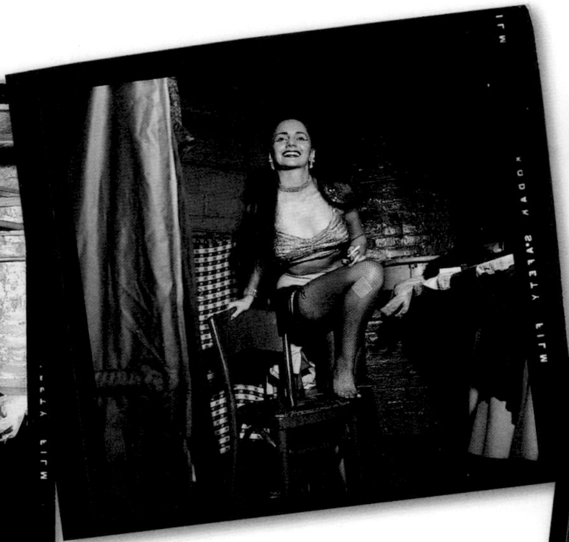
KODAK SAFETY FILM

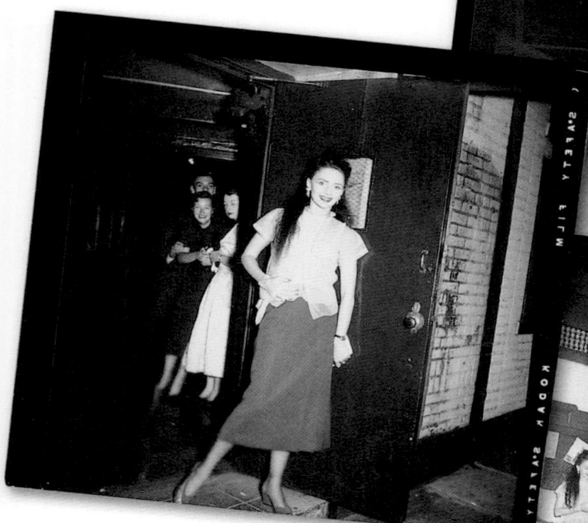
KODAK SAFETY FILM

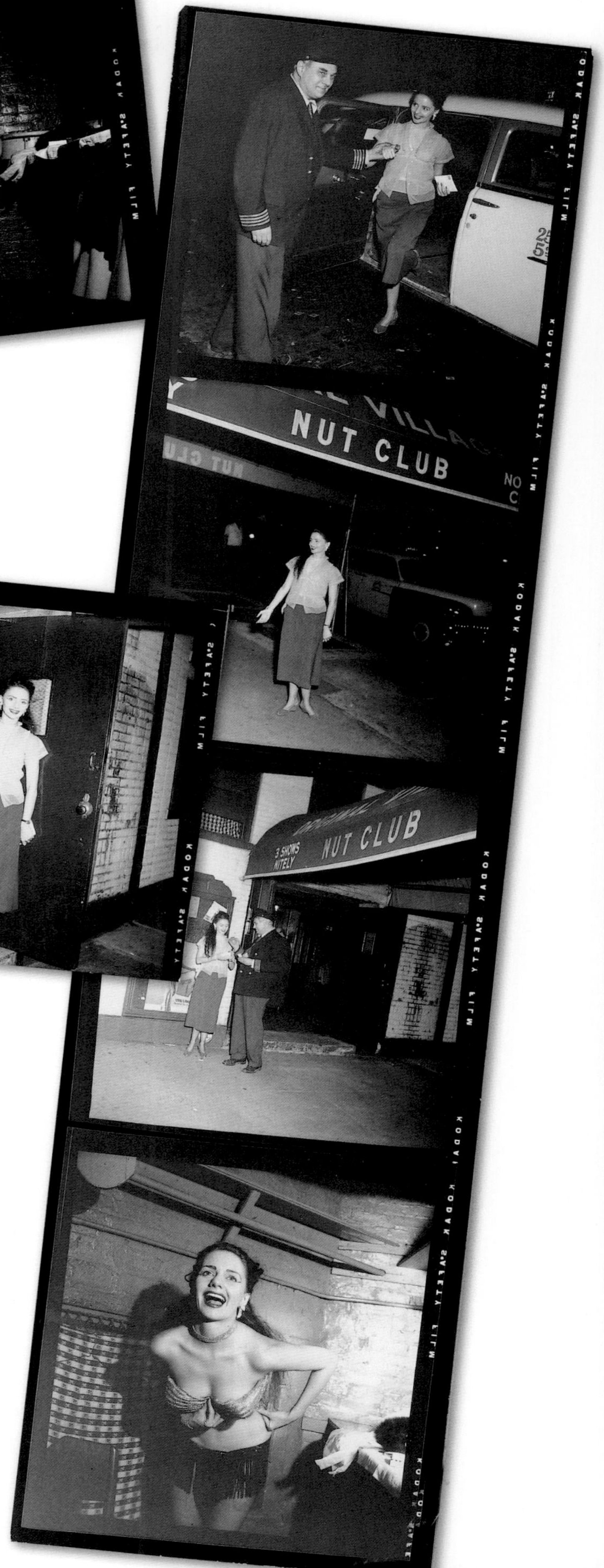
NUT CLUB
NUT CLUB
3 SHOWS NITELY
NUT CLUB
KODAK SAFETY FILM

Arlene Stevens

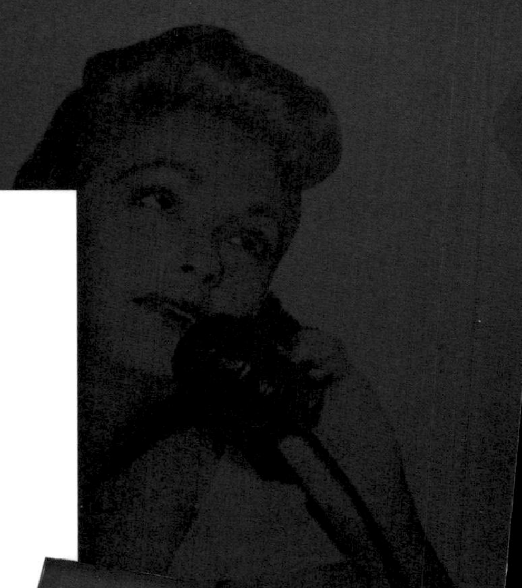

SHE'S THE PEARL IN THE OYSTER

Arlene Stevens' big act is "The Birth of a Pearl". The scene is set at the bottom of the ocean, and Arlene-as the pearl-emerges from a huge shell in the centre of the stege, naked. As she goes into her sensuous dance, she finfs her clothes in a brass-bound chest, puts them on, dances some more, takes them off again, then climbs back into her shell which closes tightly to a last spasmodic kick.

Arlene was born in Fort Worth, Texas. While in her teens, the family moved to California. Arlene was working as a salesgirl, got into show business on a dare,in Los A ngeles. Once started, she kept right on going, worked out the Birth of a Pearl" routine which has been a hit in Las Vegas, Tennessee, Louisiania, Georgia, Kansas and Texas, and latterly in good old New York.

Vital statistics: she's 5'5", measures 36-25-36.

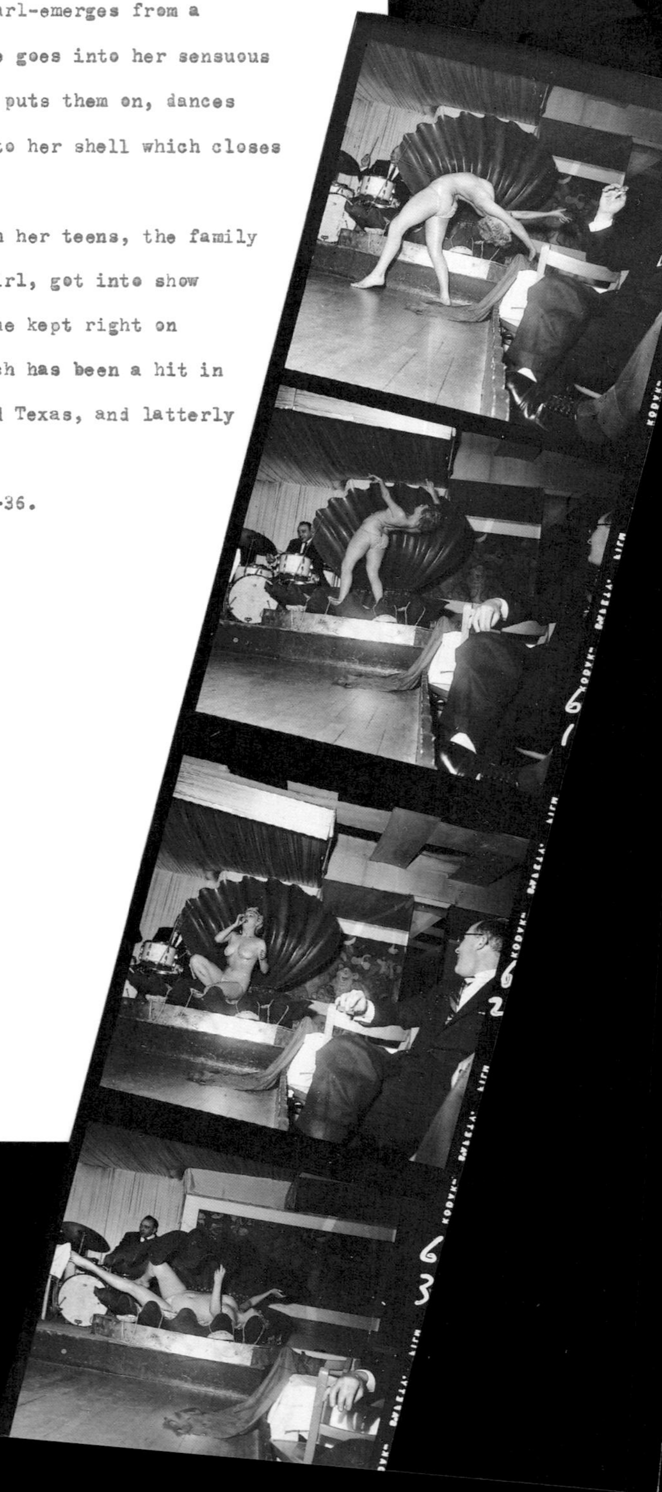

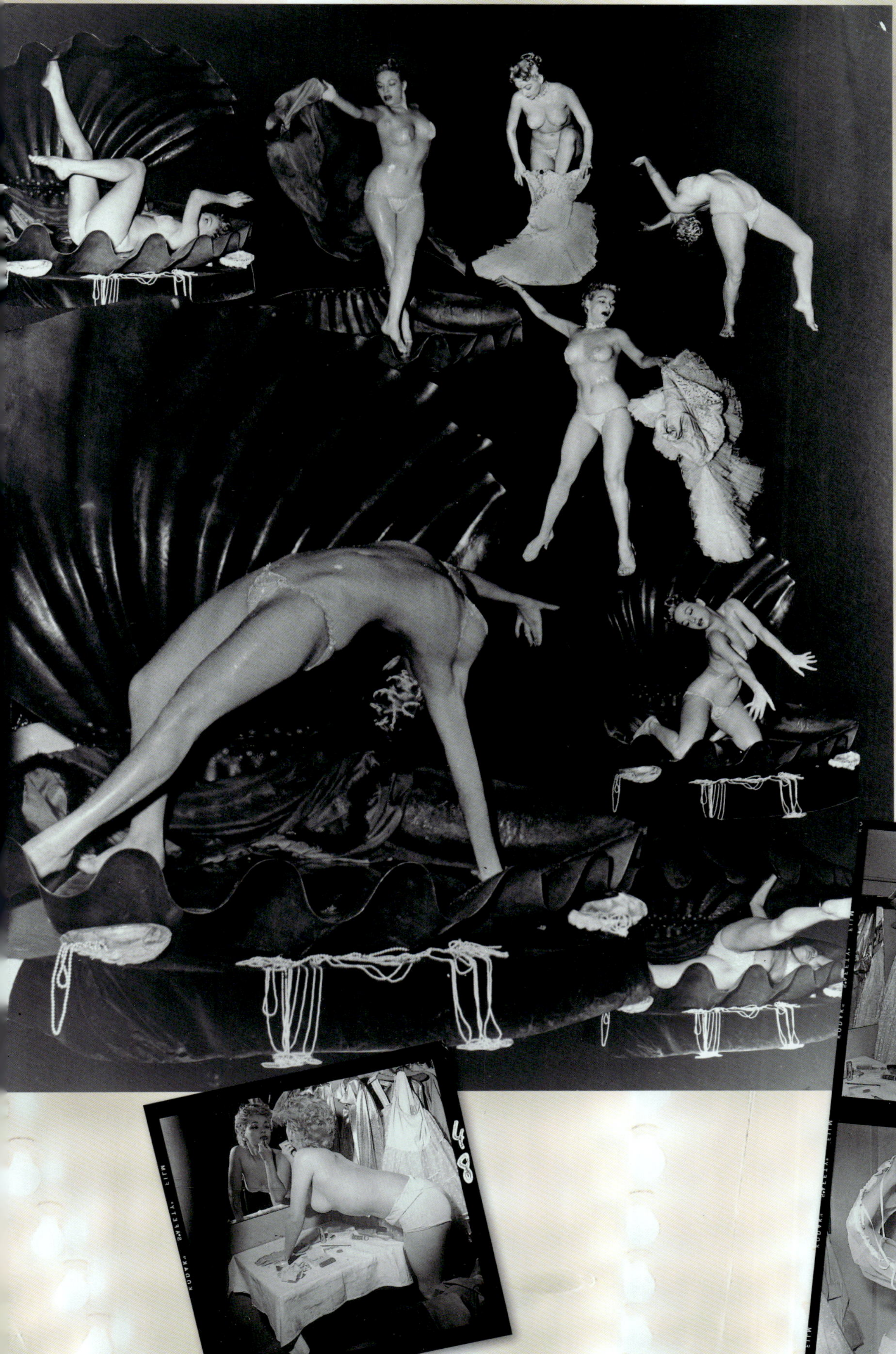

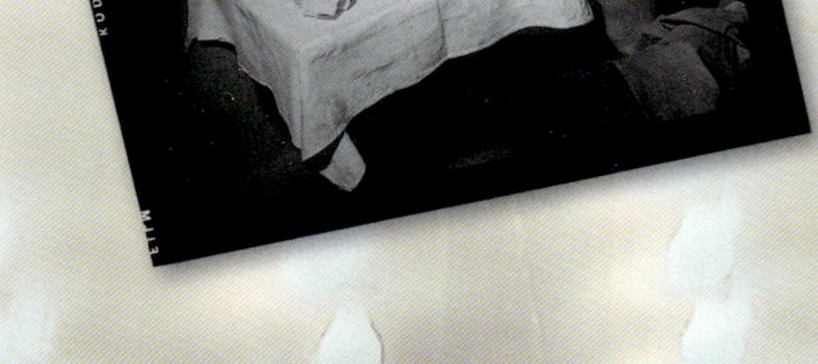
48

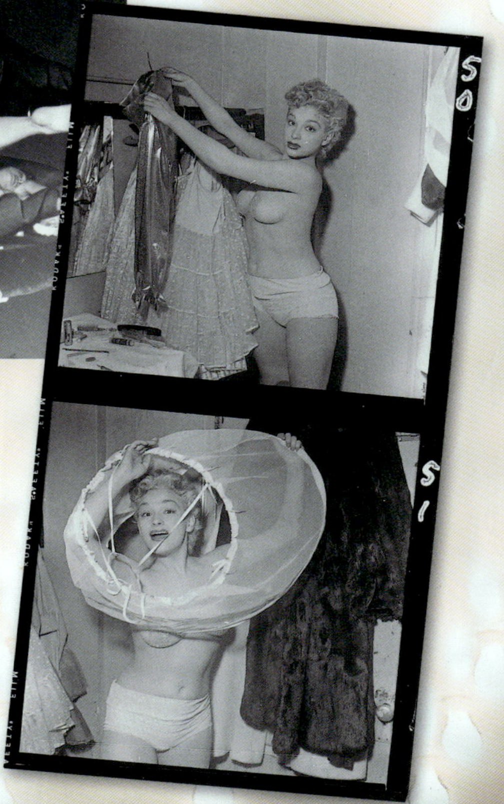
50
51

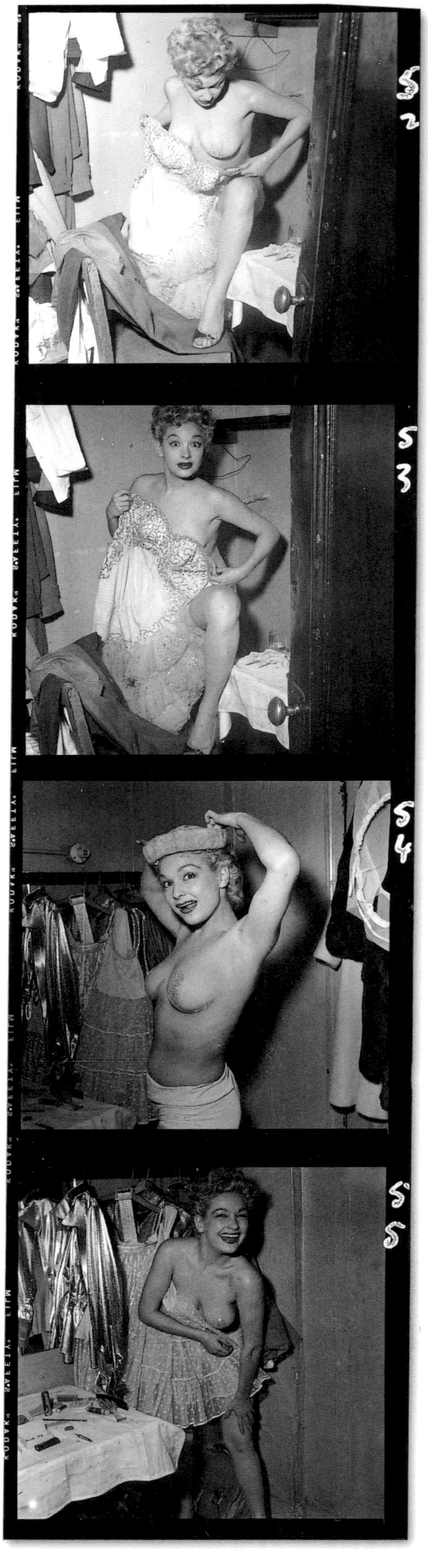
52
53
54
55
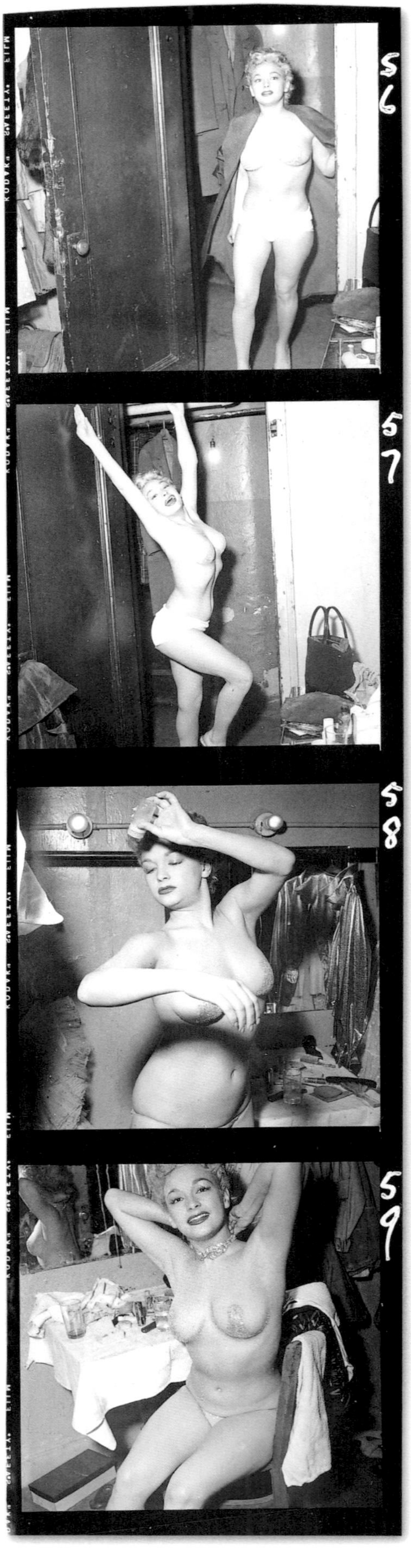
56
57
58
59
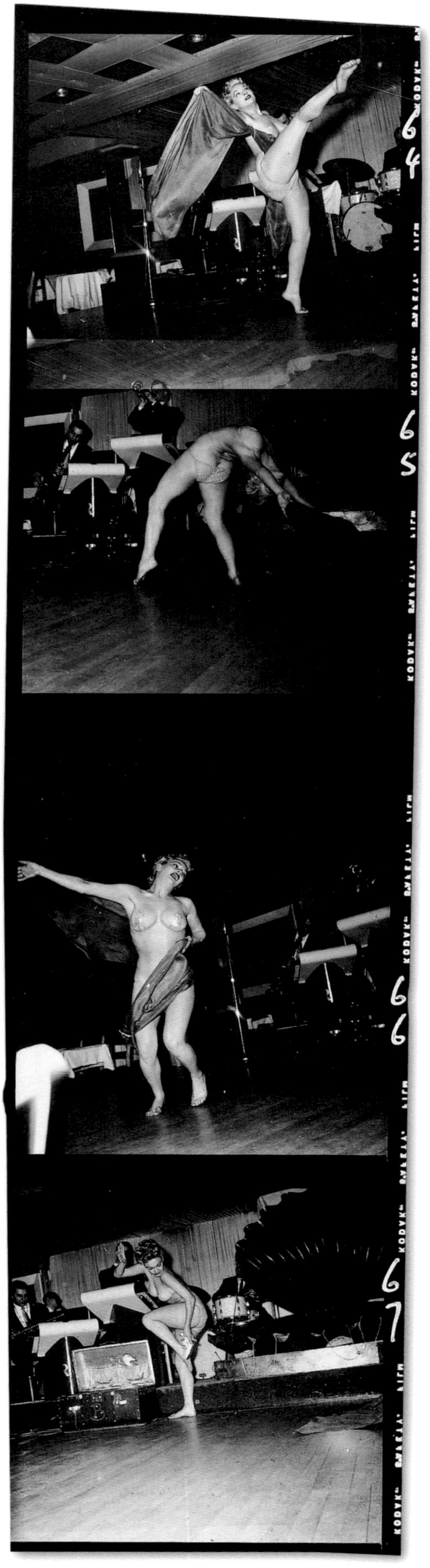
64
65
66
67

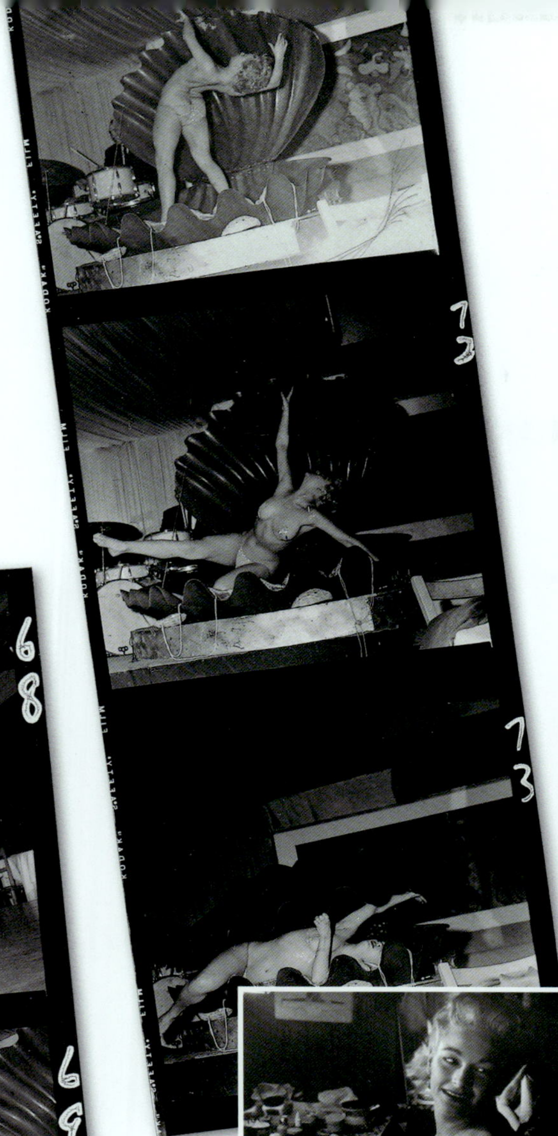
72
73

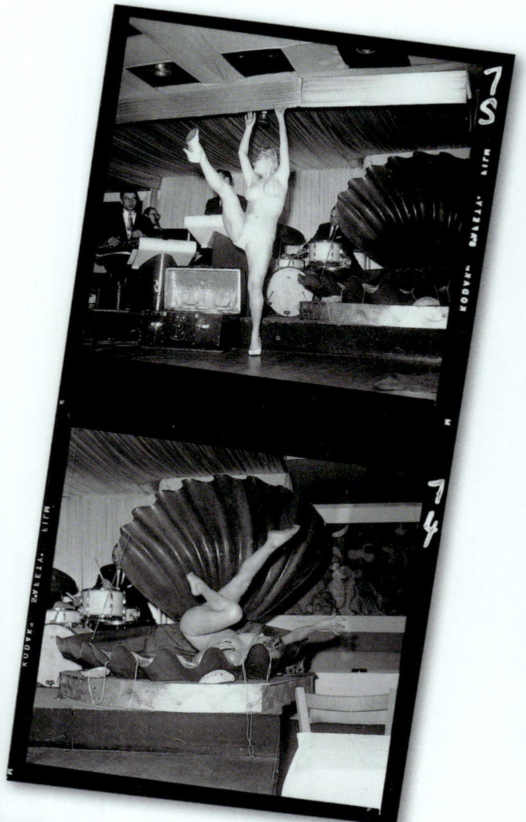
75
74

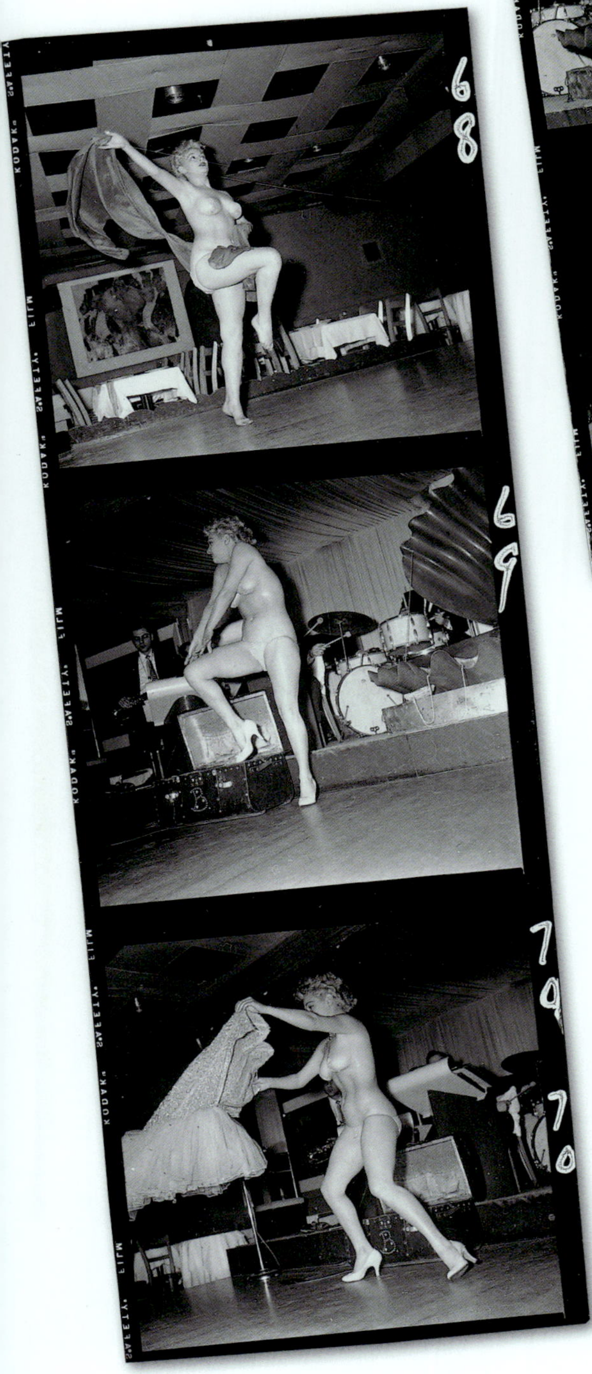
68
69
70

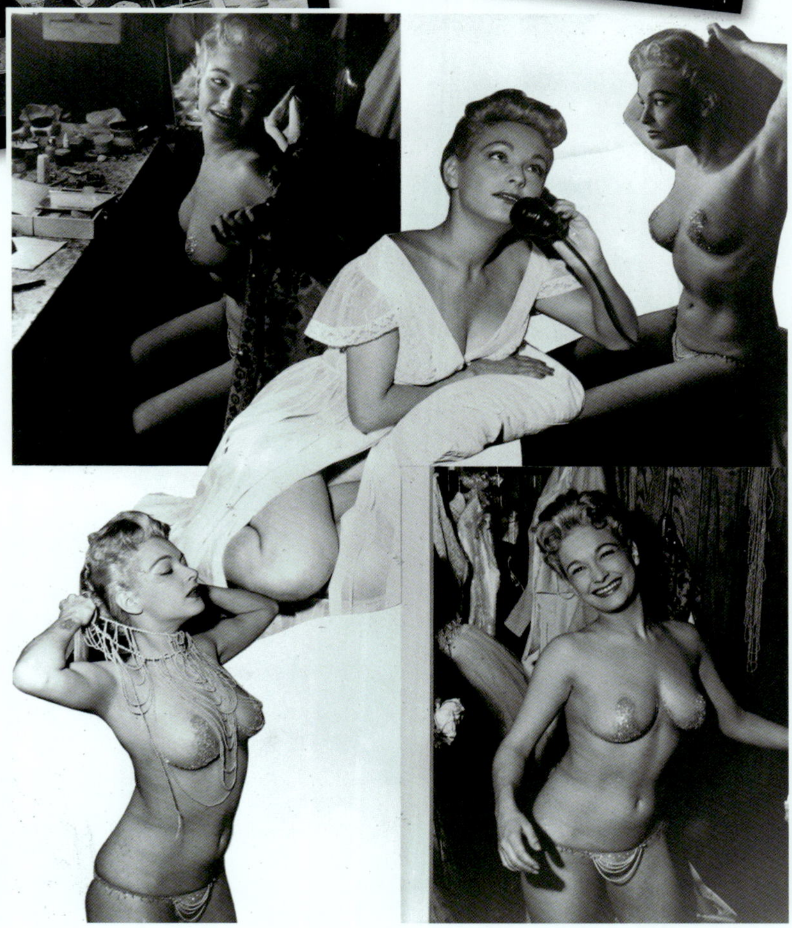

Betty Howard

BETTY HOWARD

From Daytona Beach, Florida, comes the latest star in burlesque heaven. She's Betty Howard, billed as "The Girl Who Has Everything". Well, Betty has a lot of the right things. Her measurements speak for themselves-38-25-36 and she's 5'5" tall. Until recently Betty measured 40" around the you-know-where, but she has been dieting and took off 35 lbs., now measures 38" around the top-deck. Her fans like her better that way, purrs Betty.

Betty has been a dancer from a very early age, took up stripping as "the easiest, most exciting and interesting way to wind up with a fat bank book in a short time."

Betty travels around the country in her Cadillac, towing a 34' luxury trailer in which she lives. She has played in Florida, California, Louisiana, mid-west, east coast. Has also displayed her charms in Havana, Honululu, Montreal. Not bad for a 23-year-old. Her particular combination of red hair, and blue, blue eyes, goes well under the spotlights. Everywhere that Betty goes, her dog goes too. The dog's name: "Sexy." What else ?

This gal does her own routines and designs her own costumes. The kid's talented. She also has a large collection of photographs of herself, which is easy to understand-she is probably the most accomodating stripper in the country to photographers, for she hands out cards which read: "Always willing and ready to pose at any time."

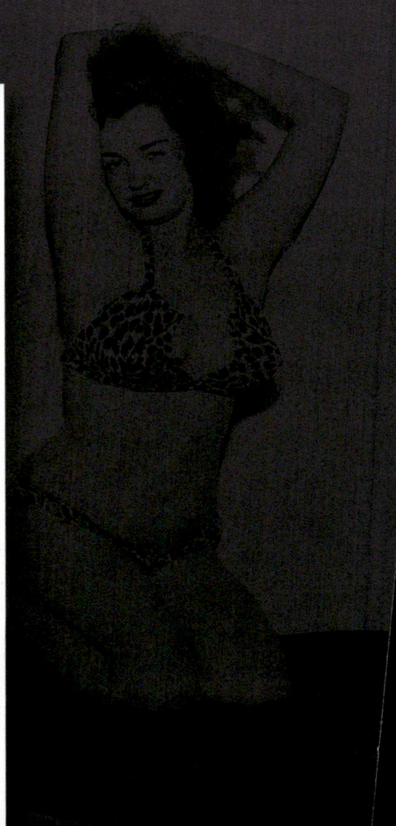

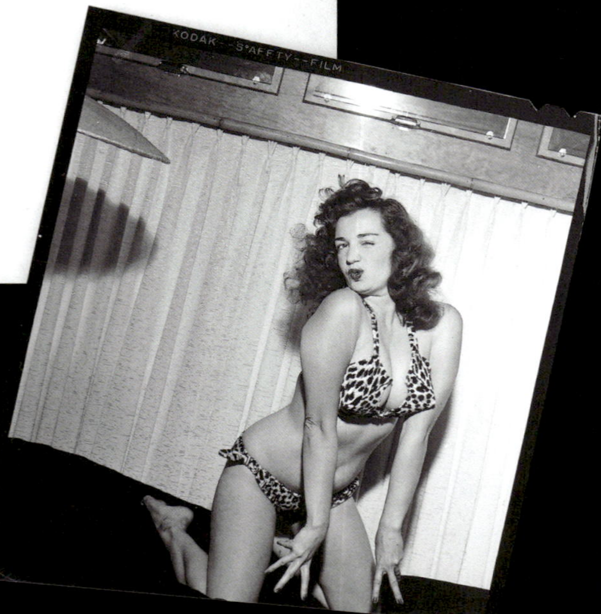

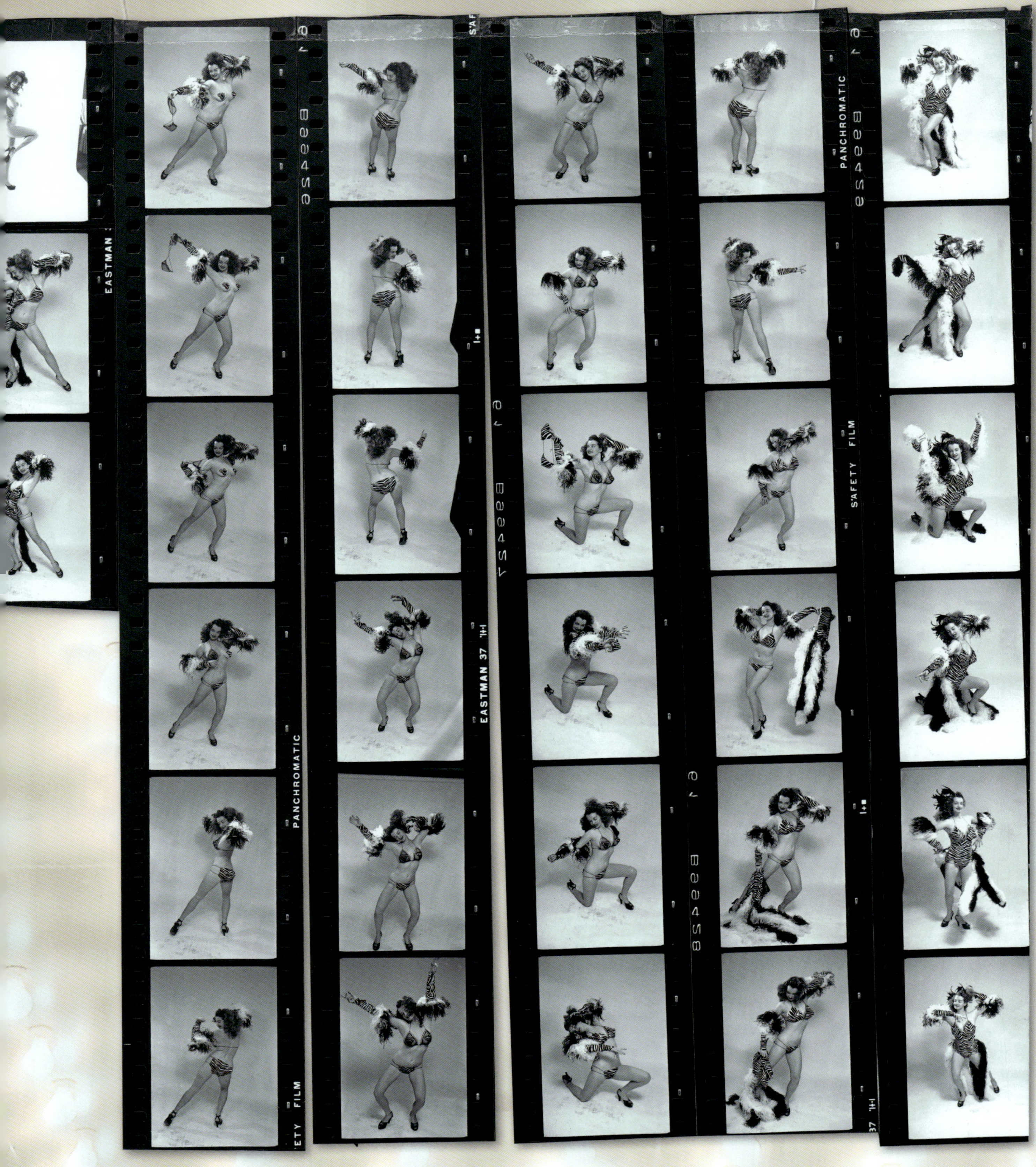
EASTMAN
PANCHROMATIC
SAFETY FILM
EASTMAN 37

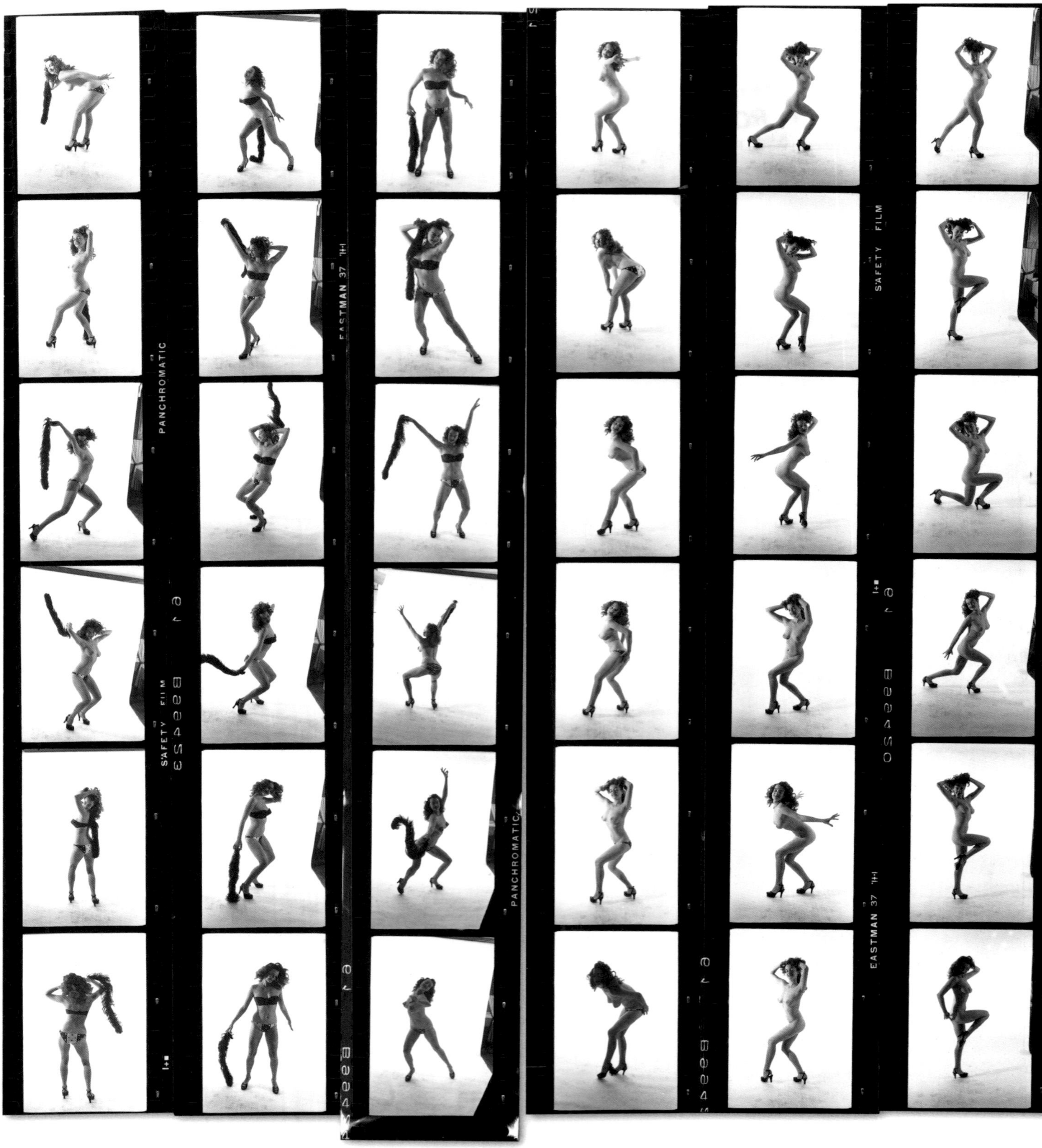

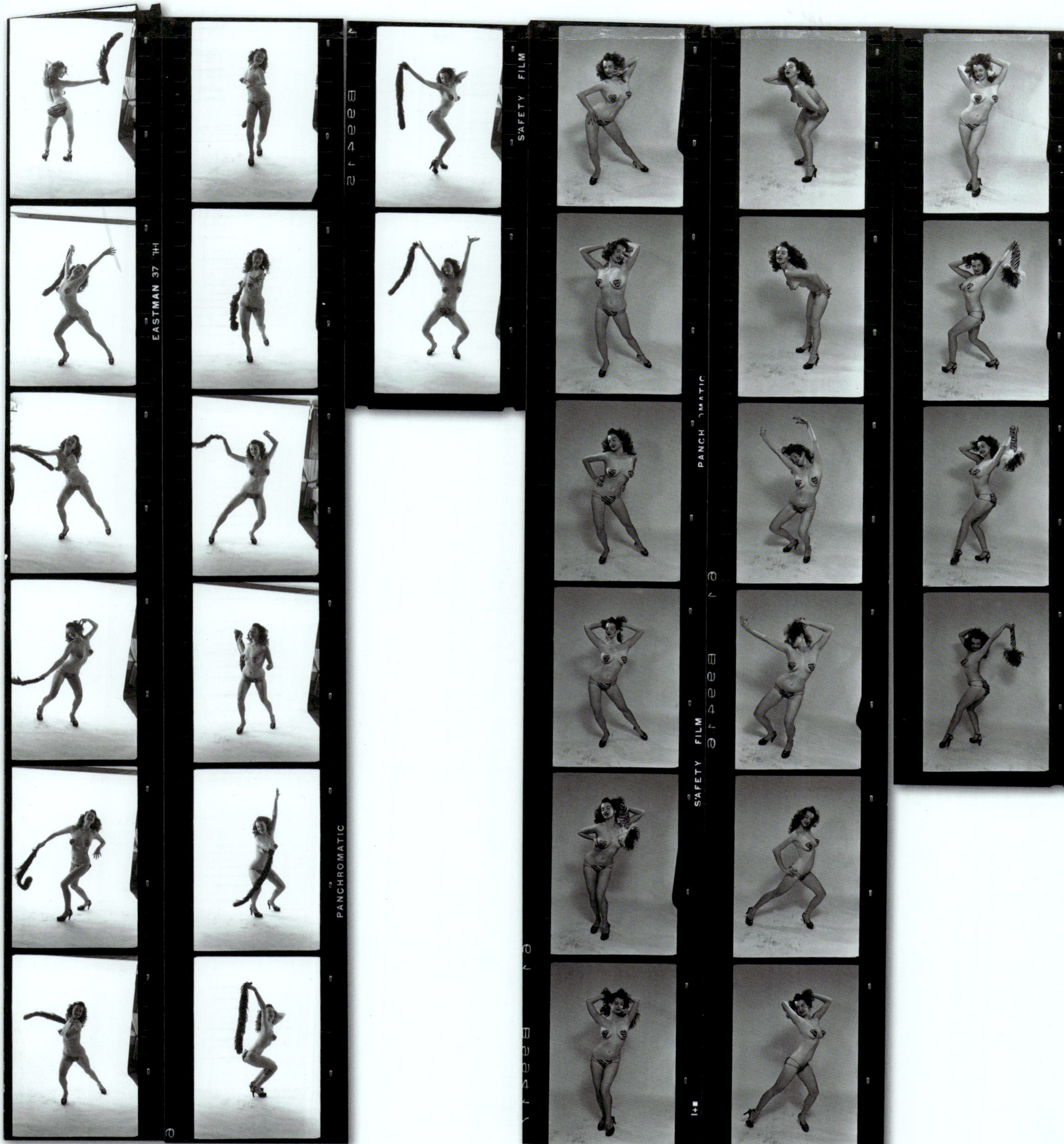
EASTMAN 37
PANCHROMATIC
SAFETY FILM
PANCHROMATIC
SAFETY FILM

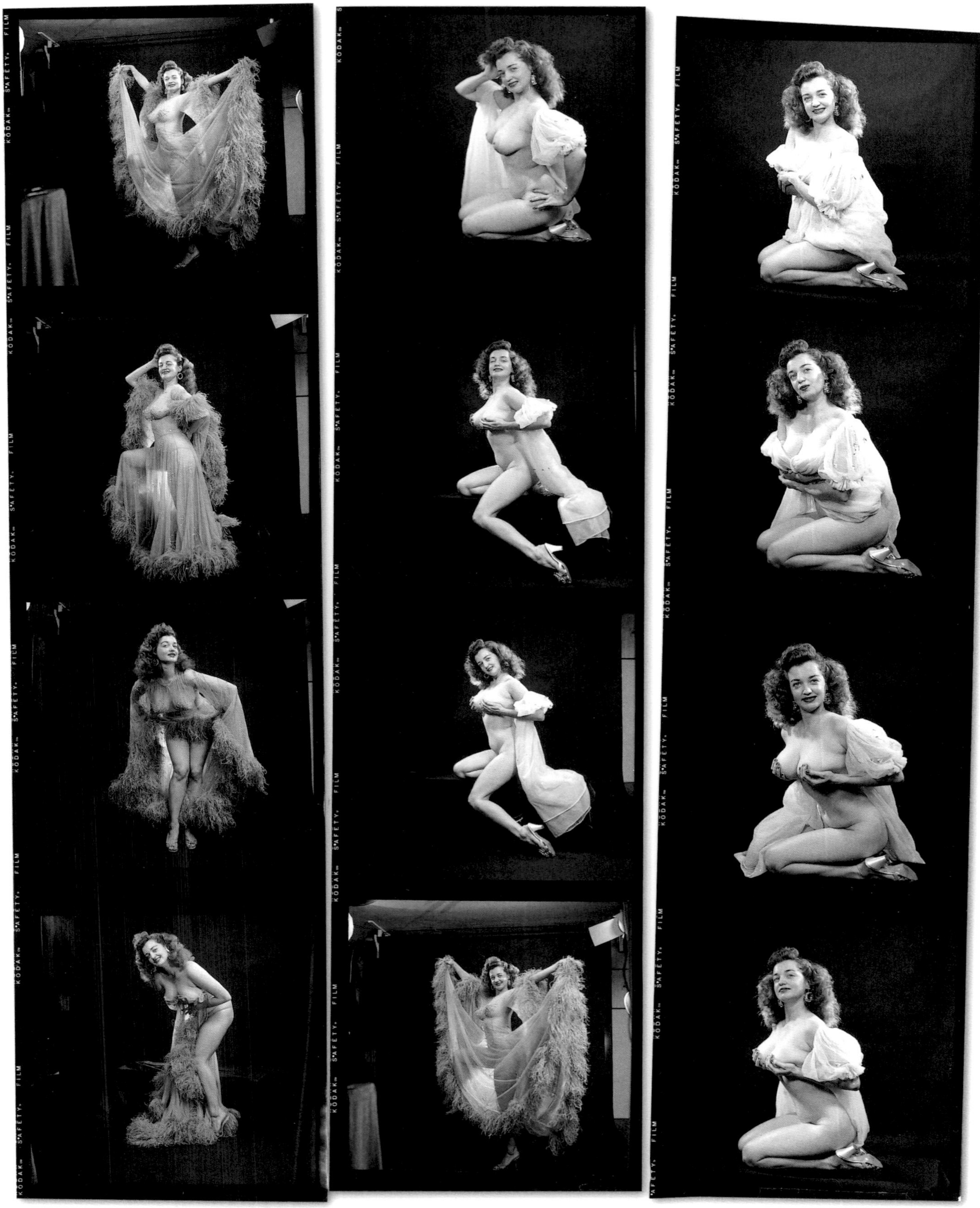

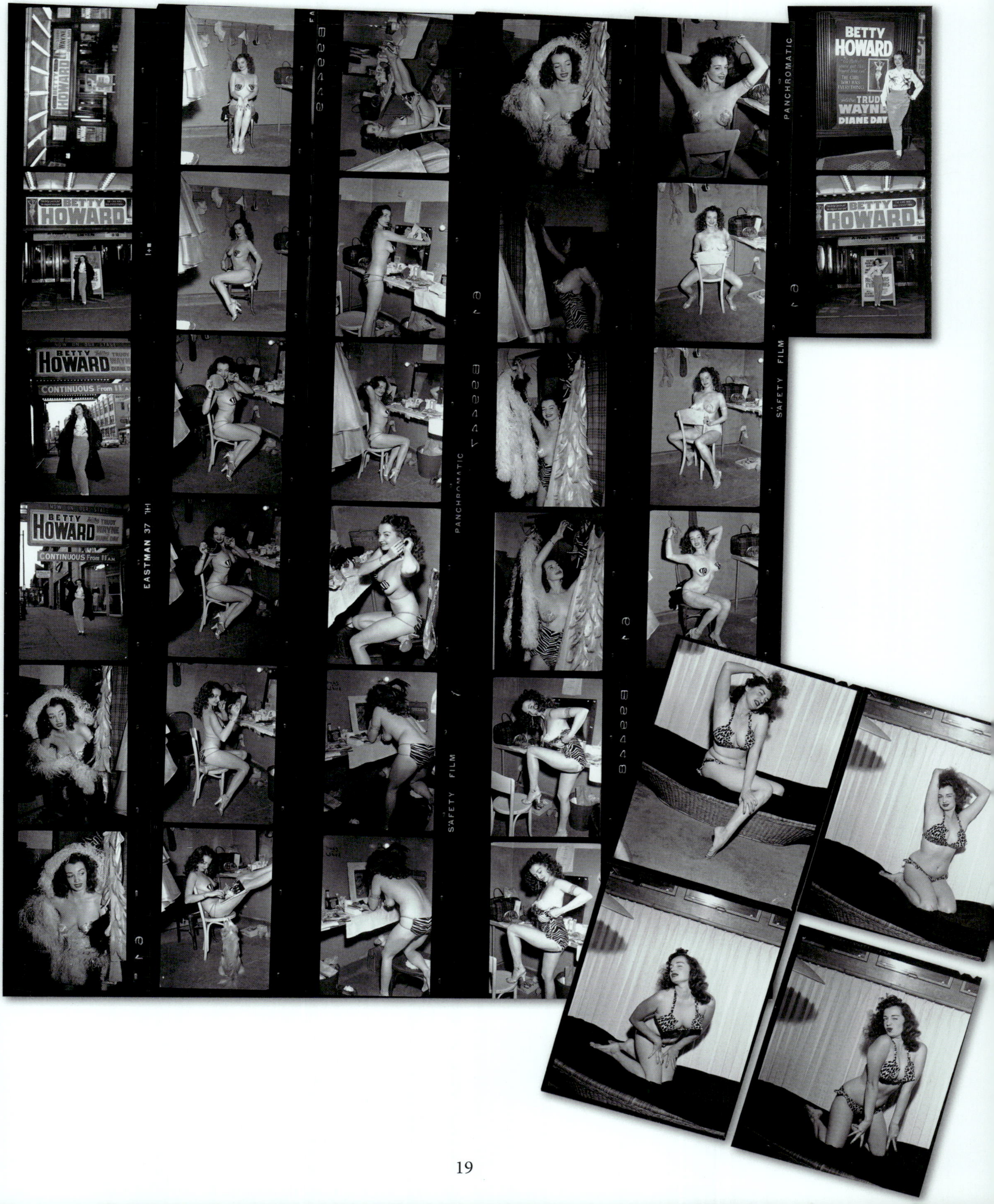
BETTY
HOWARD
THE GIRL WHO HAS EVERYTHING
TRUDY
WAYNE
DIANE DAY
NOW ON OUR STAGE
CONTINUOUS From 11 A.M.
EASTMAN 37
PANCHROMATIC
SAFETY FILM

Blaze Star

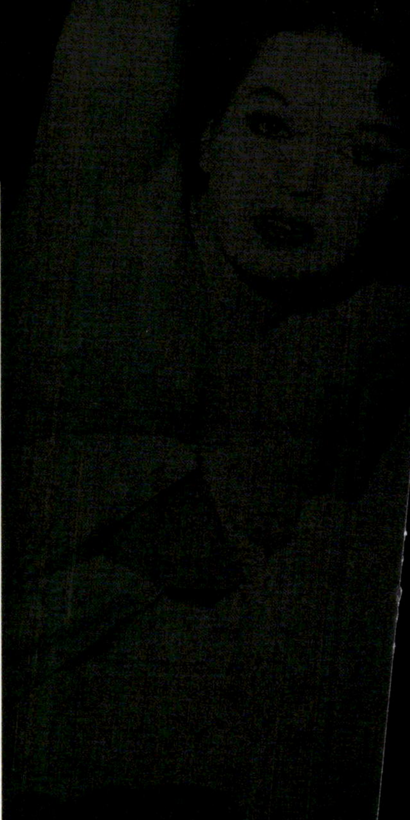

BLAZE STAR

Blaze Starr comes from West Virginia, where, she says, girls get their beaytiful legs by running up and down them thar hills. Discobered by a theatrical agent behind the counter in a donut shop, Blaze soon proved she is a crowd pleaser, Her jungle drim act, complete with dancing flames (by means of colored streamers, lights and forced air) sets the audience on fire when she dances. Her rise to stardom has been meteoric. Termed "The Hottest Blaze in Burlesque", this titian-haired beauty lives in Baltimore, works mainly on the east coast- Baltimore, Philadelphia and New York. One of a family of ten children, al West Virginia is proud of her.

Blaze is 5'6" tall, measures 38-24-37.

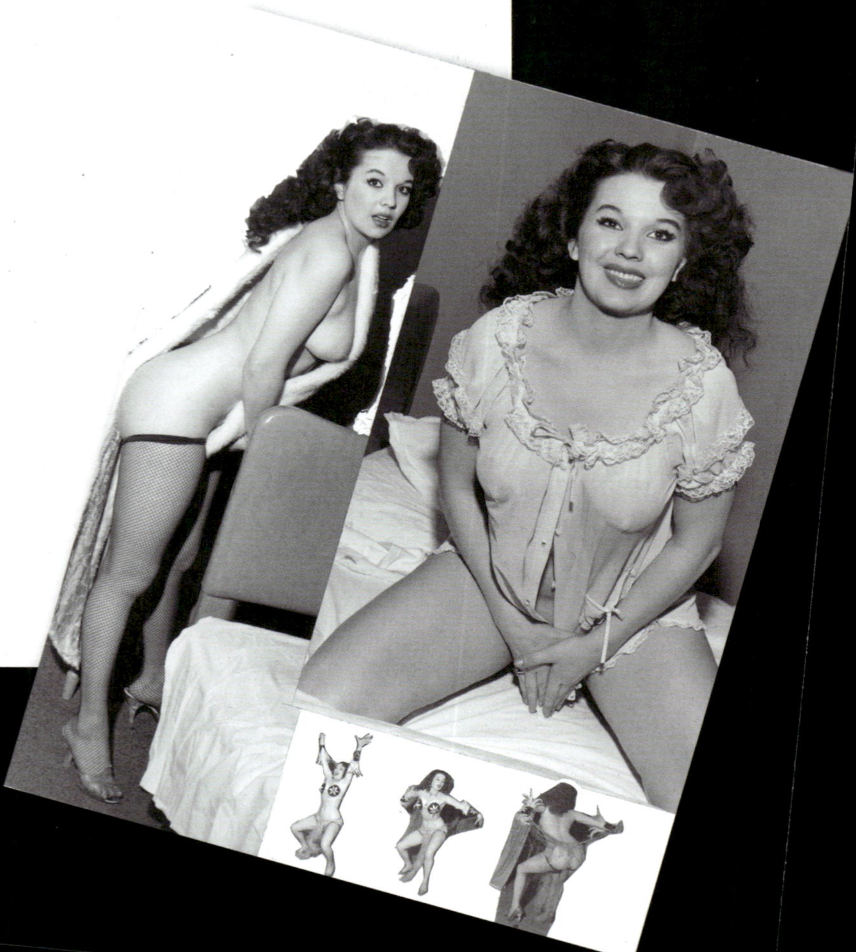

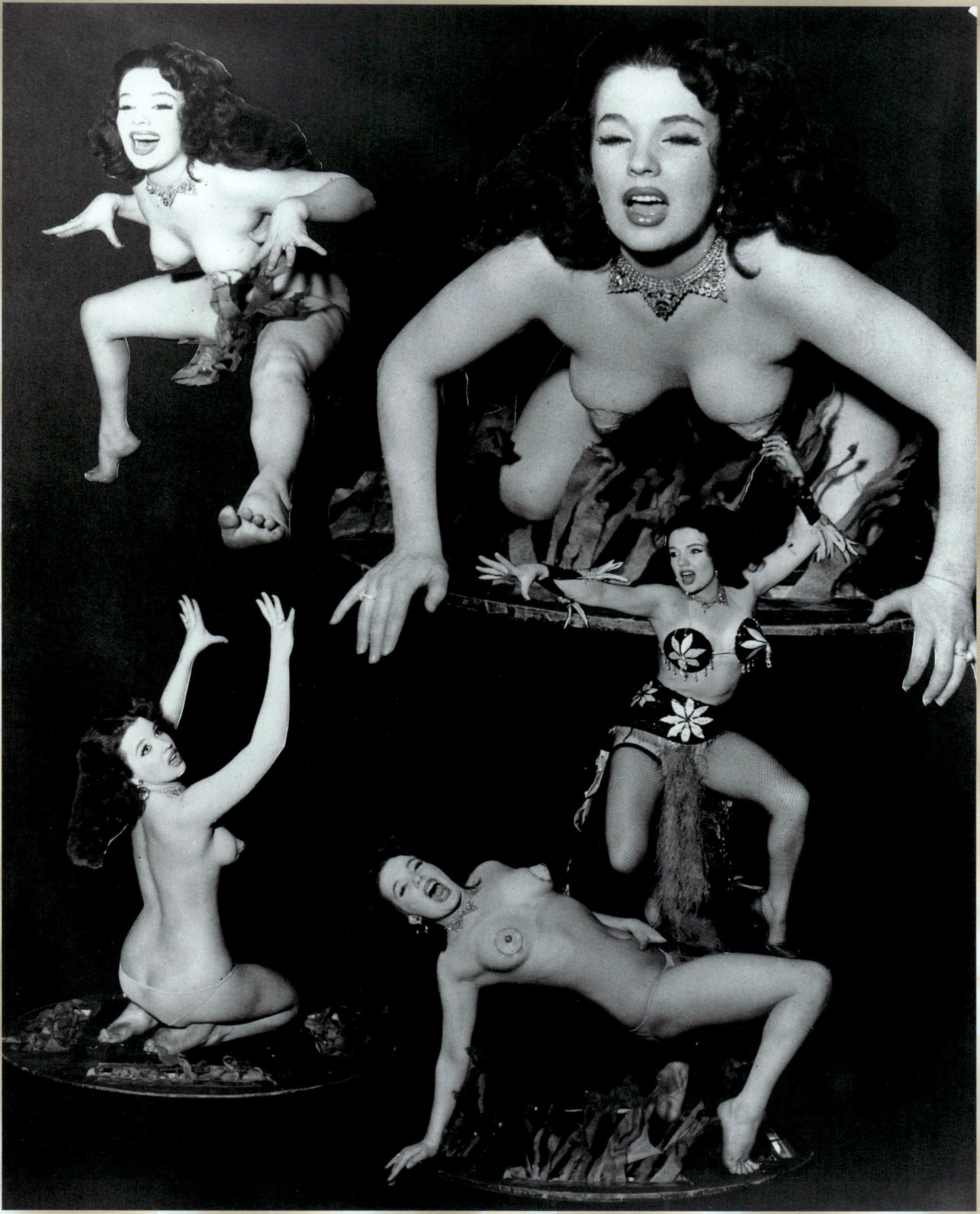

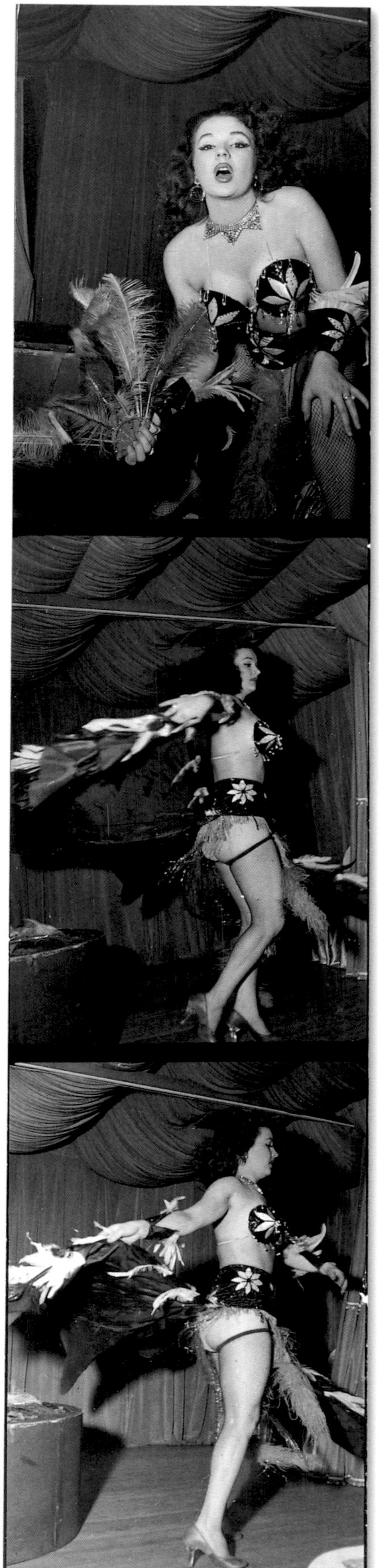
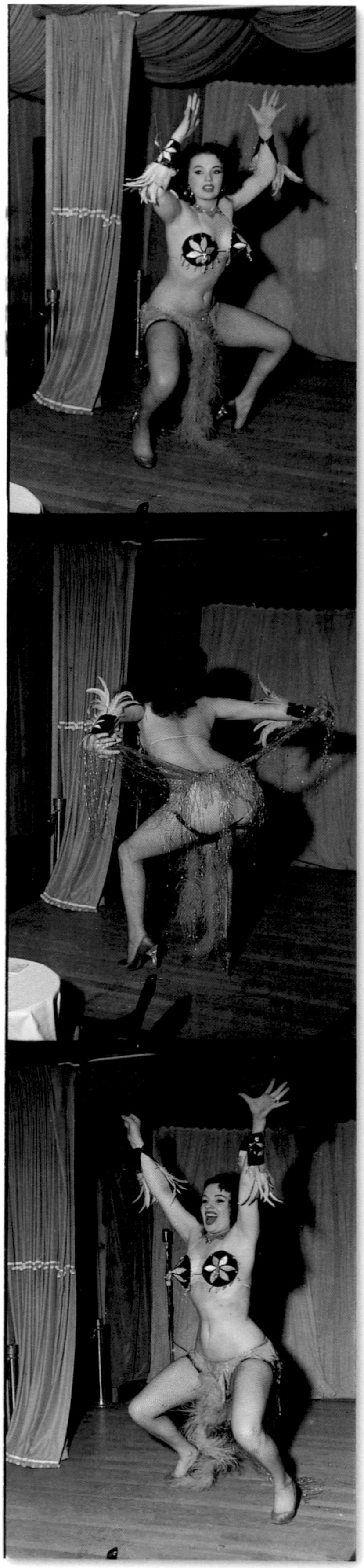
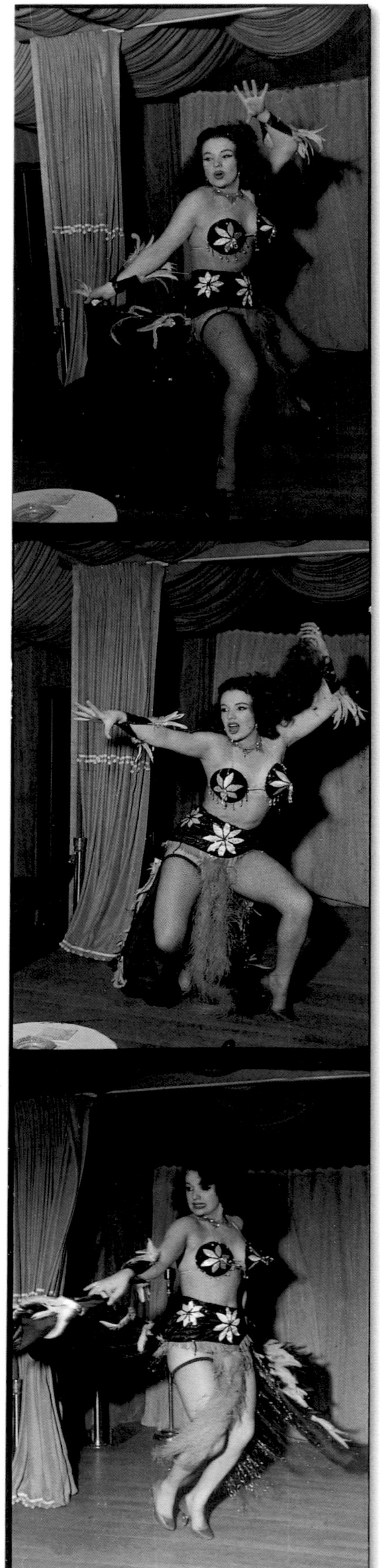

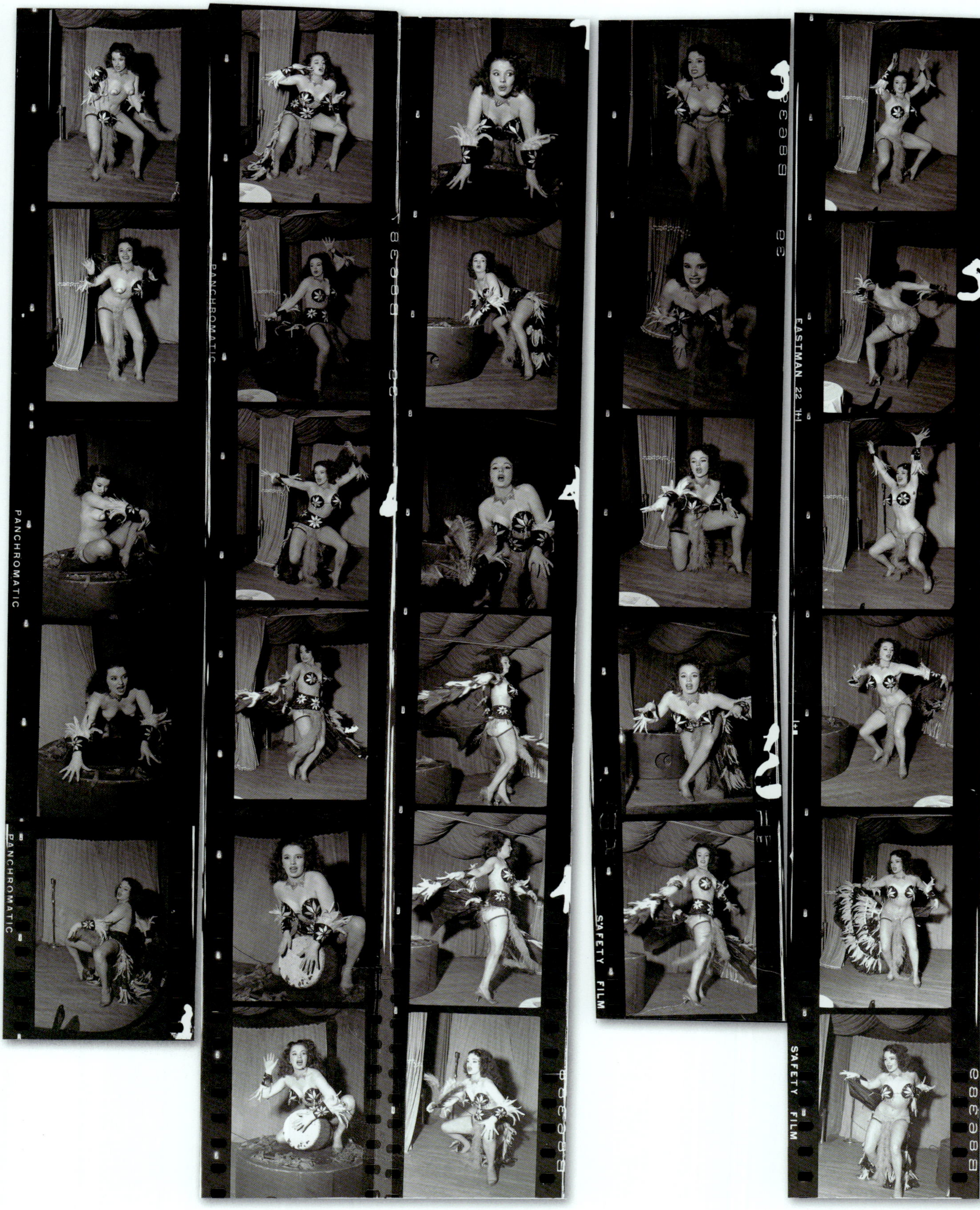
PANCHROMATIC
PANCHROMATIC
PANCHROMATIC
EASTMAN 22
SAFETY FILM
SAFETY FILM

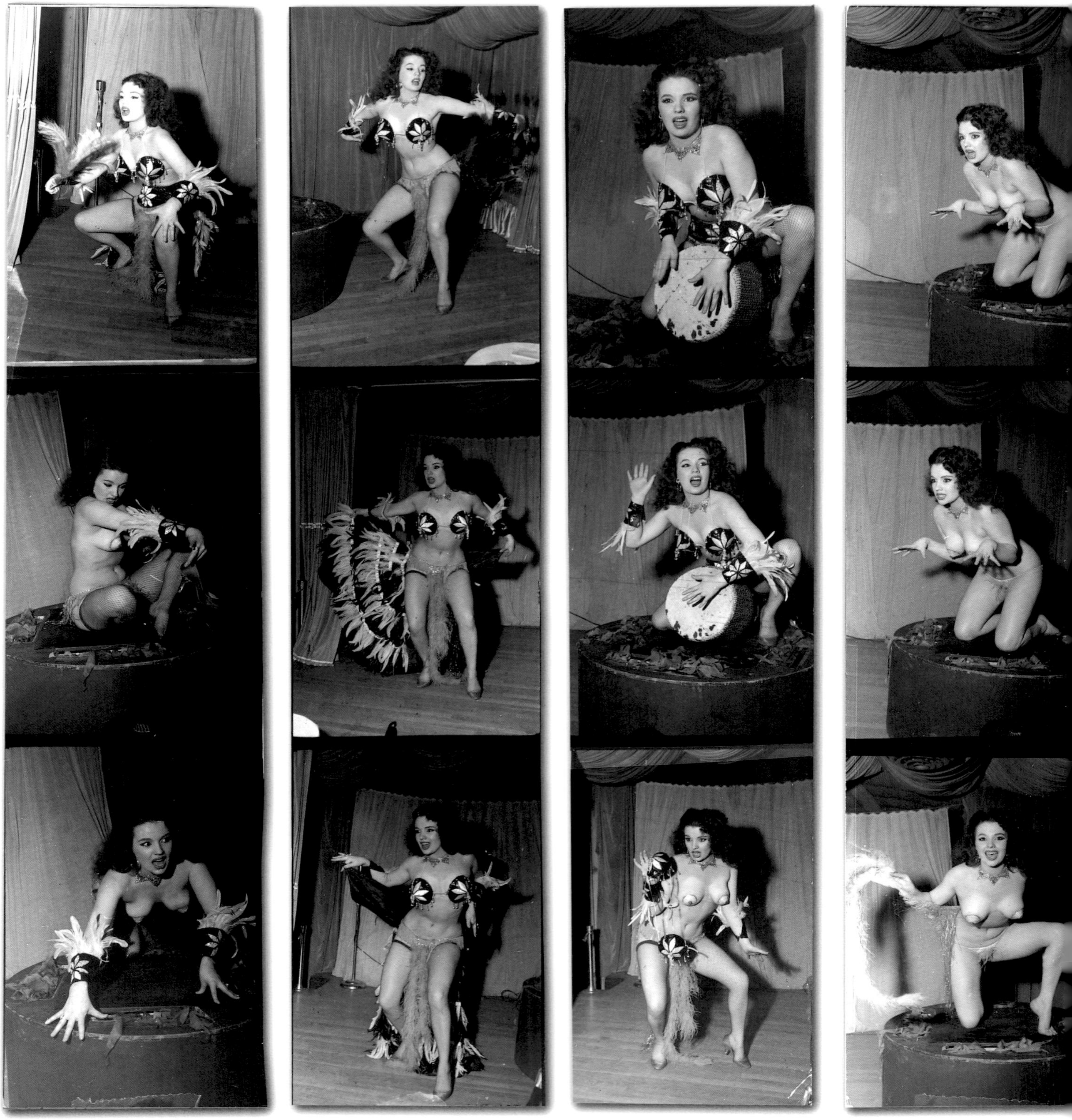

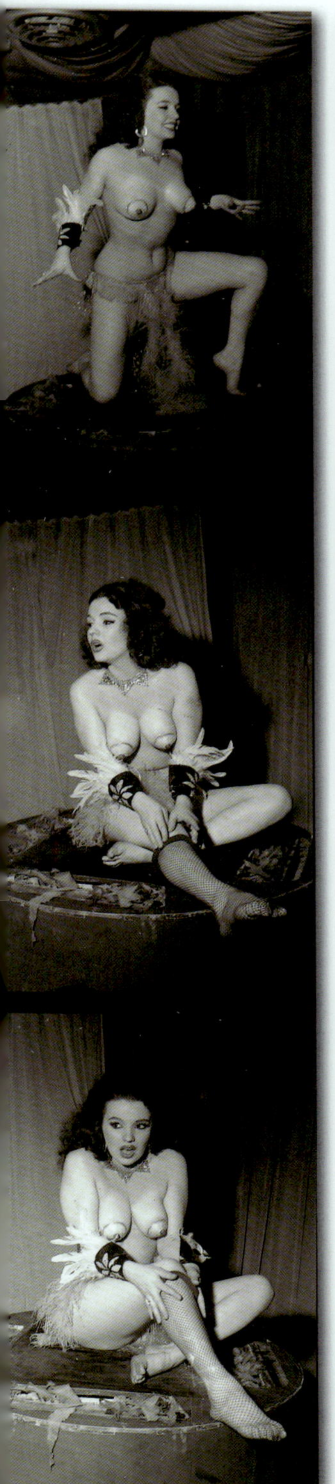

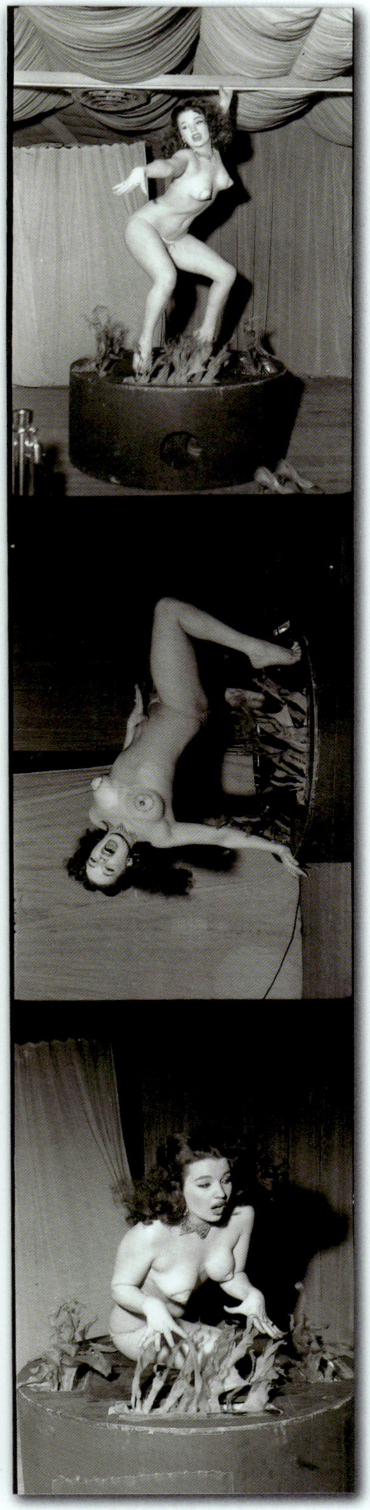

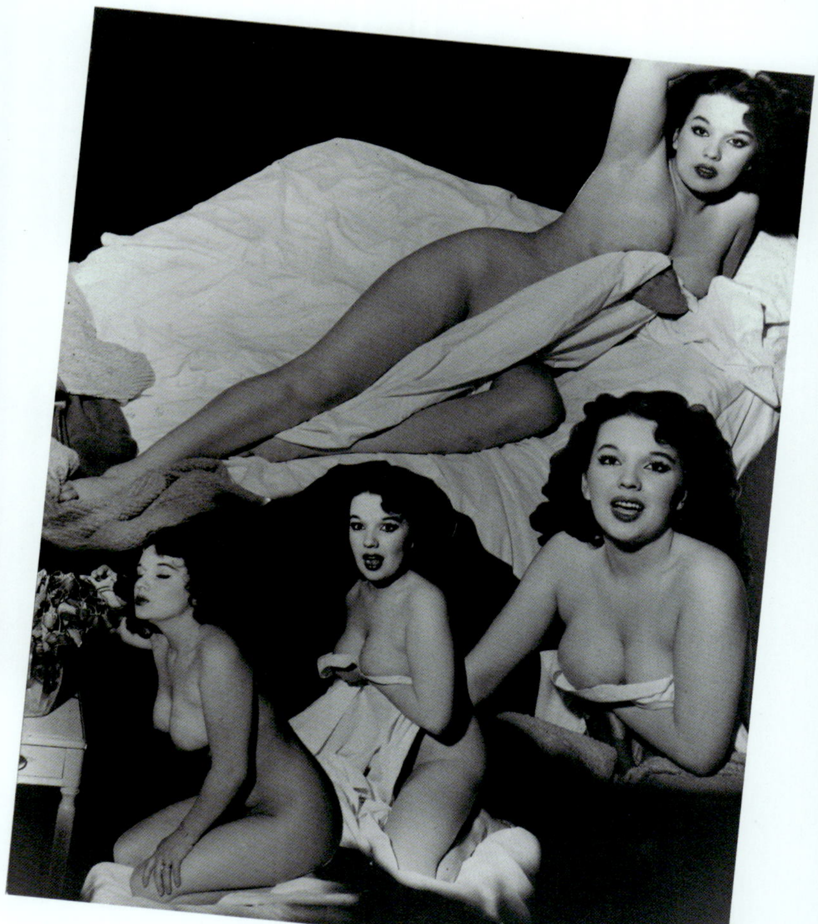

Bonnie Boyia

BONNIE BOYIA

Minsky headliner-Bonnie Boyia- comes right out and says it: "Strippers make better wives." Showgirls, our pretty expert tells us, have learned to cope with any hardship- even a man!

"Believe me, I know! ", Bonnie insists. "If a man has what it takes to win the love of a pin-up queen, he can be assured that his attentions will become her spotlight, and his affection the only applause she'll ever need."

"Moreover, no husband of a stripper could ever say 'My wife doesn't understand me. What does a man really mean when he says these hackneyed words ? Maybe that his wife is inhibited. I think so- and what woman can make a go of show business and not be outgoing and uninhibited ?

"She's learned to please men, to understand them . And she's tired of the glitter and the glamor. She can fulfill every man's real dream- by being a lady in public, but a courtesan in the bedroom !"

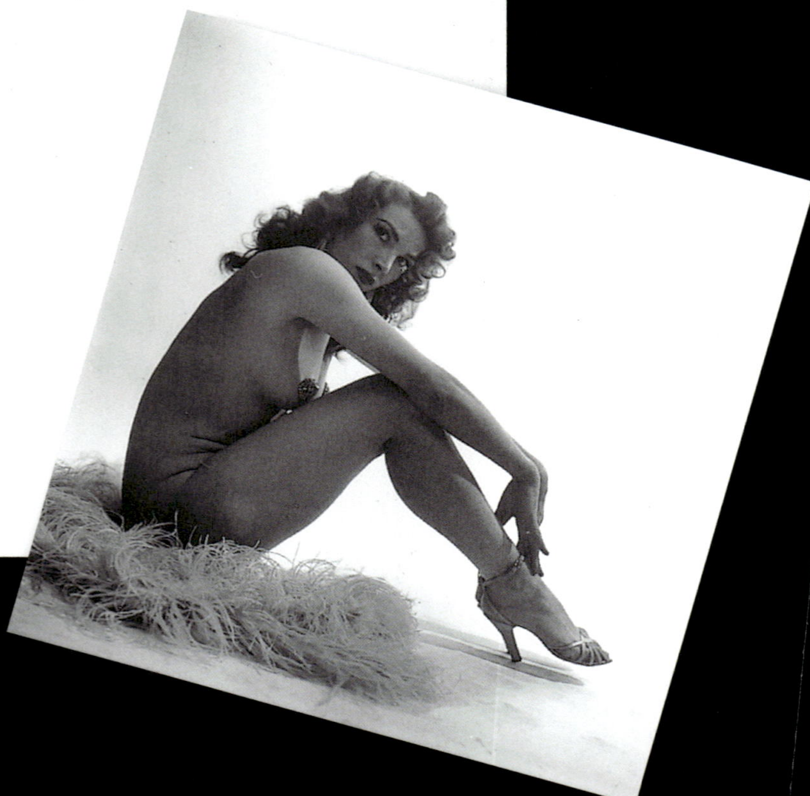

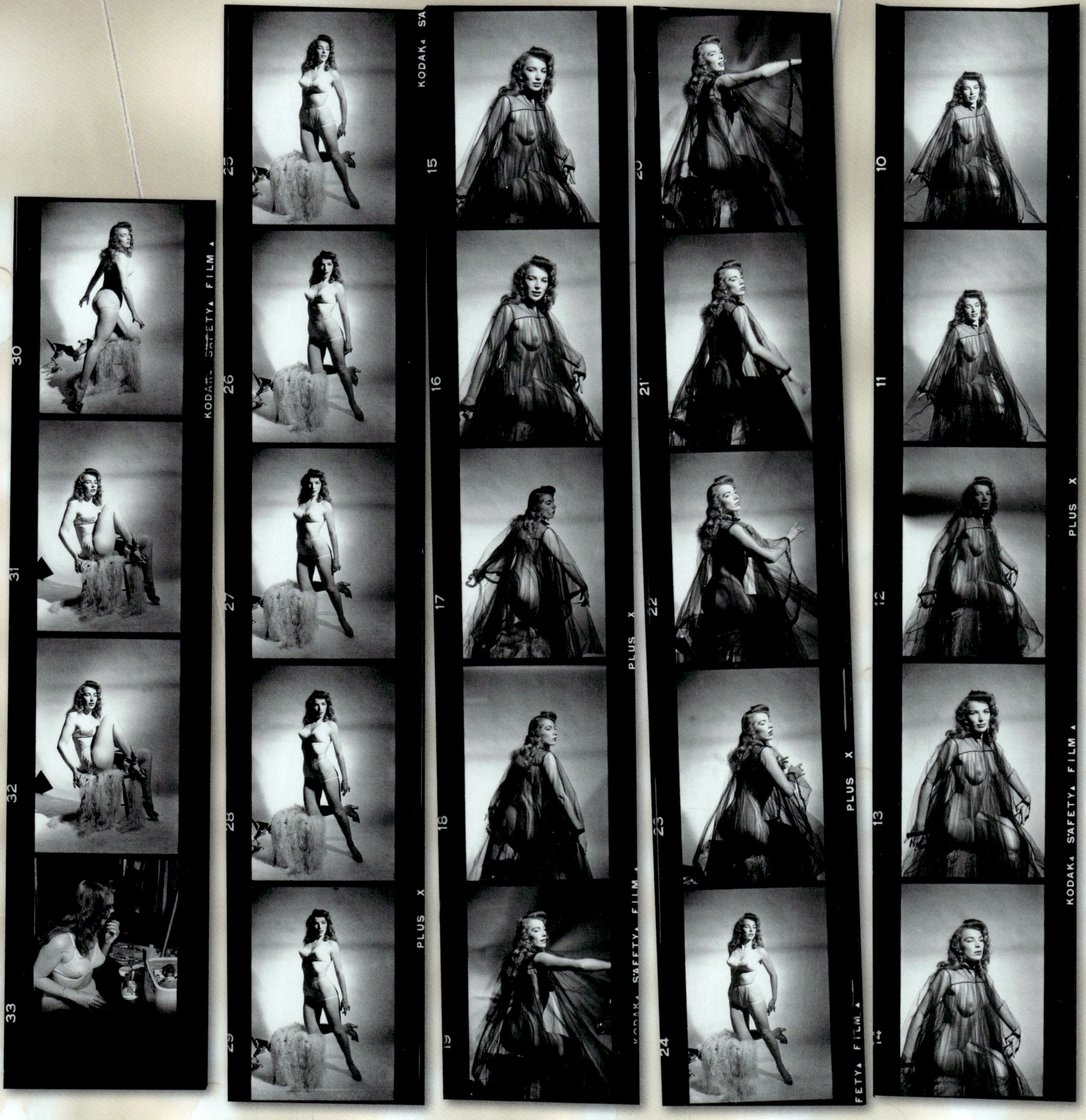
KODAK SAFETY FILM
PLUS X

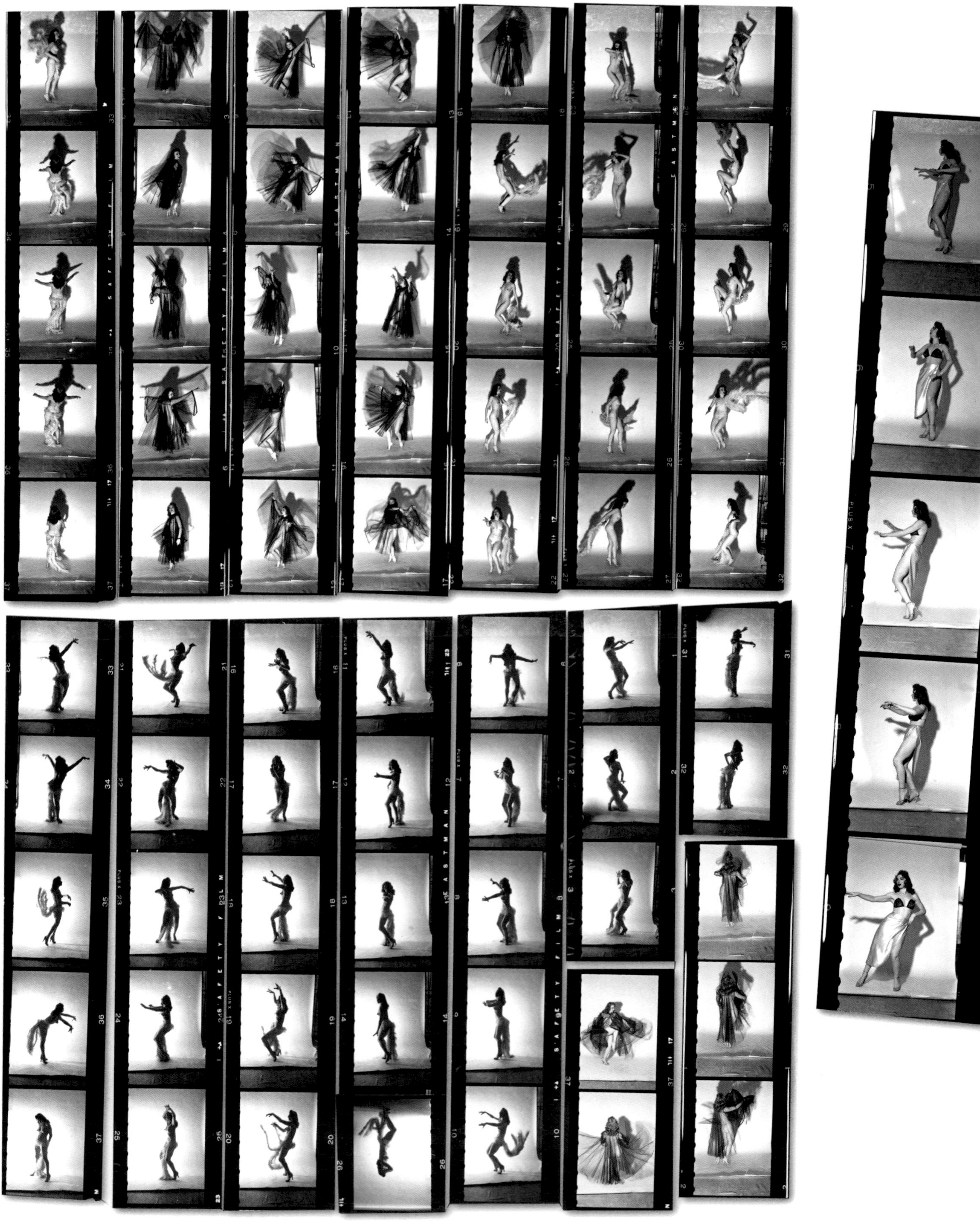

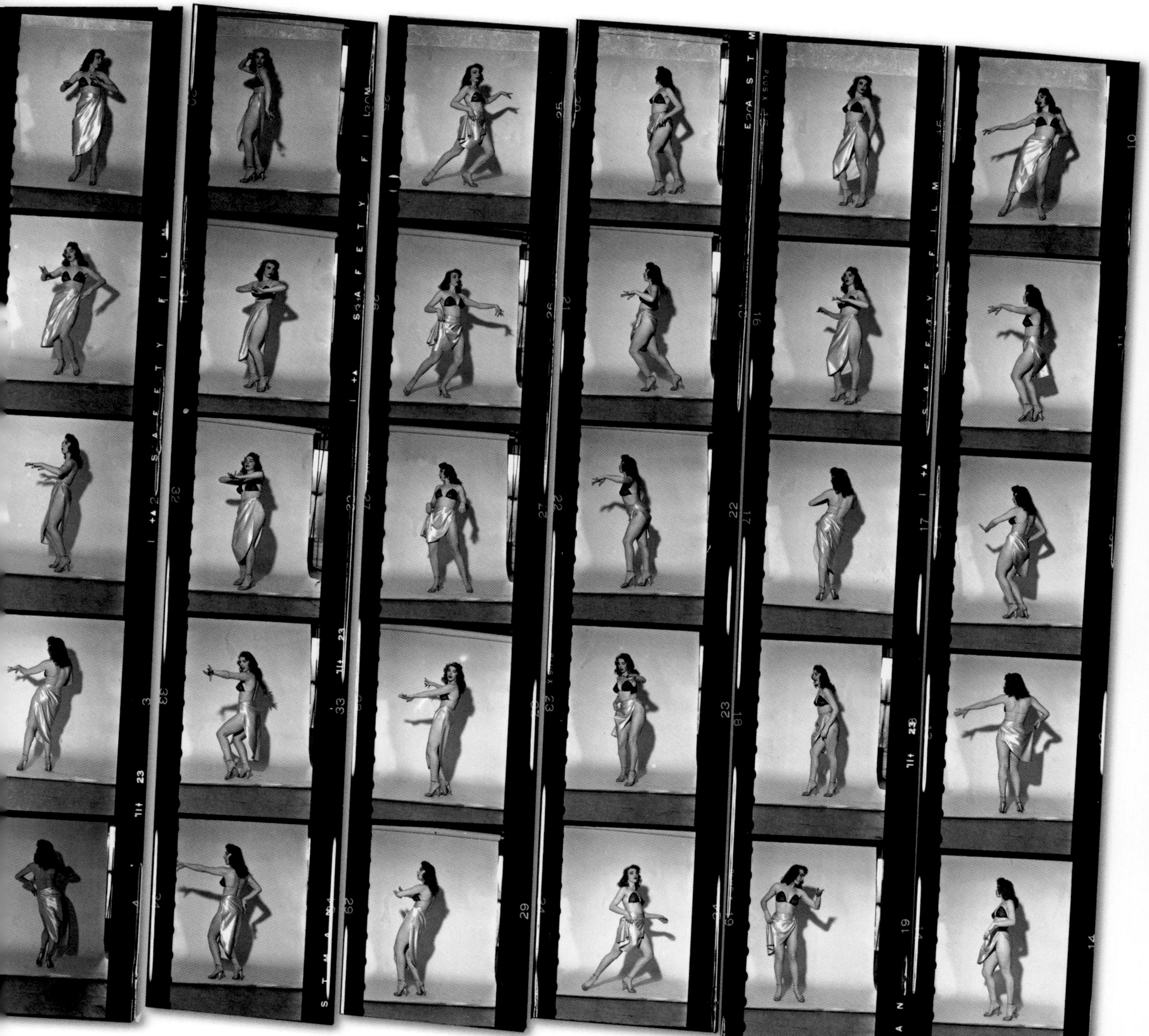

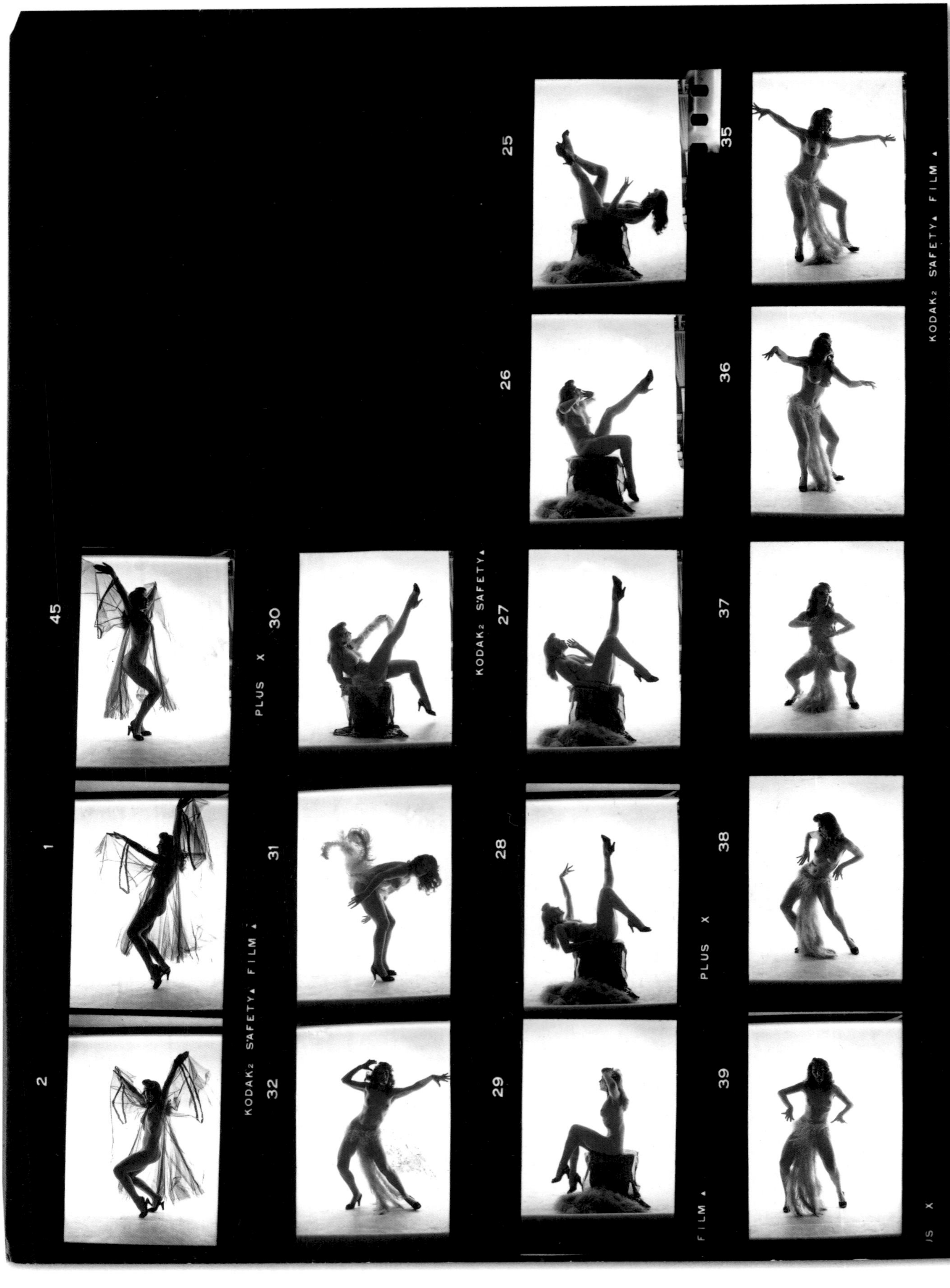
KODAK SAFETY FILM
PLUS X

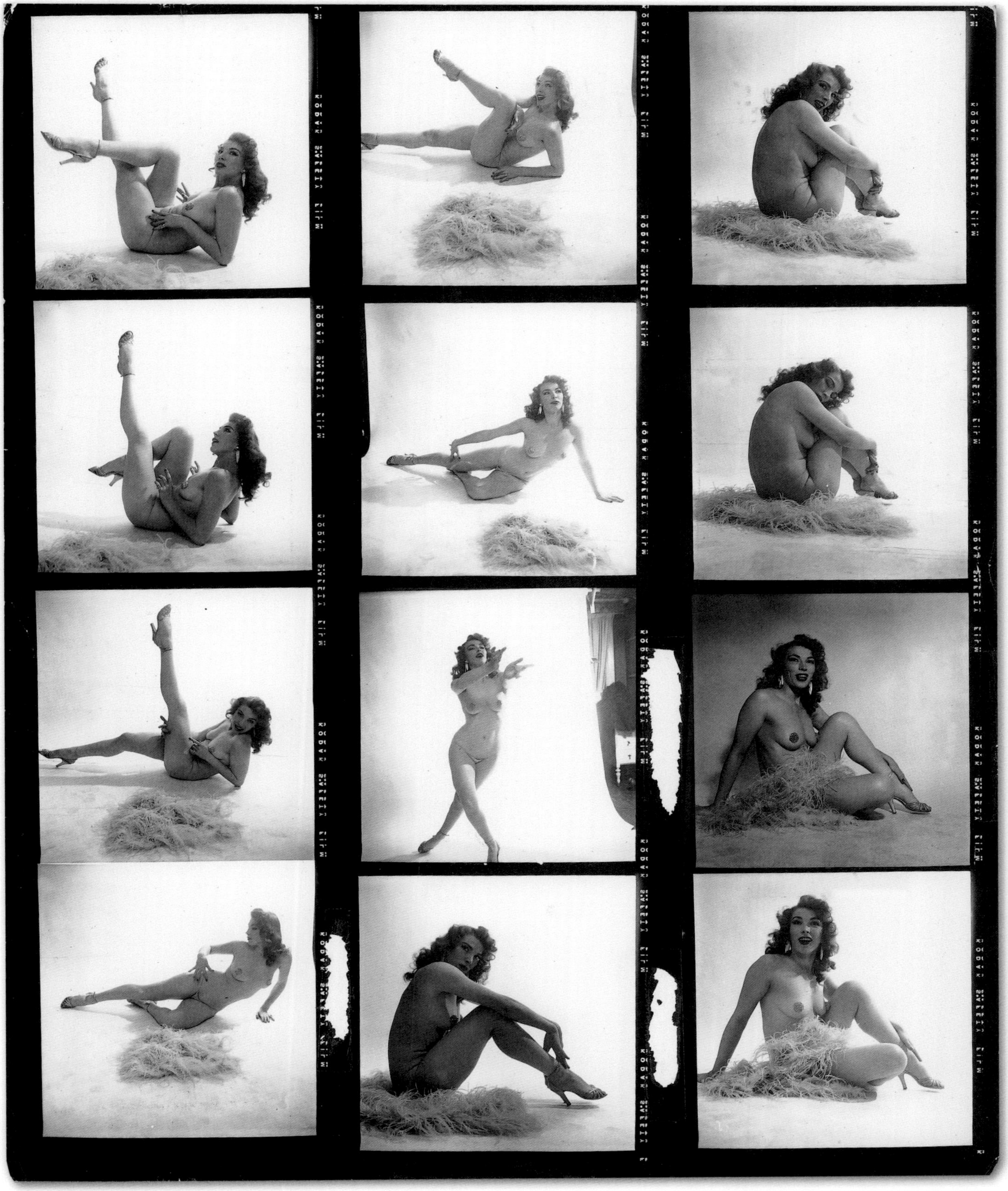

Brandy Martin

BRANDY MARTIN

Brooklyn born Brandy Martin began life in show business as an acrobatic dancer, turned to stripping because the pay is more regular and better. First time she stripped in public: "I died a thousand deaths, but not any more."

Brandy's costume consists of many parts which "must be put on correctly: takesx much longer to get it on than to take it off. My biggest expense is costumes...I pay $250 for each gown ... and I wear it for only two minutes."

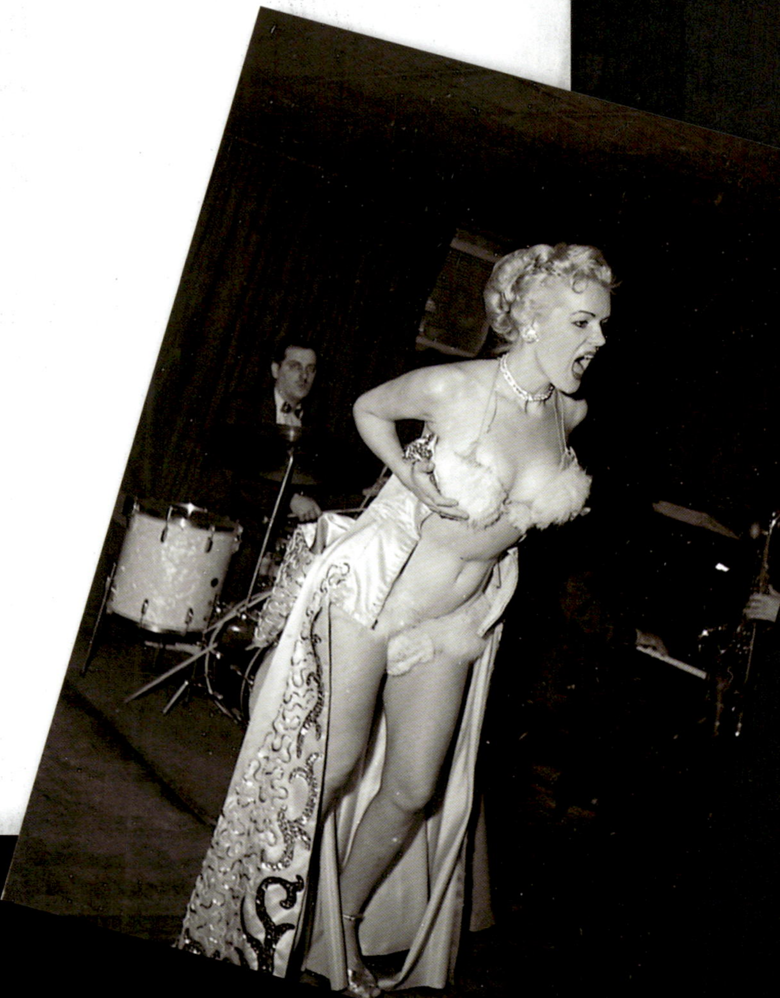

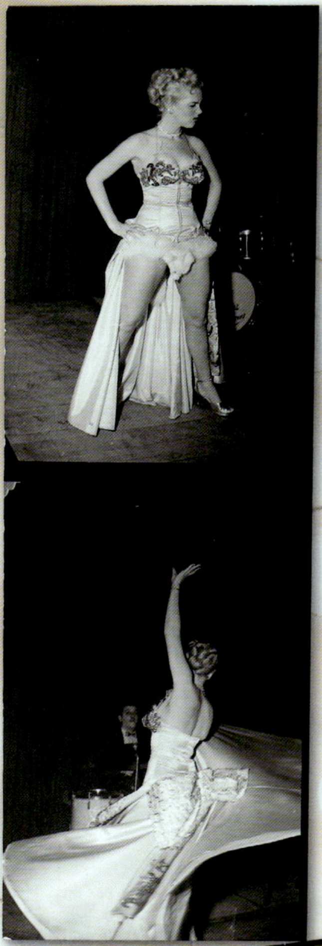

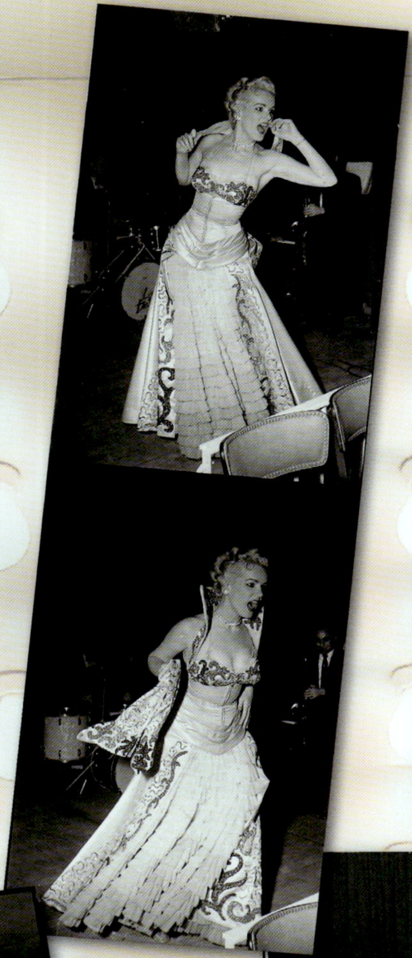

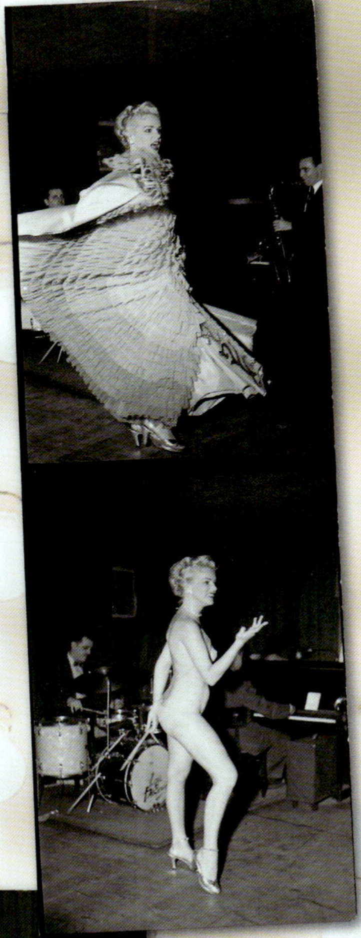

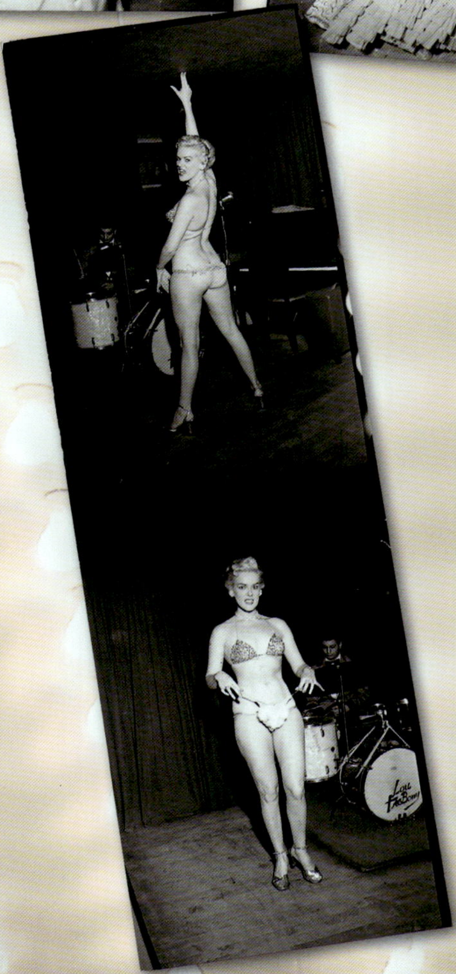

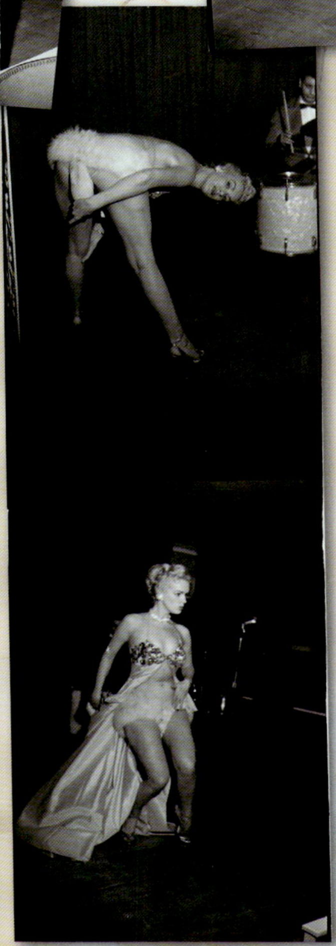

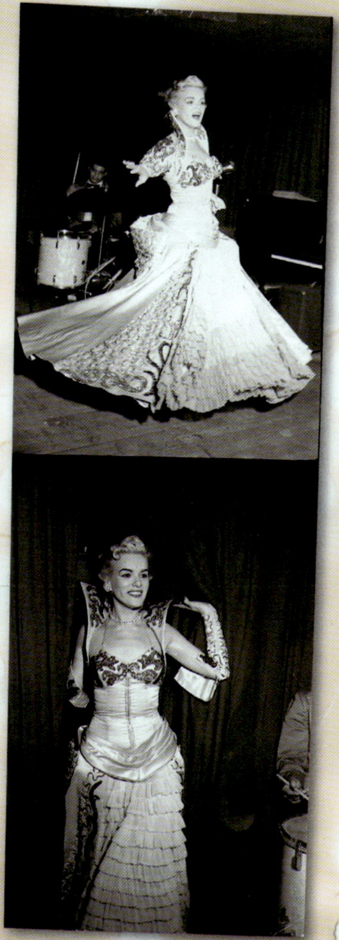

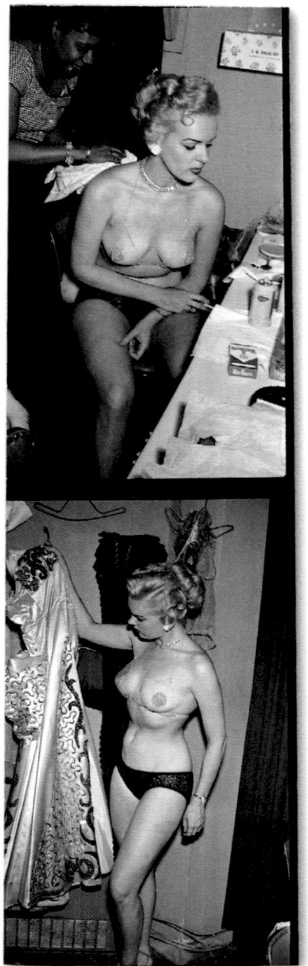
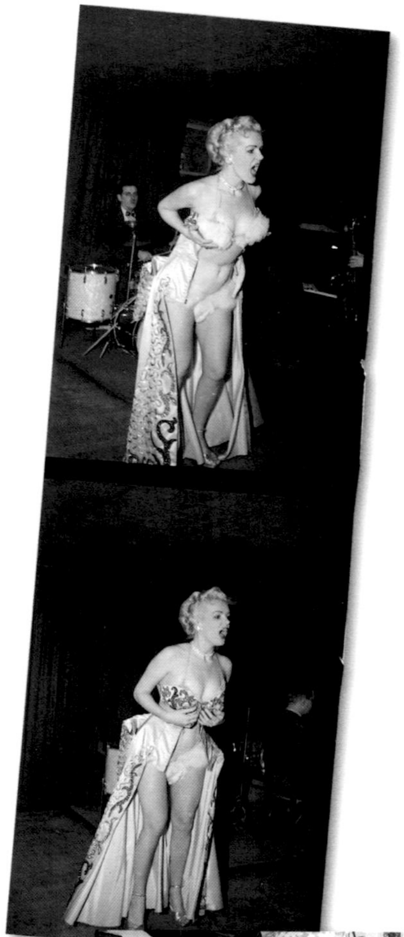
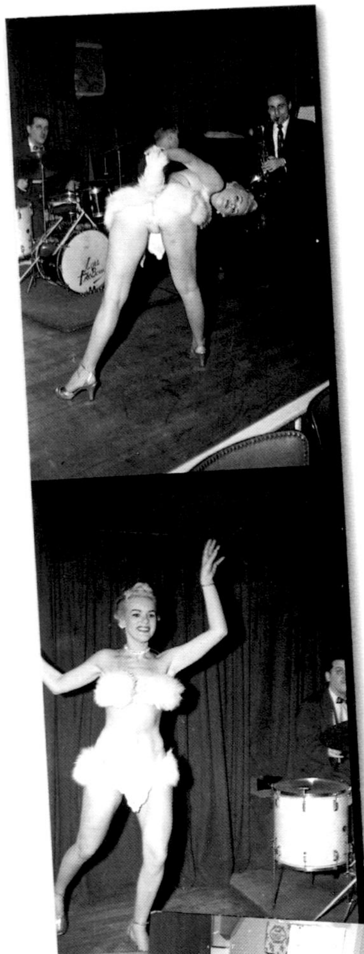
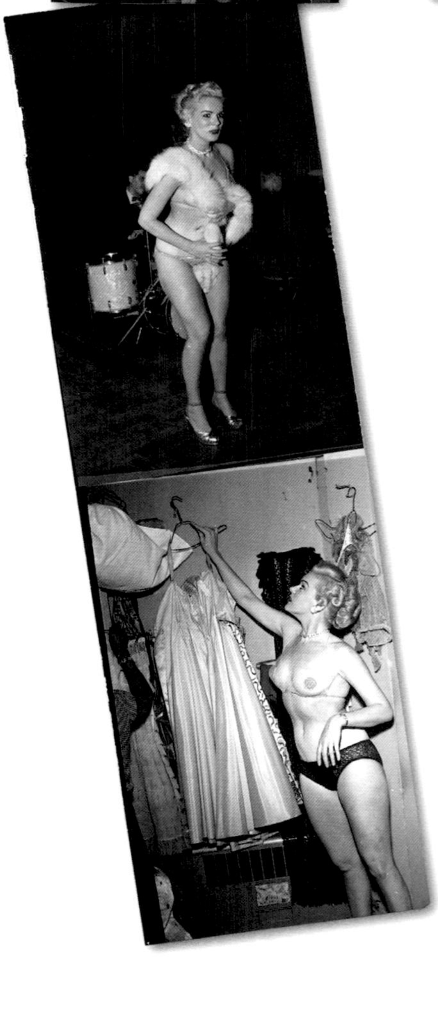
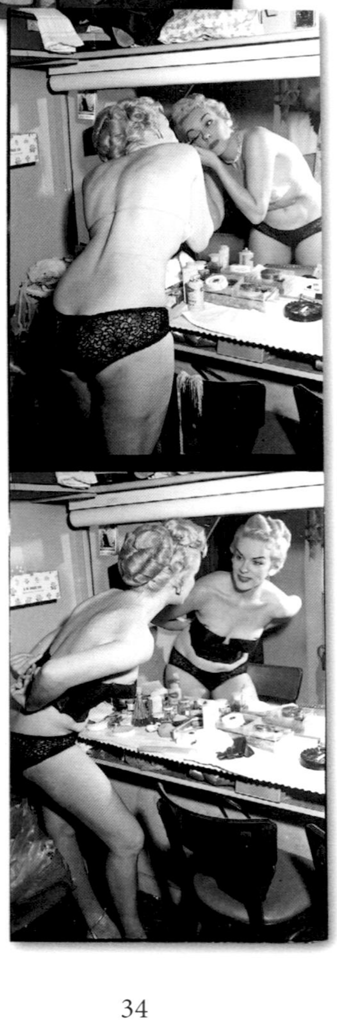
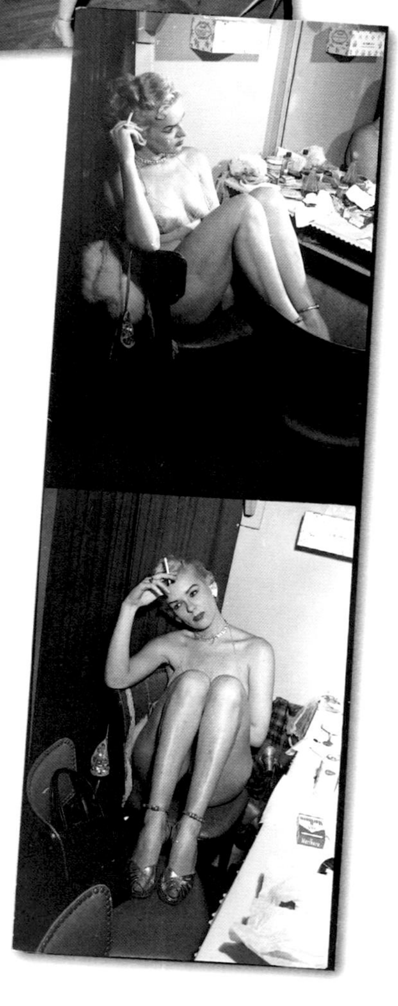

Brandy Martin

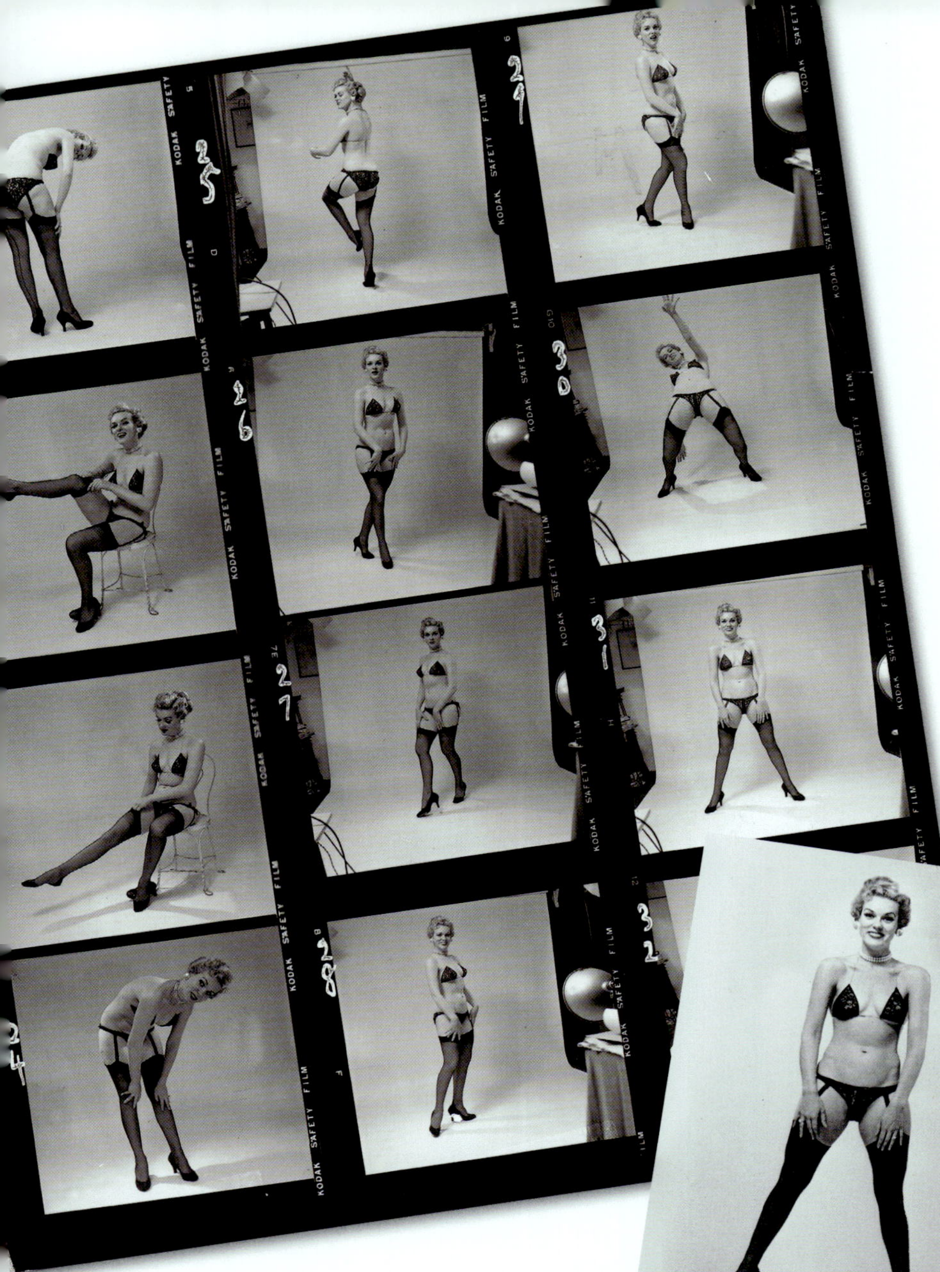

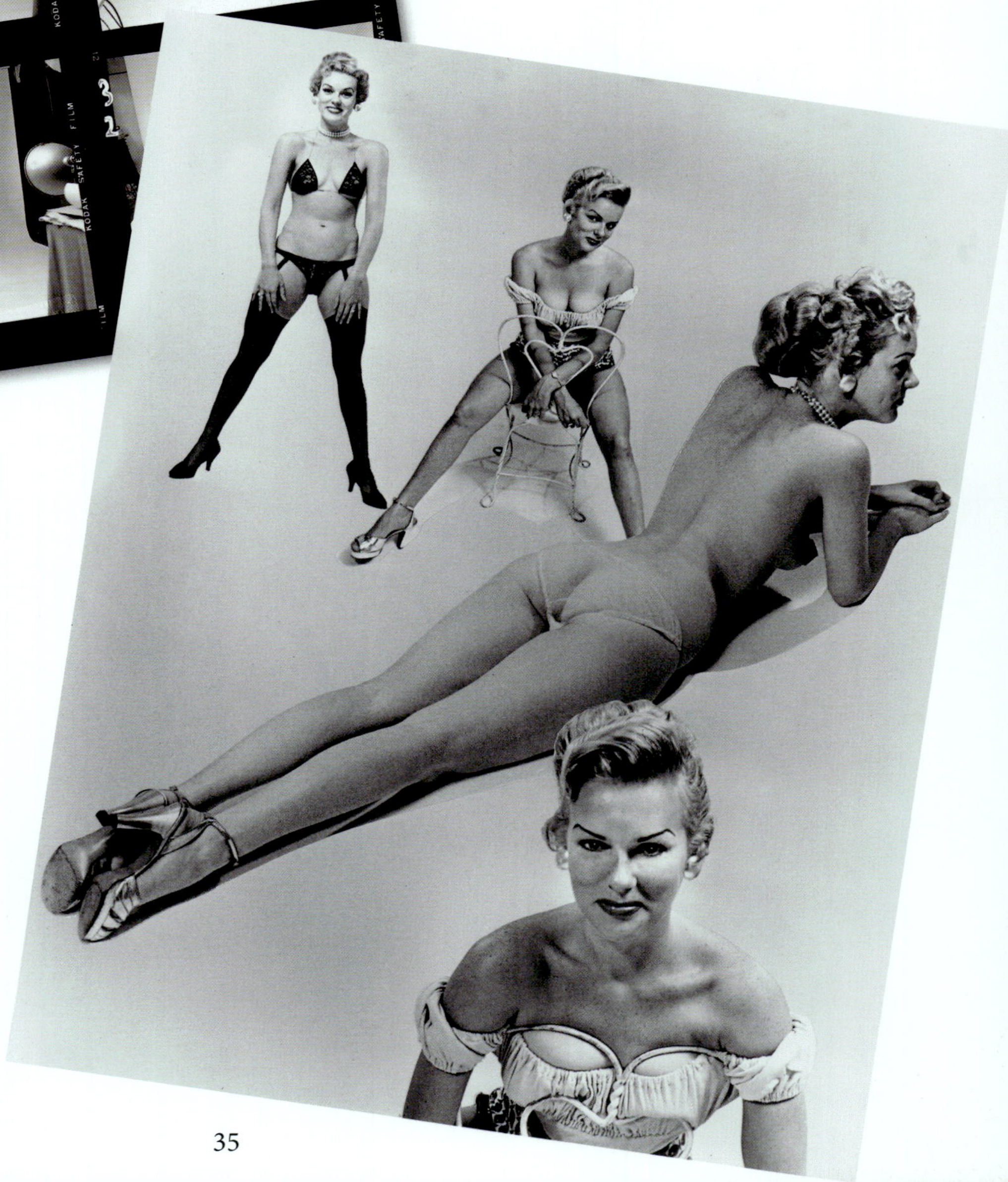

Bubbles Darlene

BUBBLES DARLINE

Born Virginia Lachimia, Bubbles Darline comes from Minneapolis. Her father is Macedonian, her mother Irish. She's a specialist in Afro-Cuban rhythms, spent two years in Havana, where she was known as "the blonde Catherine Dunham". Her favorite dances belong to the Caribbean Islands: Calypso, Haitian Voodoo, Afro-Cuban Mambo, the Meringue, the Cha-cha-cha.

Like other top-flight exotics, Bubbles has had extensive background in ballet, is an accomplished actress as well as a dancer. Half the effectivemess of ger act depends on her spoken lines. Her infectious good humor, her naivetee, sets the audience at ease at once.

She has two aims in life: to be a star in a Broadway musical; to find the right man."It is hard to make one man happy,"she says , "so I want to make them all happy with my art".

She's 24 years old, weighs 117 lbs, 5'3" tall, measures 37-23-35.

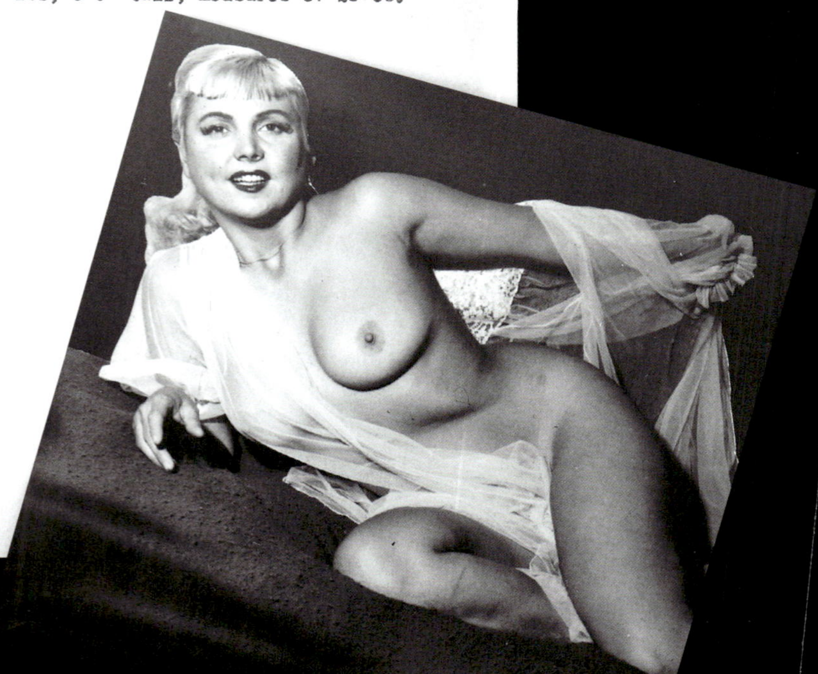

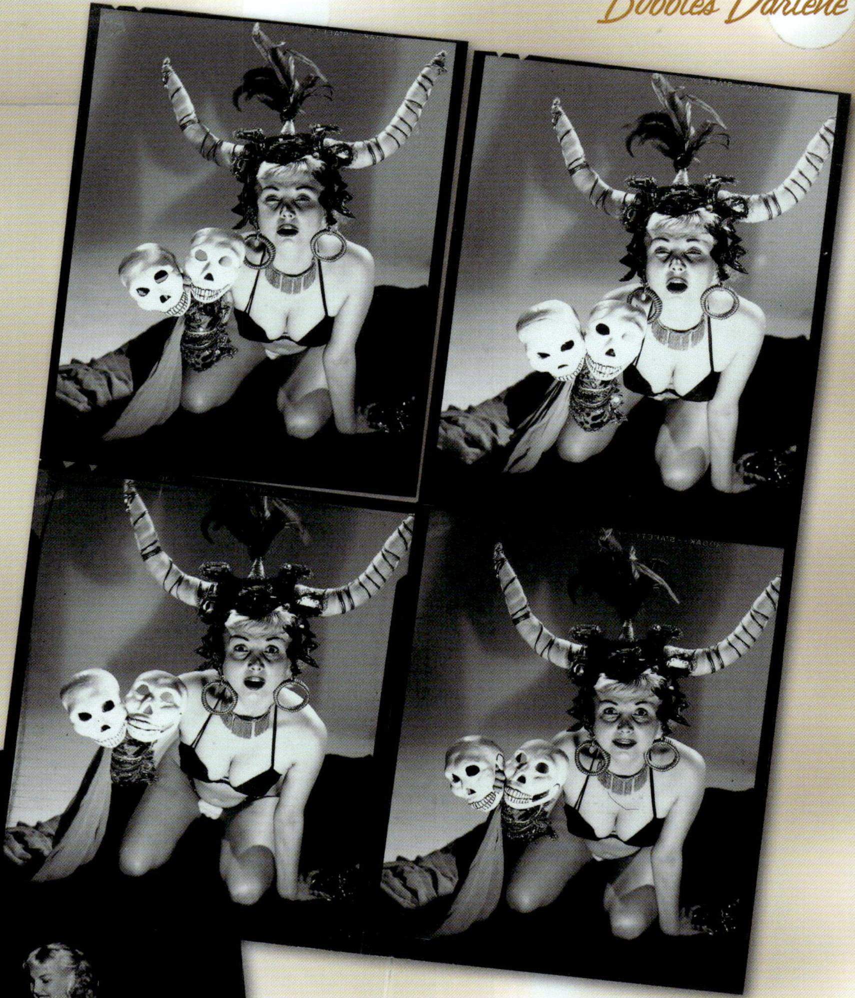

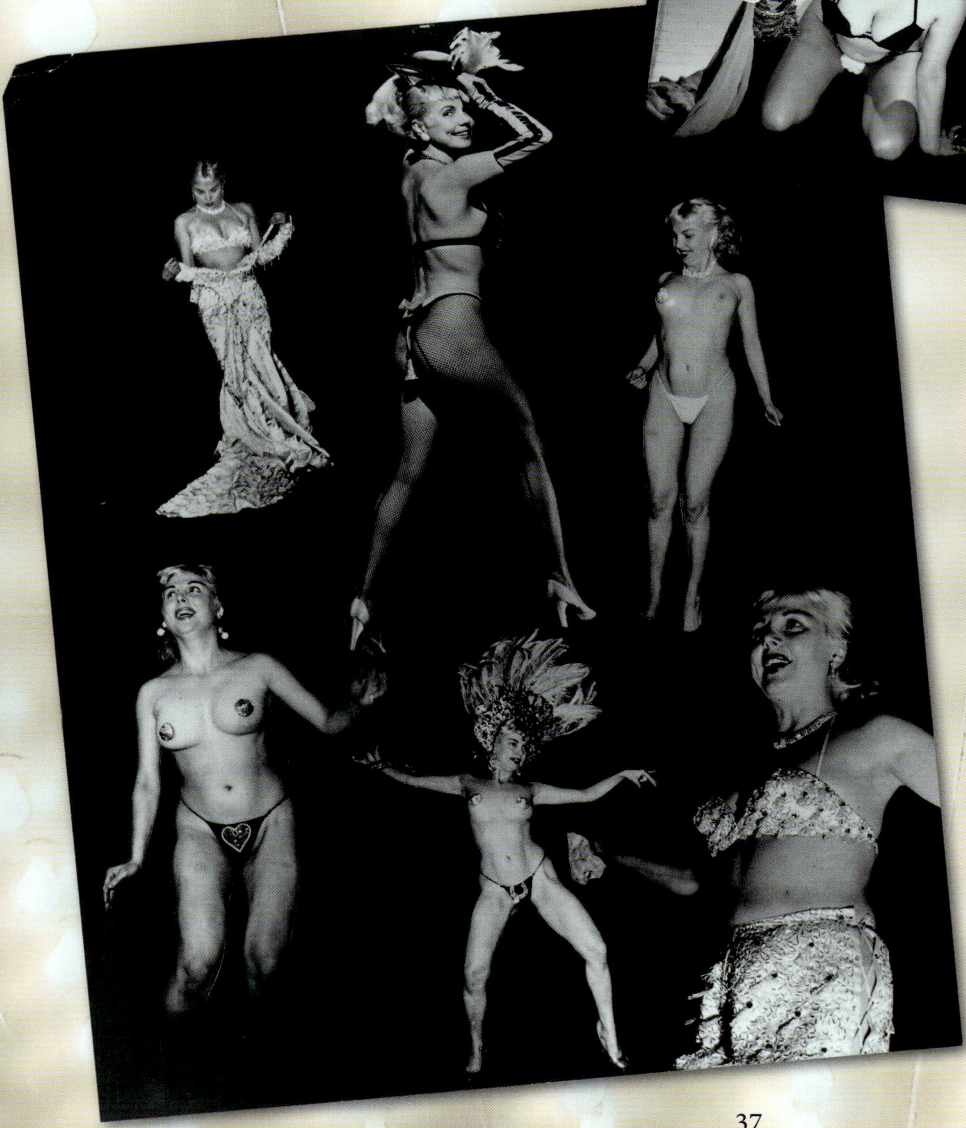

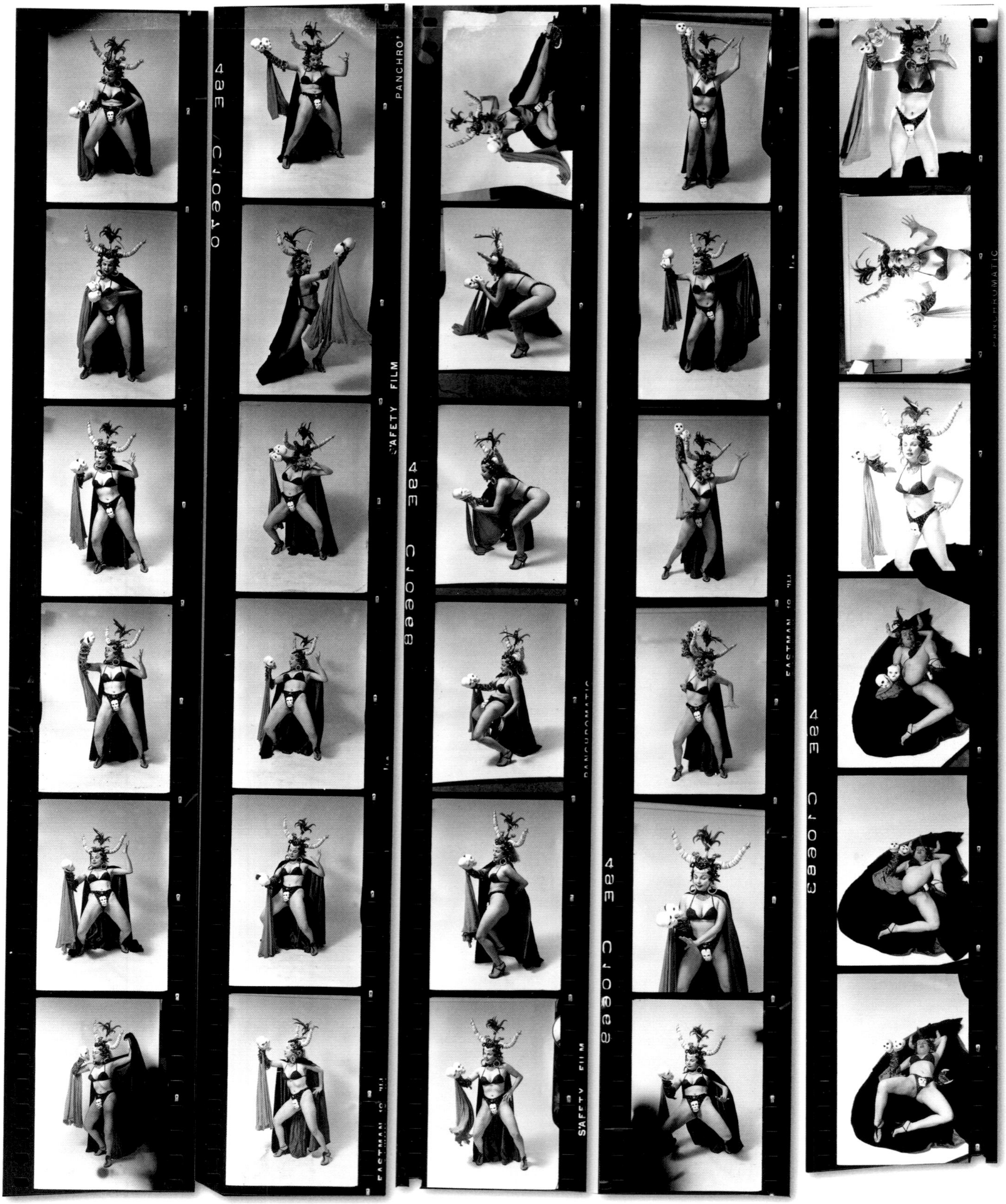
PANCHRO
SAFETY FILM
PANCHROMATIC

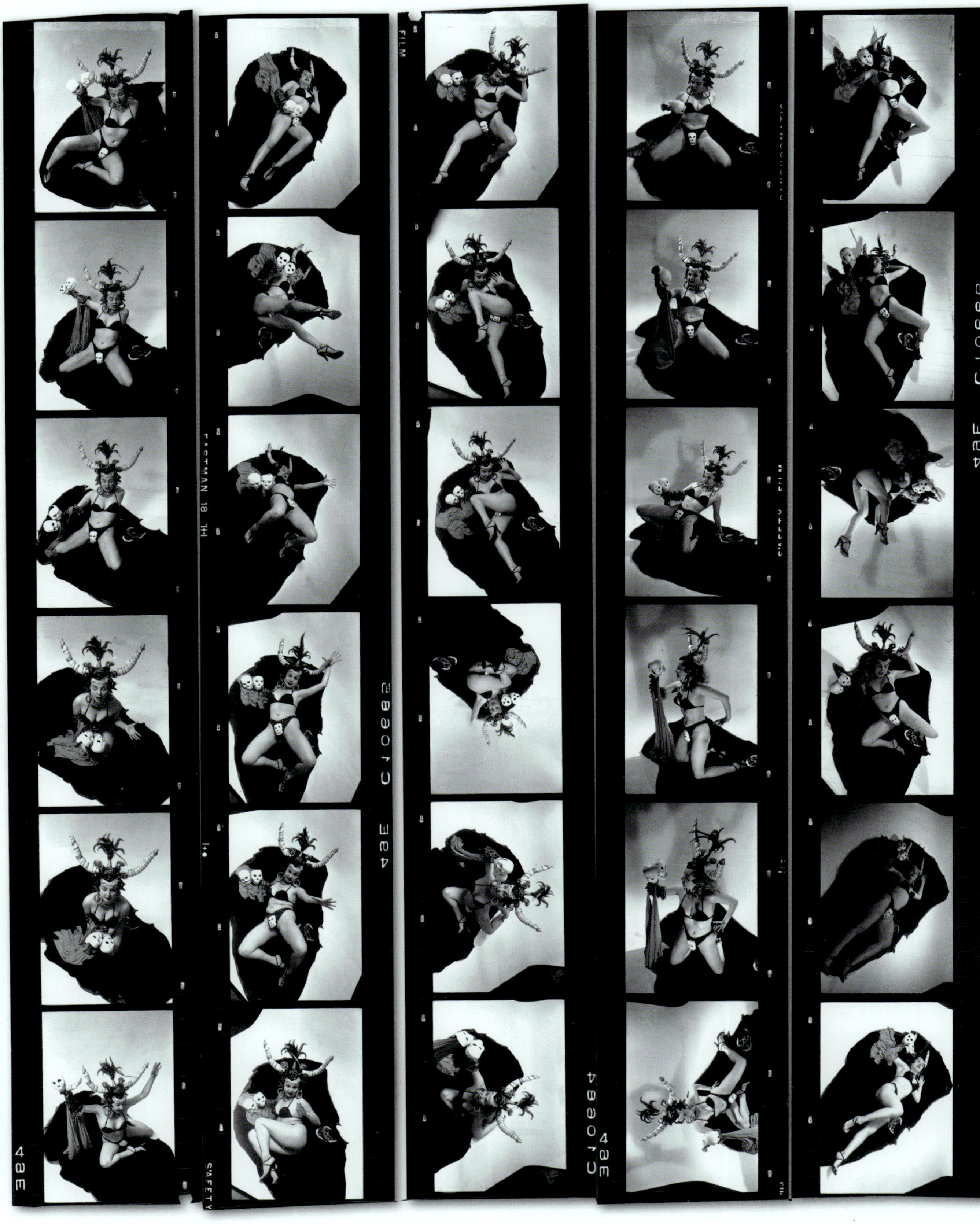

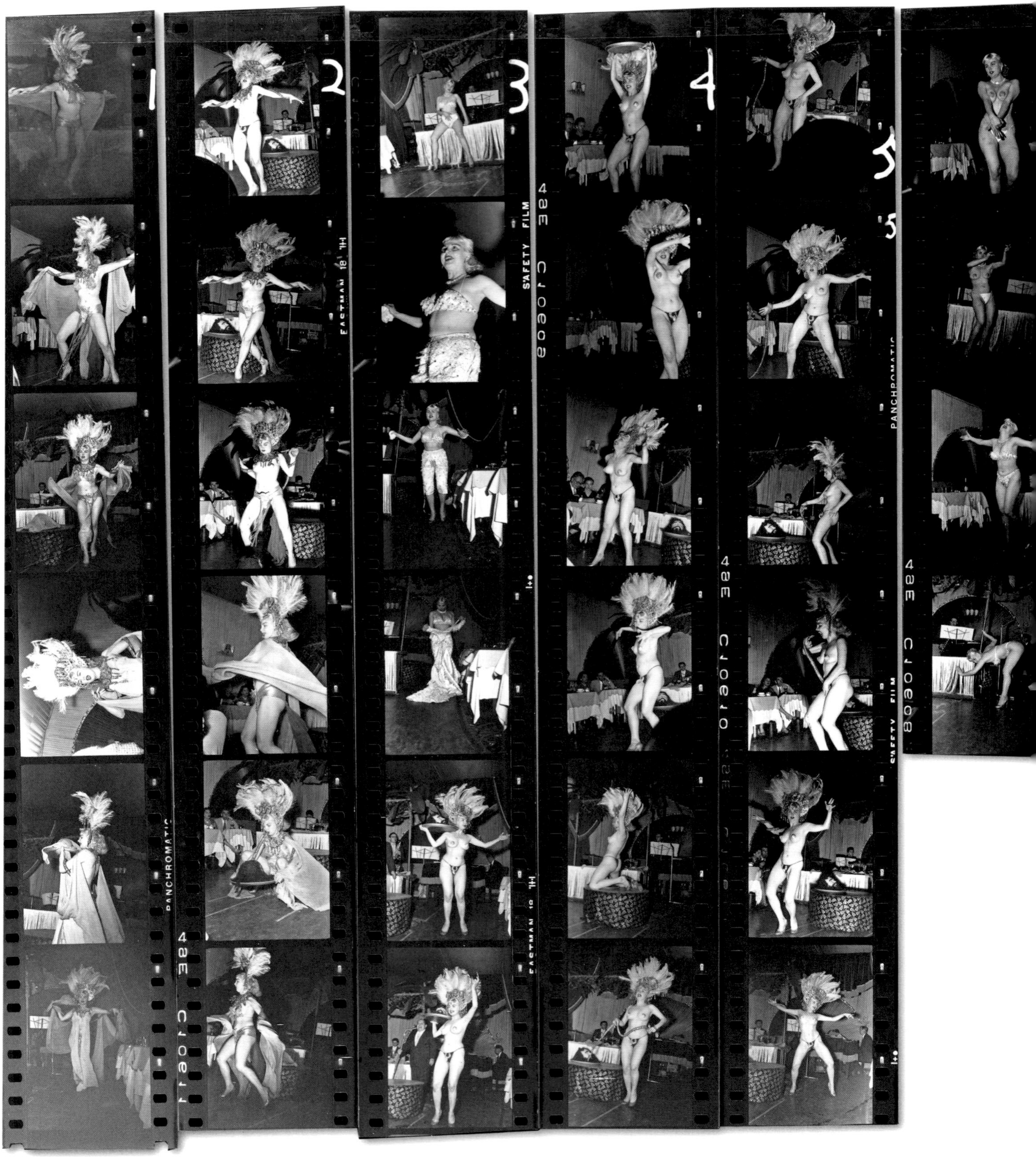
SAFETY FILM
PANCHROMATIC

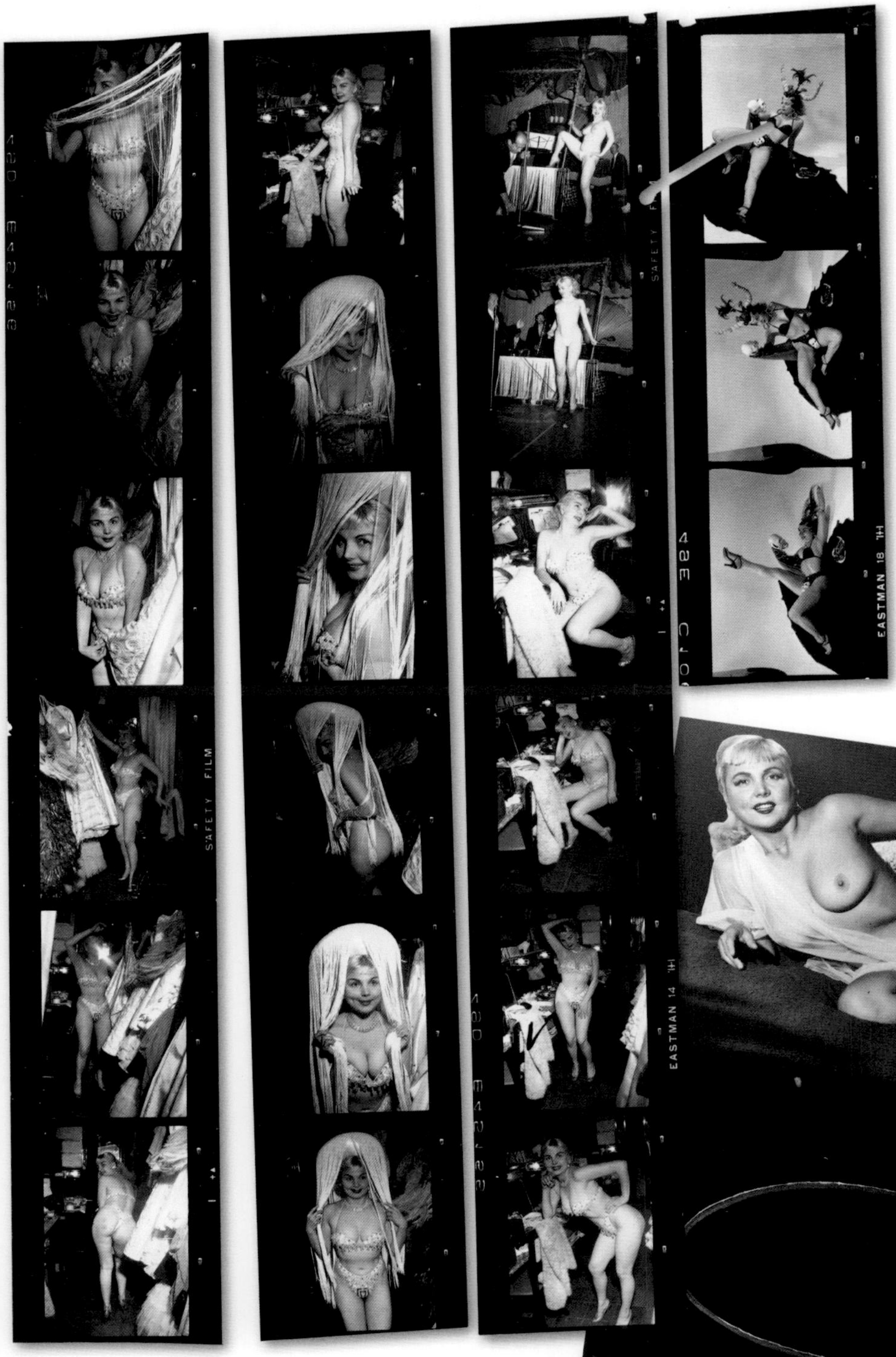
SAFETY FILM
EASTMAN 18
EASTMAN 14

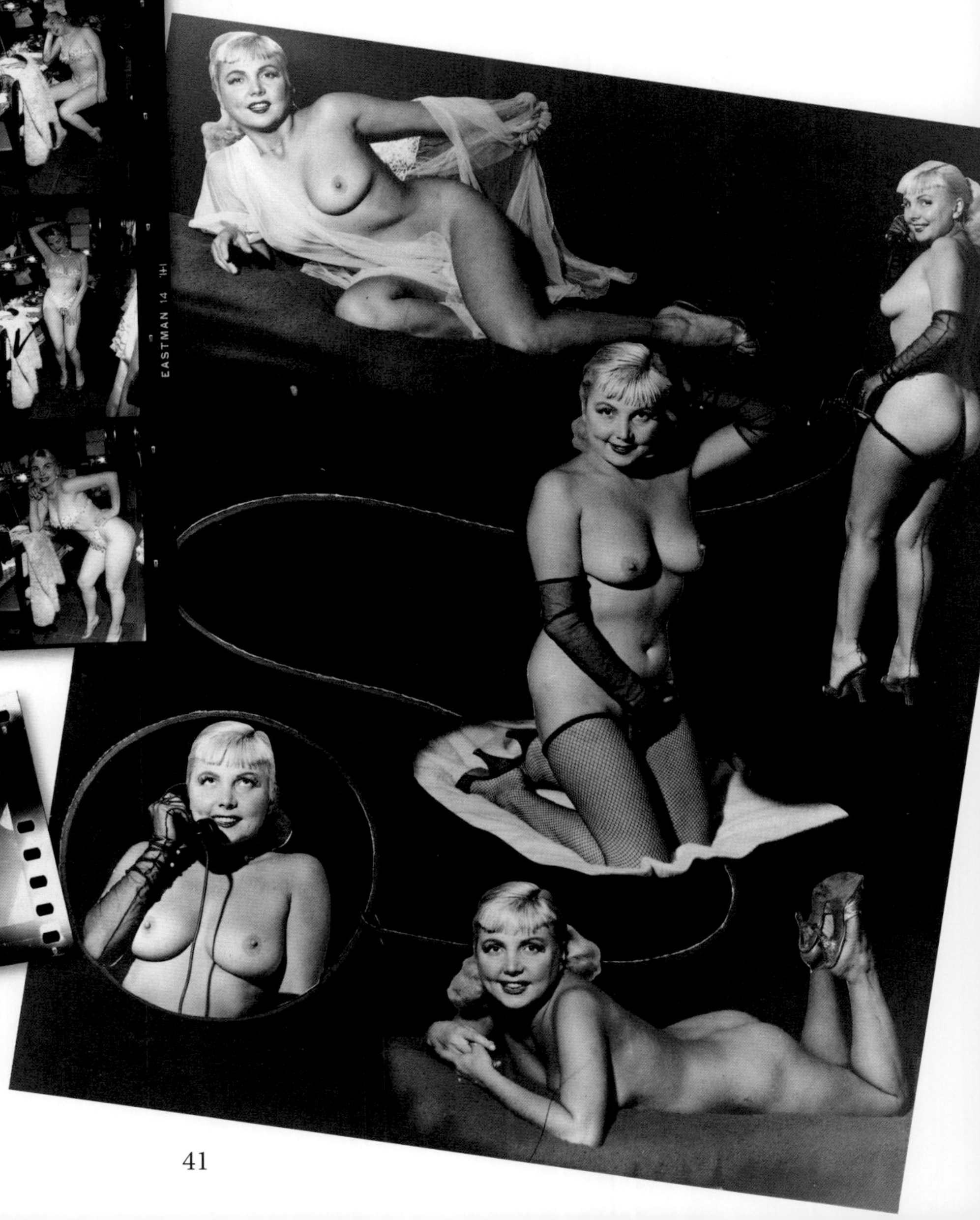

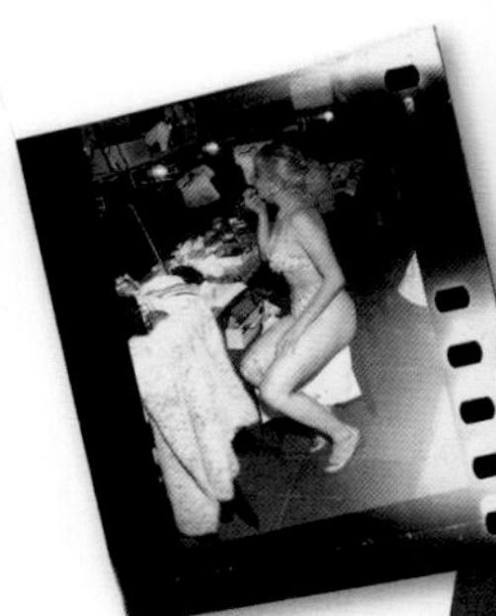

Camille

CAMILLE

Camille was an office manager in San Francisco, became bored with office routine and changed occupation to exotic dancer. Restless girl, she changes the color of her hair, too, from red to black, and back again, as the spirit moves. A talented performer, Camille plays her act straight-without props or gimmicks, depends on the fire of her personality and her dancing ability to please the customers. She's a dynamic figure that sways and struts. Her sensuous body twirls rhythmically. When she bumps, six feet of well-stacked female let go. Camille has blazed a trail of success from Las Vegas to New York and then to Miami Beach. She is a vegetarian, doesn't drink, and hopes some day to go to Paris. She likrs her men tall, dark and suave.

Camille is six feet tall, measures 39-26-39.

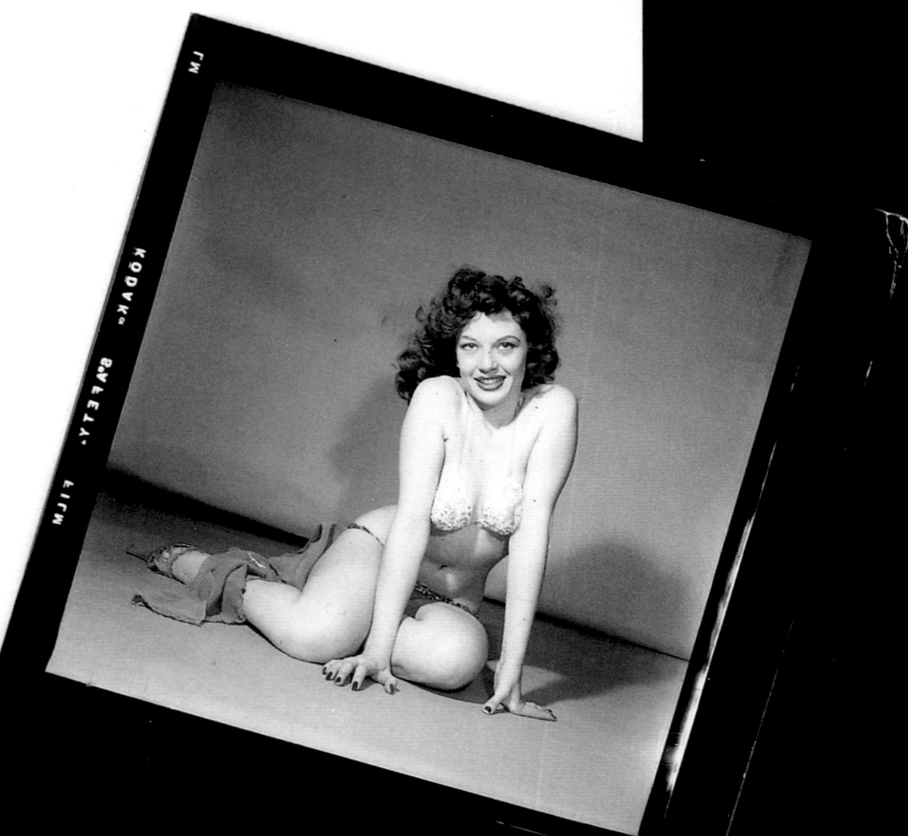

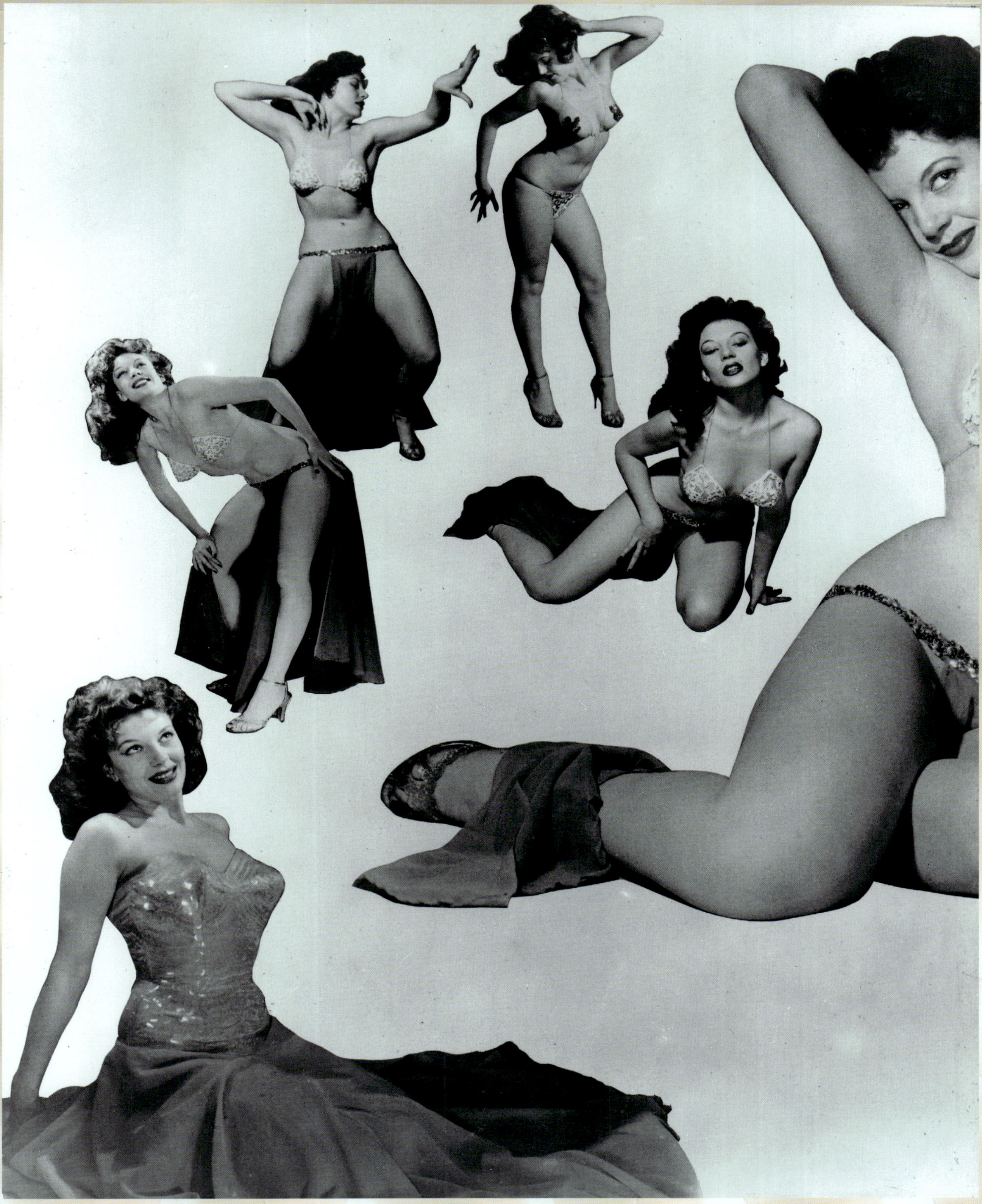

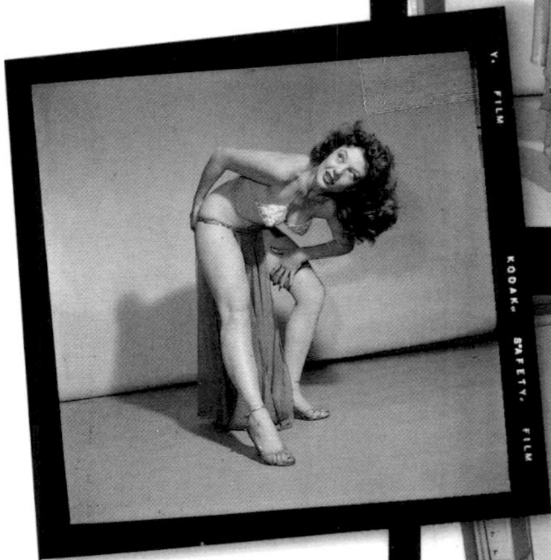

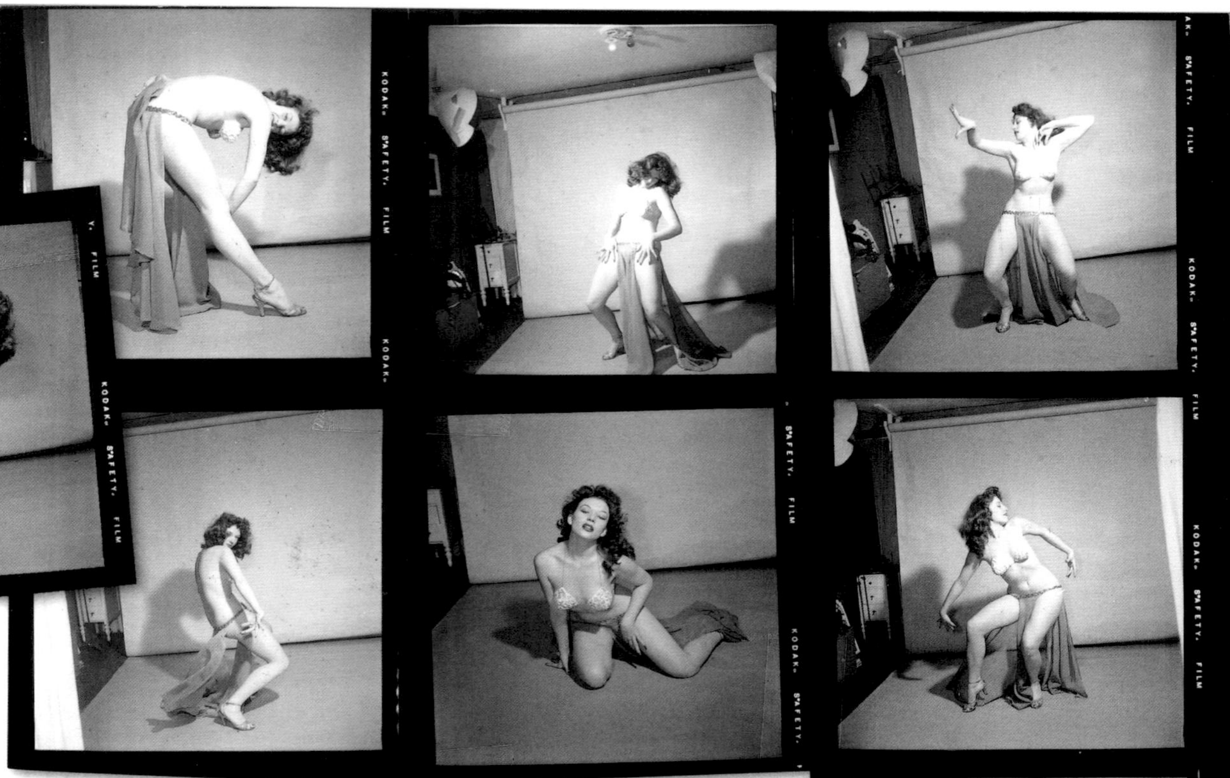

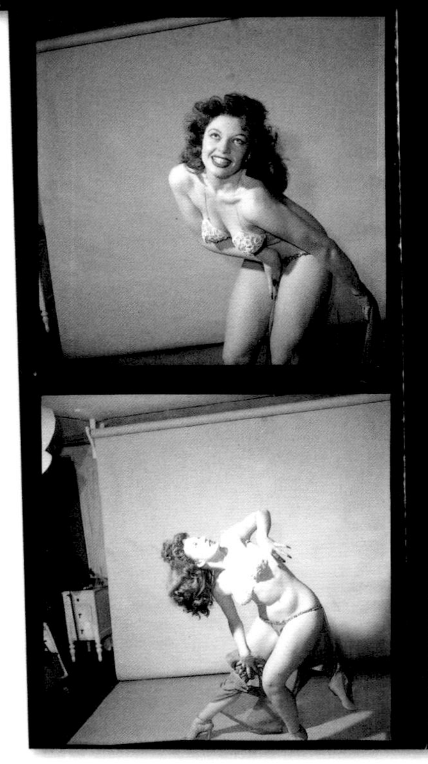

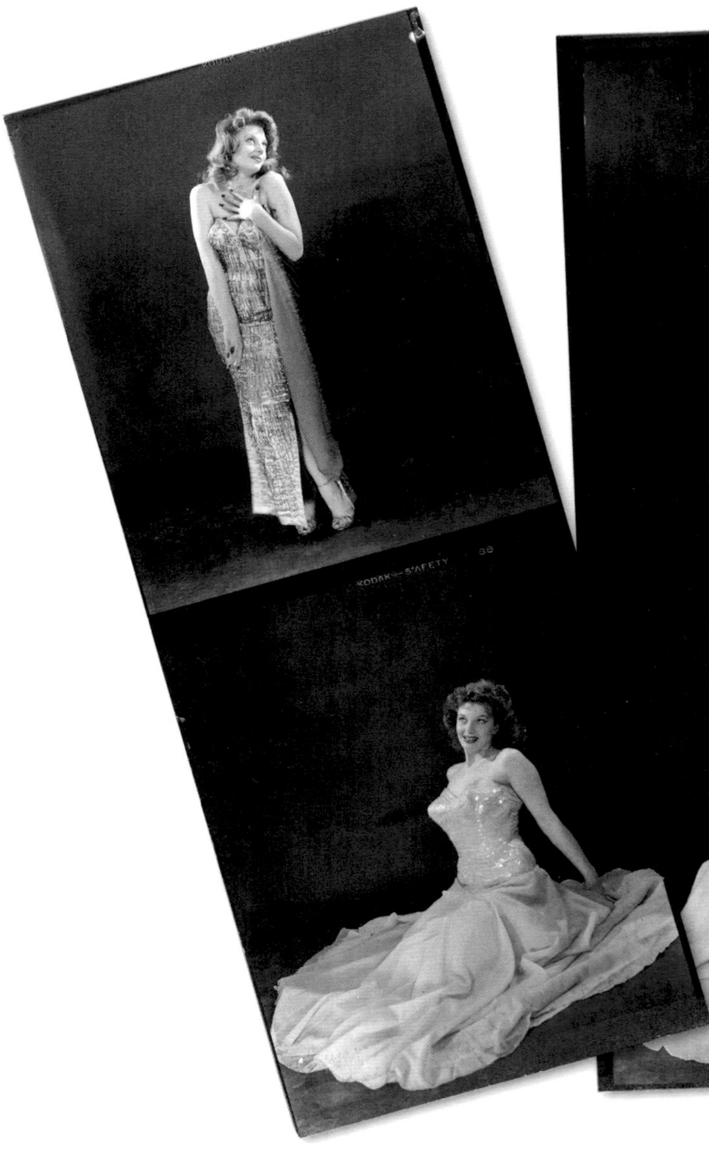

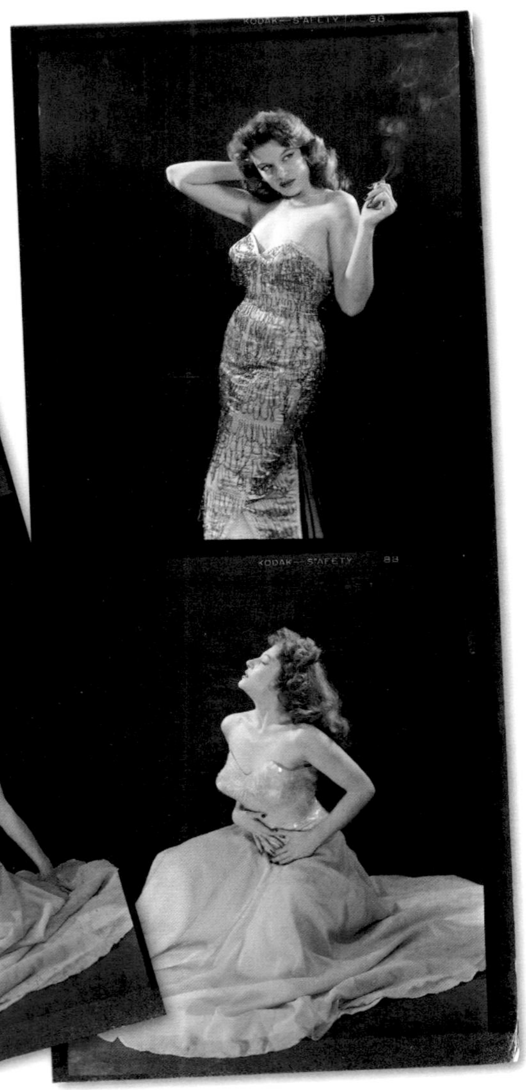

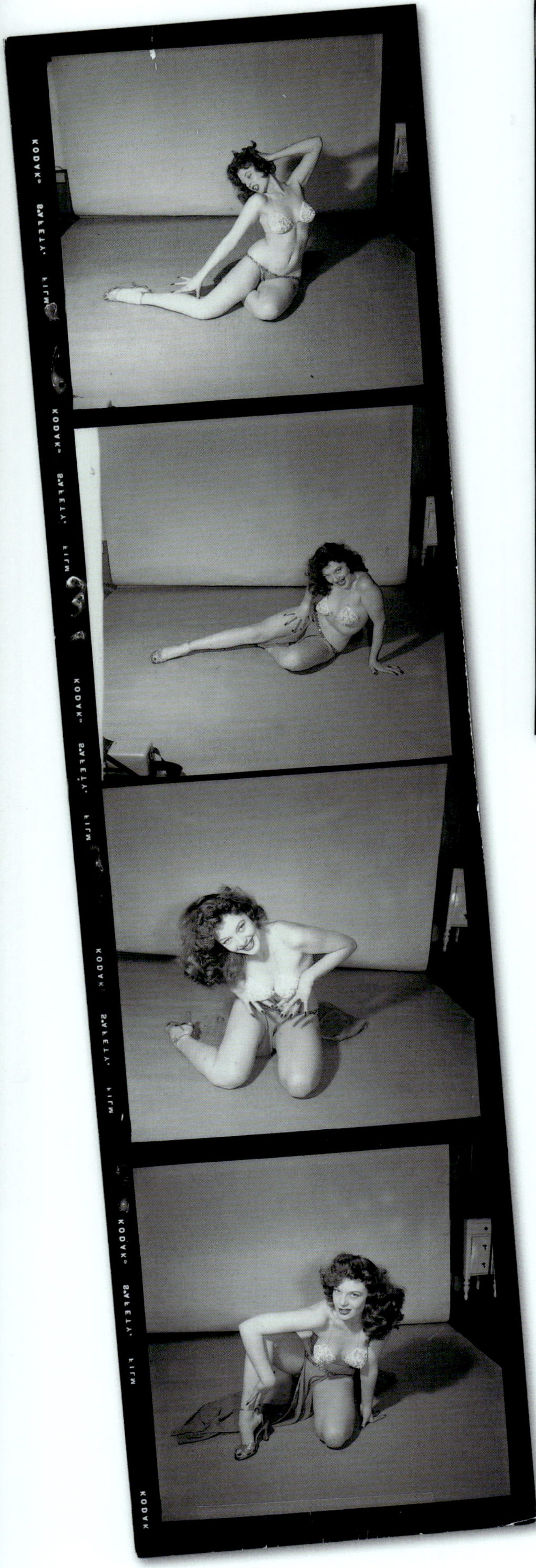

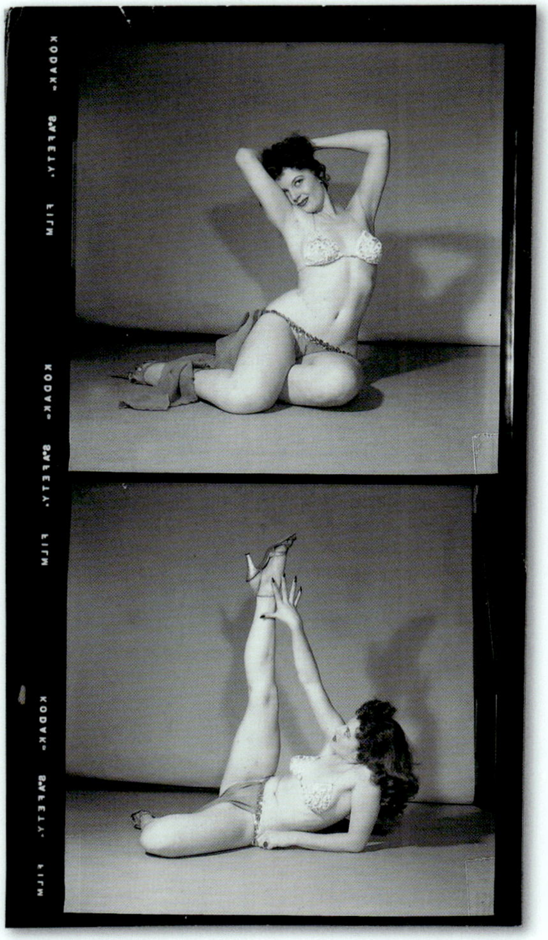

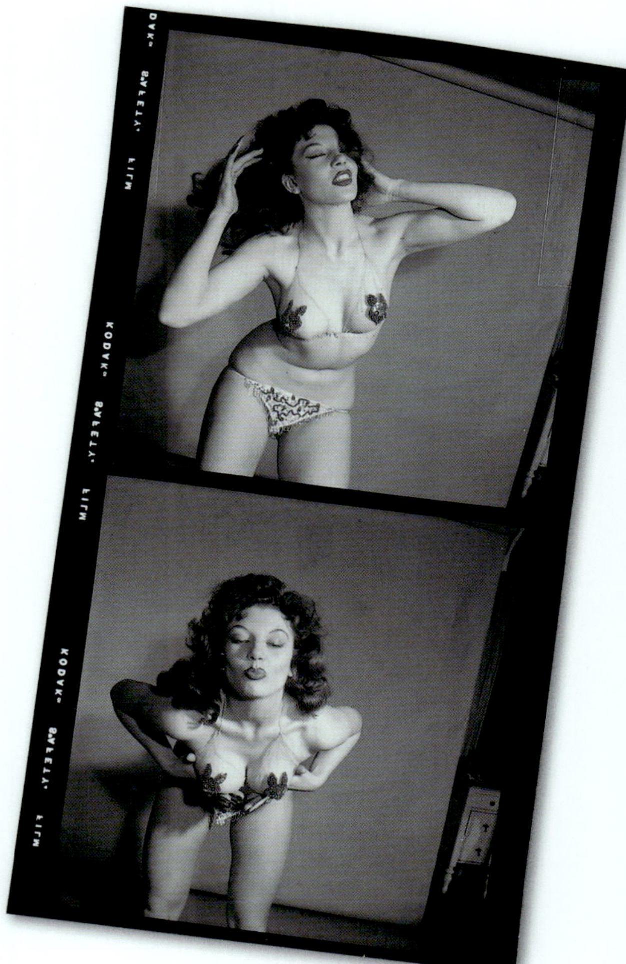

Carmela

CARMELA

Raven-haired Carmela Durso hails from Washington, D.C., where she was discovered working as a hostess in a club. One thing led to another, as the saying goes, and before she knew it, Carmela was up front doing an act with the best of them.

She's 25 years old, weighs 122 lbs., is 5'5" tall, measures 39-25-38, has worked burlesque houses of the east coast, mid-west and in Canada: CARMEN-Philadelphia, XXXXXX PALACE- Buffalo, ROXY- Cleveland, CASINO-Boston, GAYETY-Baltimore, GRAND-St. Louis, FOLLIES-Chicago, MINSKY'S-Newark, EMPIRE-Newark, CASINO-Toronto, as well as the Kain Circuit in Ohio.

CARMELA makes her own wardrobe, likes fishing, window-shopping, wants to make enough money to start a small business of her own somewhere

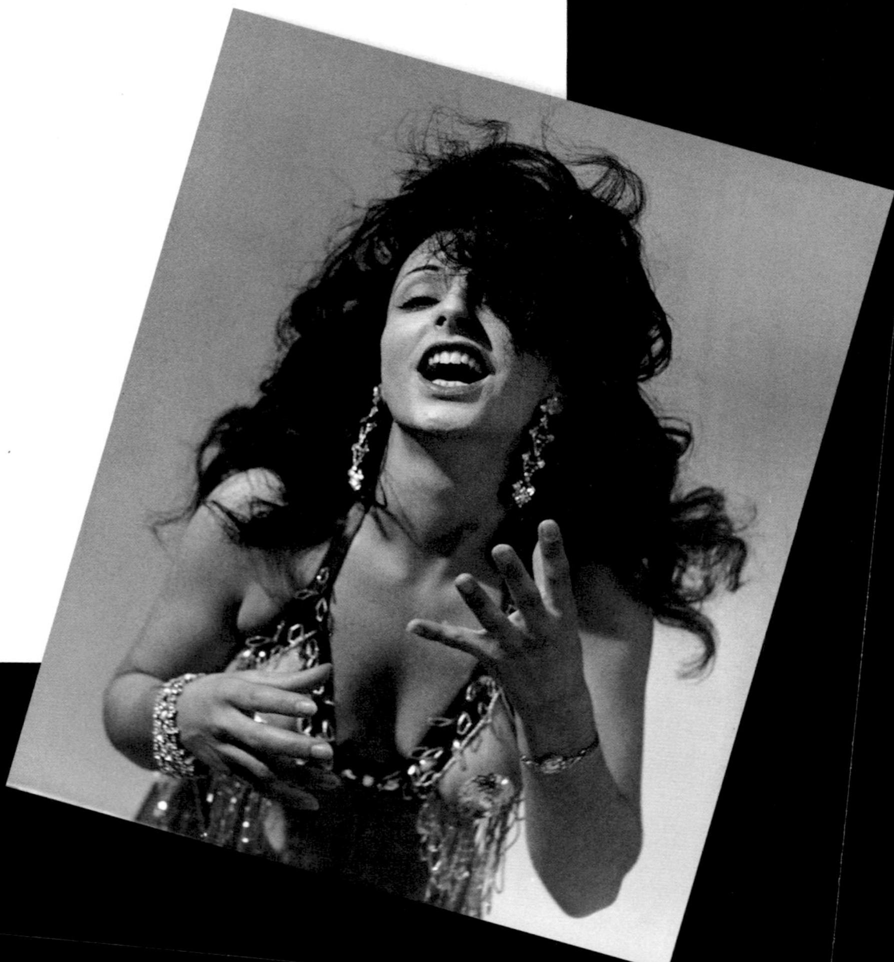

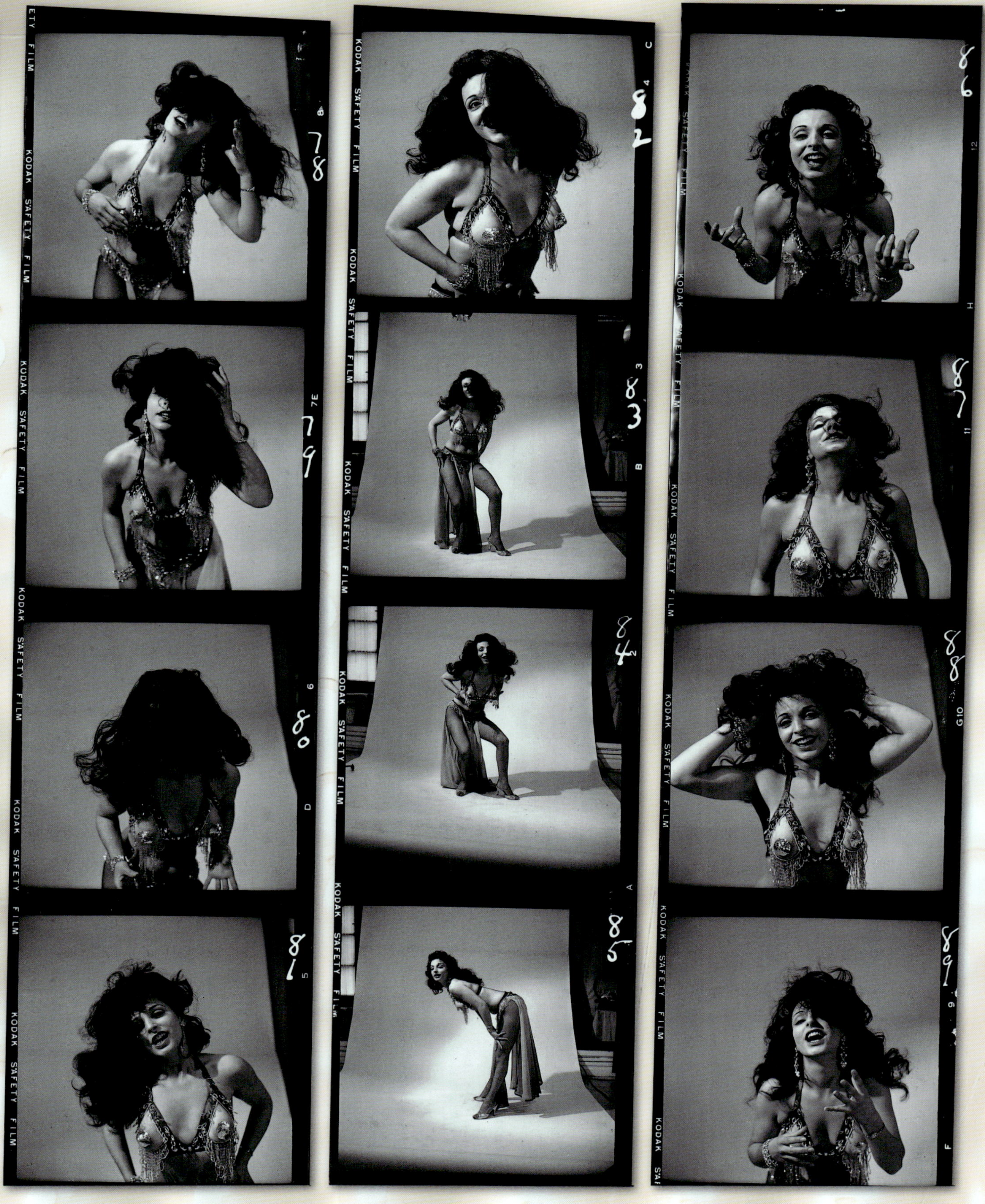
KODAK SAFETY FILM

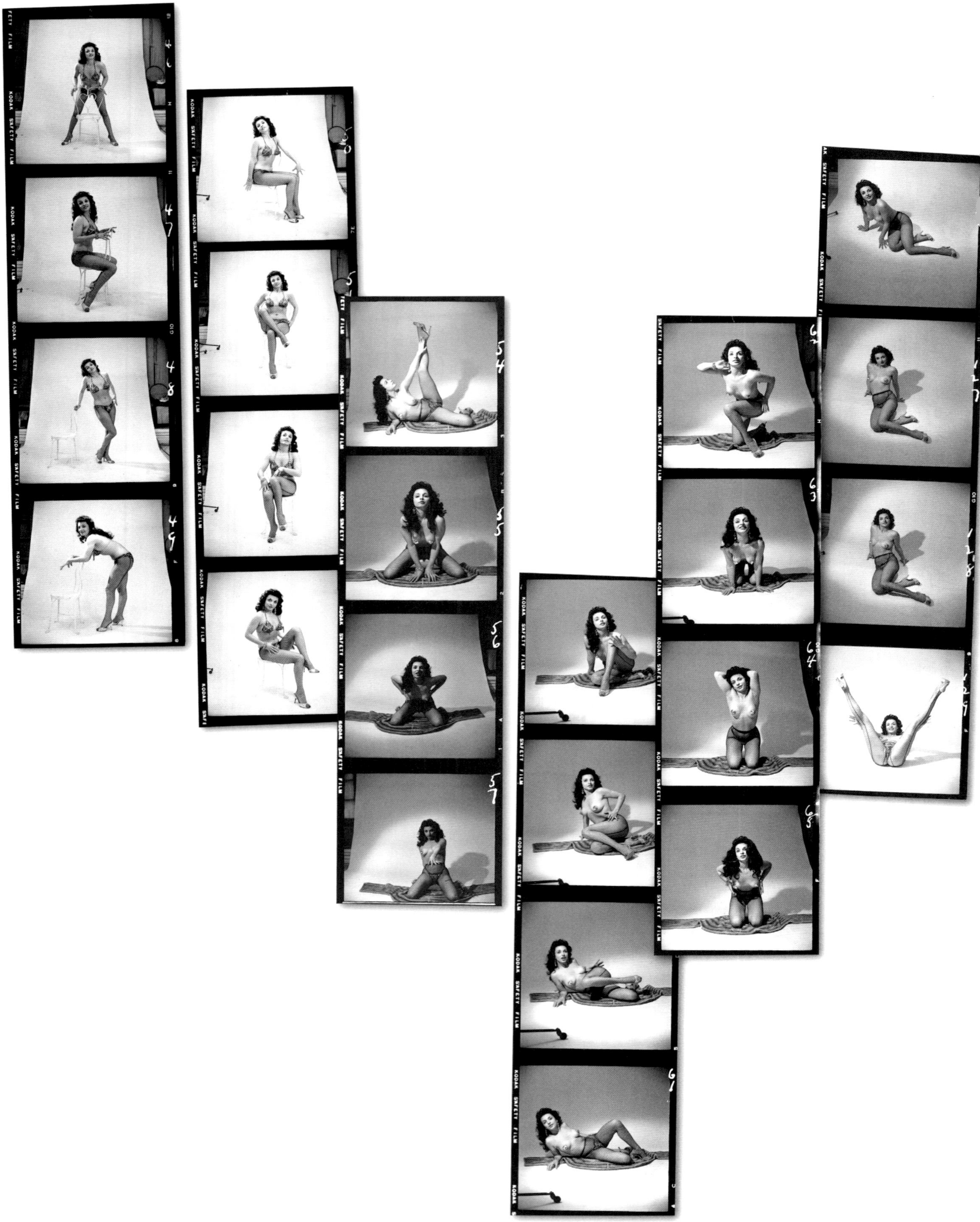

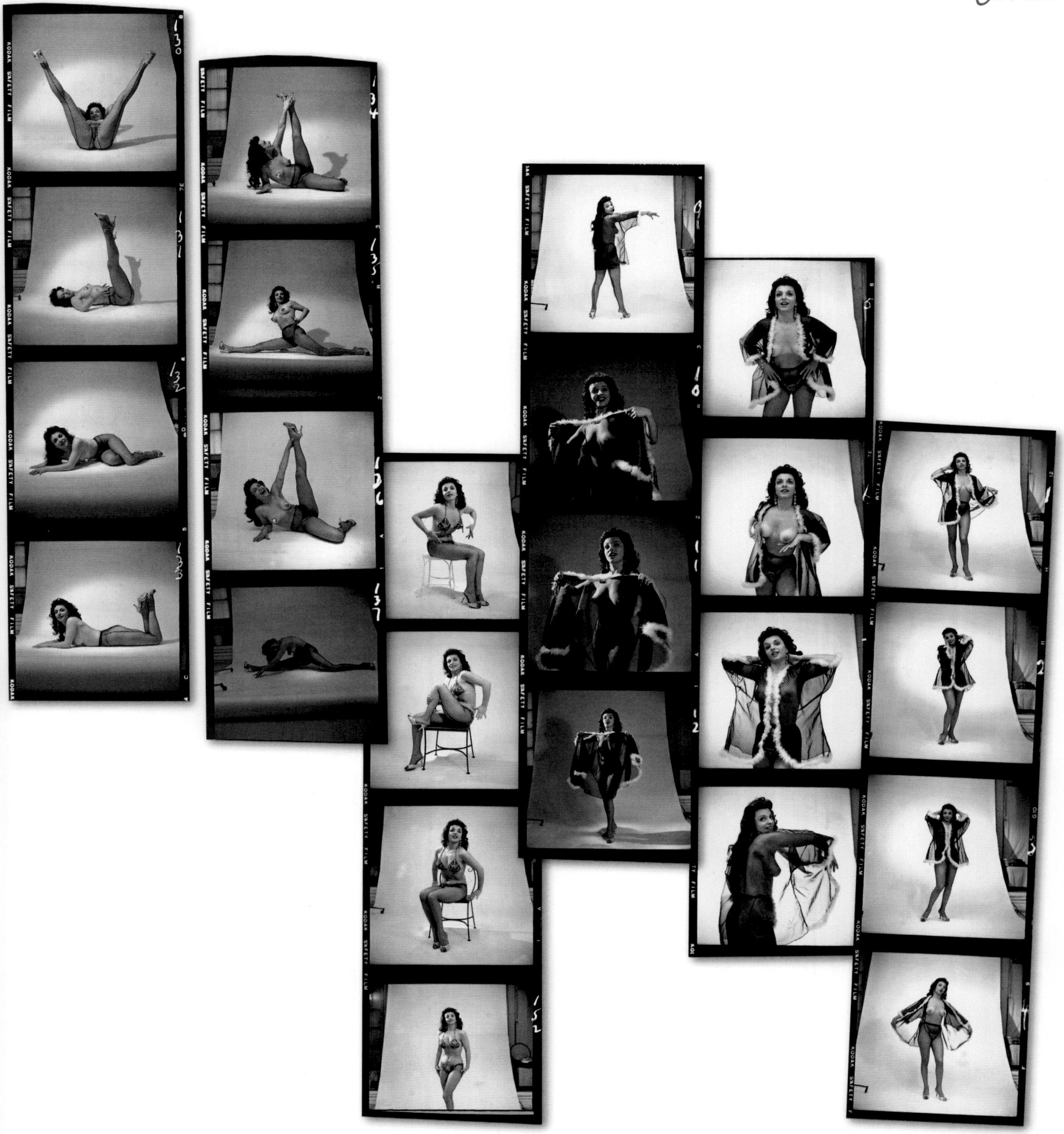

Dixie Evans

DIXIE EVANS

Dixie Evans is a natural blonde, with blue eyes- comes from Hollywood. While still in high school she modelled for some of Hollywood's top photographers. Soon after, she started stripping XXXX and was X a hit from the beginning.

She has a large collection of reprints of famous paintings and gets madeat people who express surprise that a stripper should be interested X in such things.

Matter of fact, Dixie has an act which received great acclaim on the west coast: she would come onstage in complete darkness. Then colored spots would light up the Evans' shape, unclad, motionless, but in the attitude of a famous painting of the nude figure by Michelangelo, Tintoretto, Goya, etc. This XX game of Guess Who ? is strictly for cafe society intellectuals, but it is a sidelight on the career of a famous stripper. When in New York City on a recent trip, Dixie surprised the staff of the N.Y. public library when she swept in one day and asked for their collection of famous nudes, so that la Dixie could refurbish this act in the east. Dixie still models for artists and sculptors in her spare time.

Dixie is a well-rounded personality who says: "A woman should look like a woman should look". The stripping star is 5'5" tall, weighs in at 126 lbs.

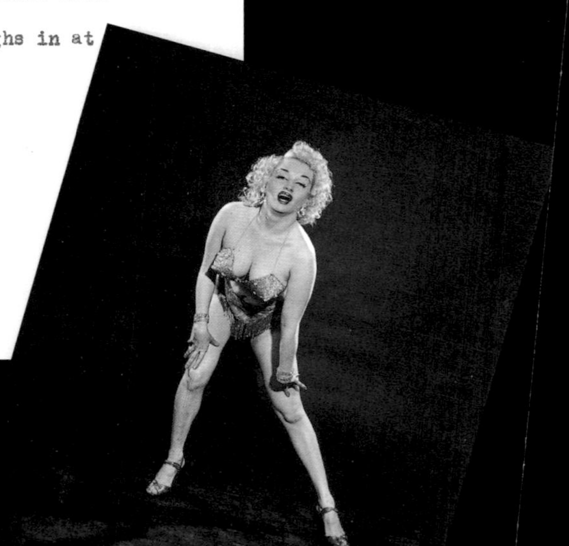

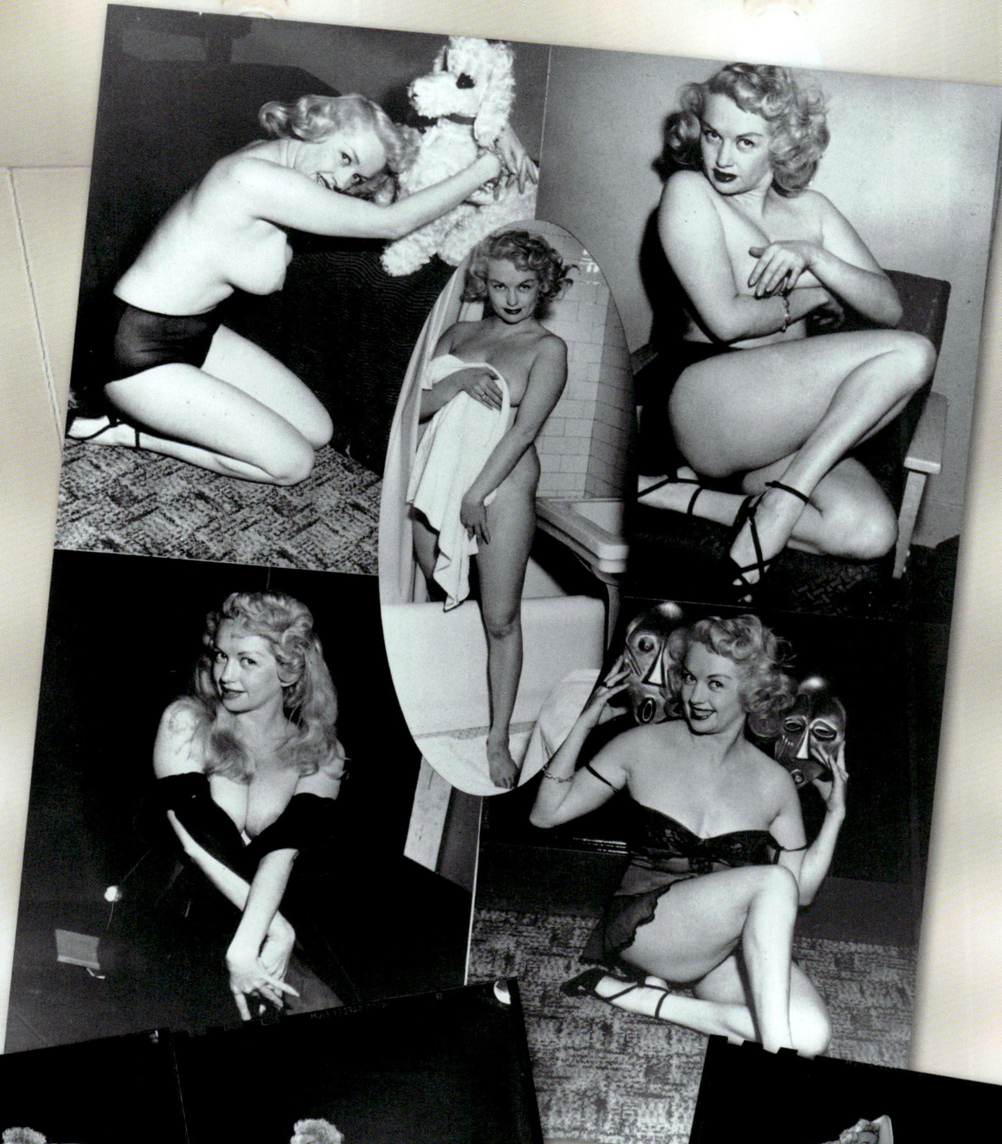

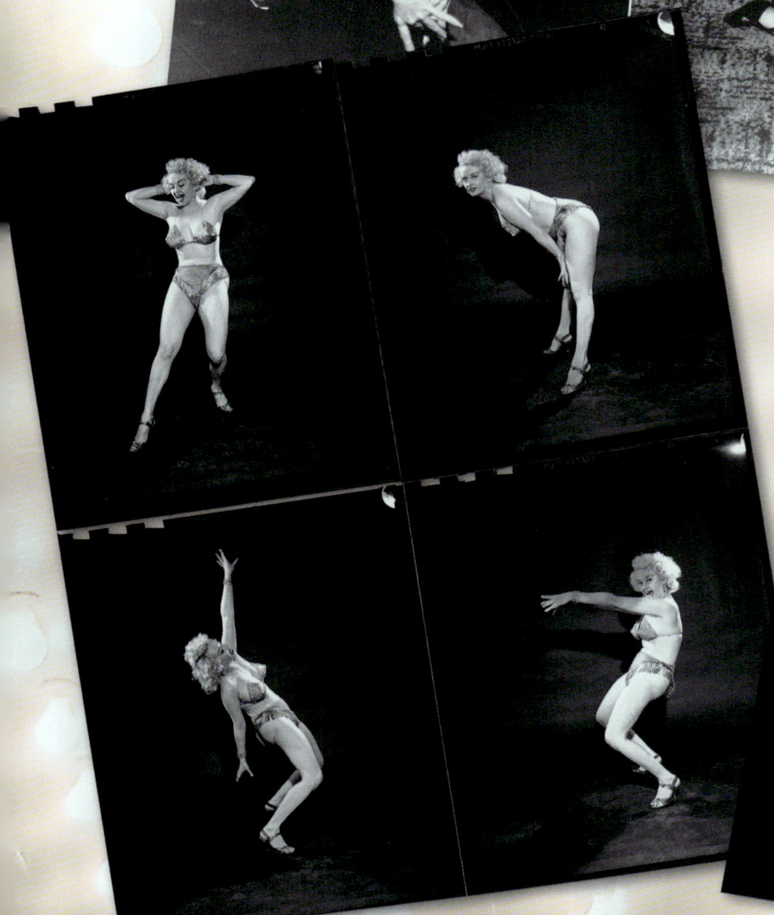

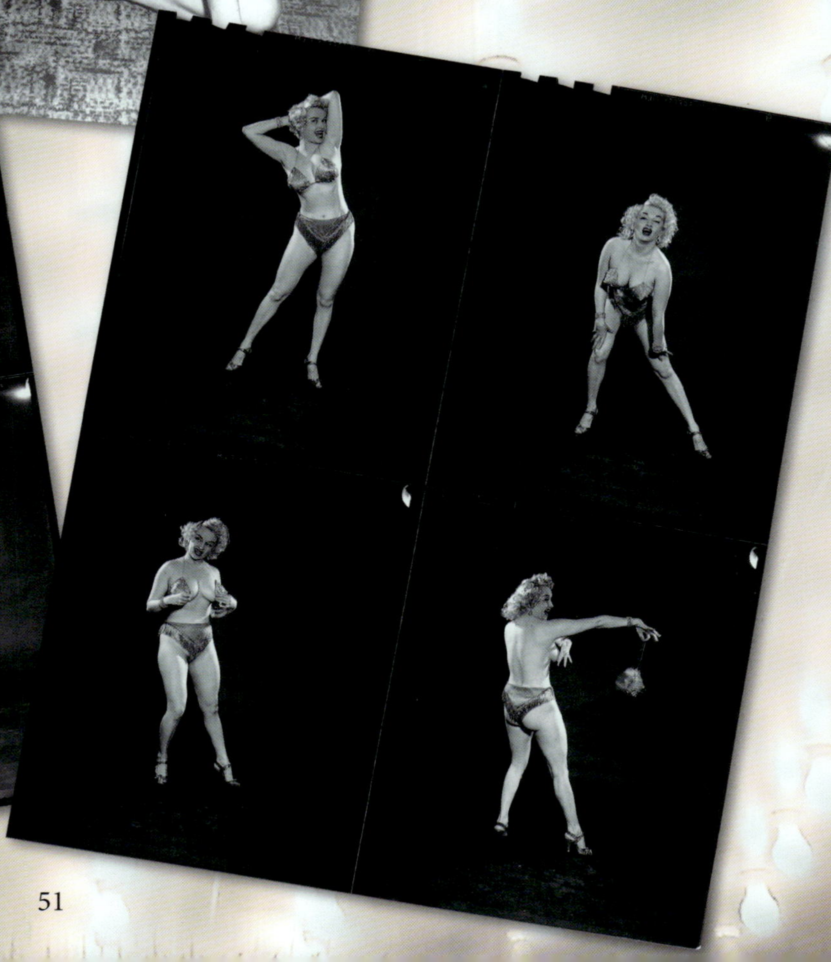

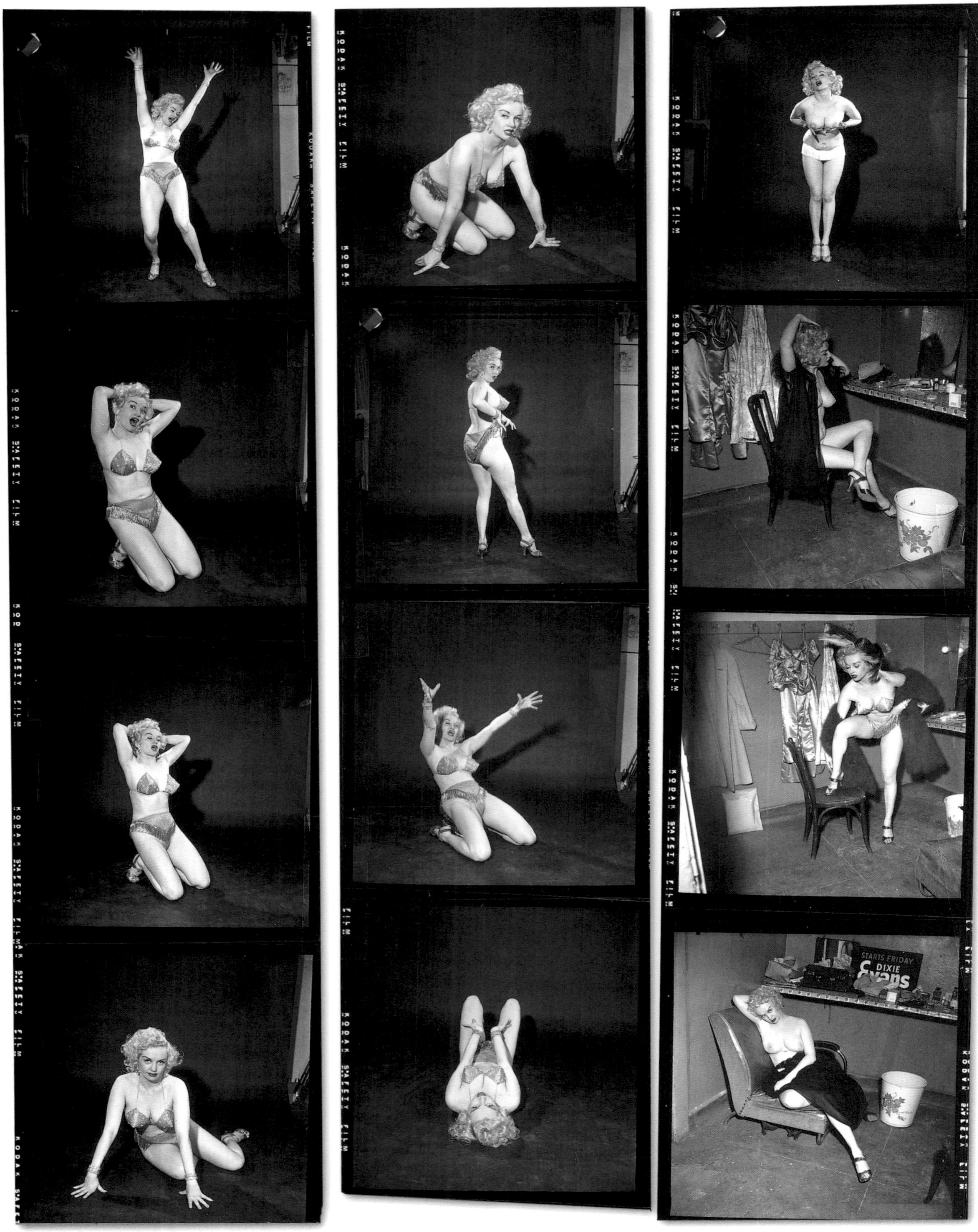
KODAK SAFETY FILM
STARTS FRIDAY
DIXIE
Evans

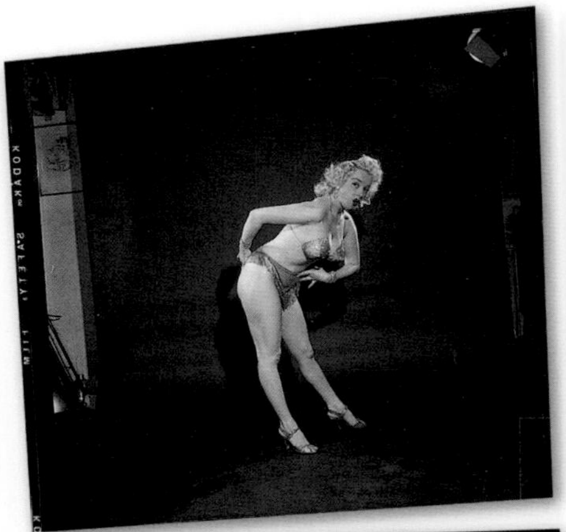
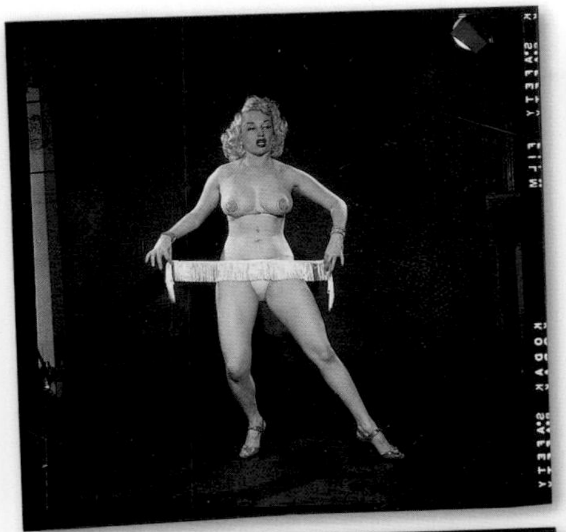
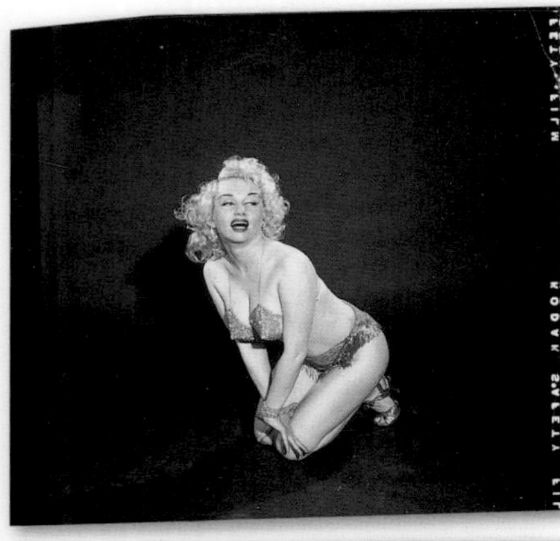
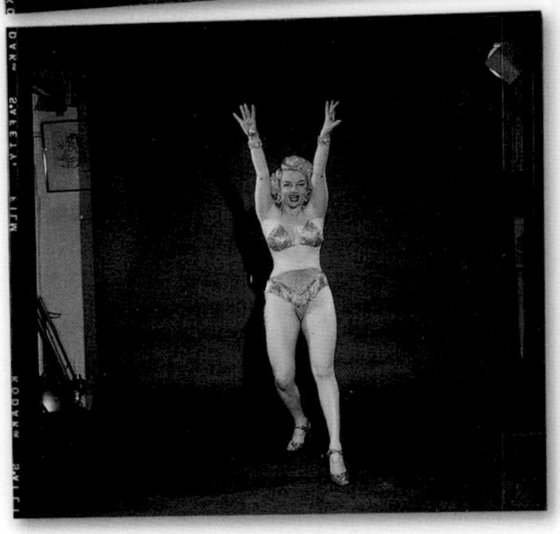
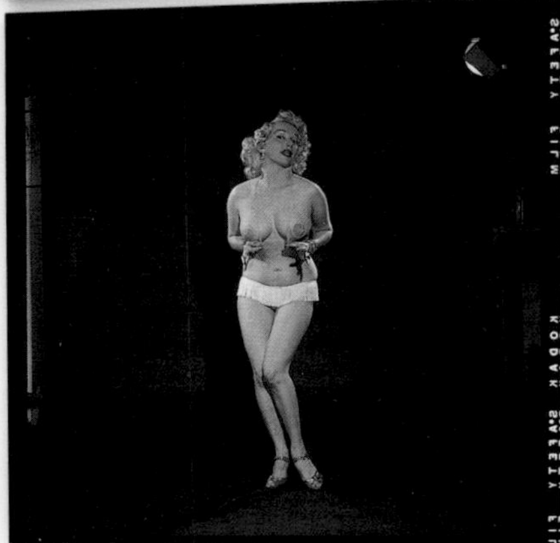
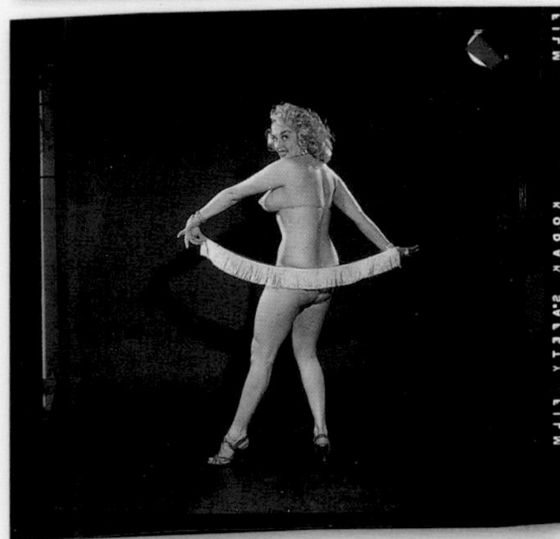
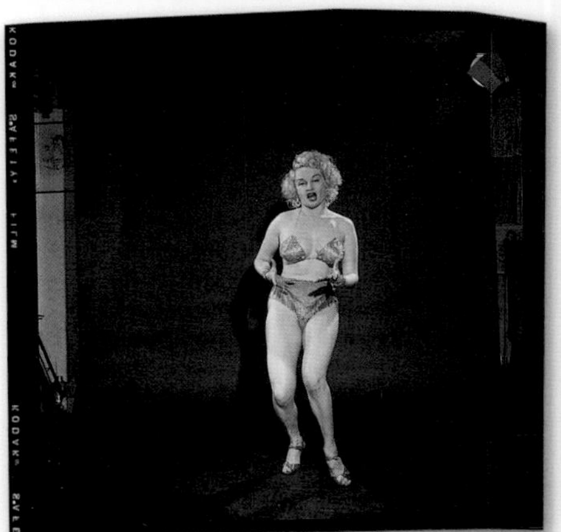
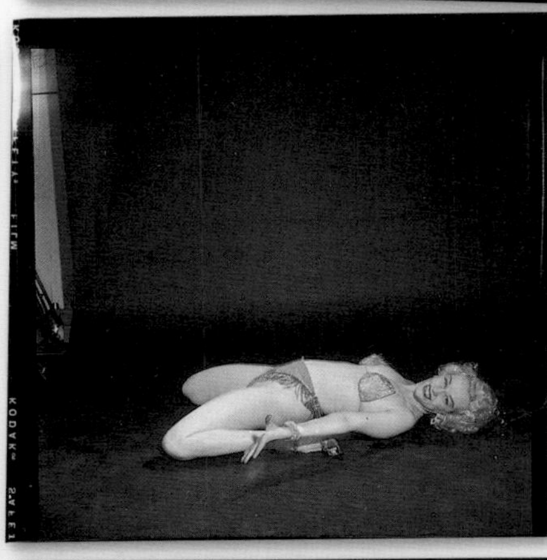
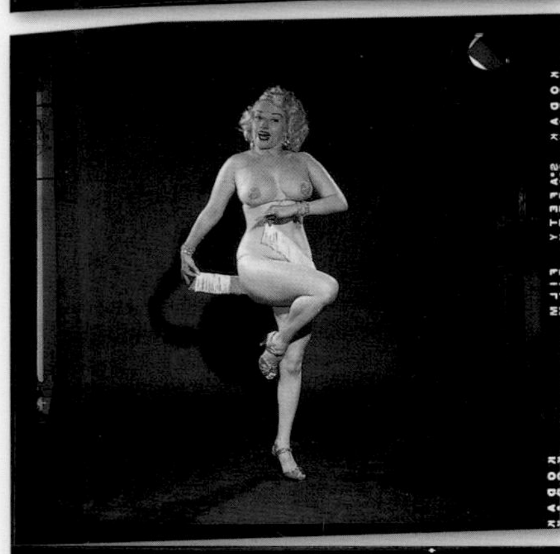
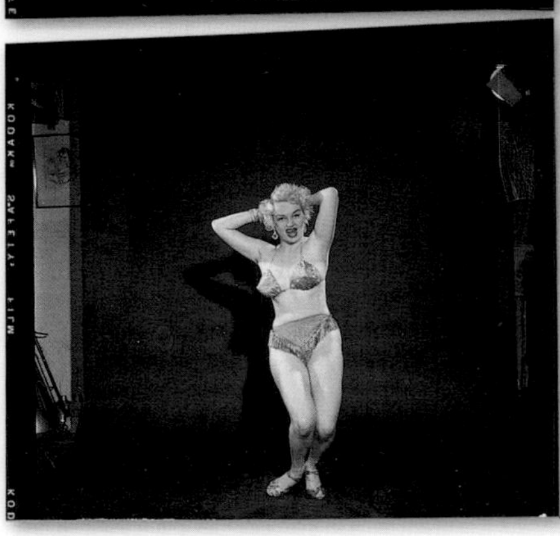
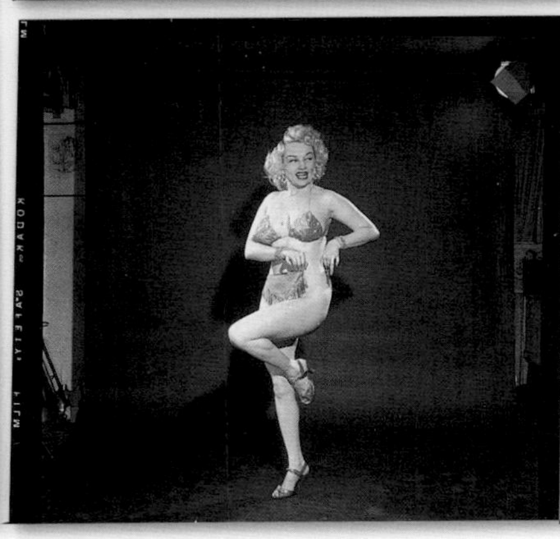
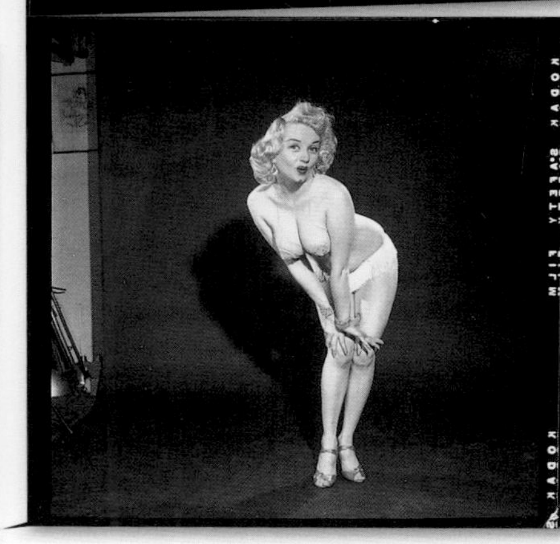

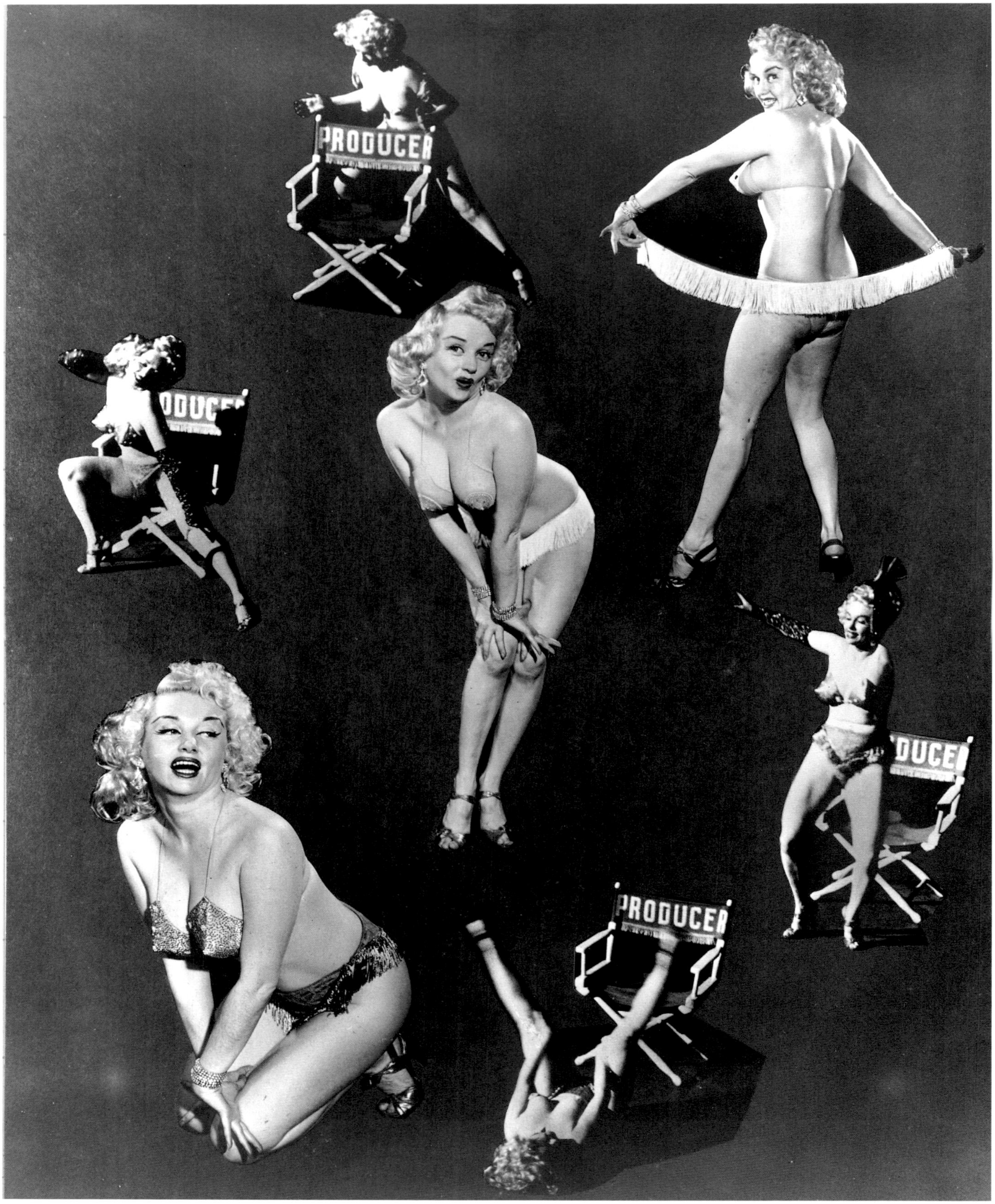
PRODUCER
PRODUCER

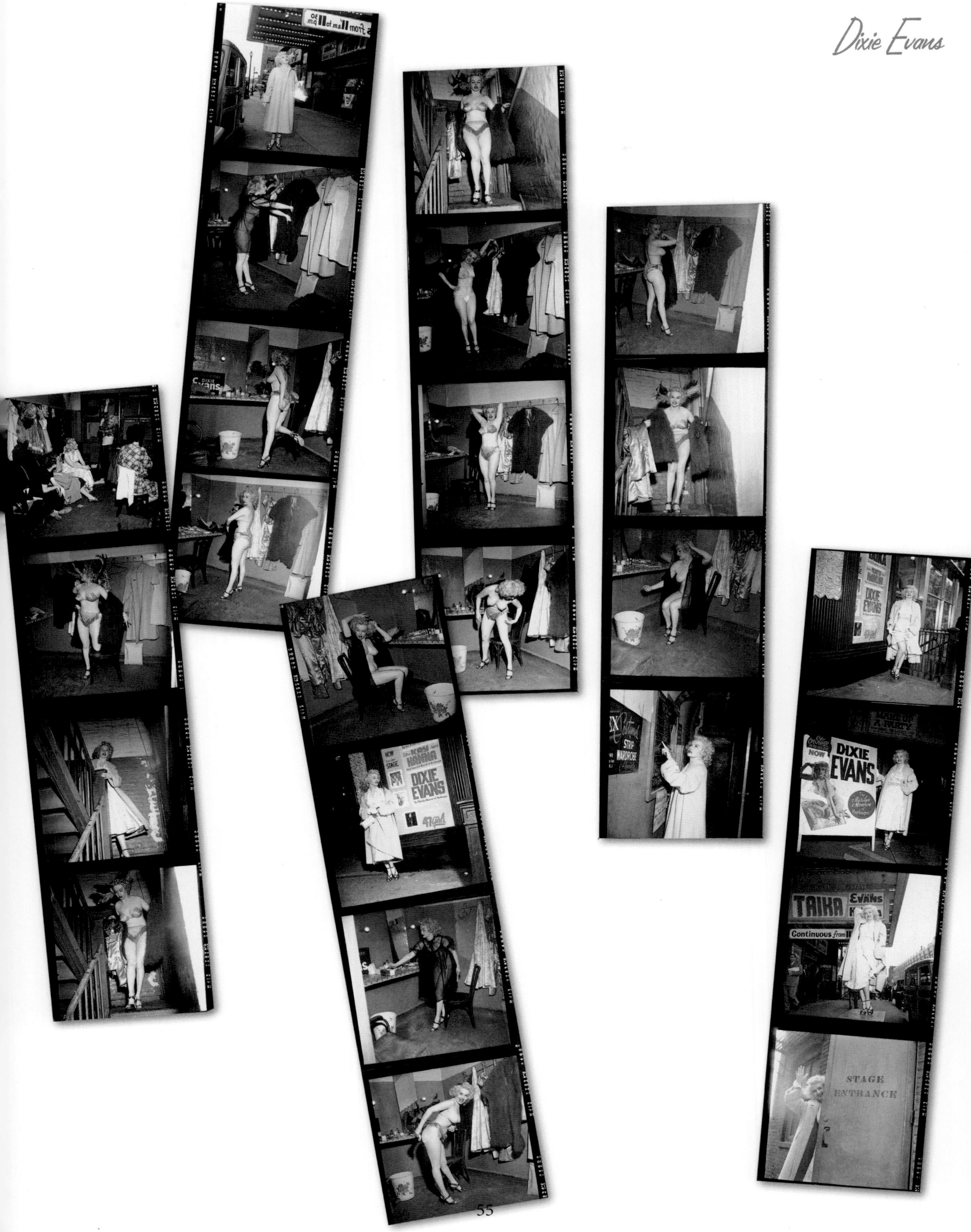
DIXIE EVANS
STRIP WARDROBE
TAIKA
EVANS
Continuous from
STAGE ENTRANCE

Princess Domay

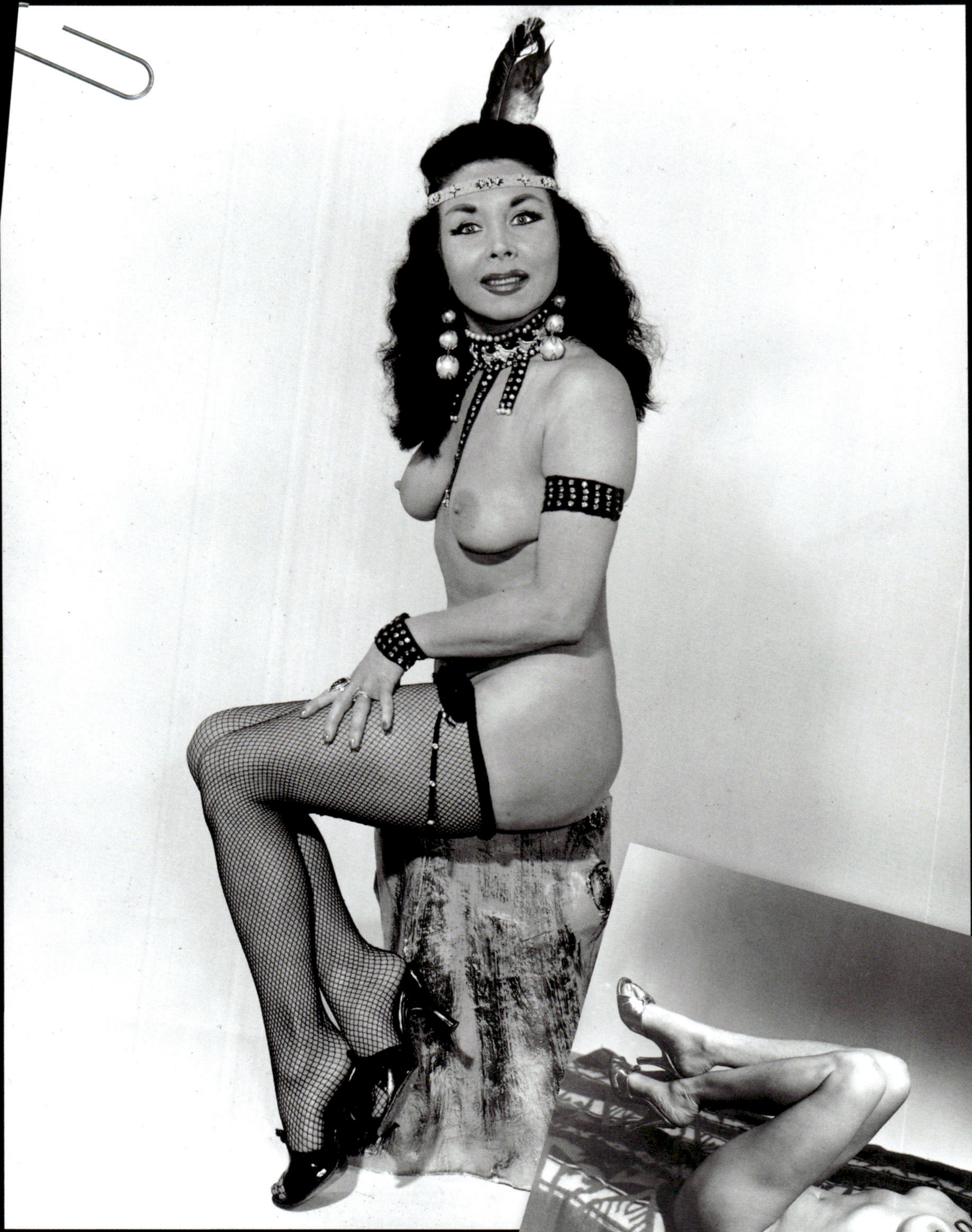

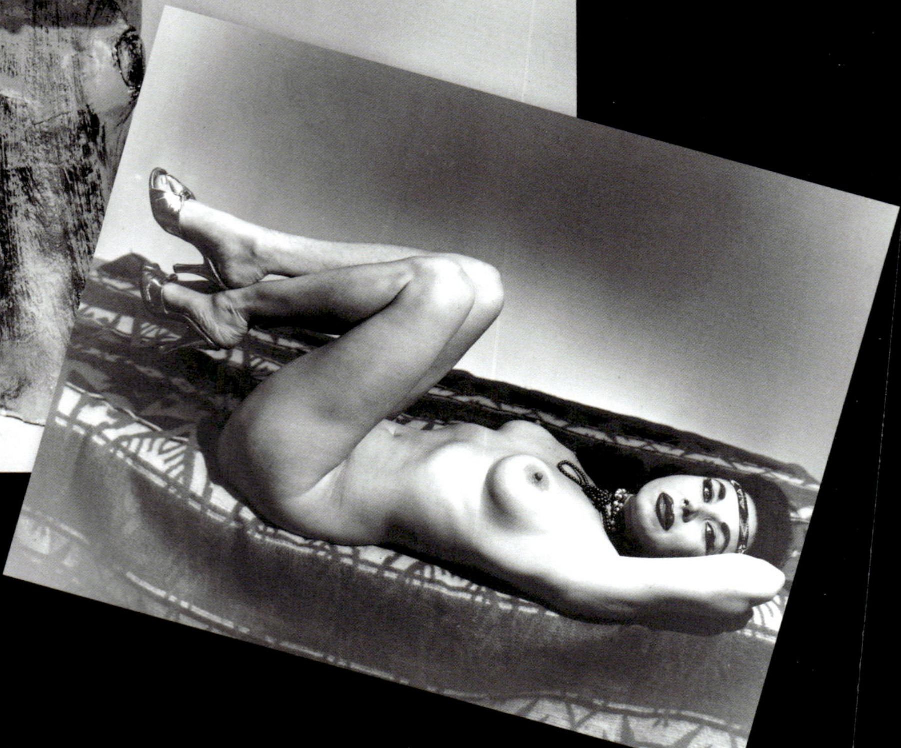

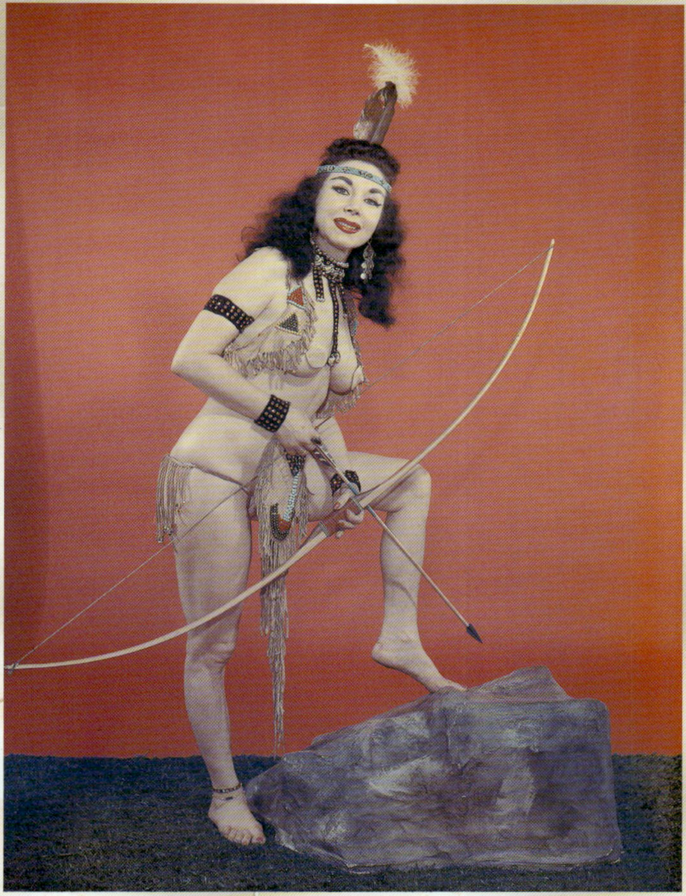

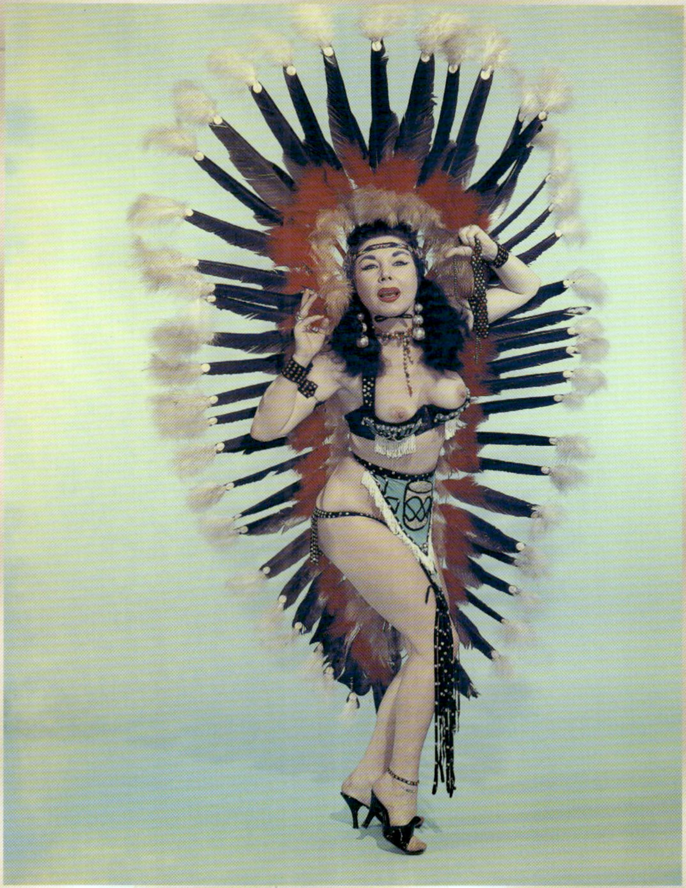

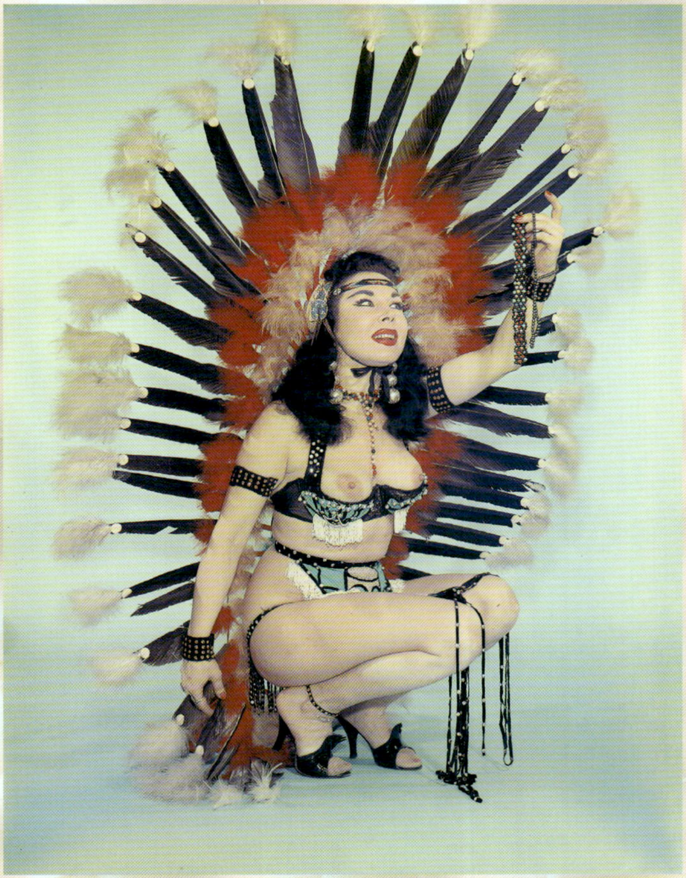

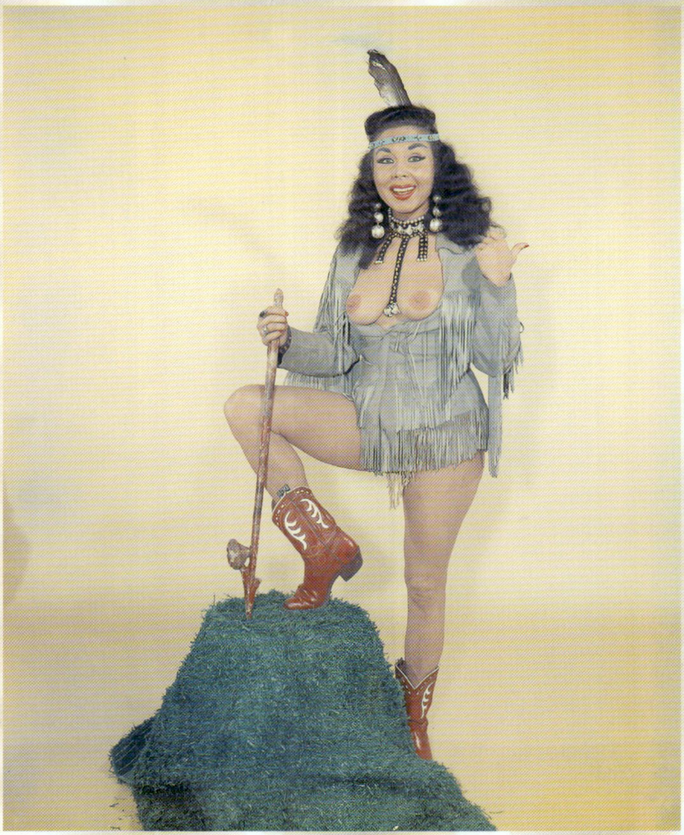

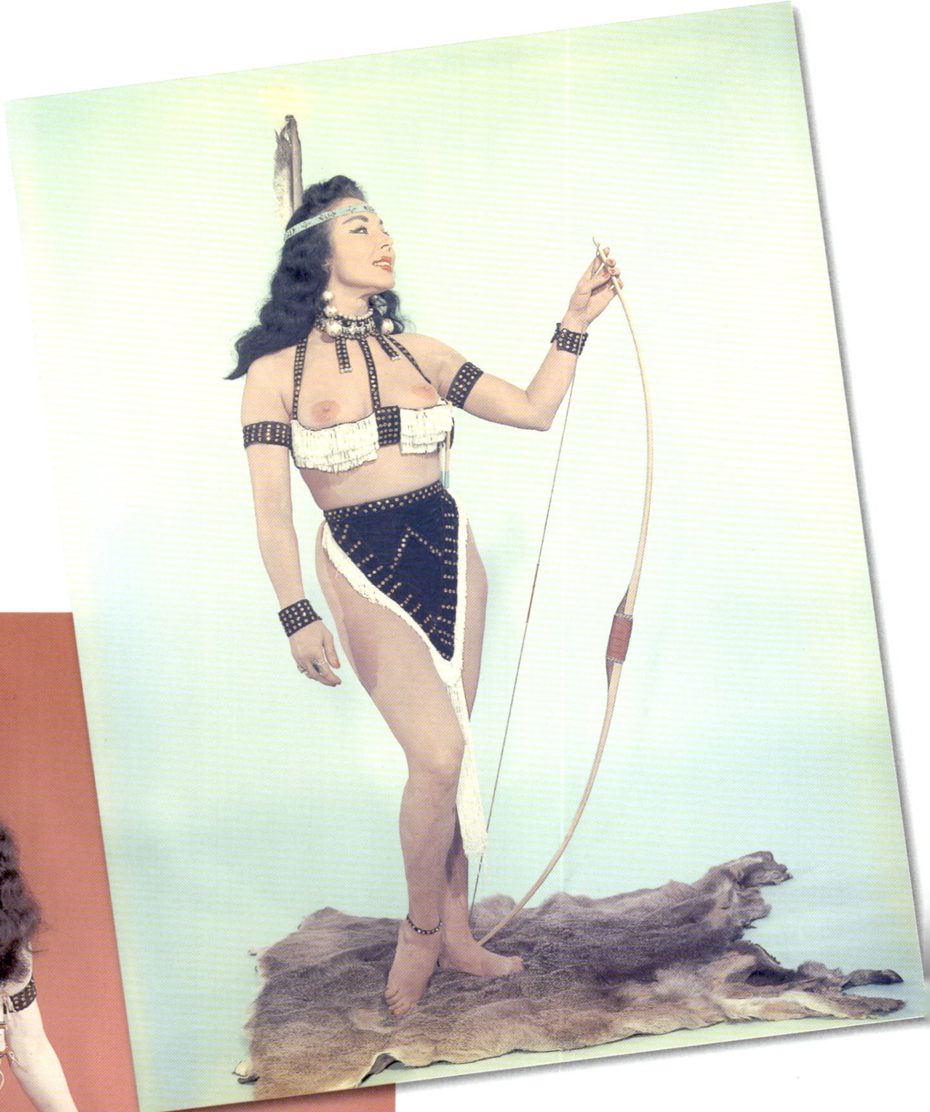

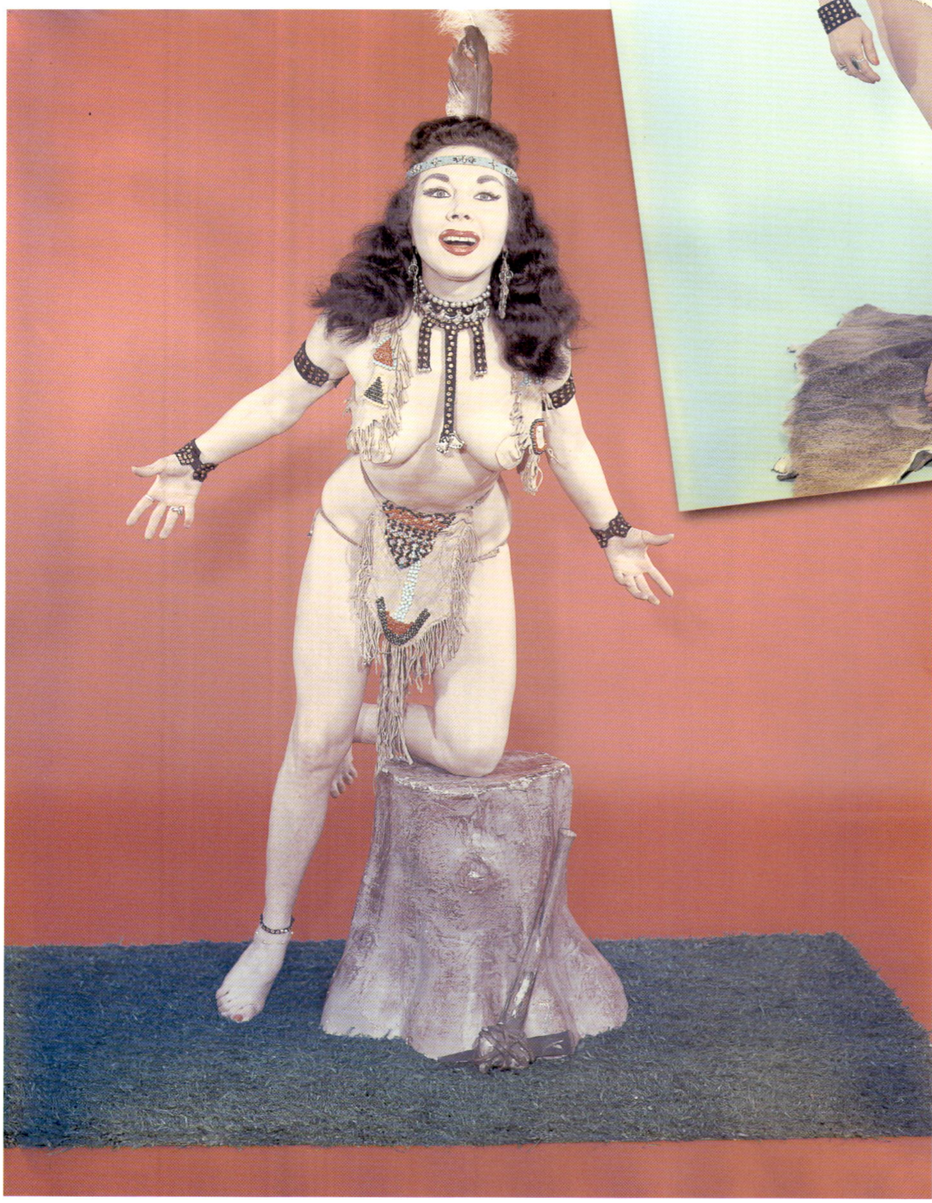

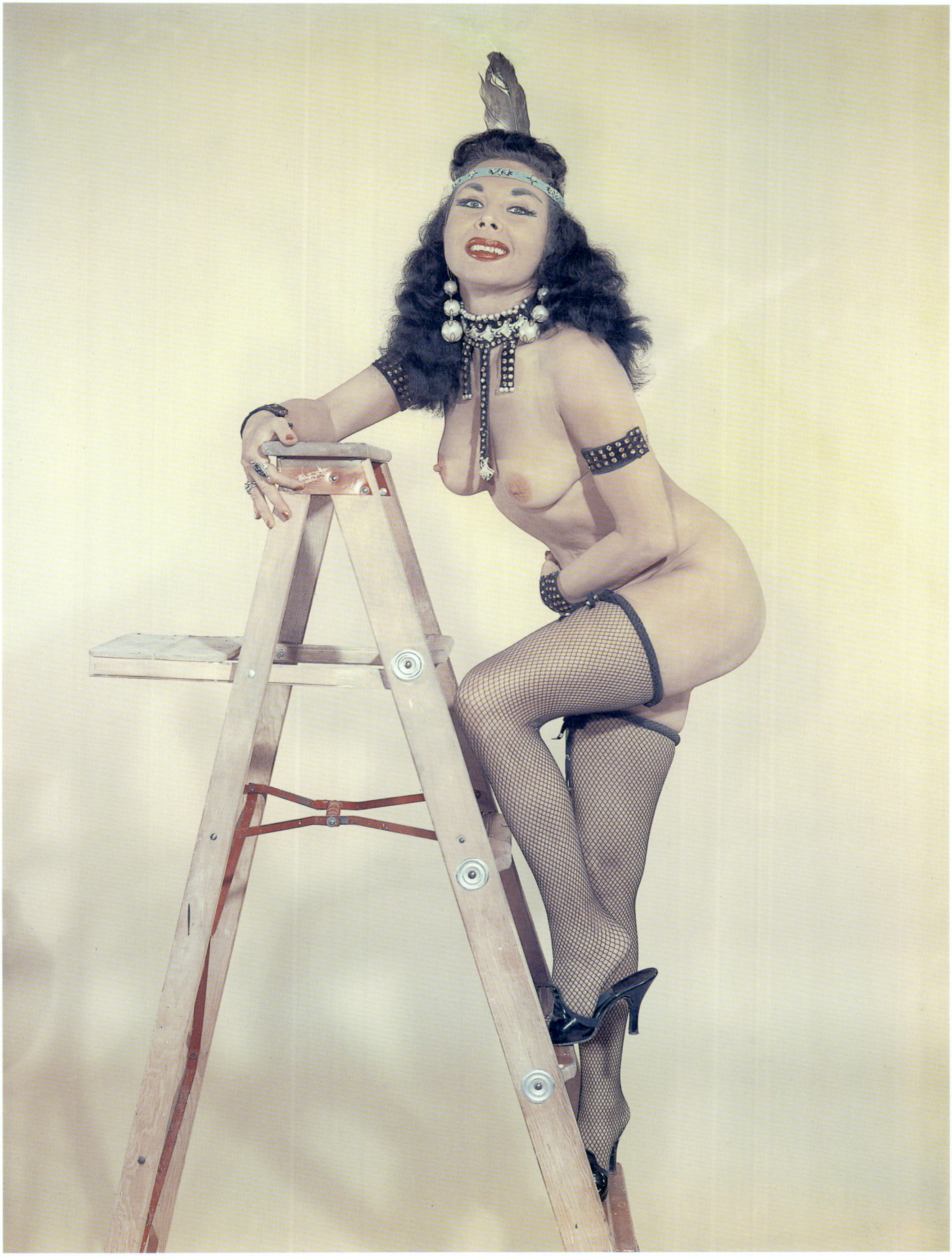

Donna Christie

DONNA CHRISTIE

You'd never know, to talk to modest Donna Christie, that she is a headliner in many an east coast night club, captivating the audience with her quiet charm and droll sense of humor. Donna is an accomplished dancer, too, which all adds up to the sum total of ONE BOMBSHELL. She does a toreador number which is right out of the bull ring. Donna comes from Rochester, N.Y., is 5'3" tall and measures 35-24-35. In her spare time she likes to paint, in fact made her living as a commercial artist at one time. But now she likes to dance as she gets around more in this business, and, let's face it, the pay is better.

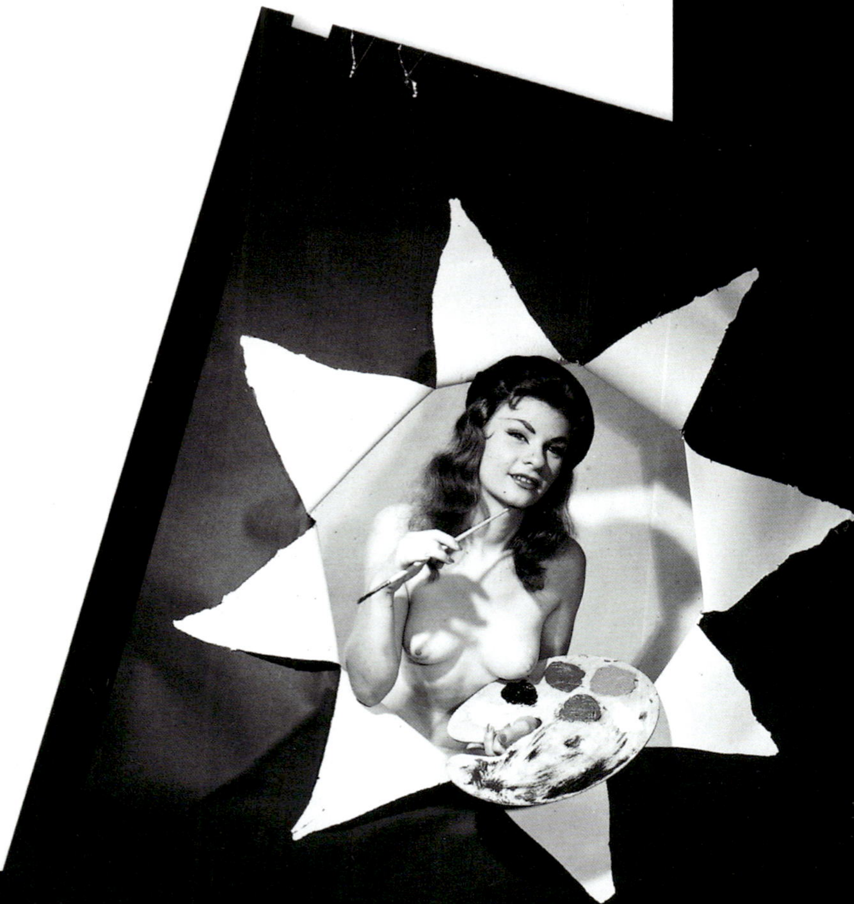

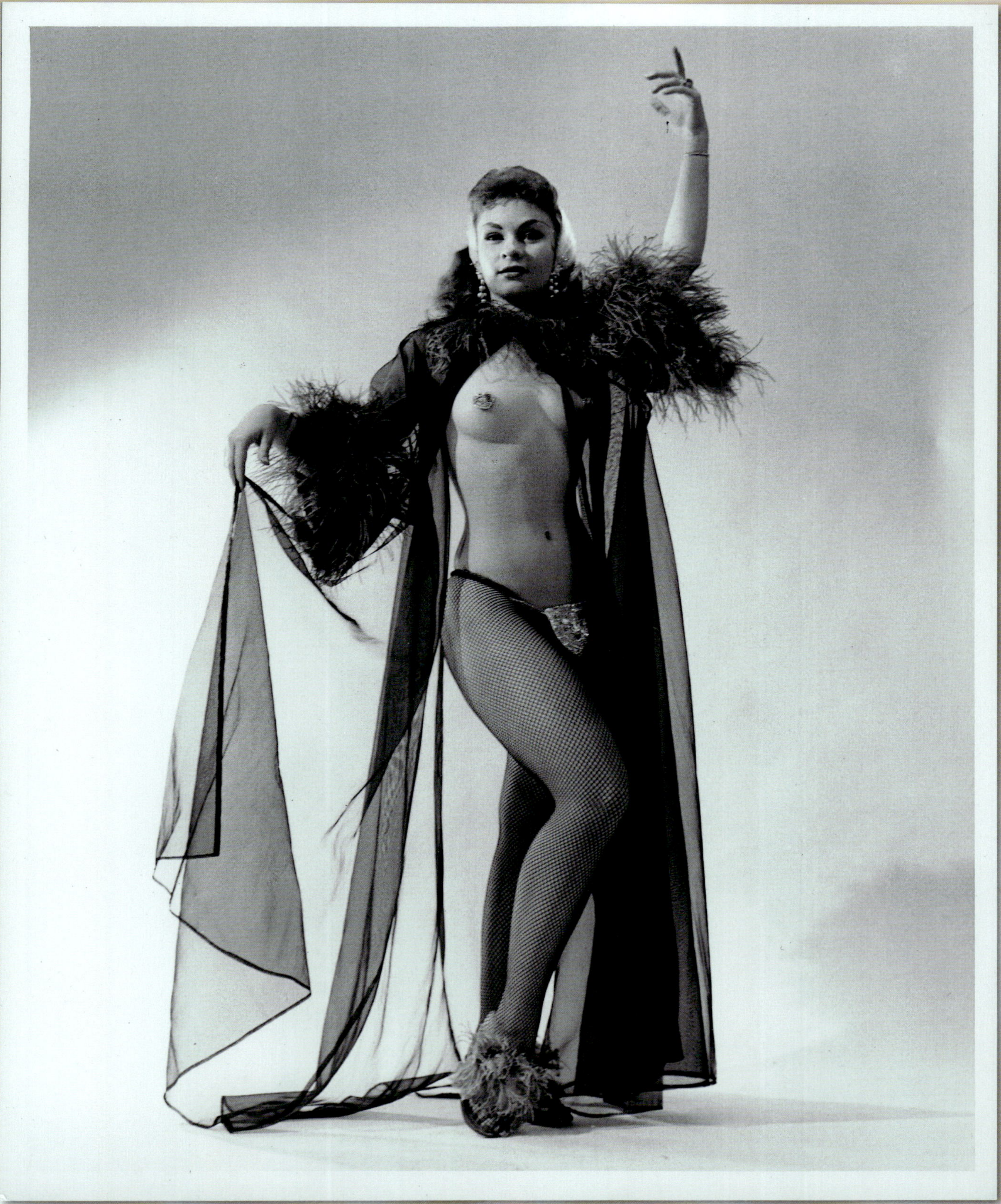

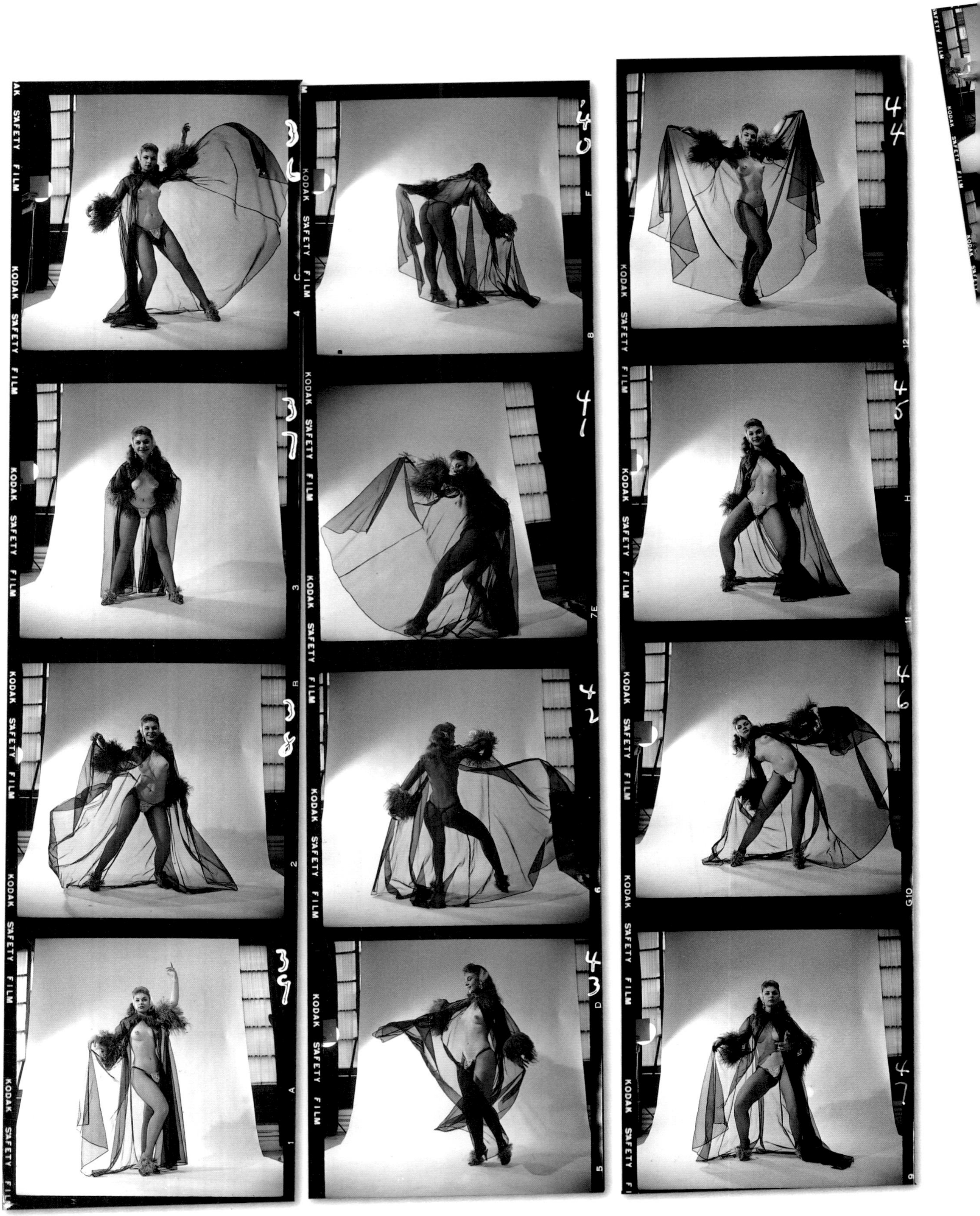

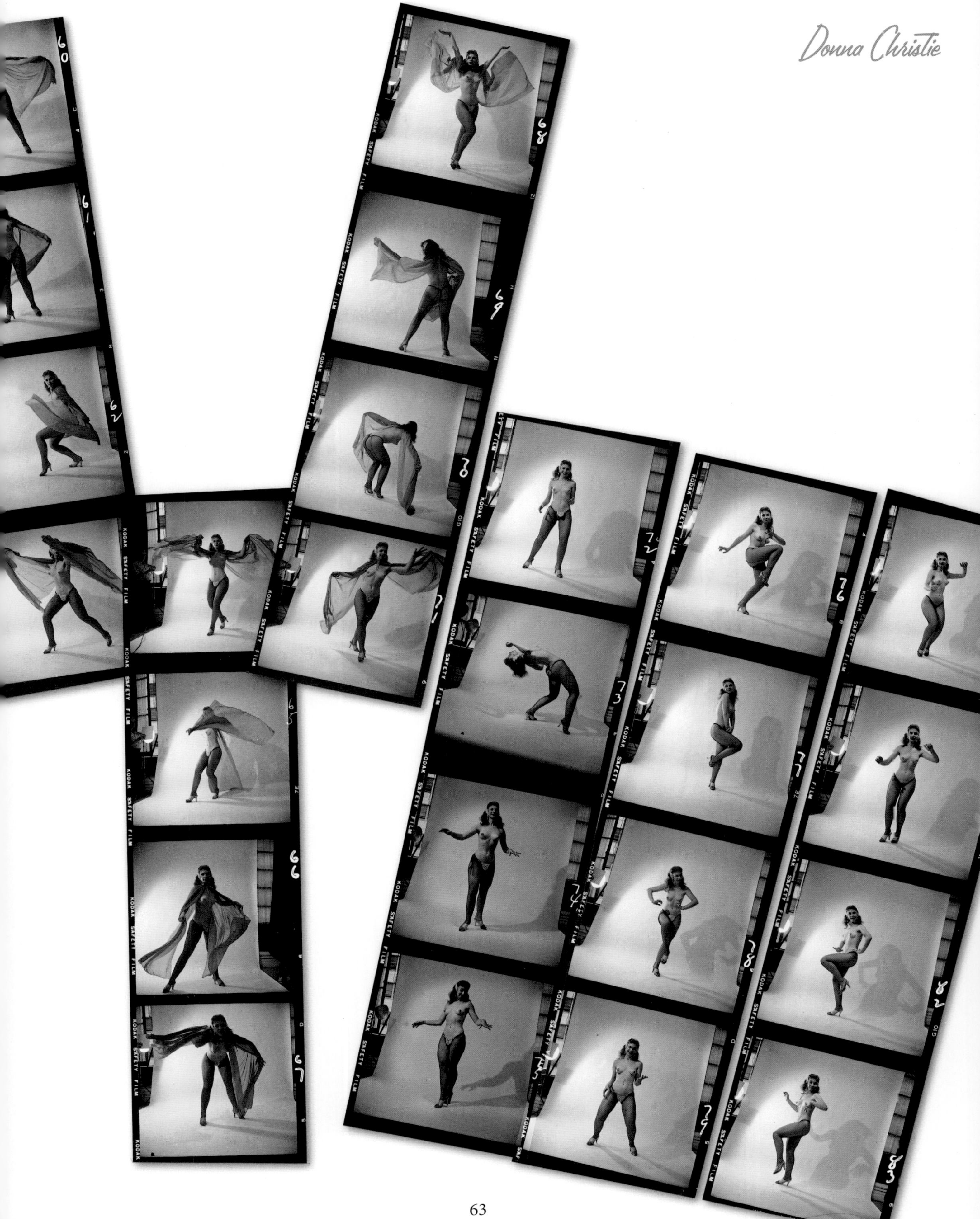

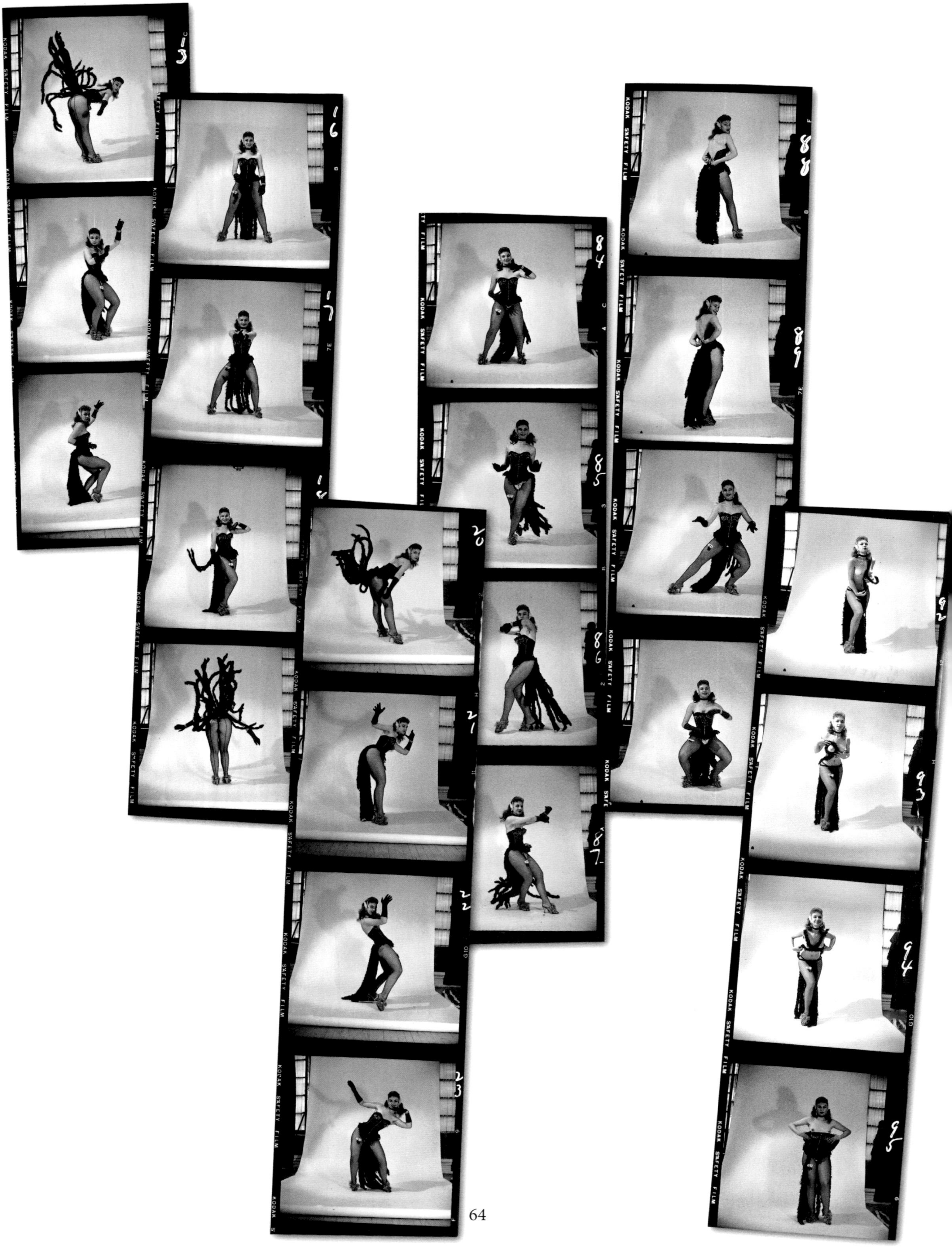
KODAK SAFETY FILM

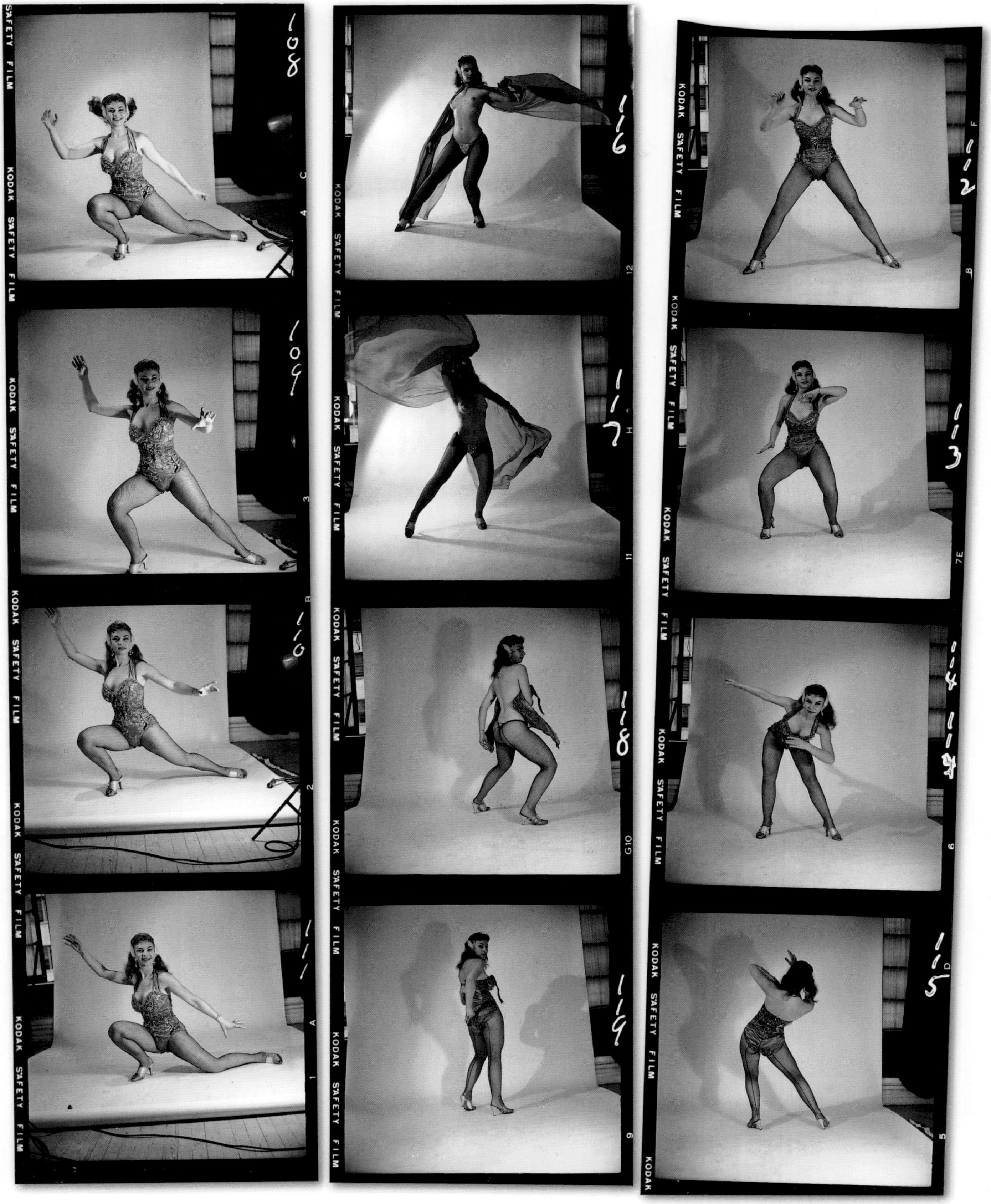
KODAK SAFETY FILM
108
109
110
111
116
117
118
119
112
113
114
115

Evelyn West

Evelyn West

A stripper may say, just like any other female: "I haven't got a thing to wear," but, she does have to have the clothes to take off. Here, we present Evelyn West, the Gal with the $50,000 Treasure Chest, getting ready for her act. Her 126 lbs. are stacked like this: $39\frac{1}{2}$-26-36. She is 5'4$\frac{3}{4}$" tall, Originally from Petersburg, Illinois, she is a graduate of Earl Carroll's Chorus on the west coast.

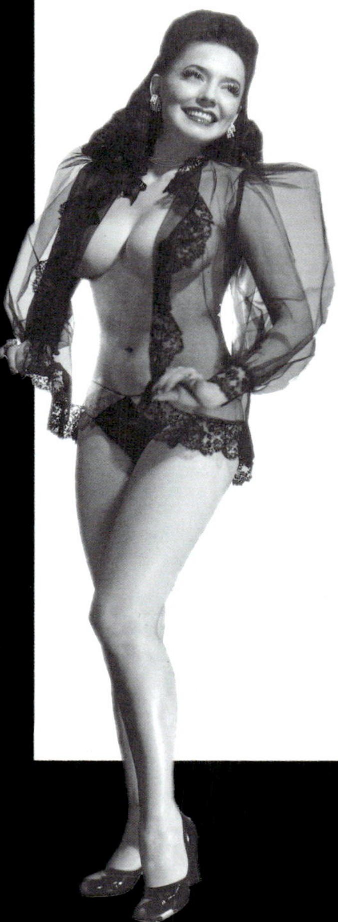

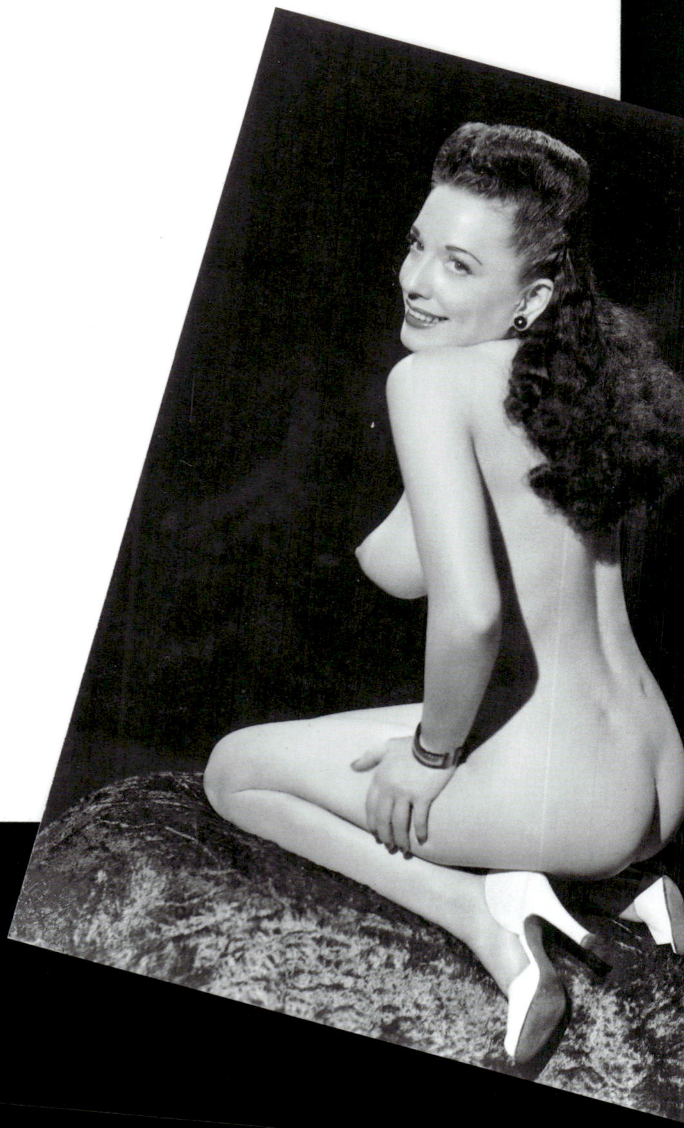

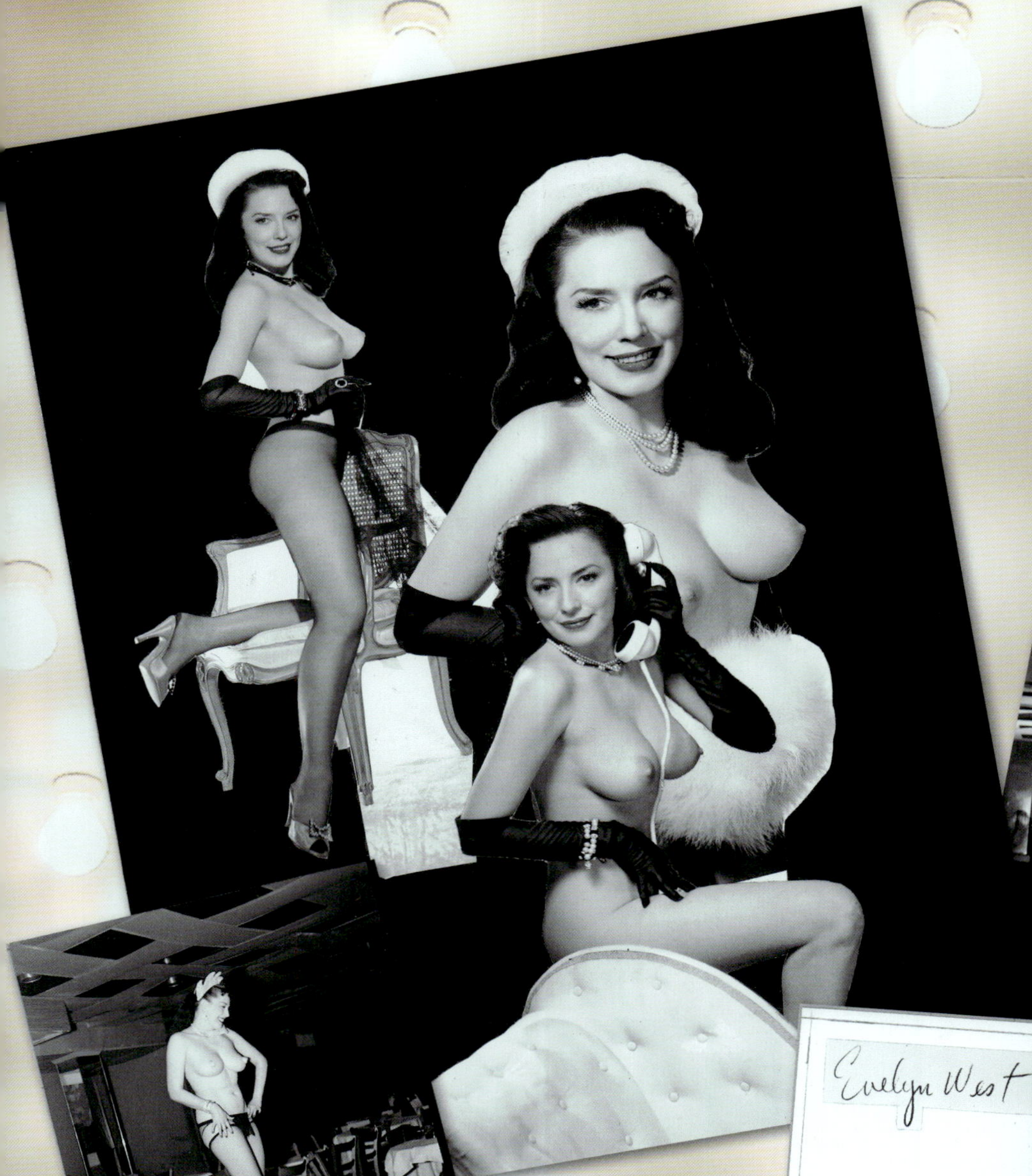

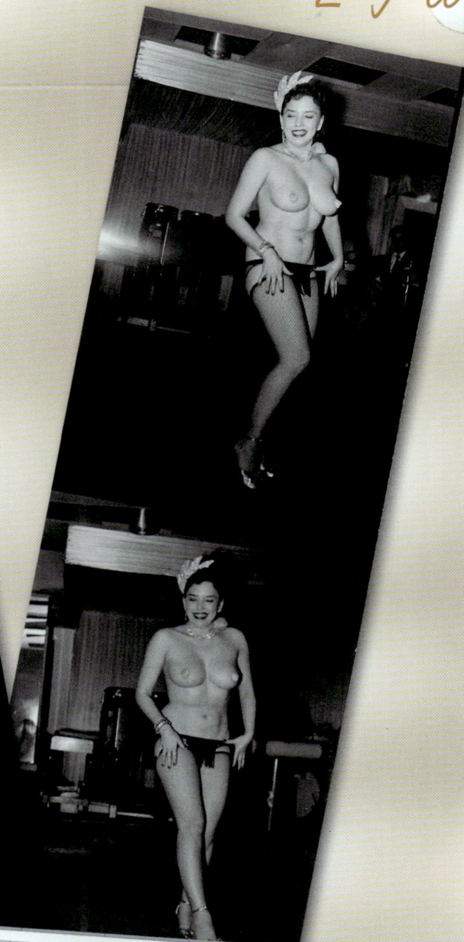

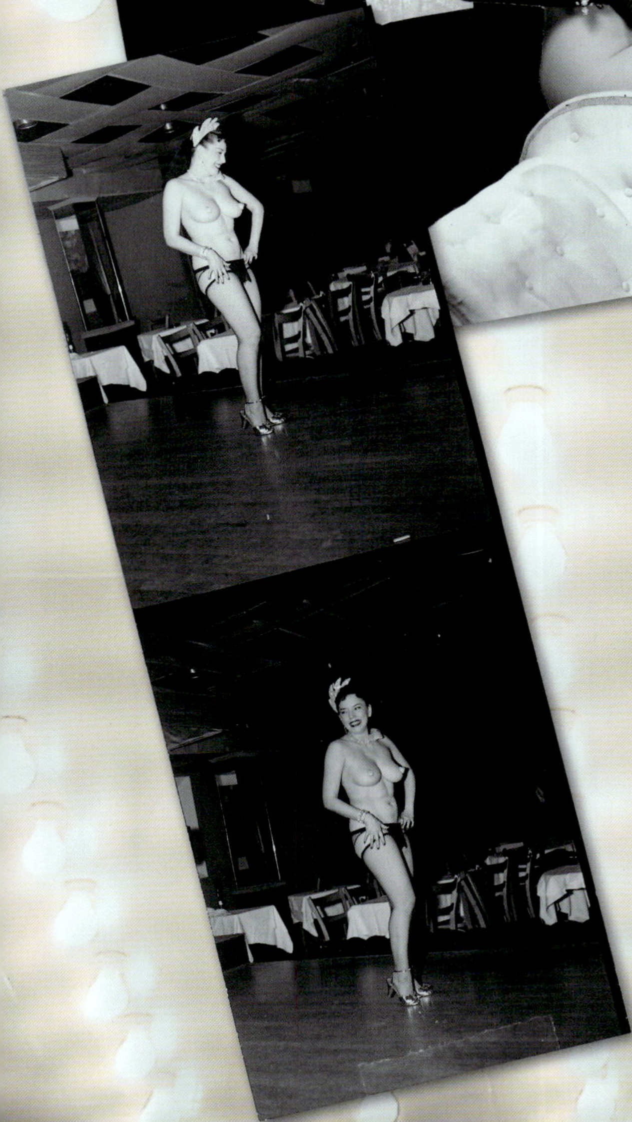

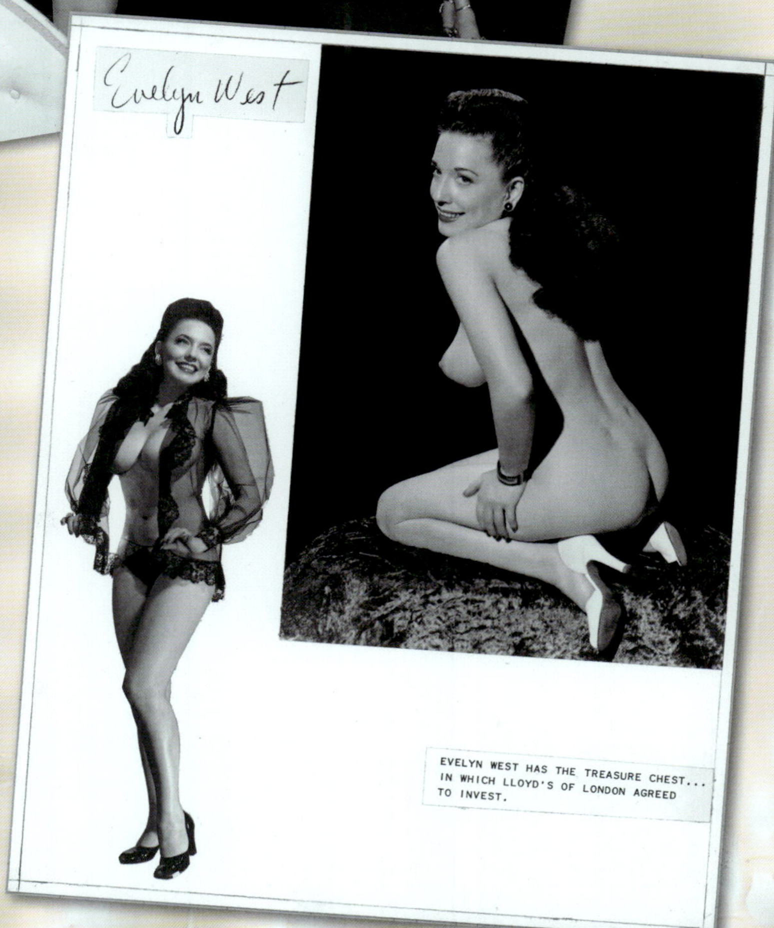
Evelyn West
EVELYN WEST HAS THE TREASURE CHEST...
IN WHICH LLOYD'S OF LONDON AGREED
TO INVEST.

Gilda

GILDA

Gilda's credo:

Ladies and gentlemen, the management of is proud to present Gilda and her Crowning Glory. As you may know, Gilda is the former Shirley Jean of Our Gang Comedies. A great many people have asked her why she is no longer in pictures. One of the many reasons is: there are too many girls who will do anything to get a job in the movies. Gilda will now give you her impressions of one of these girls trying to get a job with one of the big casting directors in Hollywood.

Vital statistics: 5'5" tall, 37½-24-36, 118 lbs.

Gilda: " I think that every woman has a secret ambition to strip... only we strippers are a little more honest about it. Why do you think women go in for frilly underclothes X if it isn't to show them off to someone ?"

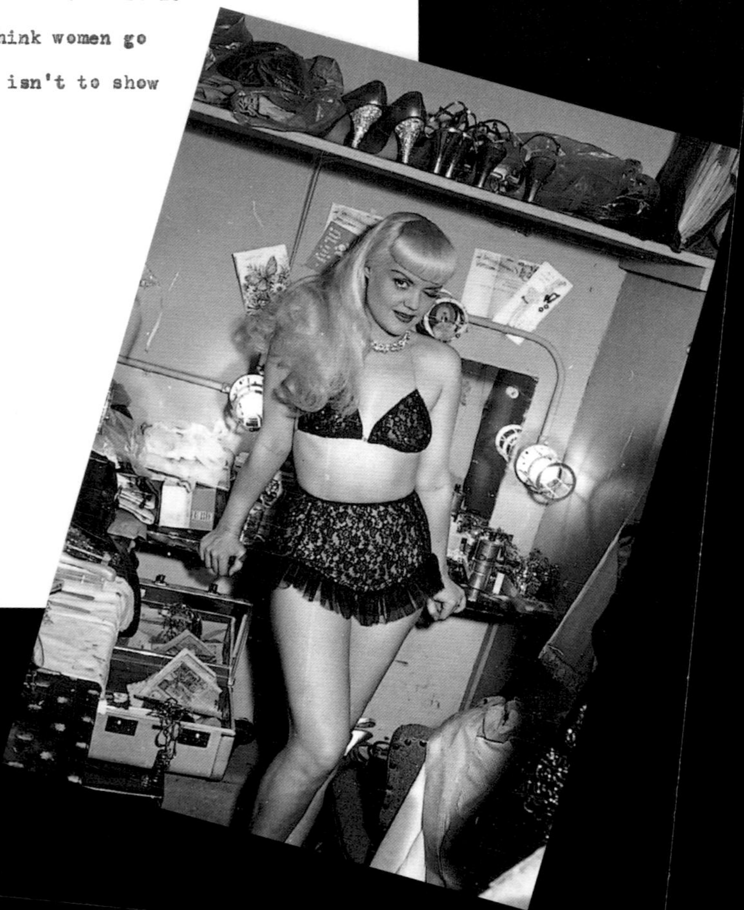

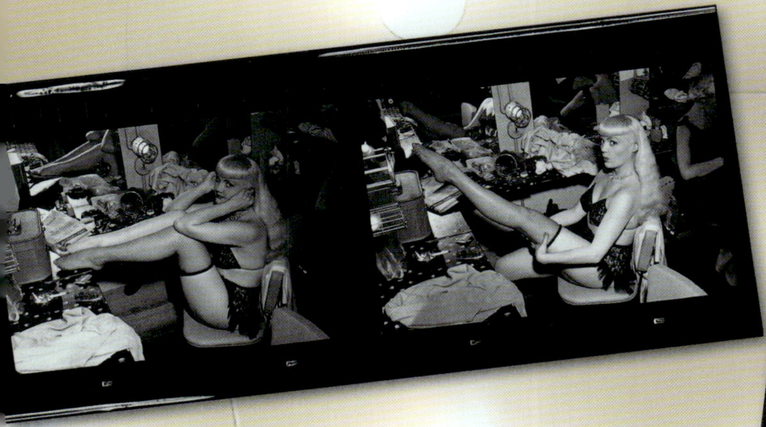

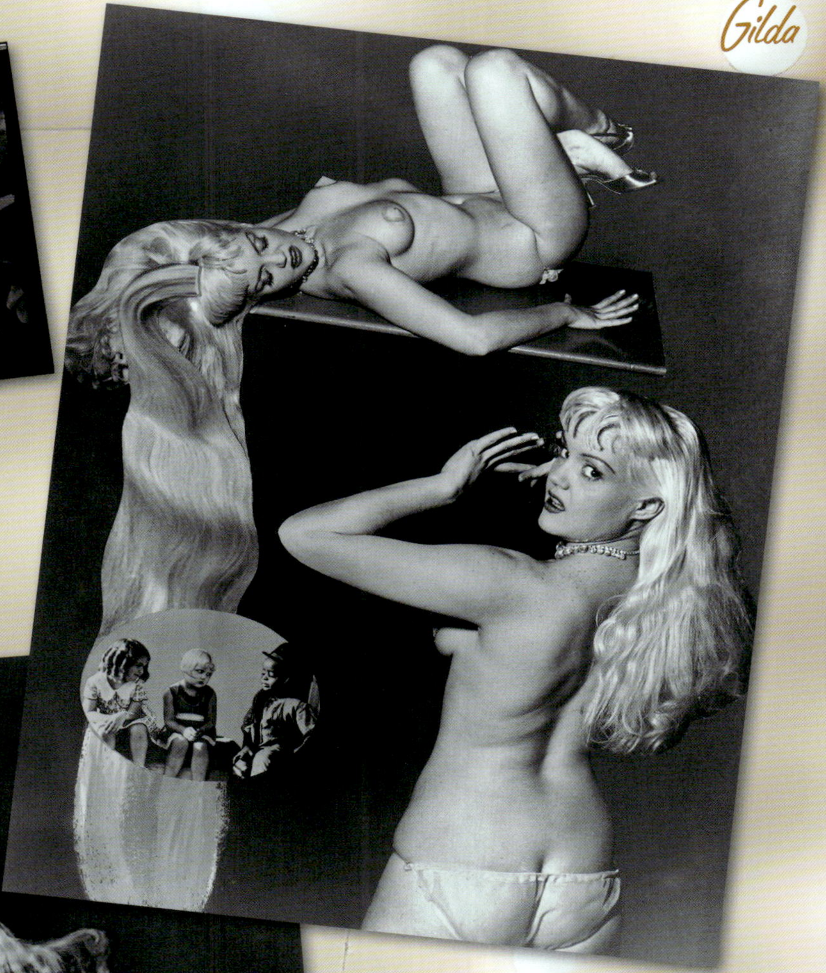

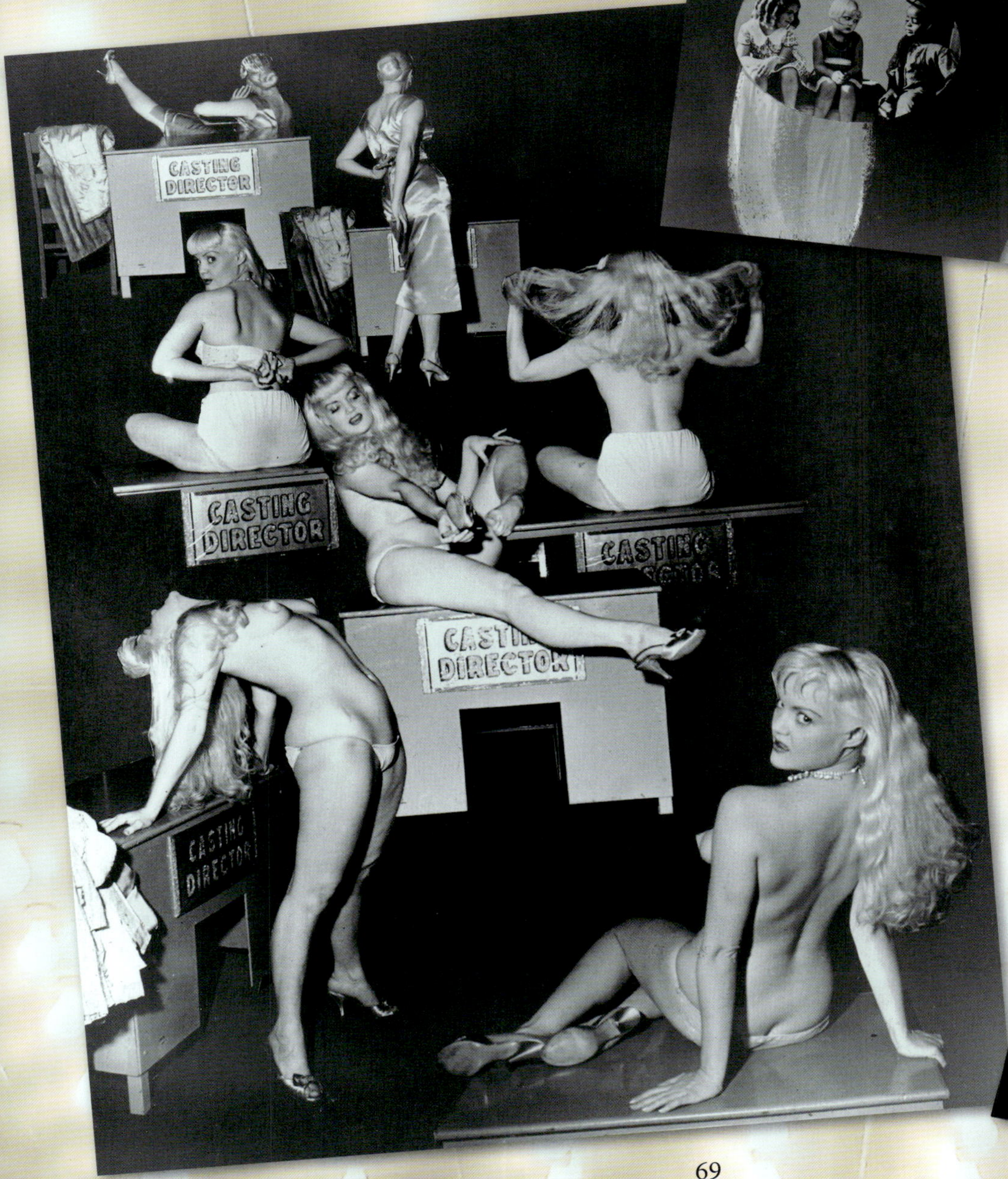
CASTING DIRECTOR
CASTING DIRECTOR
CASTING
CASTING DIRECTOR
CASTING DIRECTOR

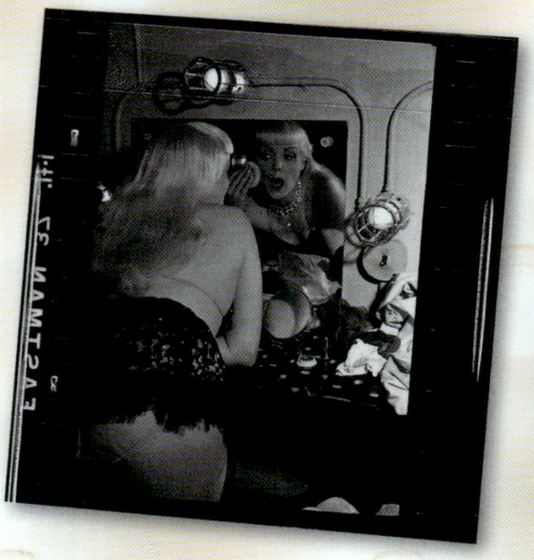

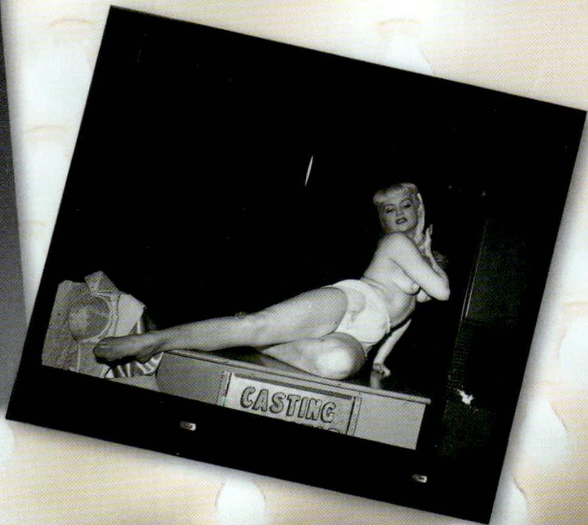
CASTING

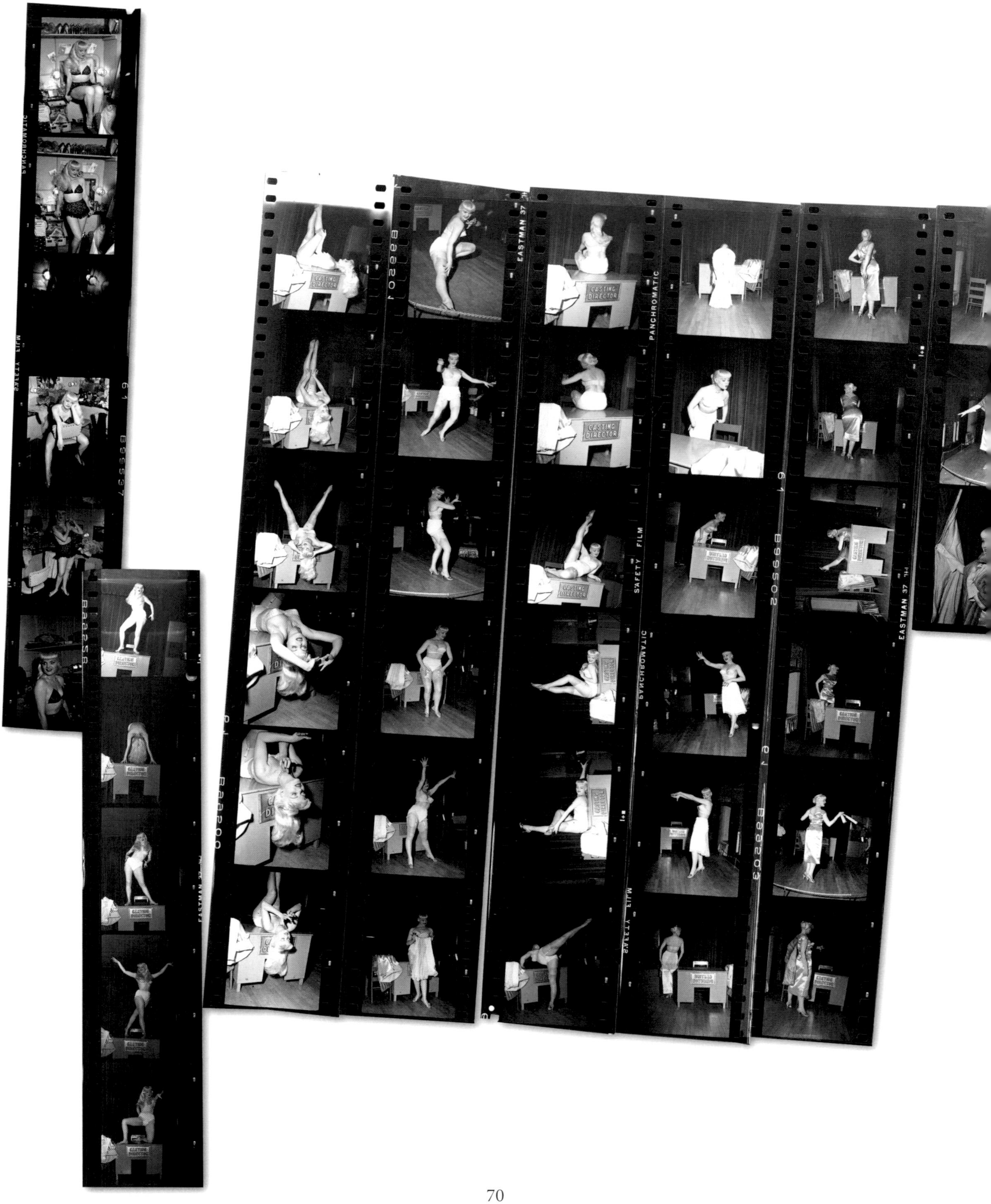
EASTMAN 37
PANCHROMATIC
SAFETY FILM
CASTING DIRECTOR

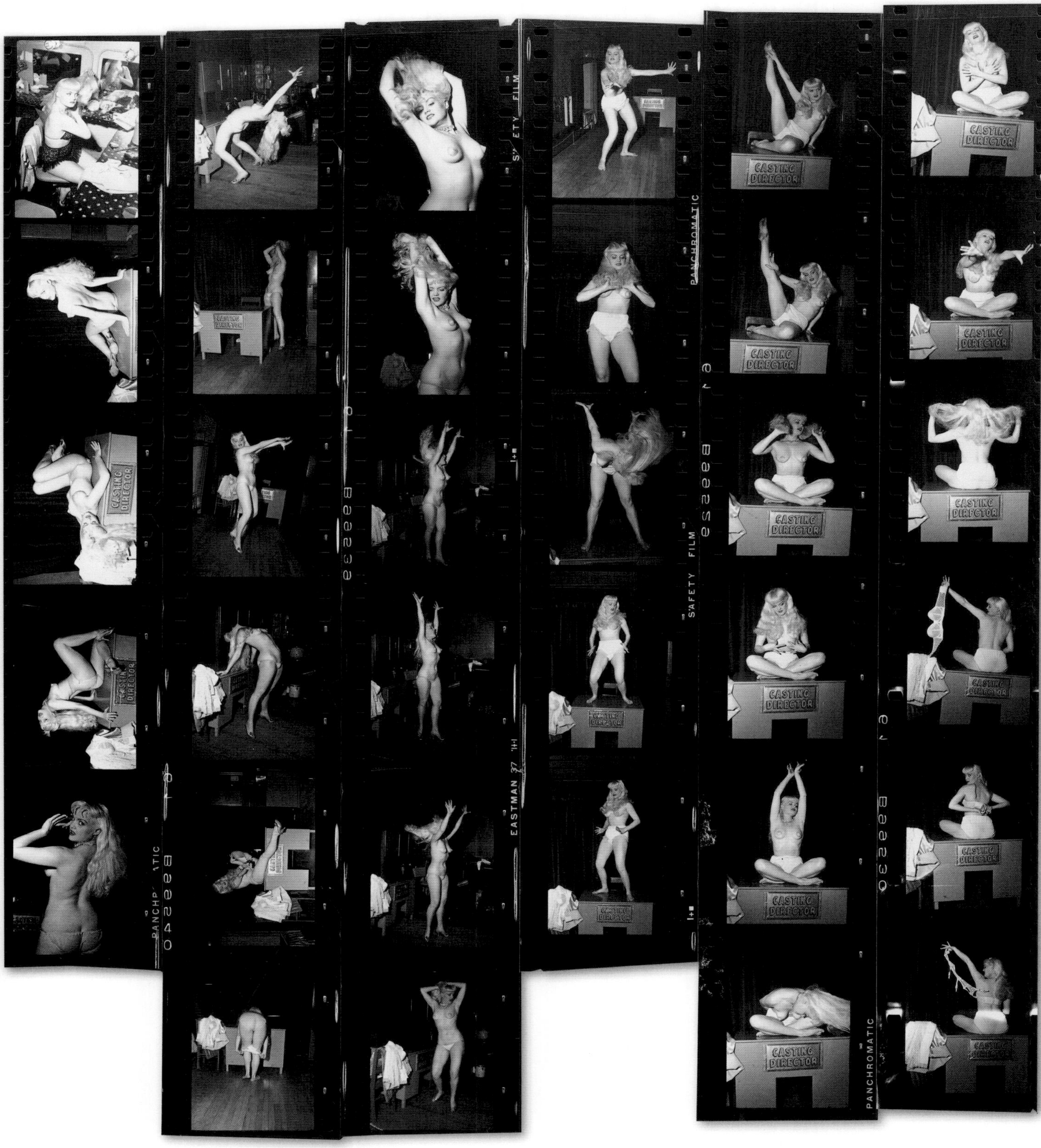
CASTING DIRECTOR
SAFETY FILM
PANCHROMATIC
EASTMAN

Irma "The Body"

IRMA

Generously endowed by Nature, Mary Goodneighbor of Prospect Park,
New Jersey, entered show biz via modelling. Her vital statistics speak
for themselves. She's 5'9½, weighs 139, measures 39-23-39.
She has just come back from Canada where the fans voted her "Miss
Goodneighbor of 1956". In eastern U.S. where she is well-known, she
is IRMA THE BODY.

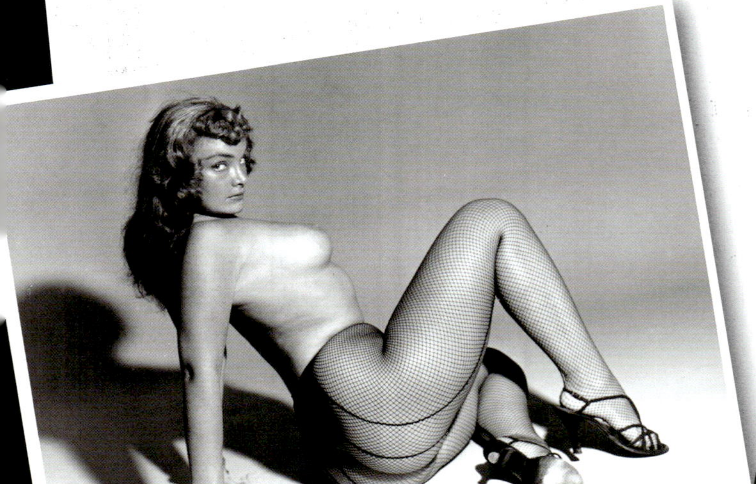

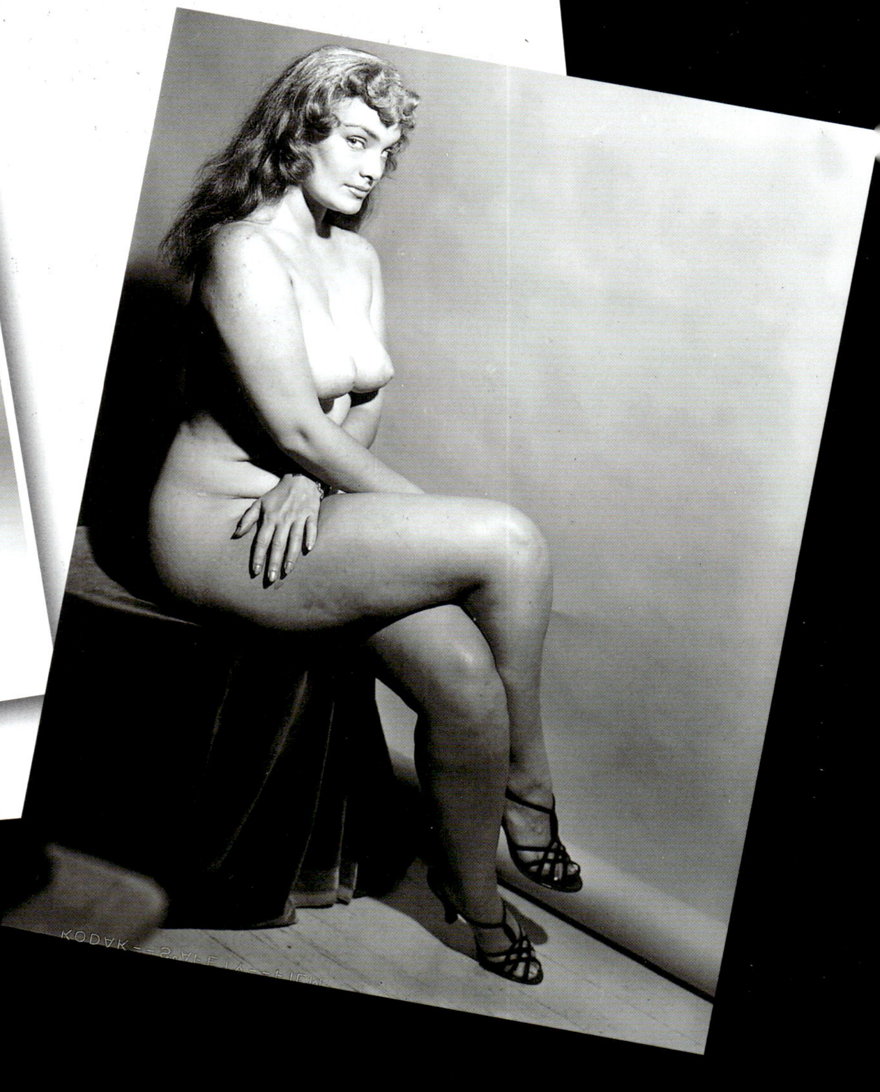

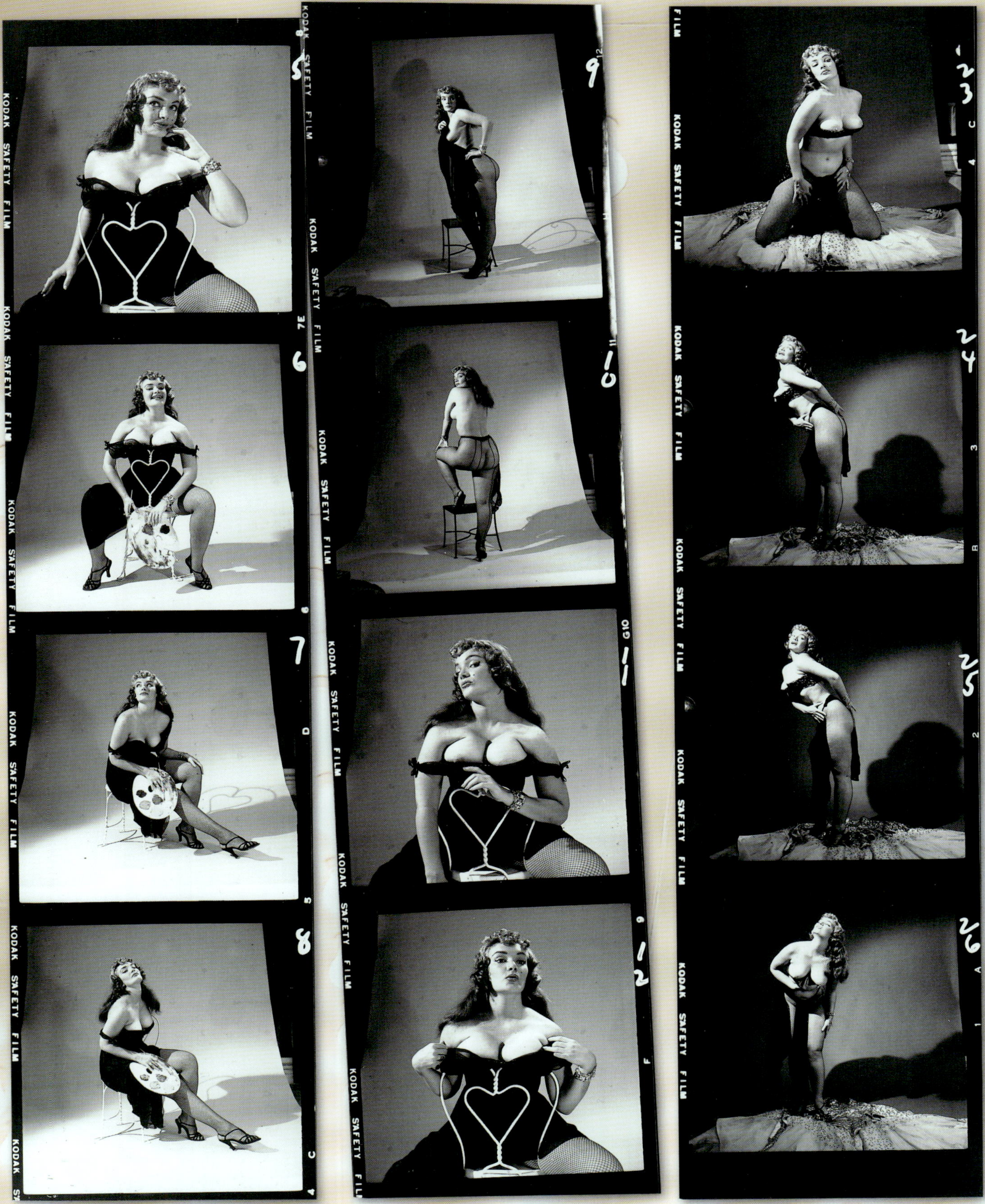
KODAK SAFETY FILM

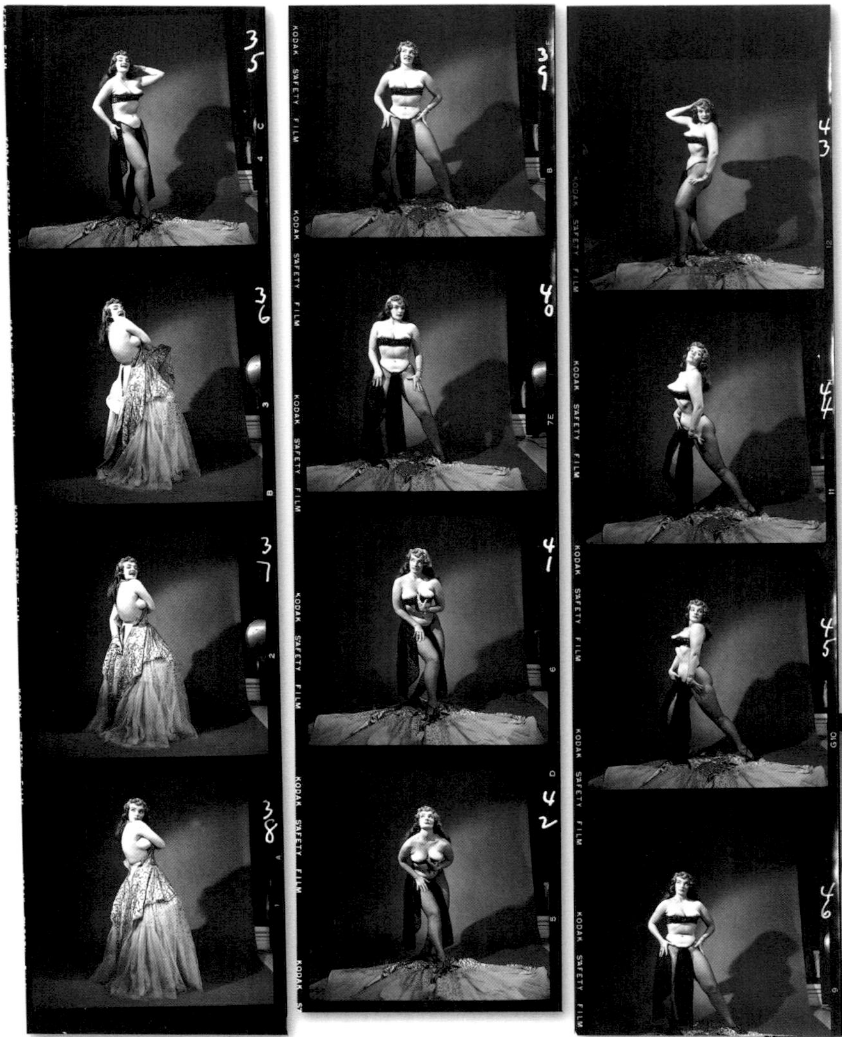

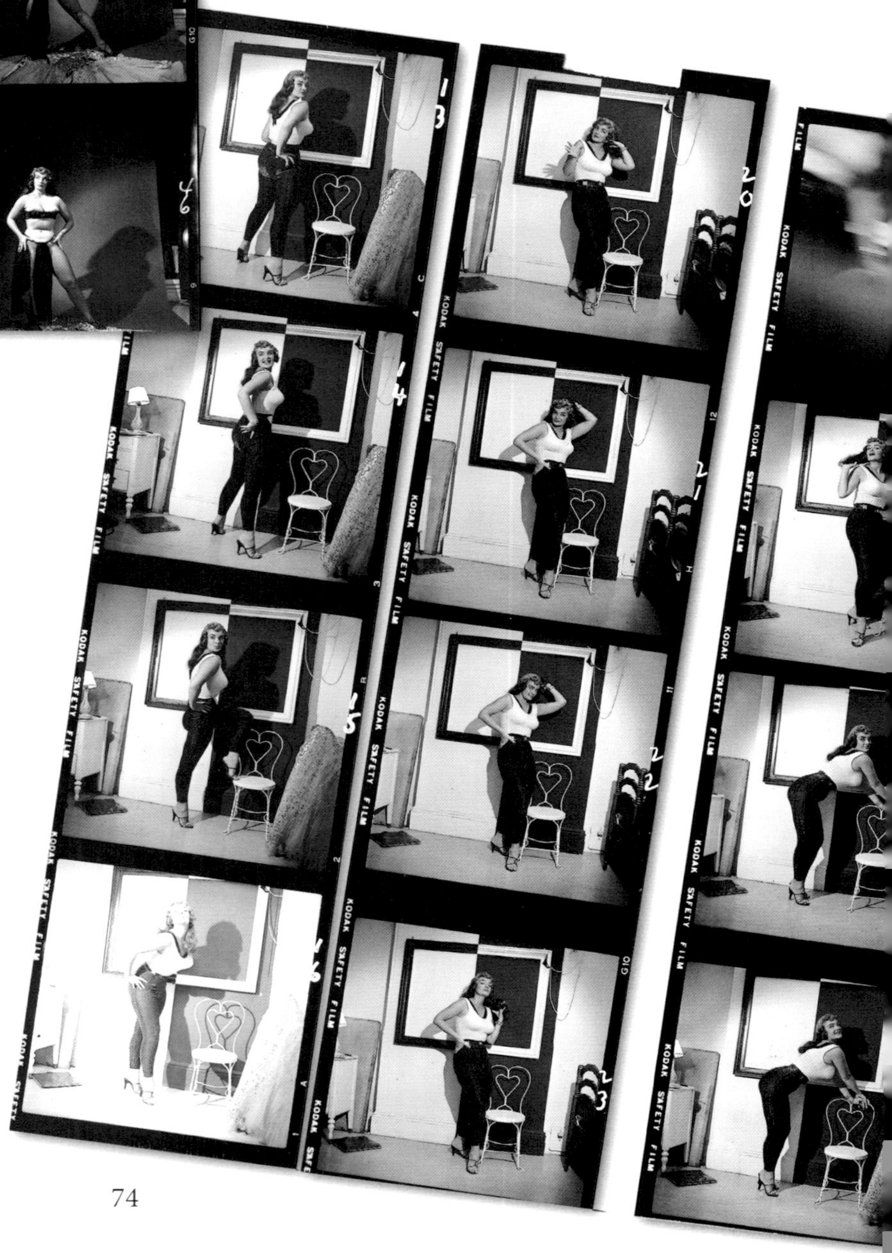

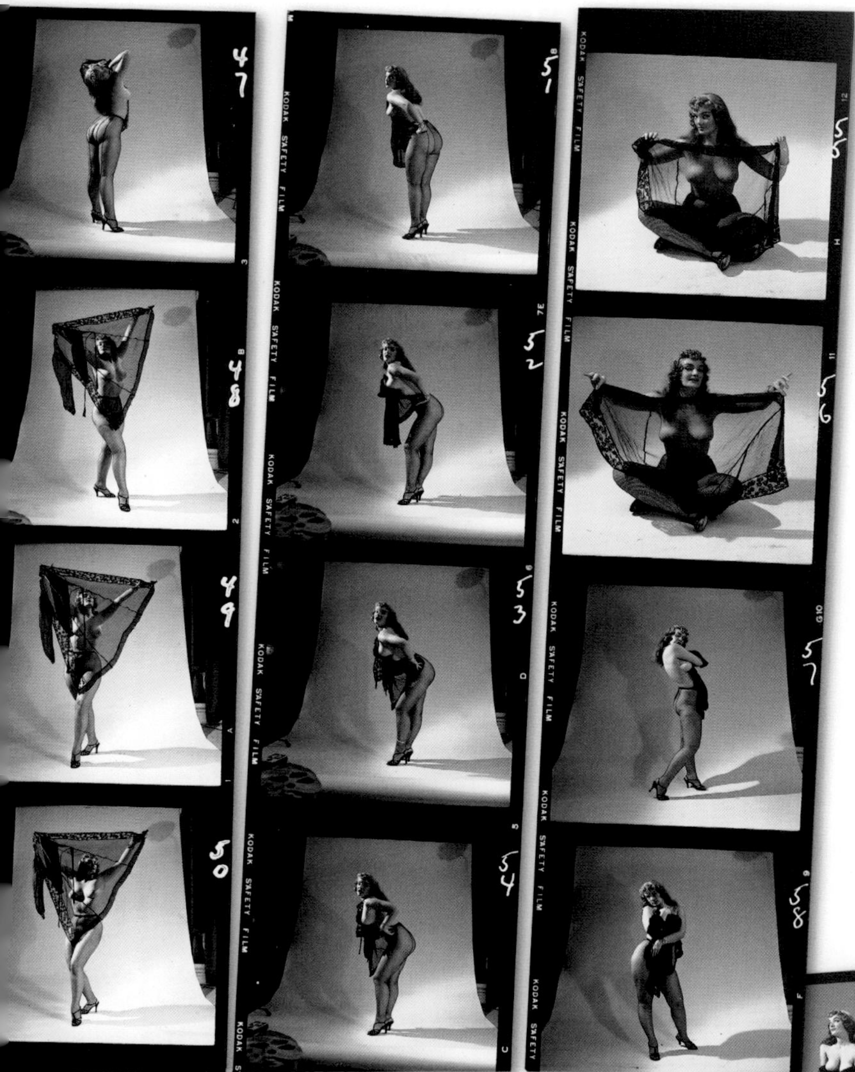

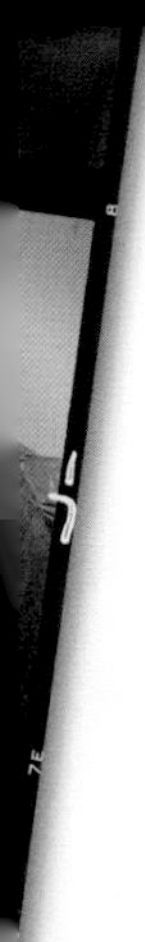

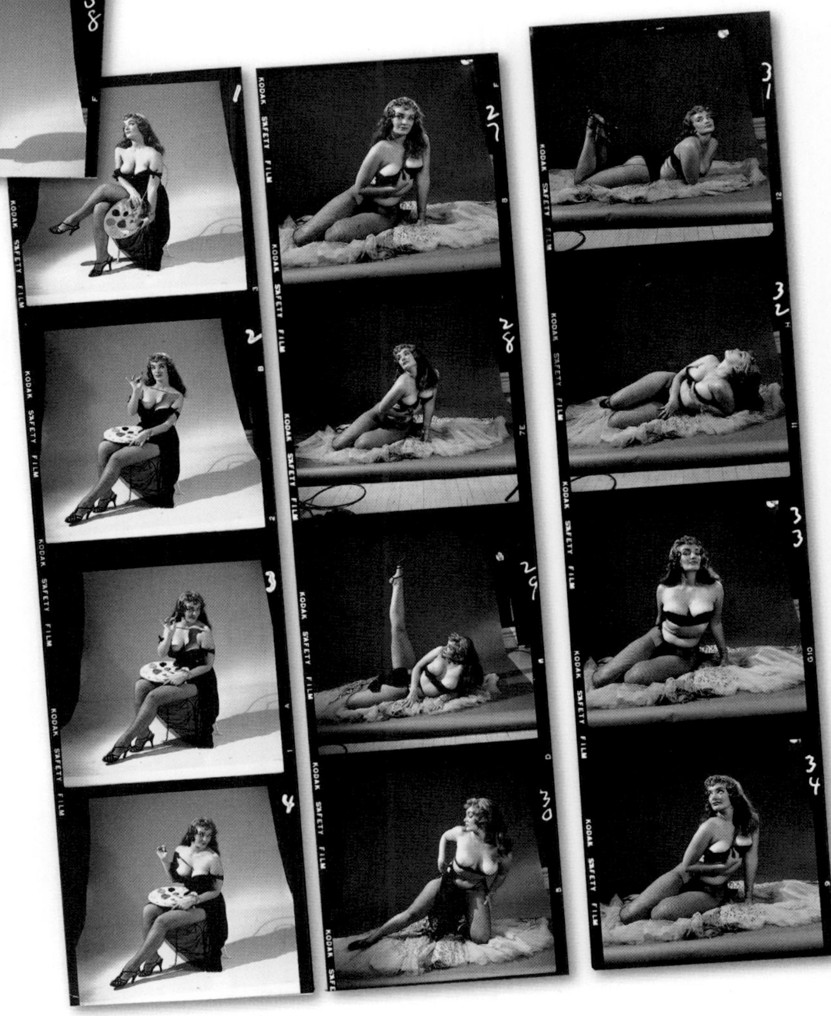

Jean Rich

3

JEANNE WHITNEY (nee Jean Rich)

Should SHE STRIP TO CONQUER ?

Here's a red hot redhead with a problem. She's Jeanne Whitney, a high voltage outlet who's all dressed up and doesn't know whether she should stay that way or not.

It all began when Jeanne was working in the chorus at the Empire Theatre in Newark, New Jersey. Whenevr the audience seemed to be getting cold, the manager would tell Jeanne maybe she ought to too a few of her clothes to the wolves. Which Jeanne would do, much to the delight of the audience and the worry of the Fire Inspector. Then top comedians began working Jeanne into their acts whenever they came to the Empire. And almost before you could button a bra, Jeanne was the toast of Newark. Fan mail began pouring into her dressing room by the bushel full. How they did love to see this girl remove her raiment. As well they might, considering....

Well, anyway, Jeanne was suddenly offered a high salary modelling job. At the same time she got a chance to make some TV movie shorts and commercials. So she left her G-string in New Jersey and did these other jobs in New York. You'll be seeing the movies on your screen, soon. She likes her new work, but she does miss the whistles, the gentlemen yelling "Take it off" and the thrill of showing students of strip the fundamentalsof life. She also gets hundreds of letters begging her to come back and take off again. Several big night-clubs have offered her a big build-up if she'll reveal her secrets on their podiums, too.

All of which naturally has the sizzling redhead in a real tizzy. Should she give up her chancy of a classy career in TV and return to the

old grind ? Or a
breathtaking achi
this were gentleme
-/Jeanne wowed th
- now she's headi
- Jeanne's breatht
- she's a born hum
- the luscious redhe
-comedians grabbed h
-isit fair for a girl
fa
Jeanne is a New Yorker.

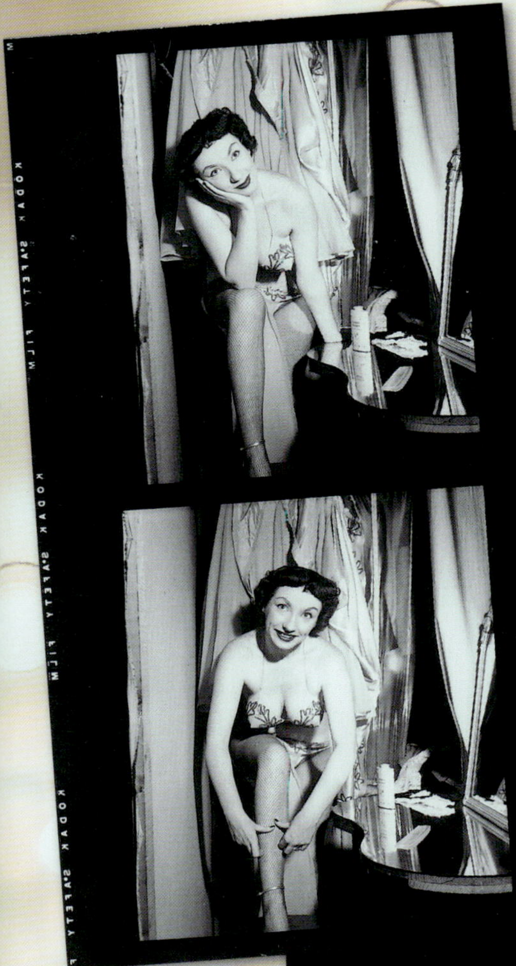

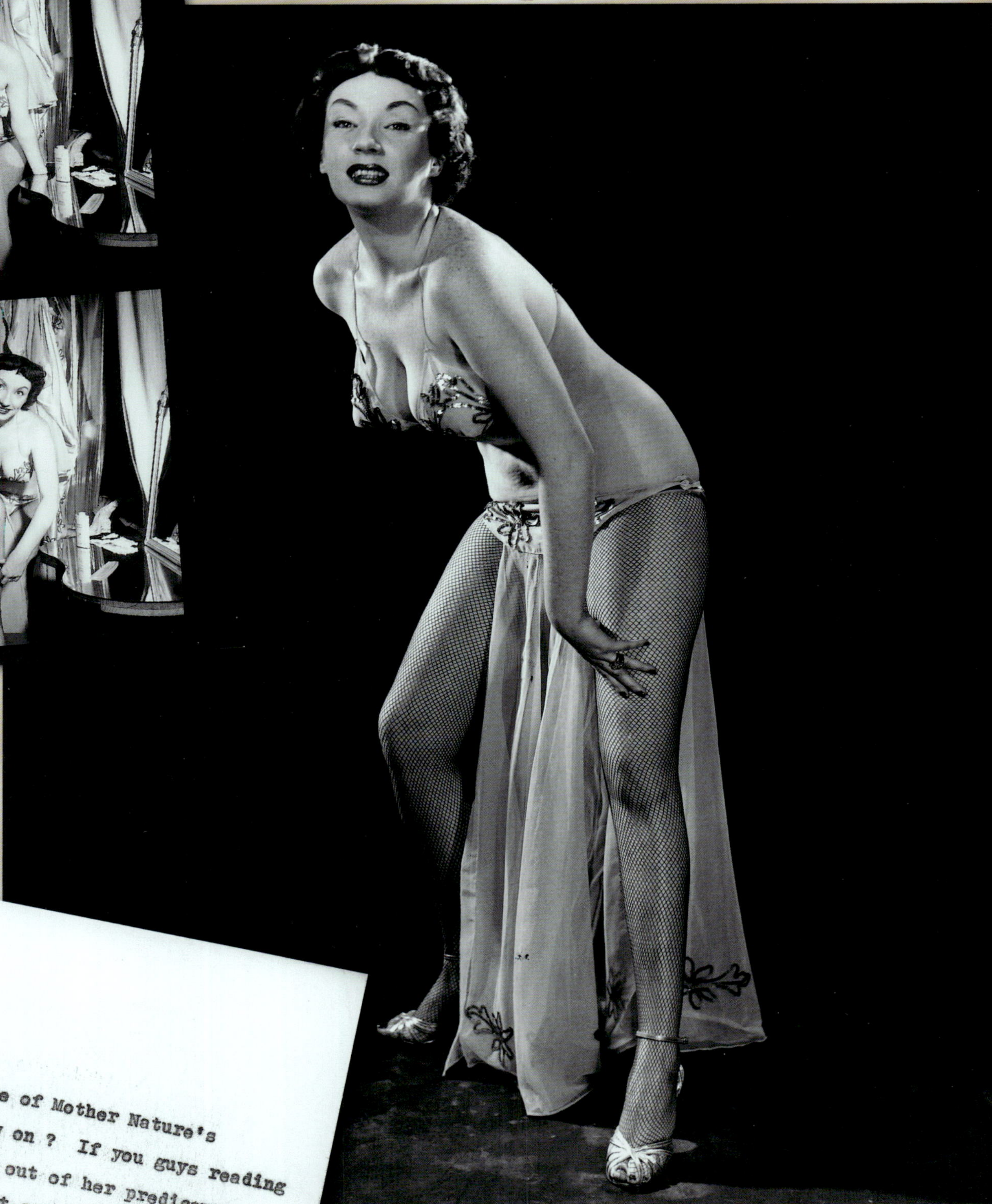

2

he decide to keep some of Mother Nature's
under cover from now on ? If you guys reading
 help the young lady out of her predicament.
ew Jersey with her act on how to peel a peach.
he Big Time in TV, but isn't sure she likes it.
ents have won her a contract for TV movies.
 is always teasing- in one way or another.
thumping 38" around the top-deck .
heir act, thus ensuringaudience attention.
rously endowed by nature to keep the
den ?

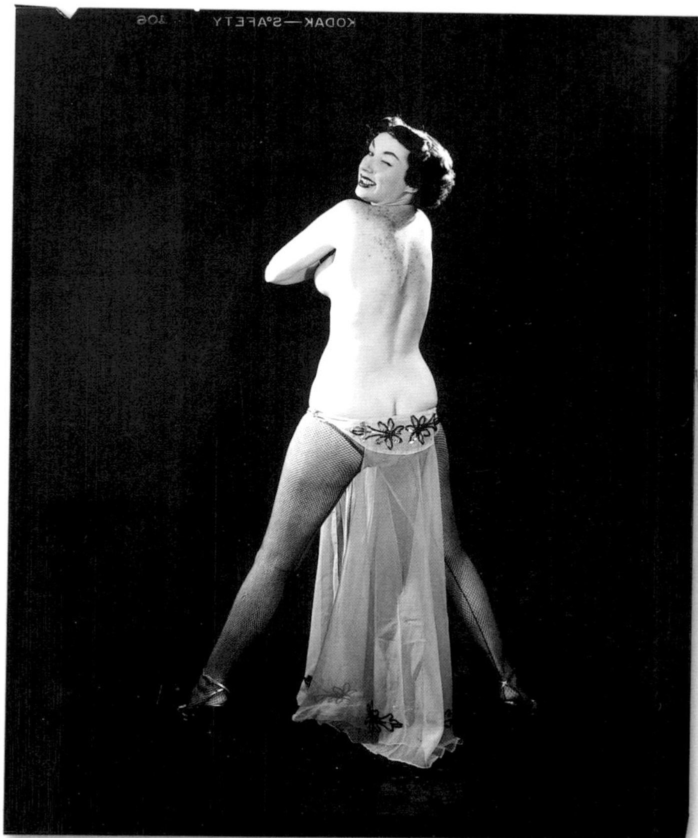

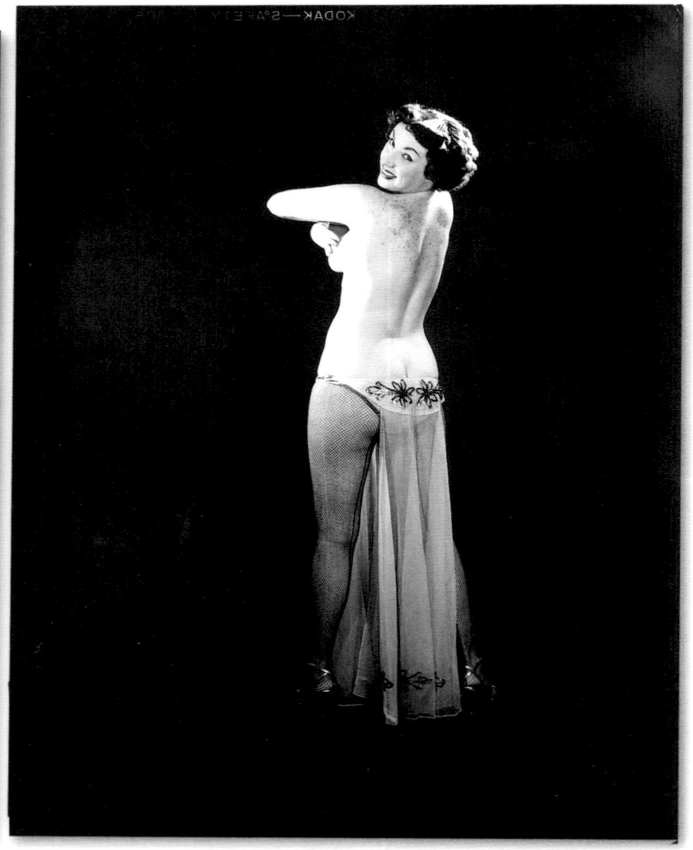

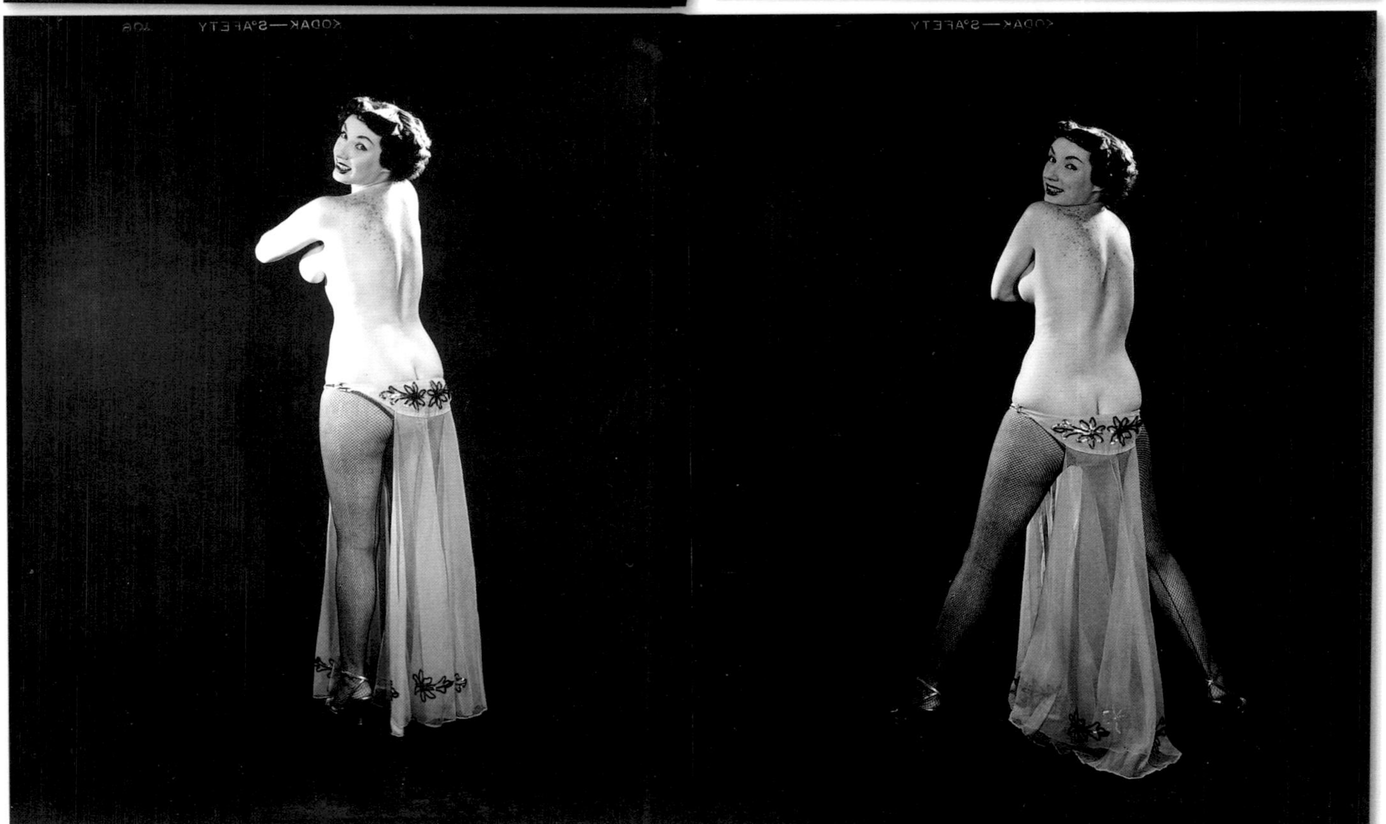

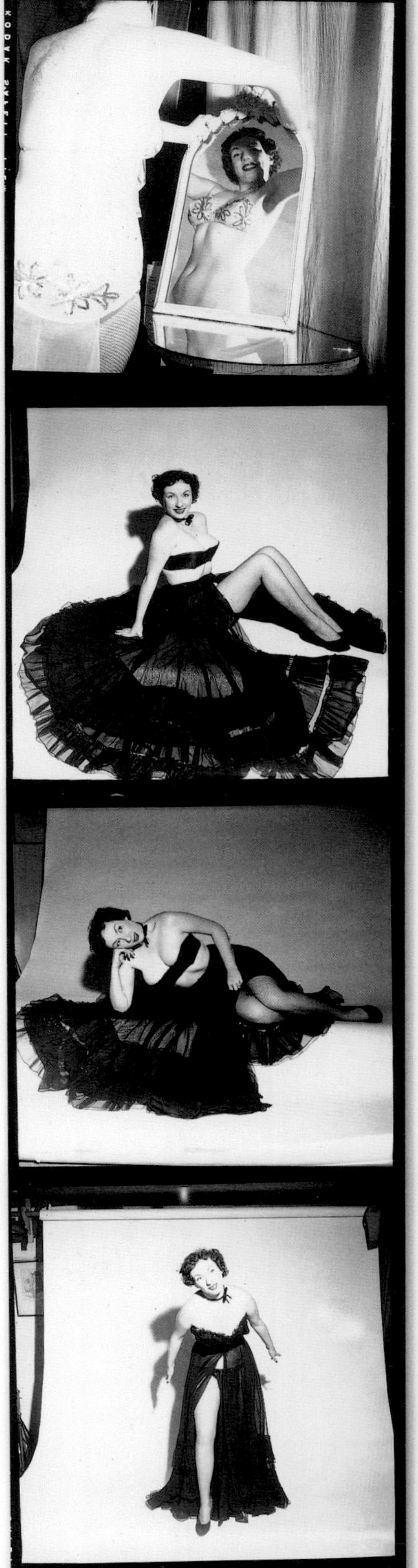

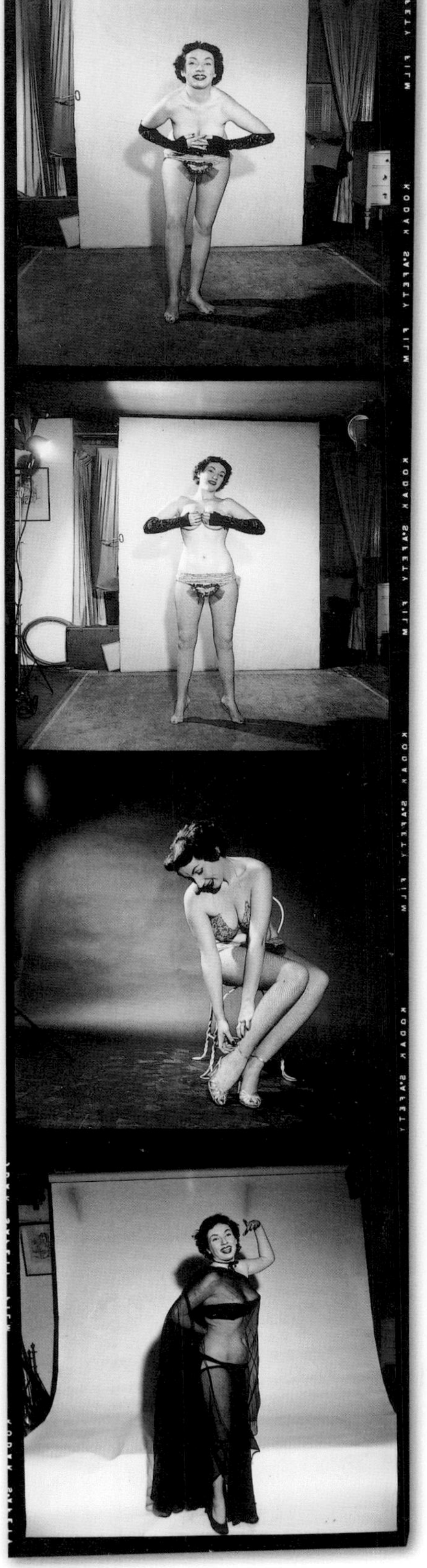

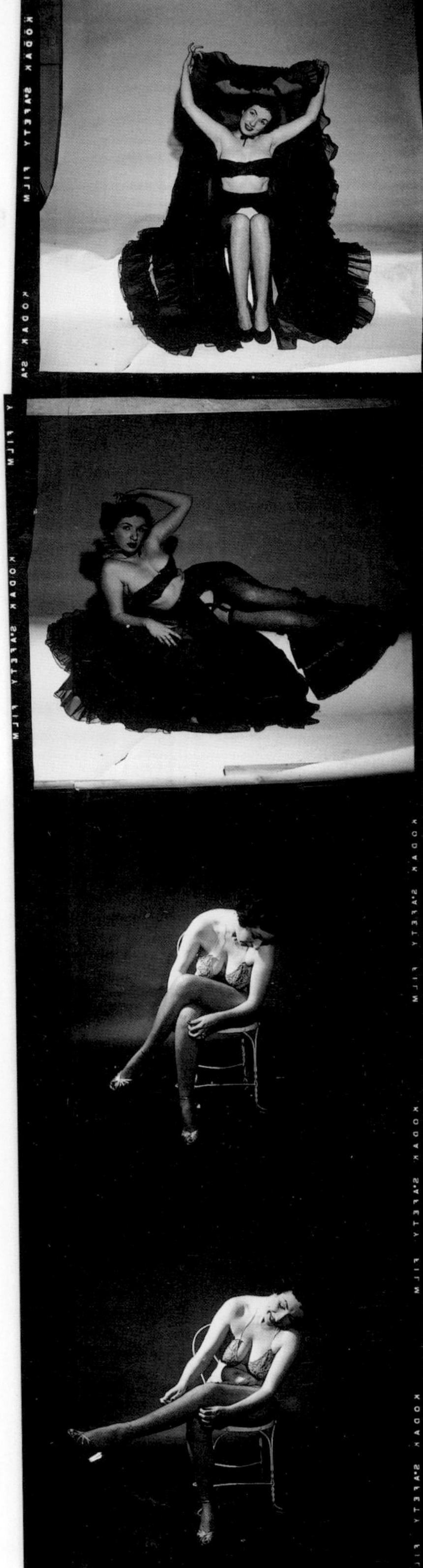

Jennie Lee

JENNIE LEE

Jennie Lee is a big girl- in any man's language. Jennie is 5'9" tall, measures 42-28-40, weighs 140 lbs. She was born in Kansas City, 25 years ago, has been a busy gal ever since she got out of High School, displaying her charms all over the country- west coast, mid-west, Mexico, Cuba, Canada. Jennie has done some dramatic roles in theatre on west coast, aspires to legit stage- comedy parts. Favorite pastime- answering her fan mail. Jennie gets about a thousand fan letters a month. She has her own following- the Jennie Lee Bazoomers. For 25¢ anyone can join this organization and gets, in return, a reply from Jennie herself, plus a membership card to this organization, plus 2 wallet-size burlesk pin-ups of La Bazoom herself.

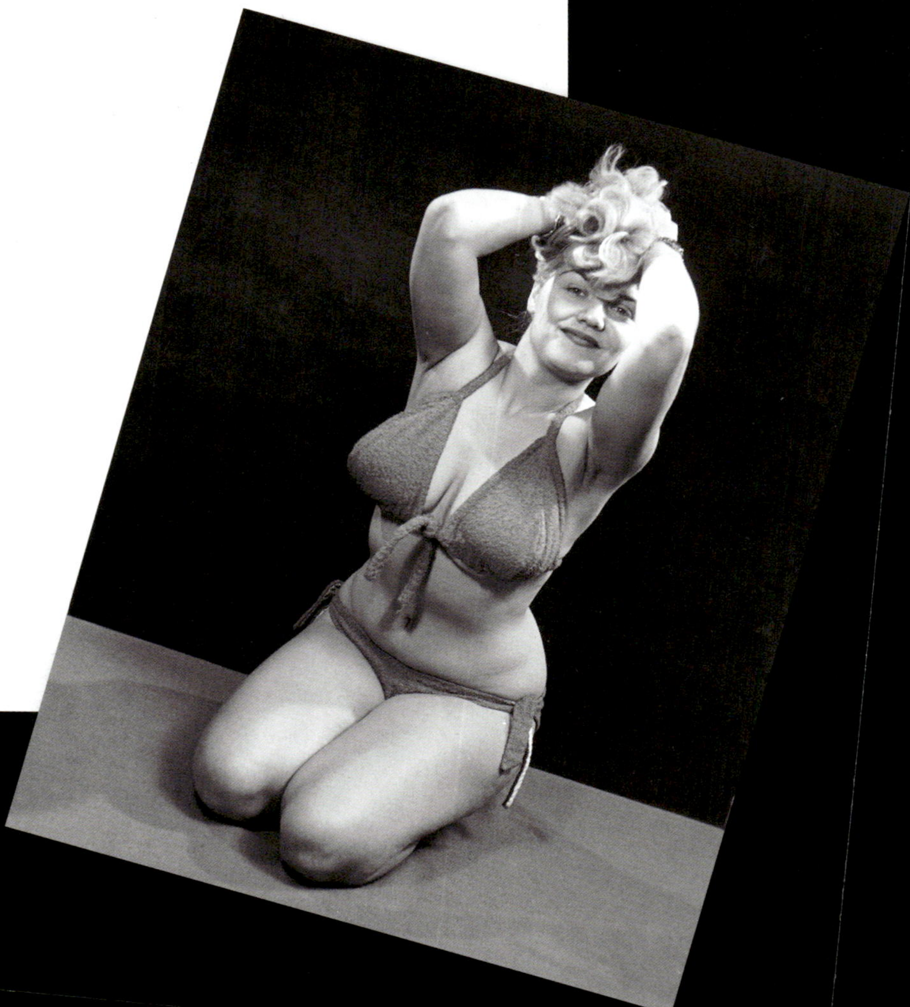

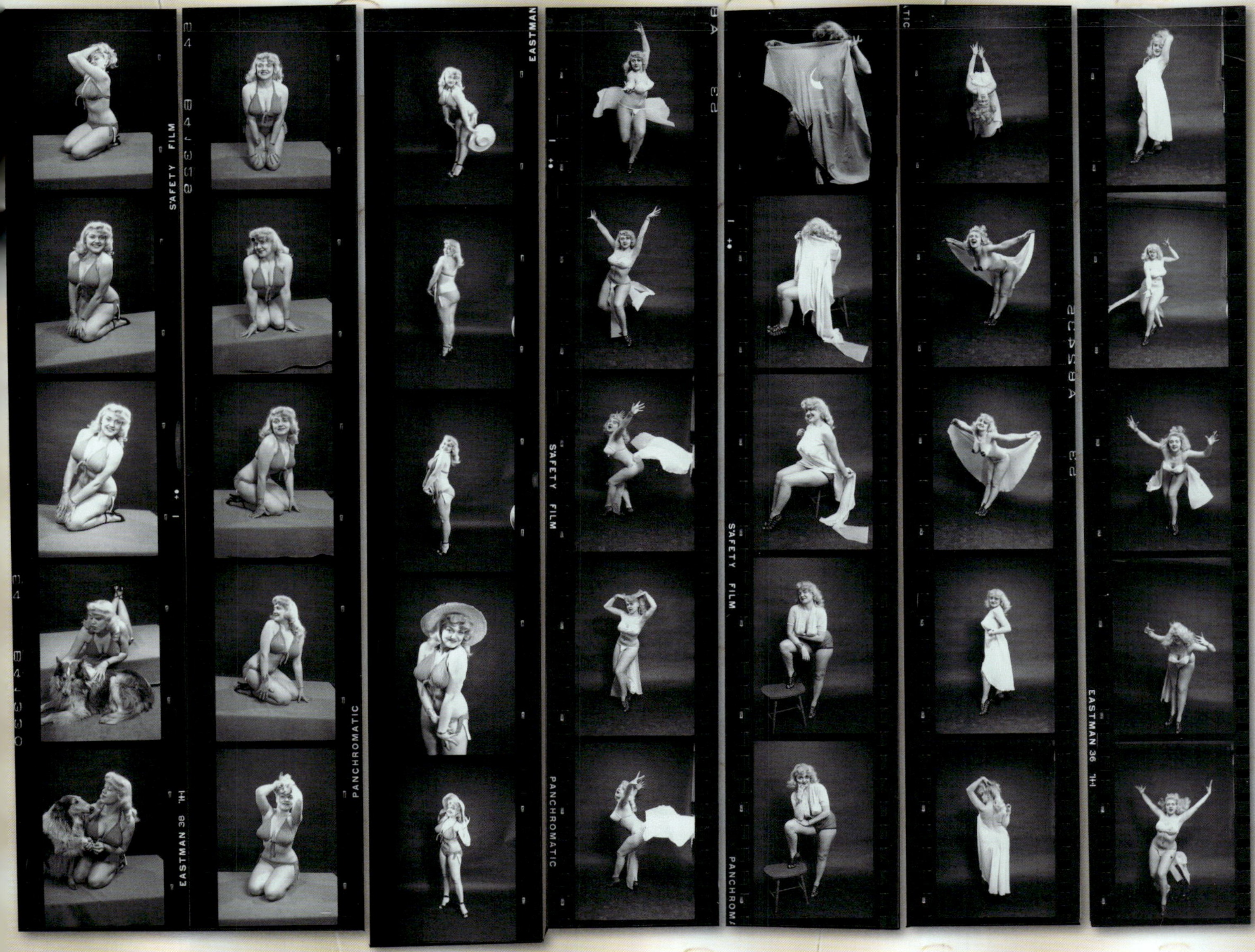
SAFETY FILM
EASTMAN 36
PANCHROMATIC
EASTMAN
SAFETY FILM
PANCHROMATIC
SAFETY FILM
EASTMAN 36

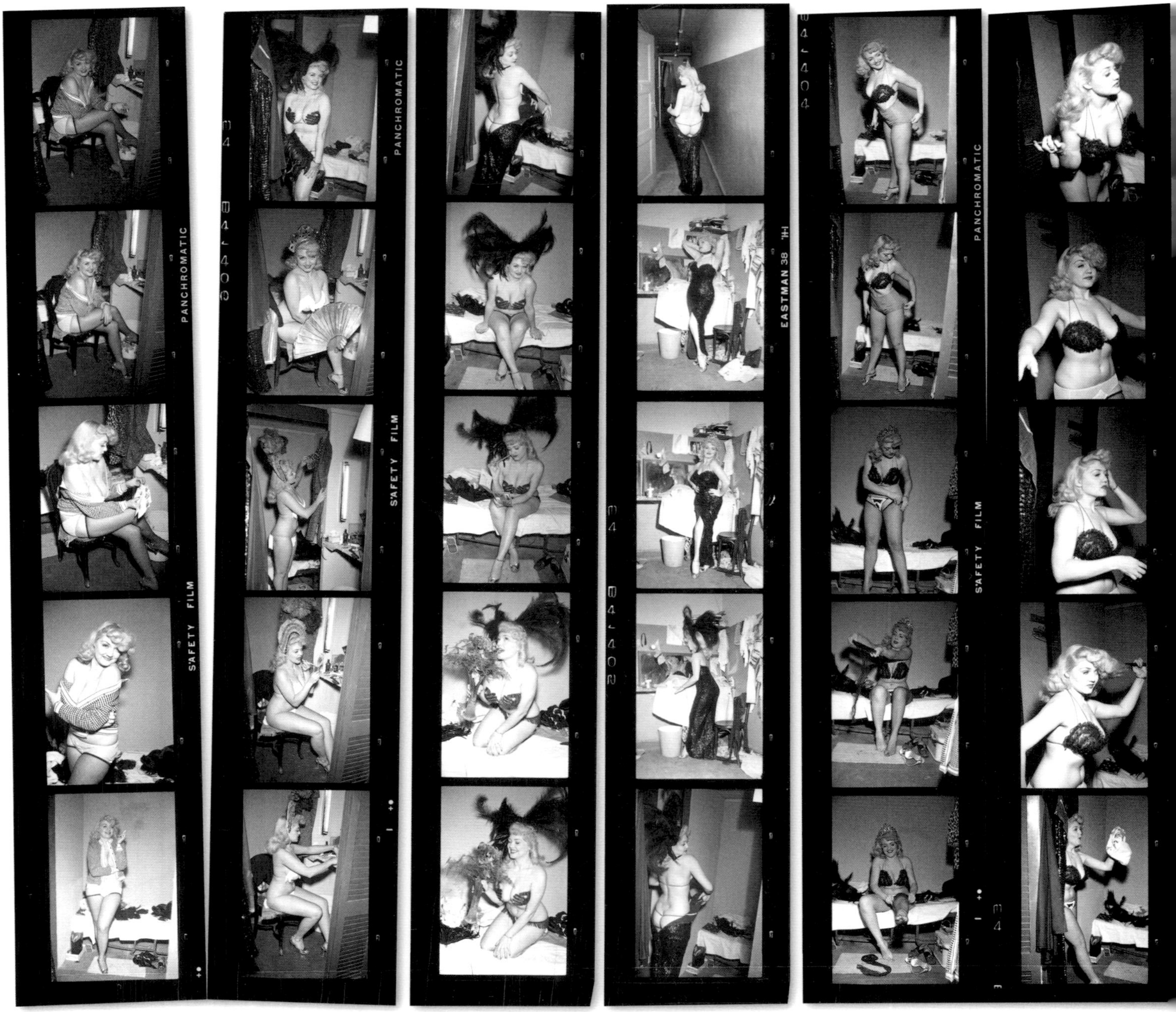
PANCHROMATIC
SAFETY FILM
EASTMAN 38

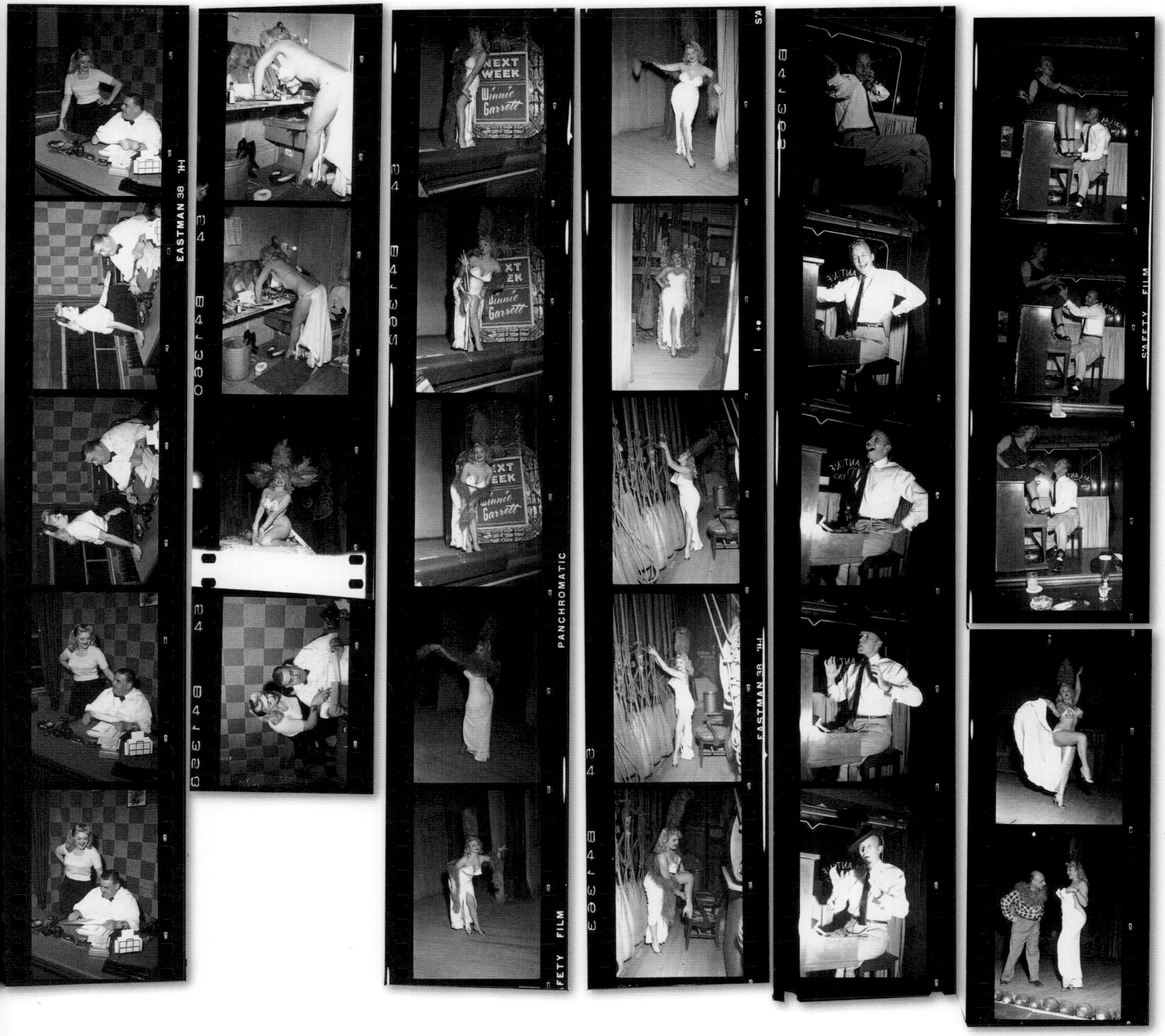
NEXT WEEK
Winnie Garrett
EASTMAN 38
PANCHROMATIC
SAFETY FILM

Jessica Rogers

JESSICA ROGERS

Jessica measures 39-27-39. She is 5'7" tall and she hails from Tampa, Florida. Her hair is blonde and her eyes blue.

Probably nobody in show biz can match Jessica Rogers when it comes to dishing out with showmanship. You could say that she is an old-timer, although from looking at these pictures, she is still young enough to wow 'em wherever she goes.

Jessica has played all over the United States and Canada, and audiences are ever prepared for something "new" each time they see her. The latest dance is a parakeet dance, conceived and executed by Jessica herself. Jessica comes onstage with parakeets properly seated. Spotlight is kept on birds during act, while Jessica sings a song, mentioning that she has "the best parakeets in town".

Jessica's routine is always a crowd pleaser. Most folks don't realize the hard work that's done.

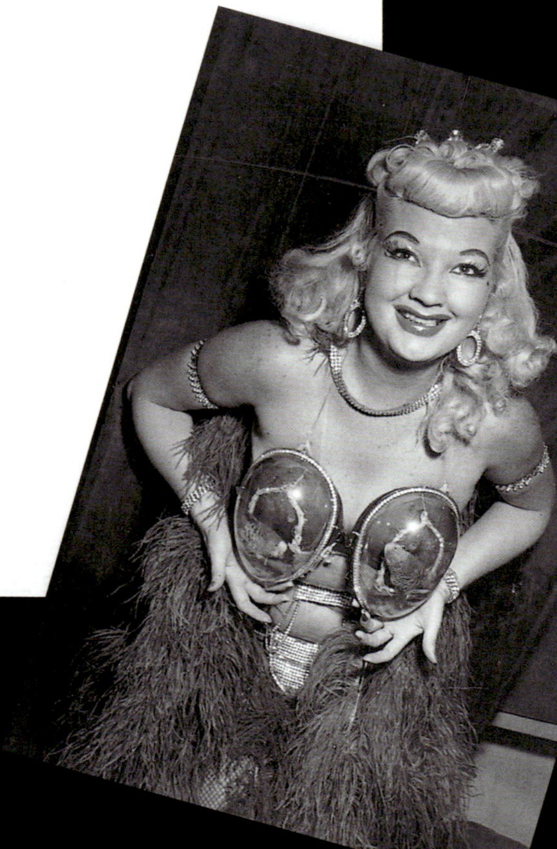

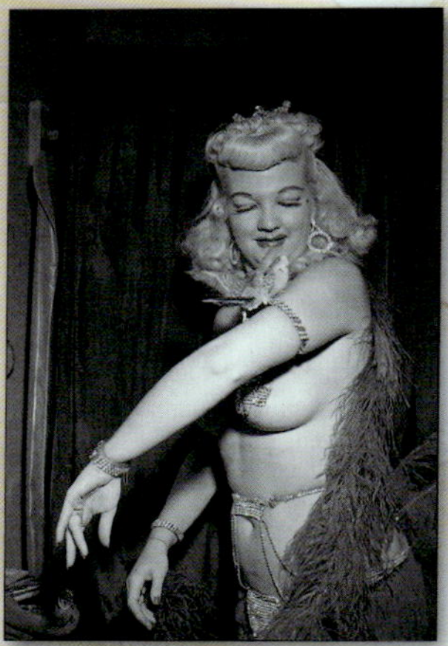
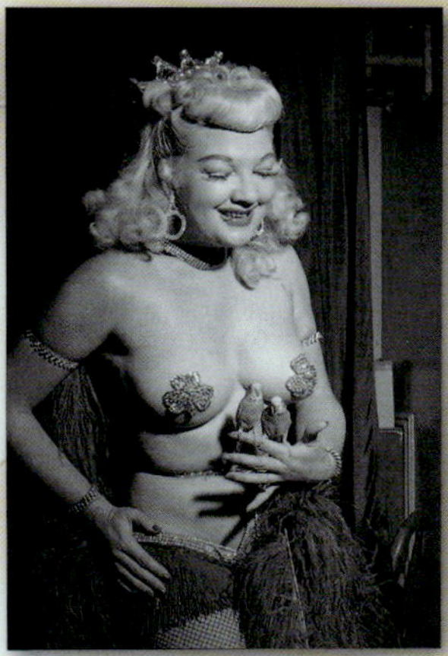
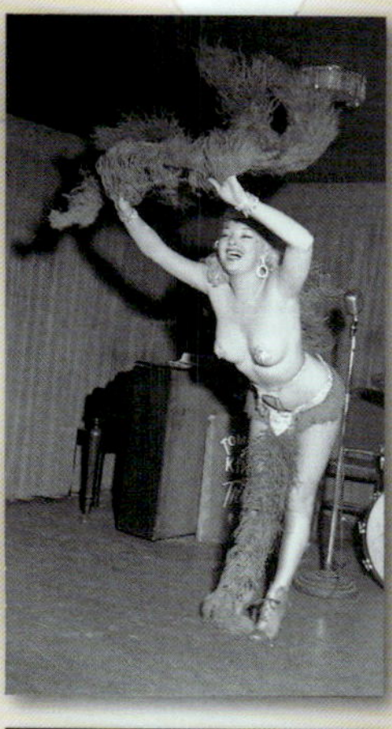
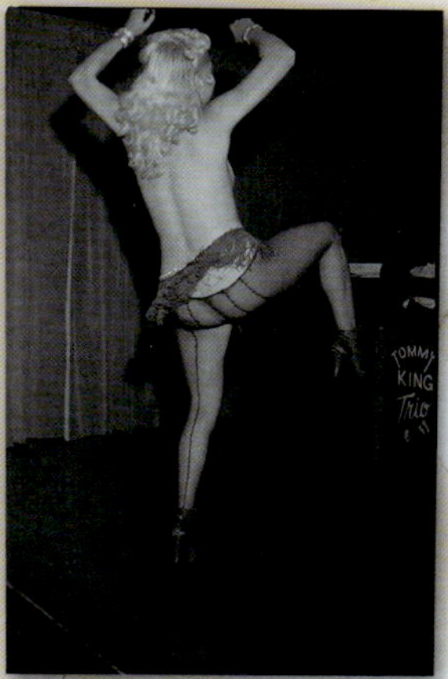
TOMMY
KING
Trio
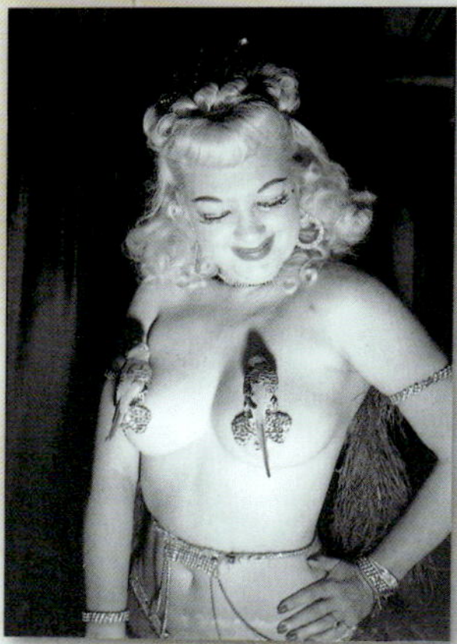
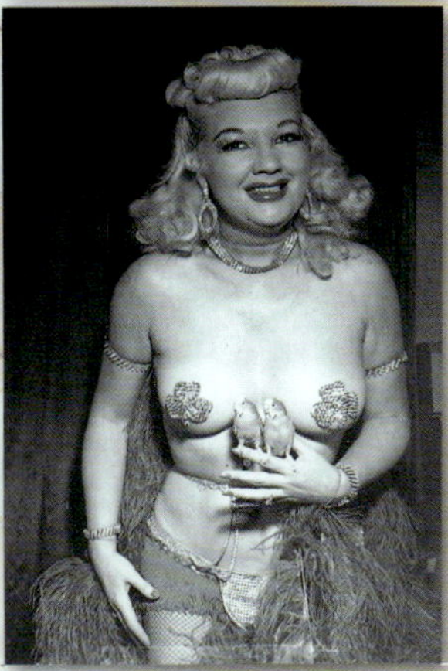
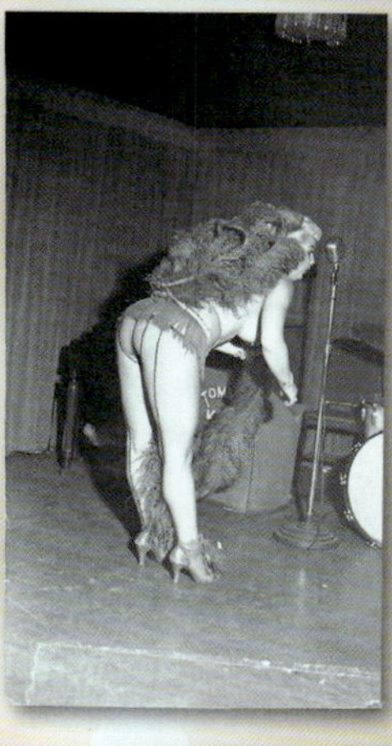
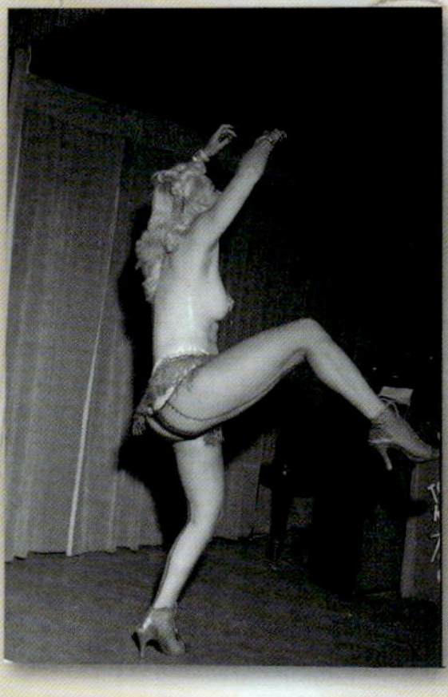
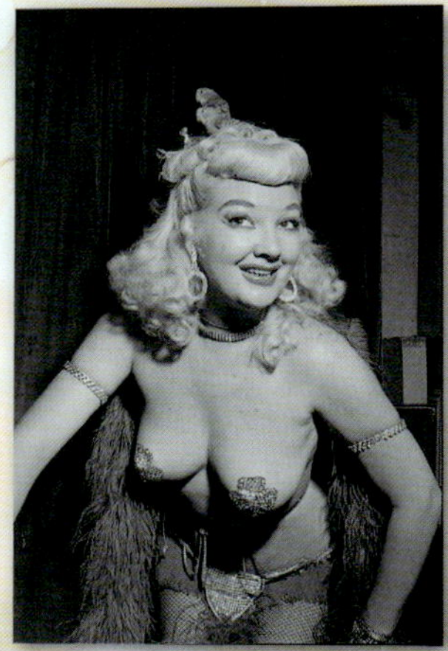
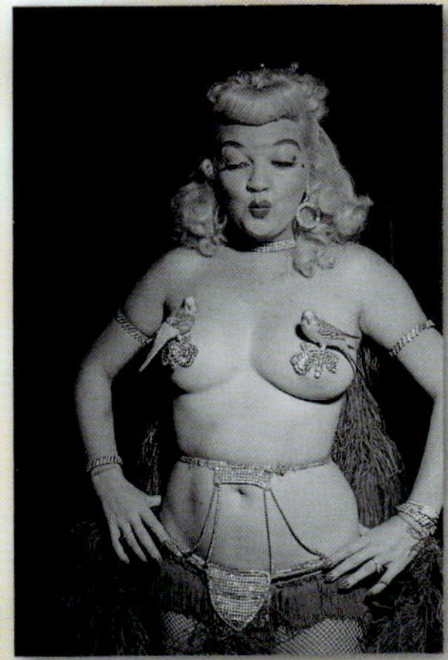
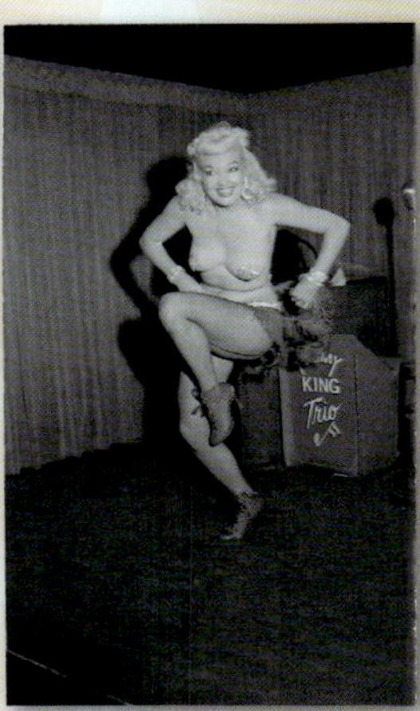
KING
Trio
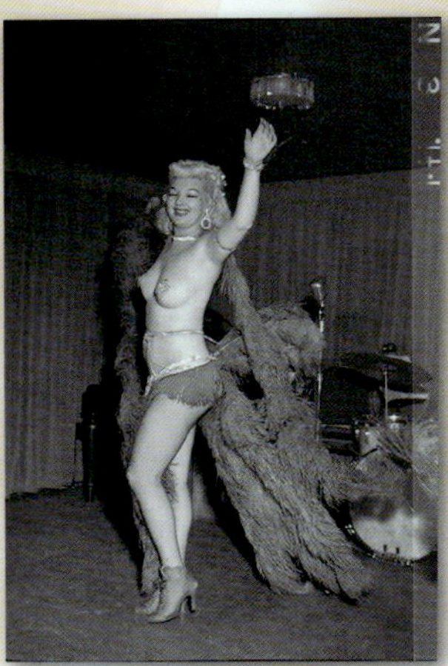
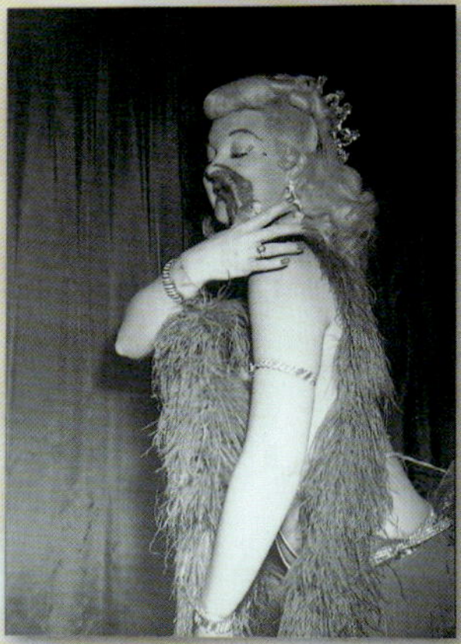
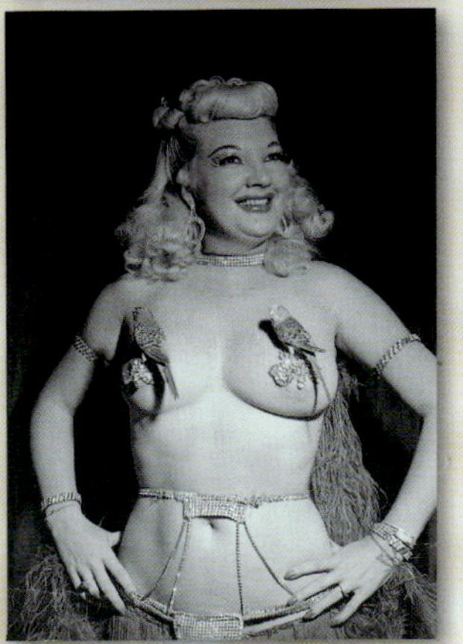
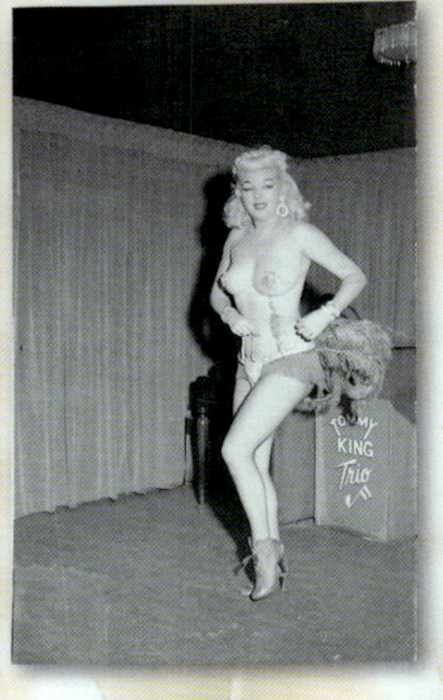
TOMMY
KING
Trio
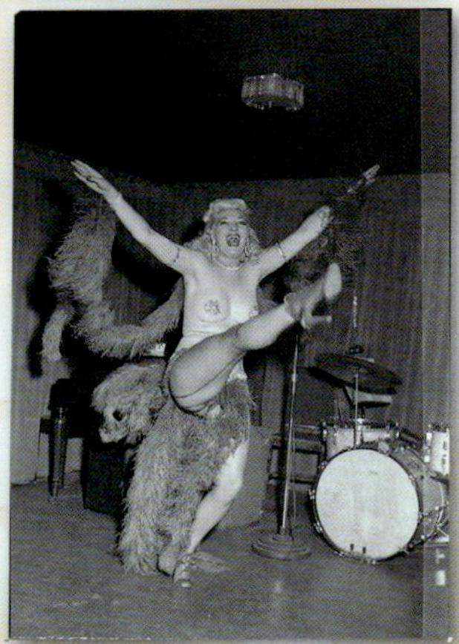

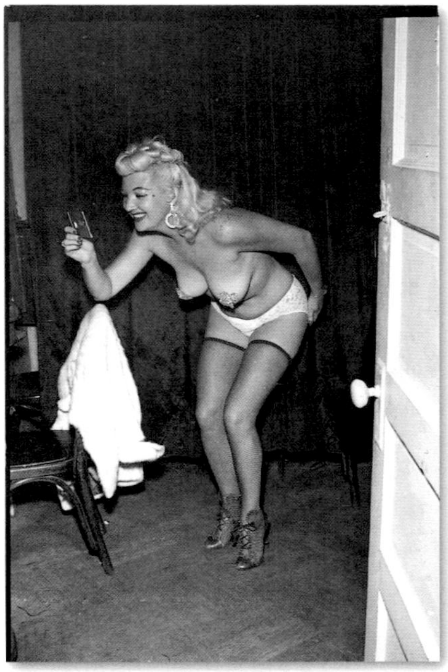
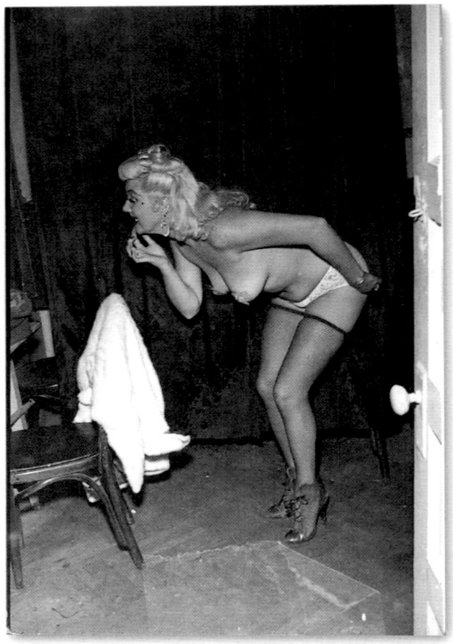
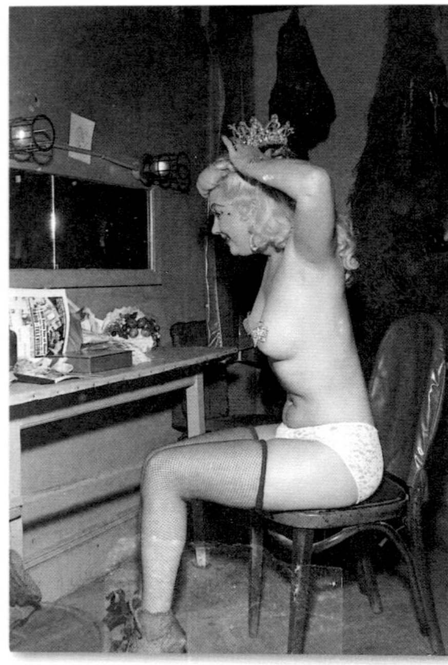
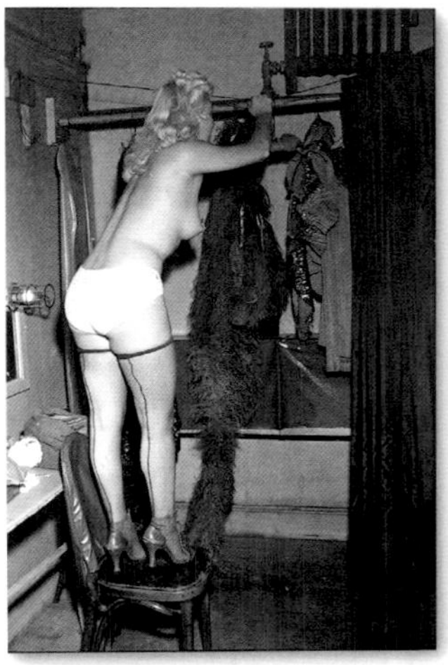
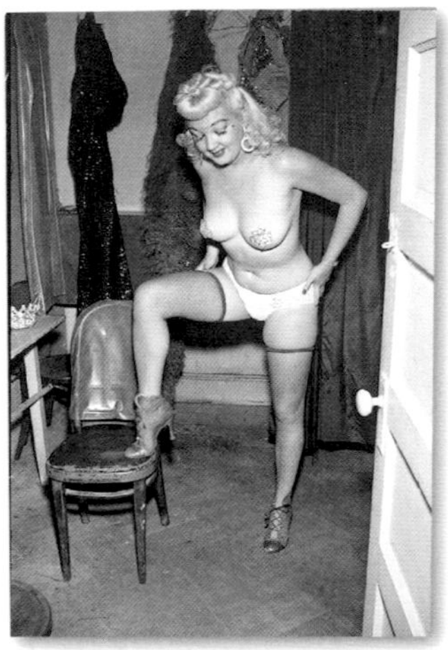
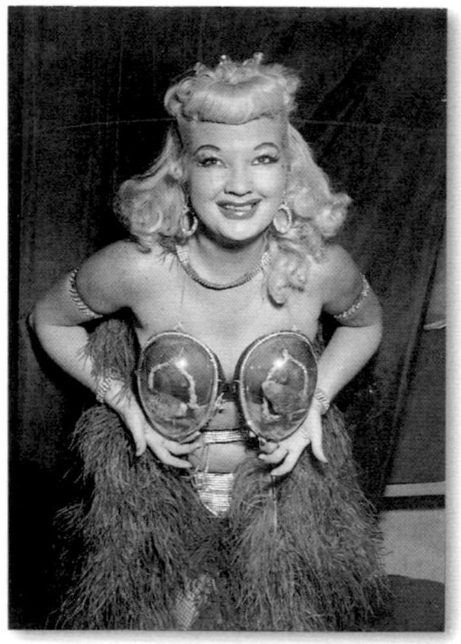
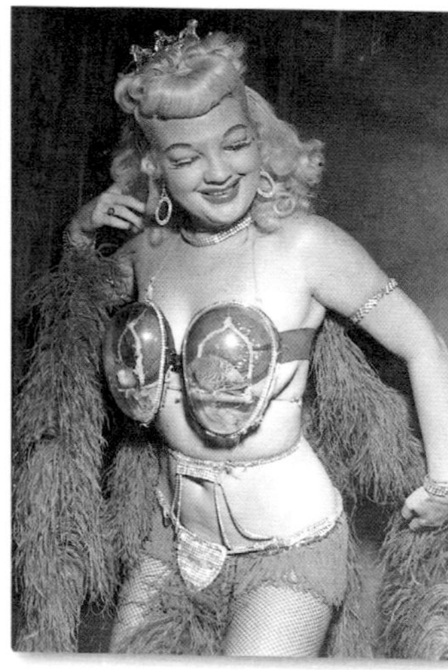
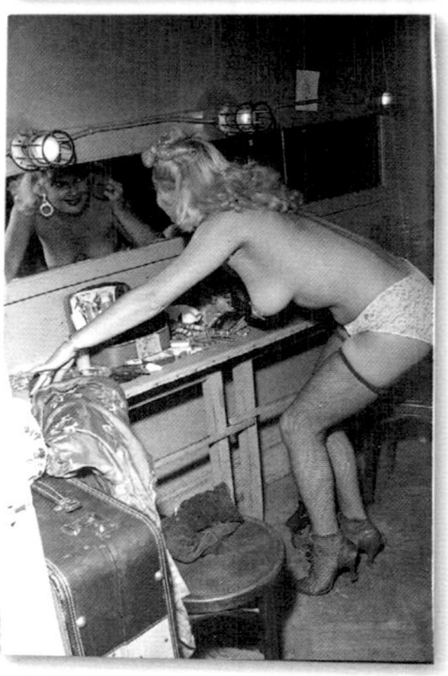
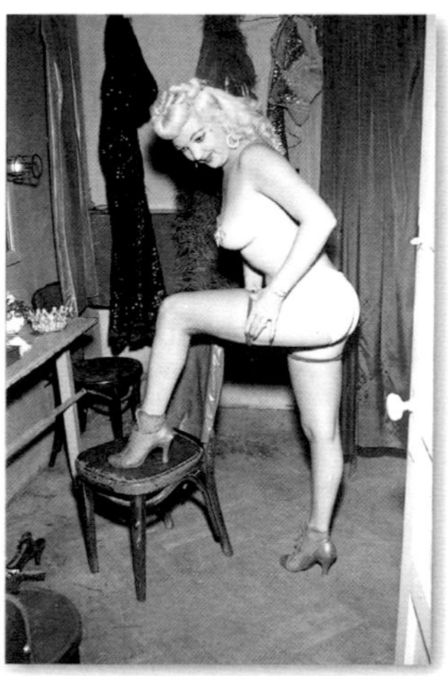
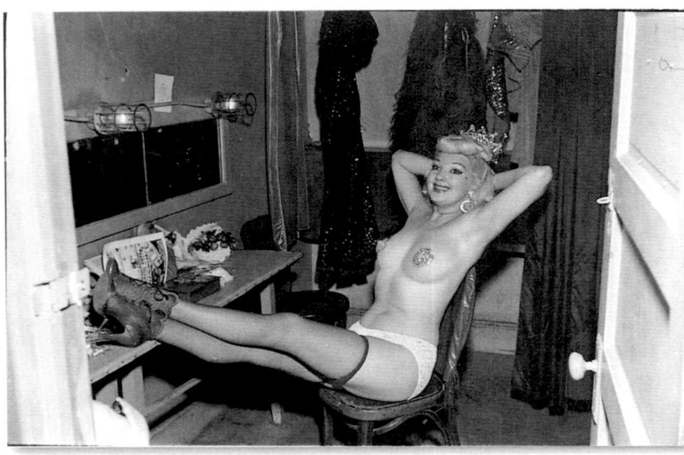

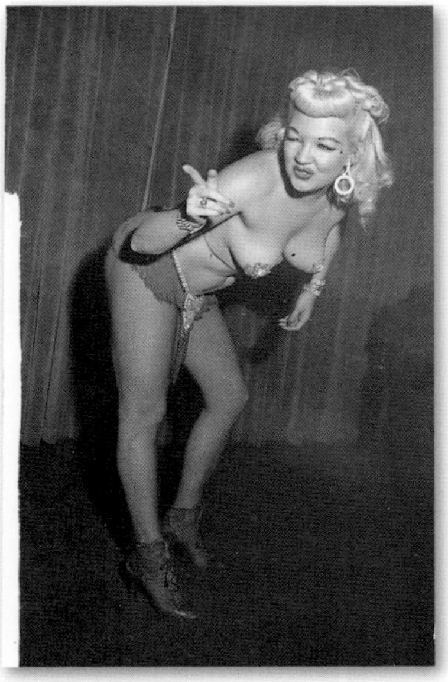

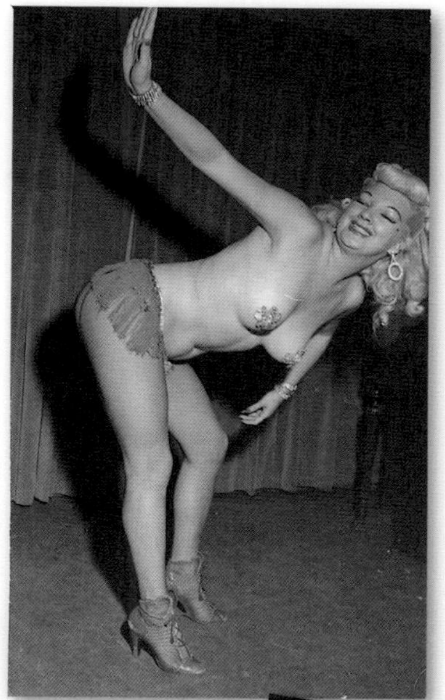

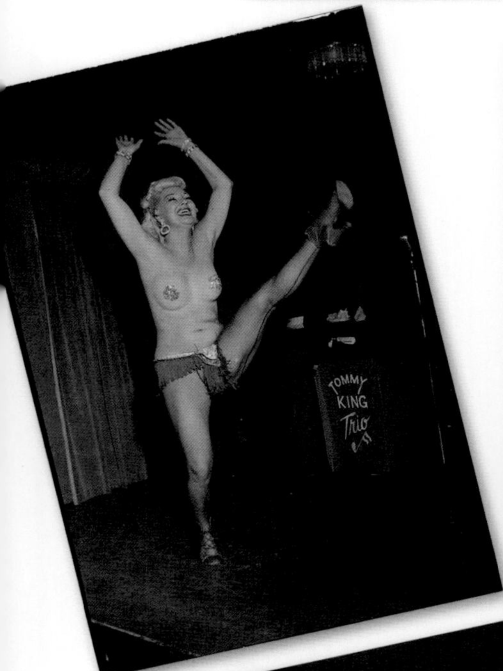
TOMMY
KING
Trio

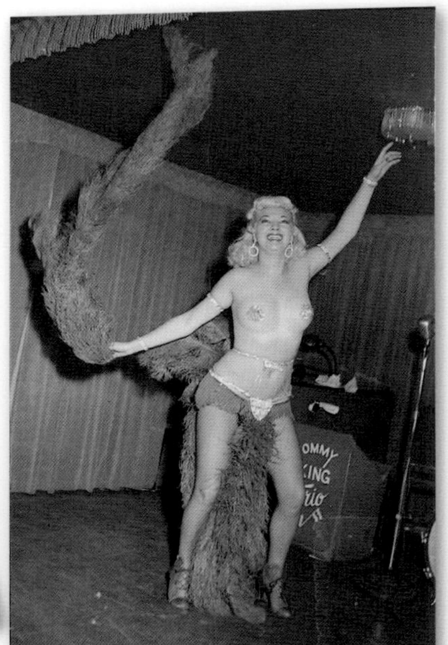

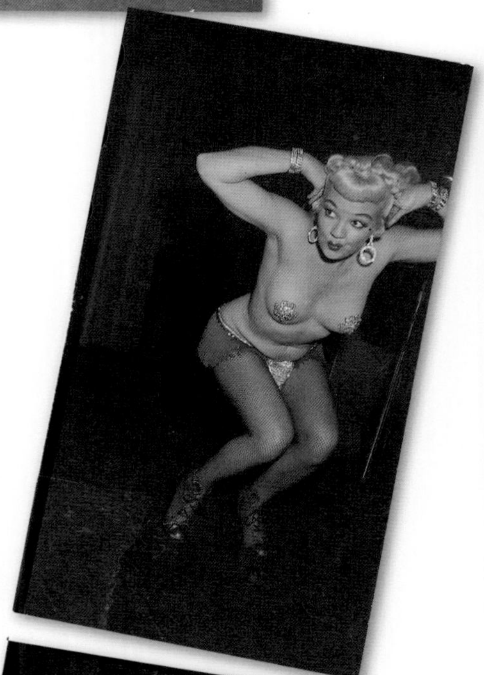

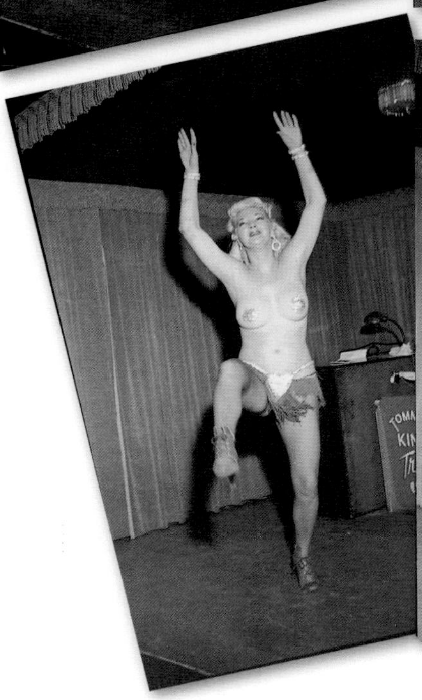

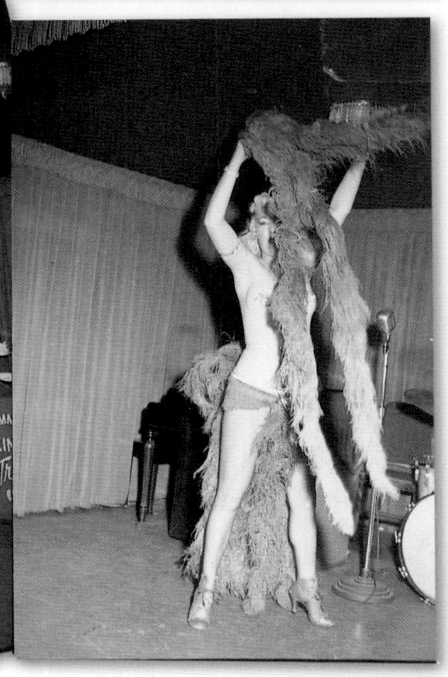

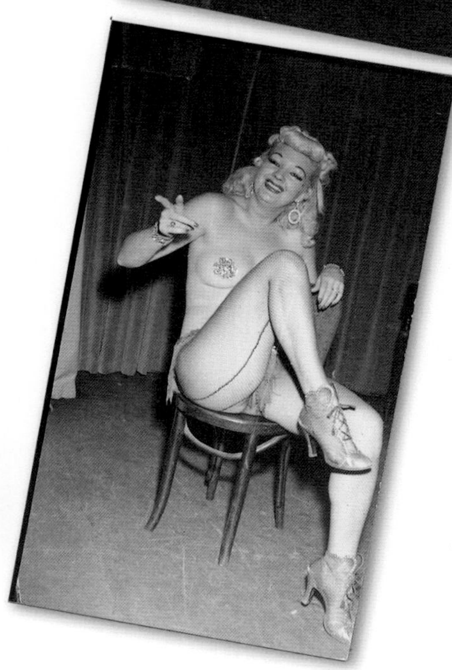

LEE SHARON

24-year-old Lee Sharon is currently appearing in a London night club. Originally from Dallas, Texas, her bewitching charm is partly due to her mixed ancestry- Lee is part French, Irish and Cherokee. Discovery in a Baltimore wee hours club led to a long engagement in Lou Walters' LATIN QUARTER in New York, then she appeared at the LATIN QUARTER in X Tokyo, subsequently returned to U.S. for engagements on the west coast.

Lee is 5'3" tall, measures 35-23-35.

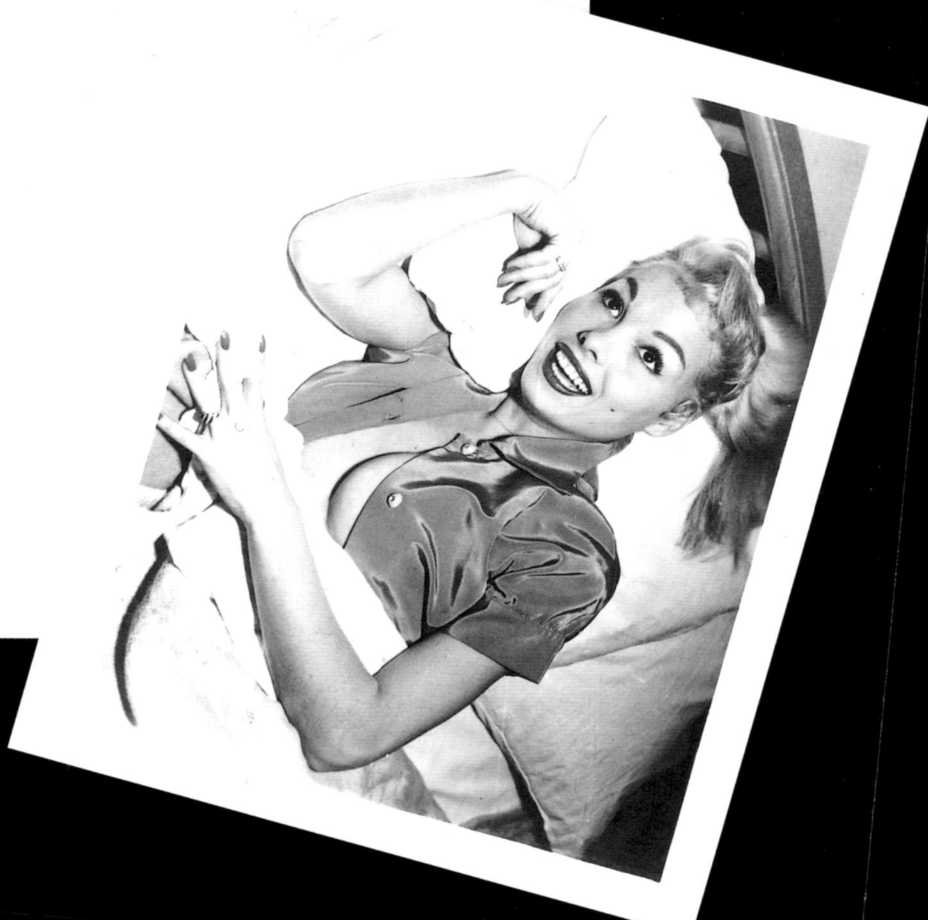

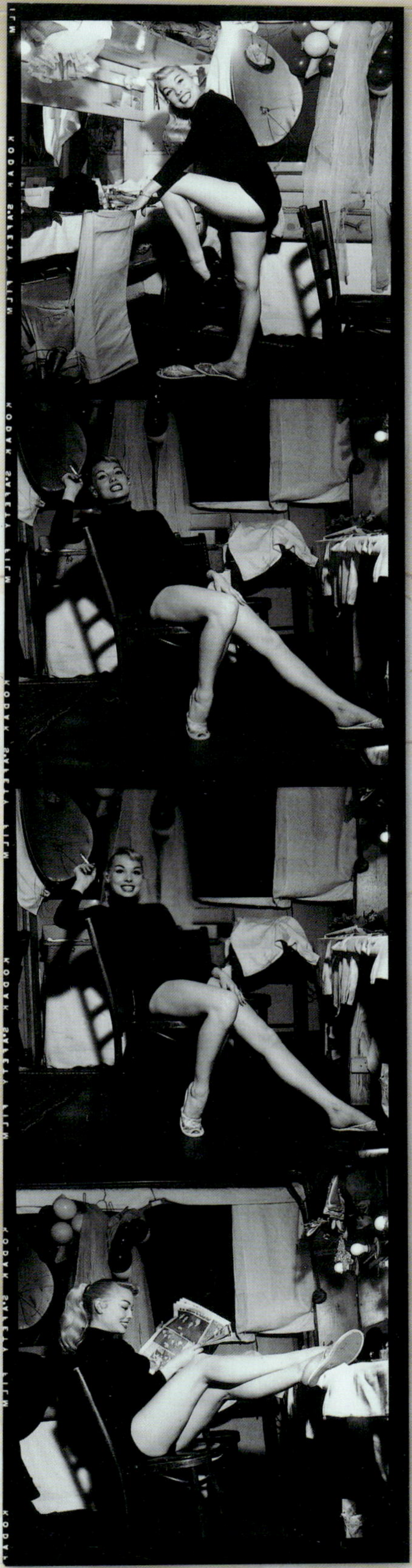

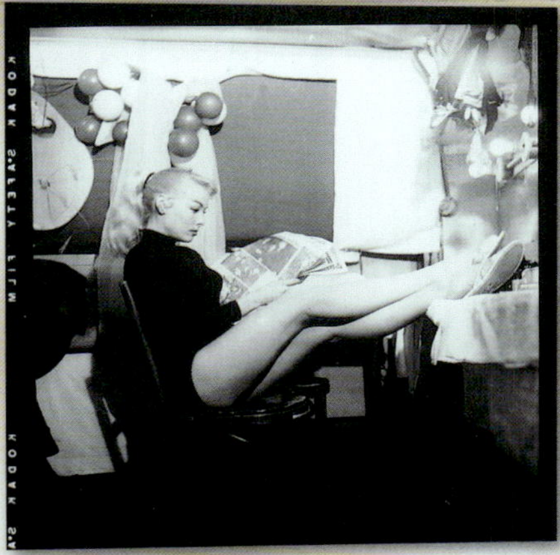

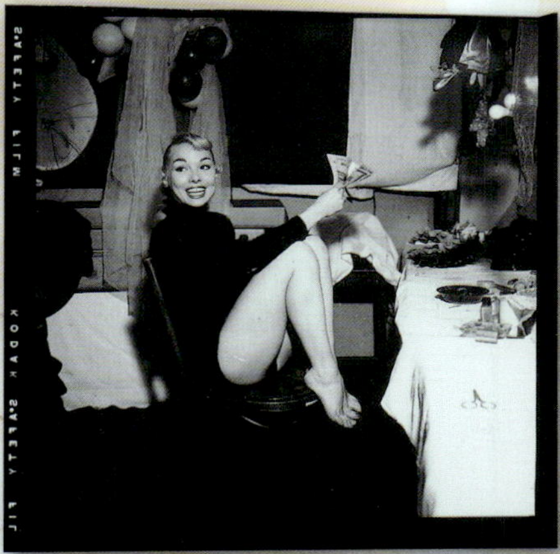

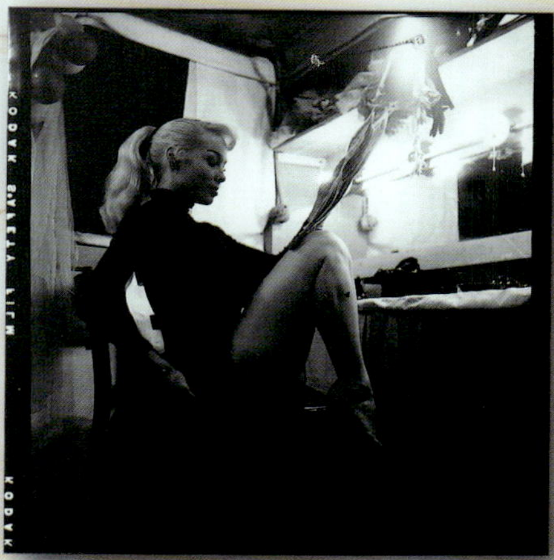

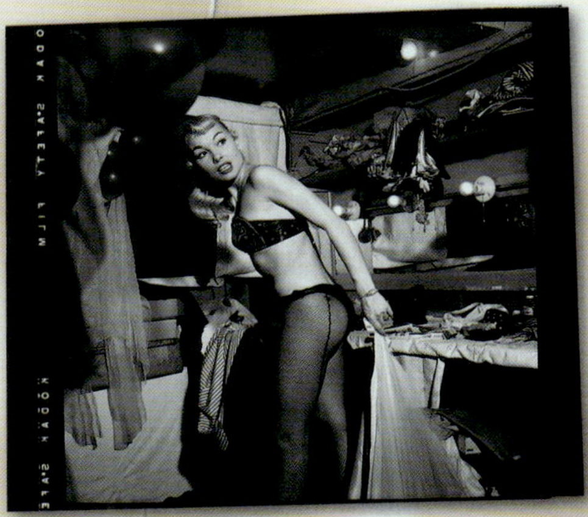

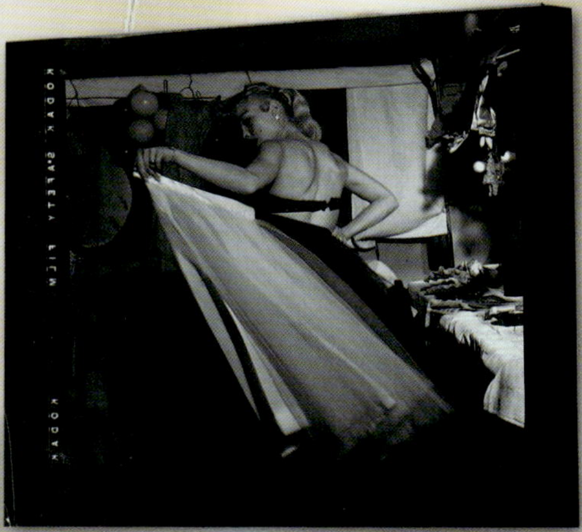

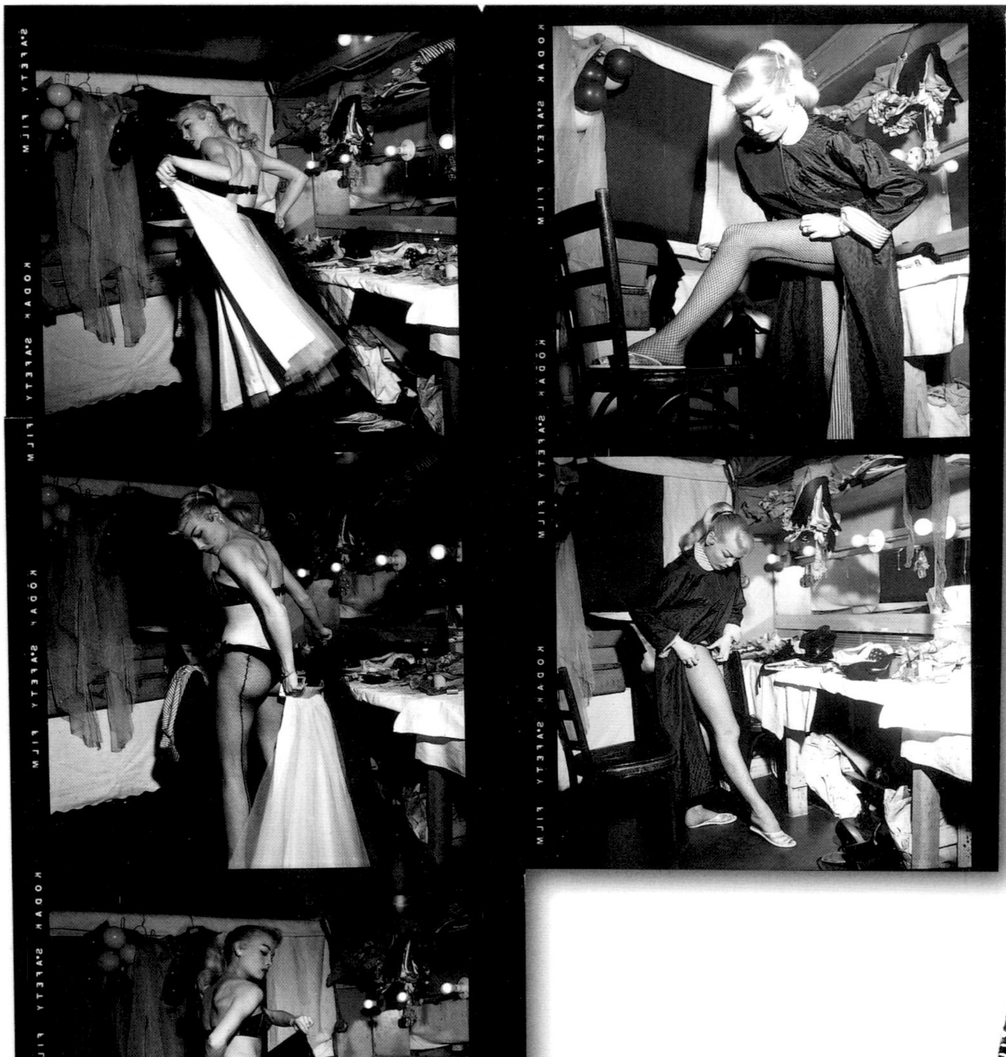

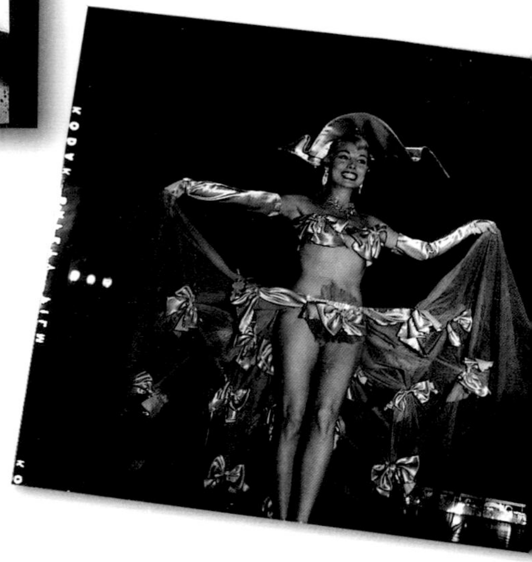

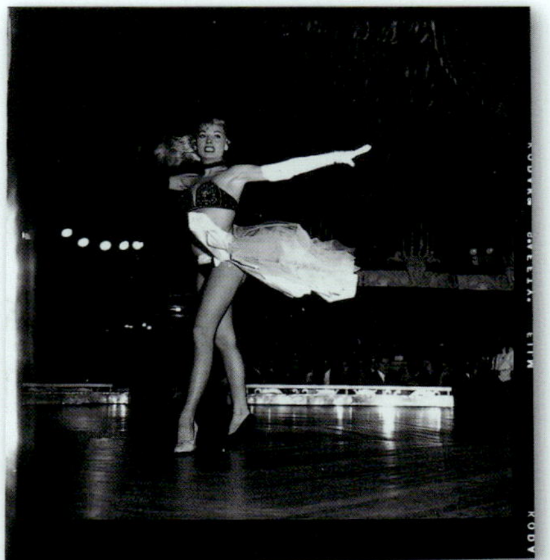
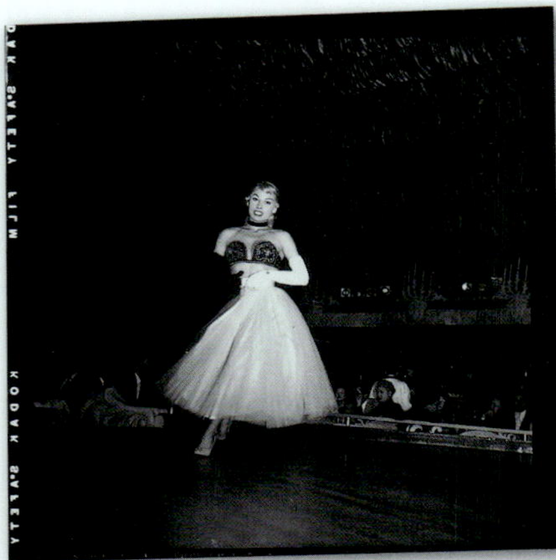
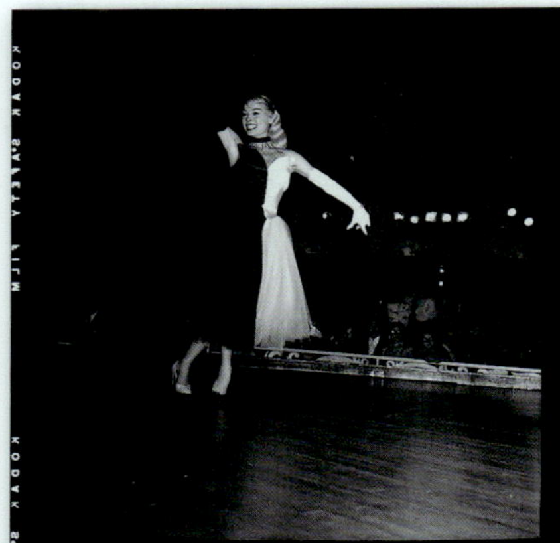
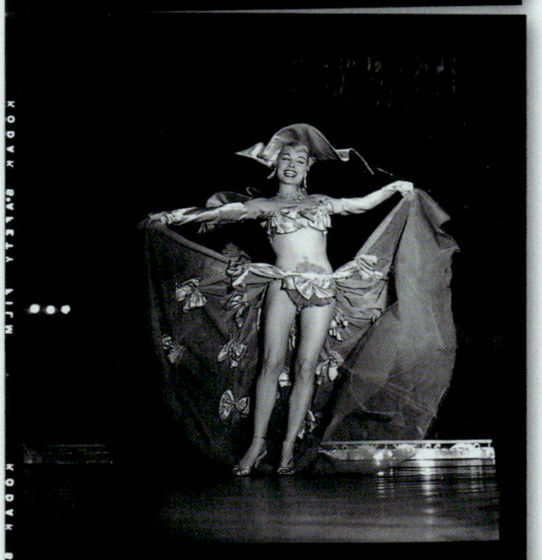
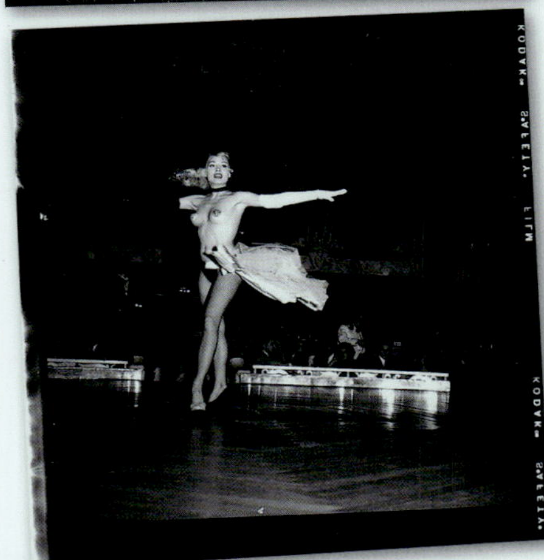
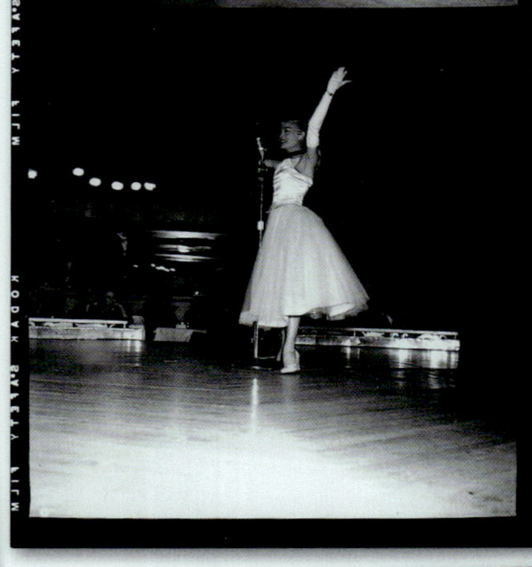
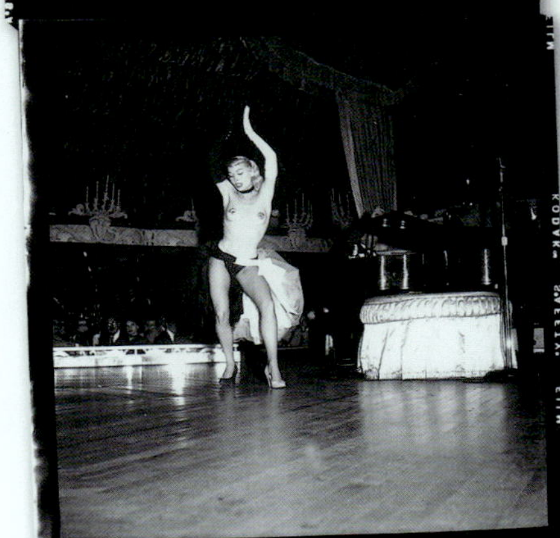
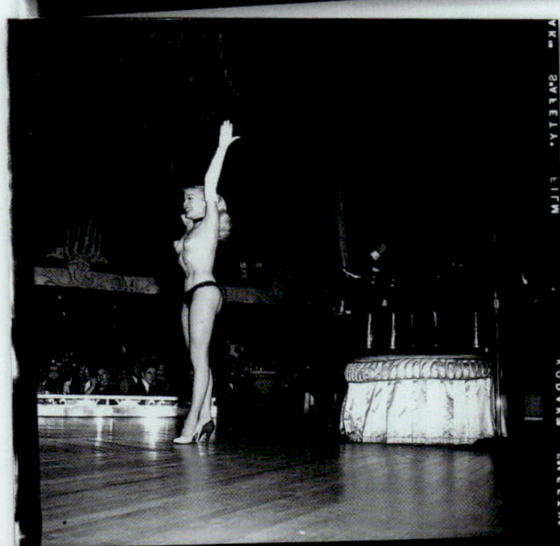
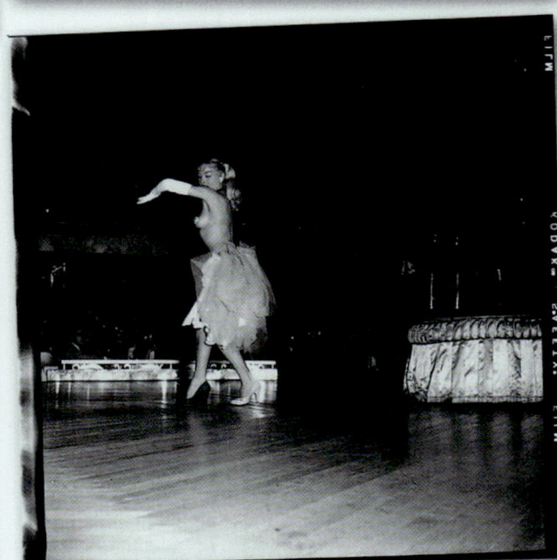
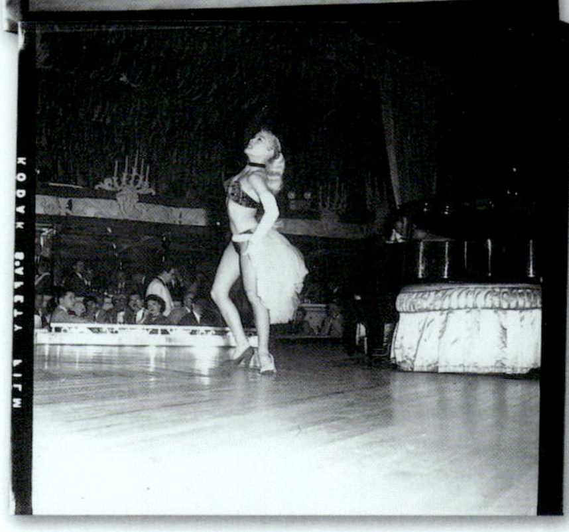
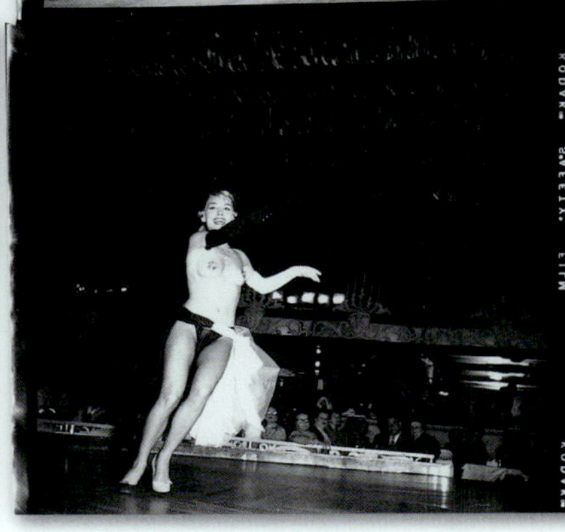
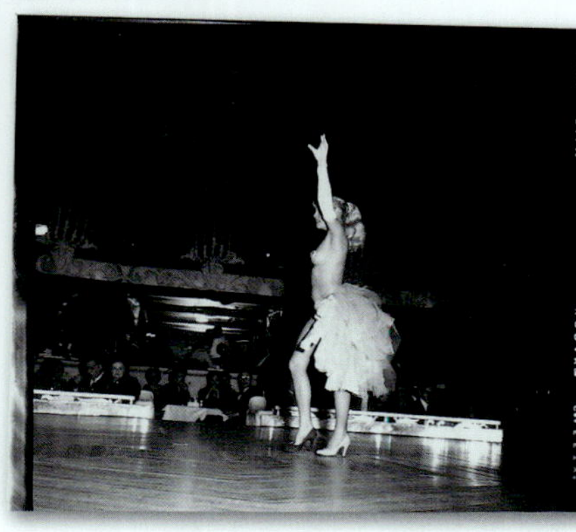

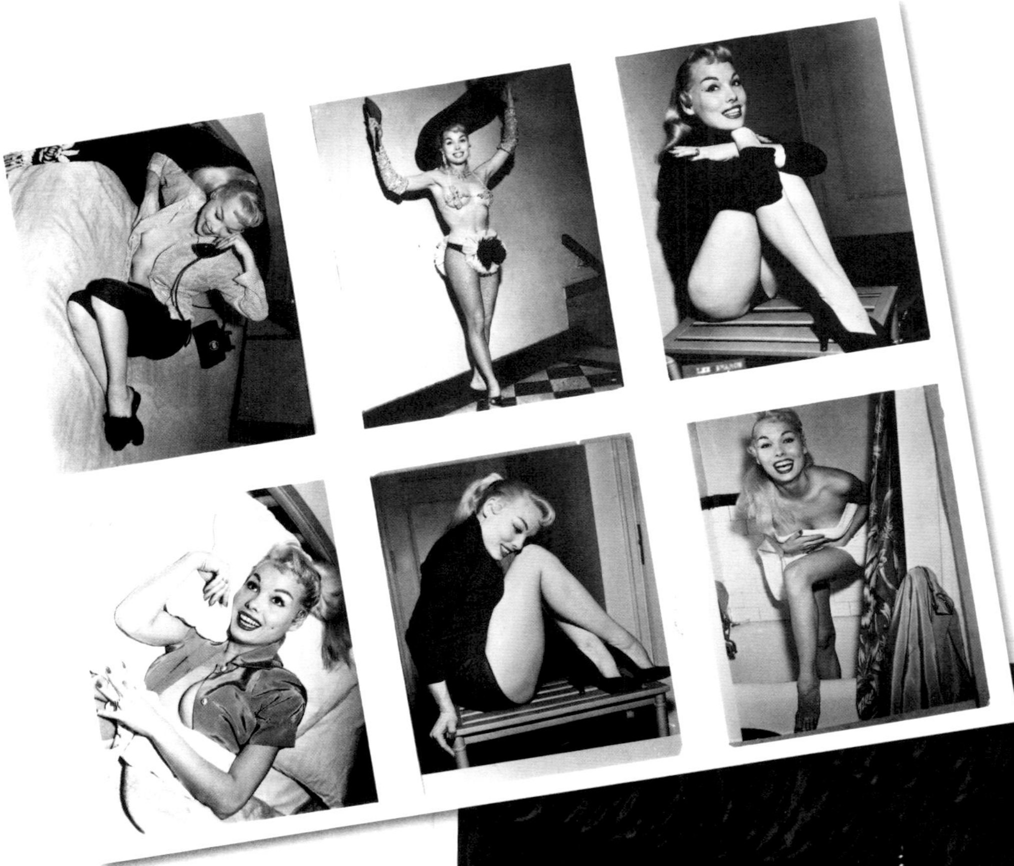

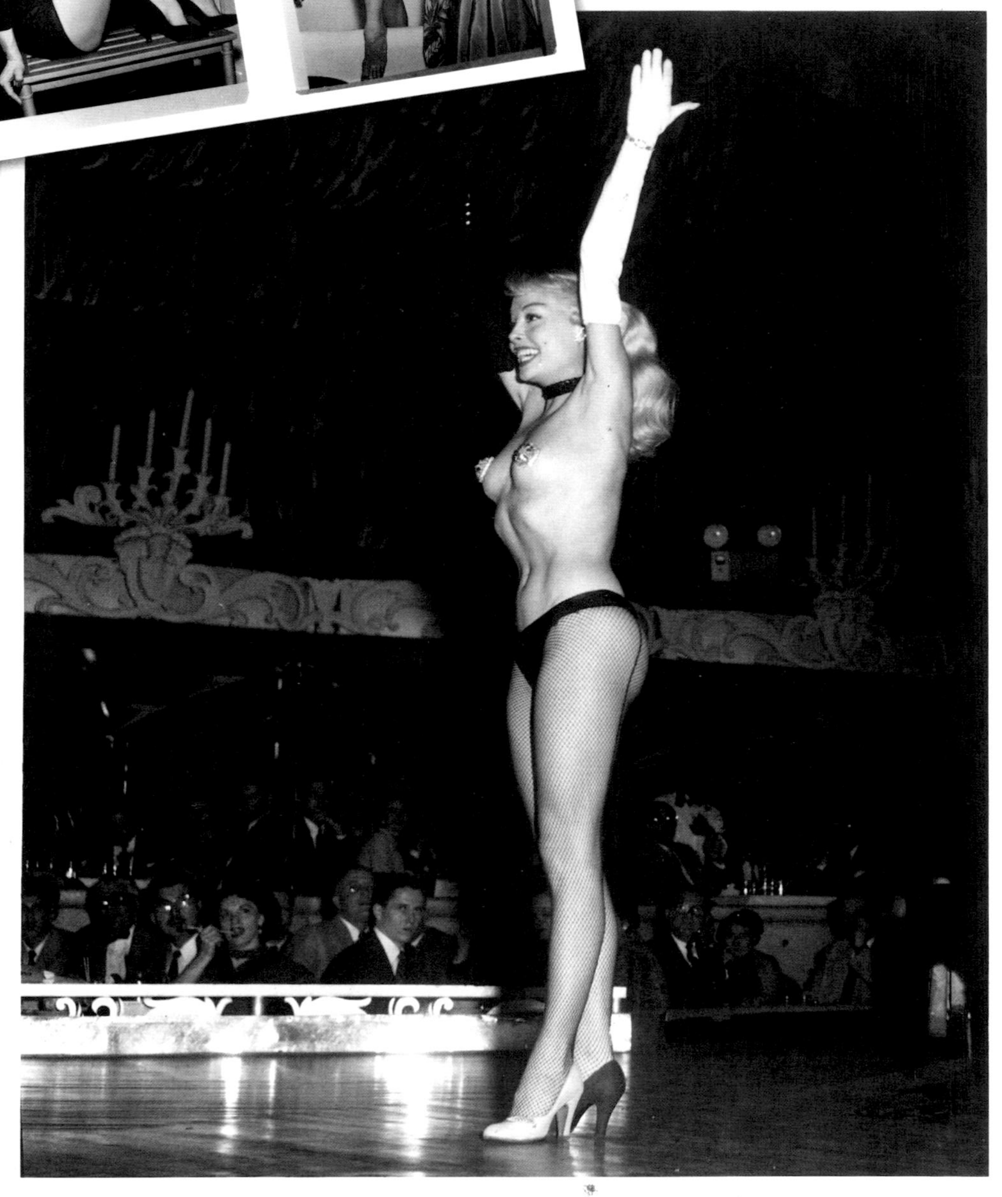

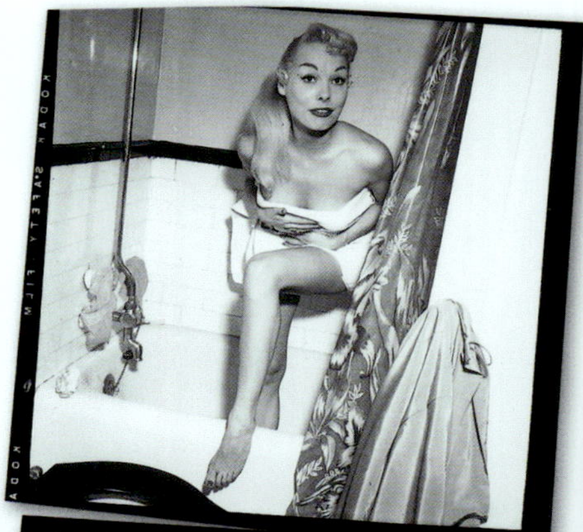
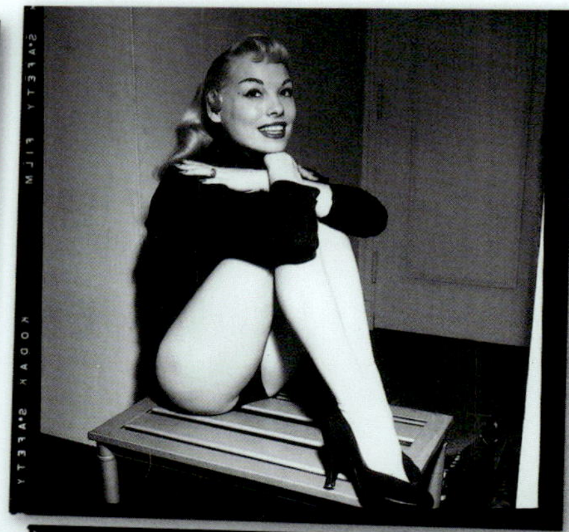
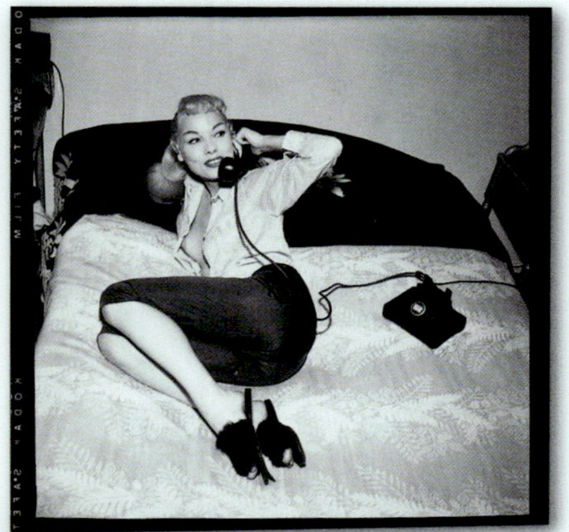
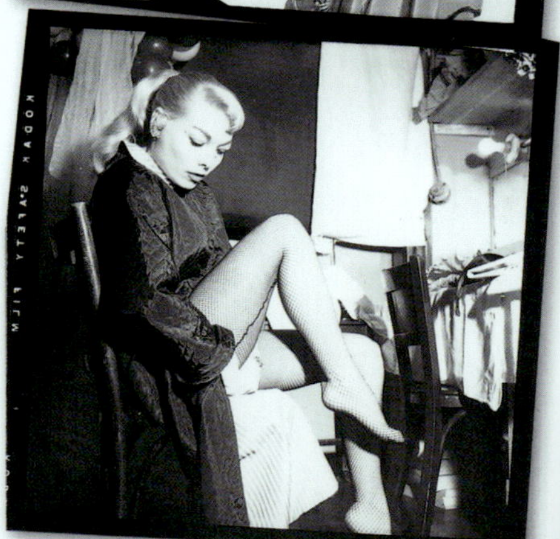
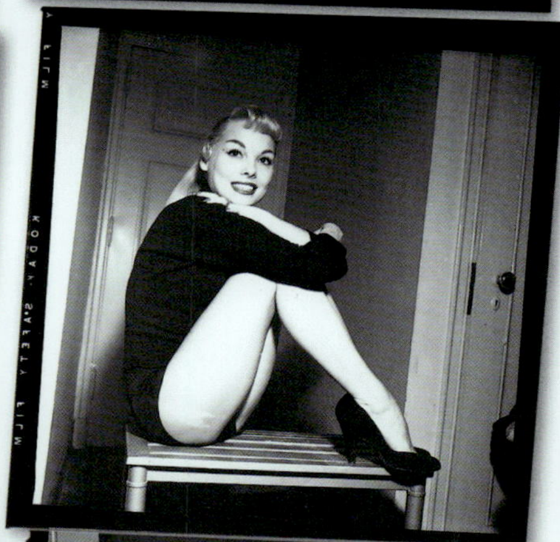
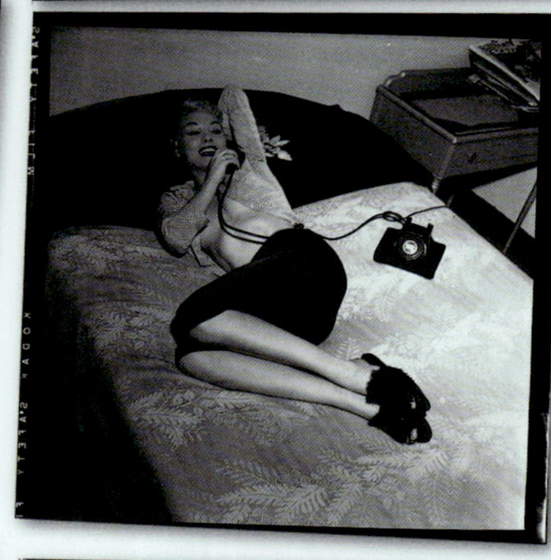
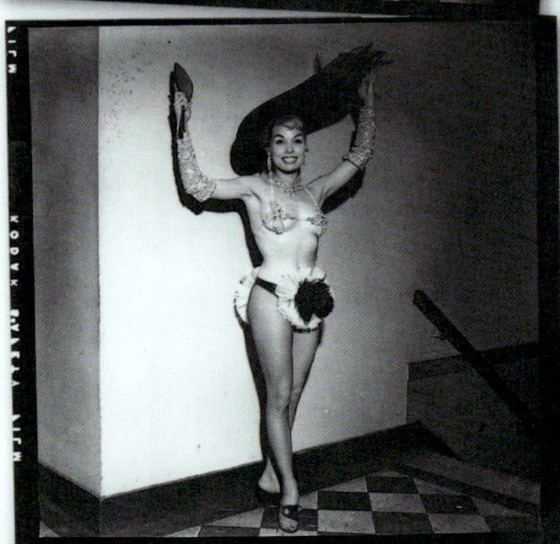
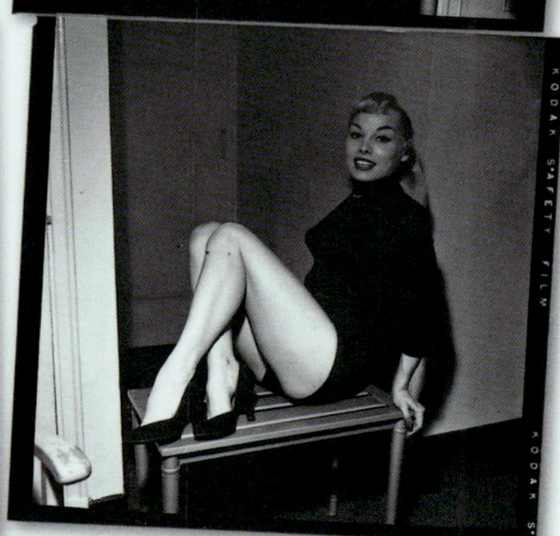
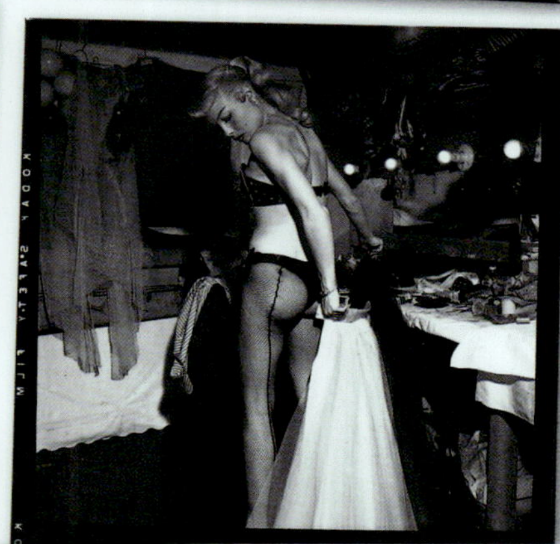
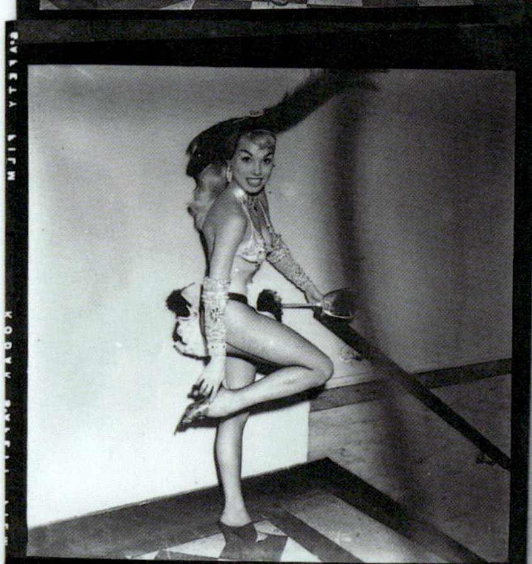
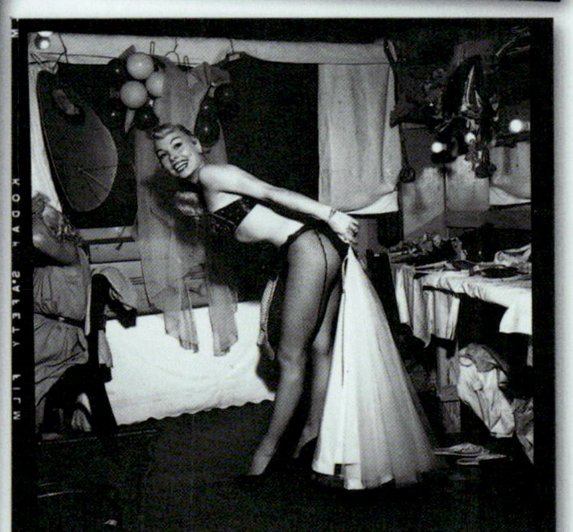
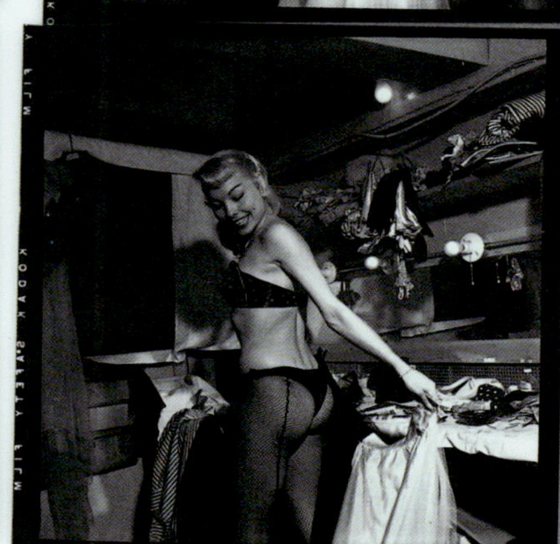

Libby Jones

LIBBY JONES

Not very long ago Libby Jones was pounding a typewriter as a secretary in an aircraft factory in Seattle. One night, while attending a burlesque theatre in Portland, she was fascinated by the performance of the feature stripper, asked for a job (on a dare). Exit secretary, enter strpper. Libby took to stripping like a duck to water. Her casually sensuous movements are the acme of provocative sex. From the moment she comes onstage in a severe, regal-looking black and white gown, she lingers over every detail, artfully loitering in the removal of flimsy silken whaddayacallits. The suspence is electric. It is high art stripping. After watch-Libby, the customers feel they've had a great experience. Libby had the covetted appointment as feature in Harold Minsky's new show at the Dunes, Las Vegas. Libby likes lean, hungry types of men. Her characteristic expression: "Men are the greatest thing since 7-Up."

She's 5'8", measures 35-35-35.

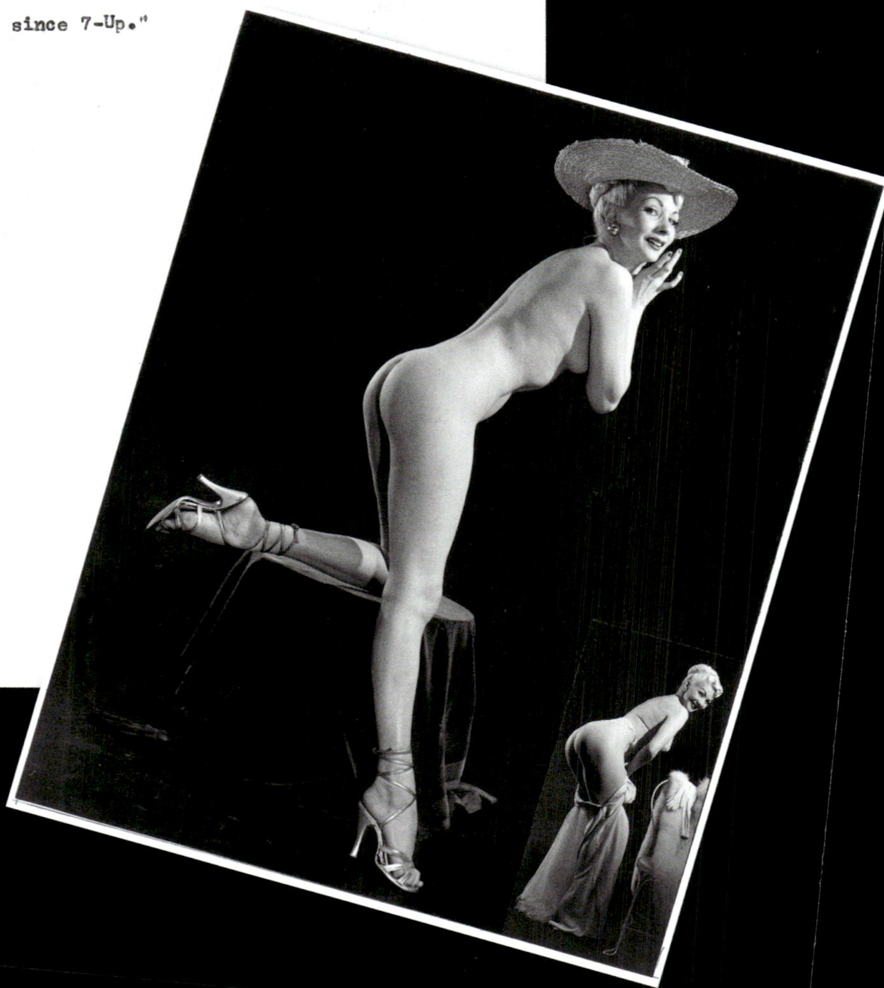

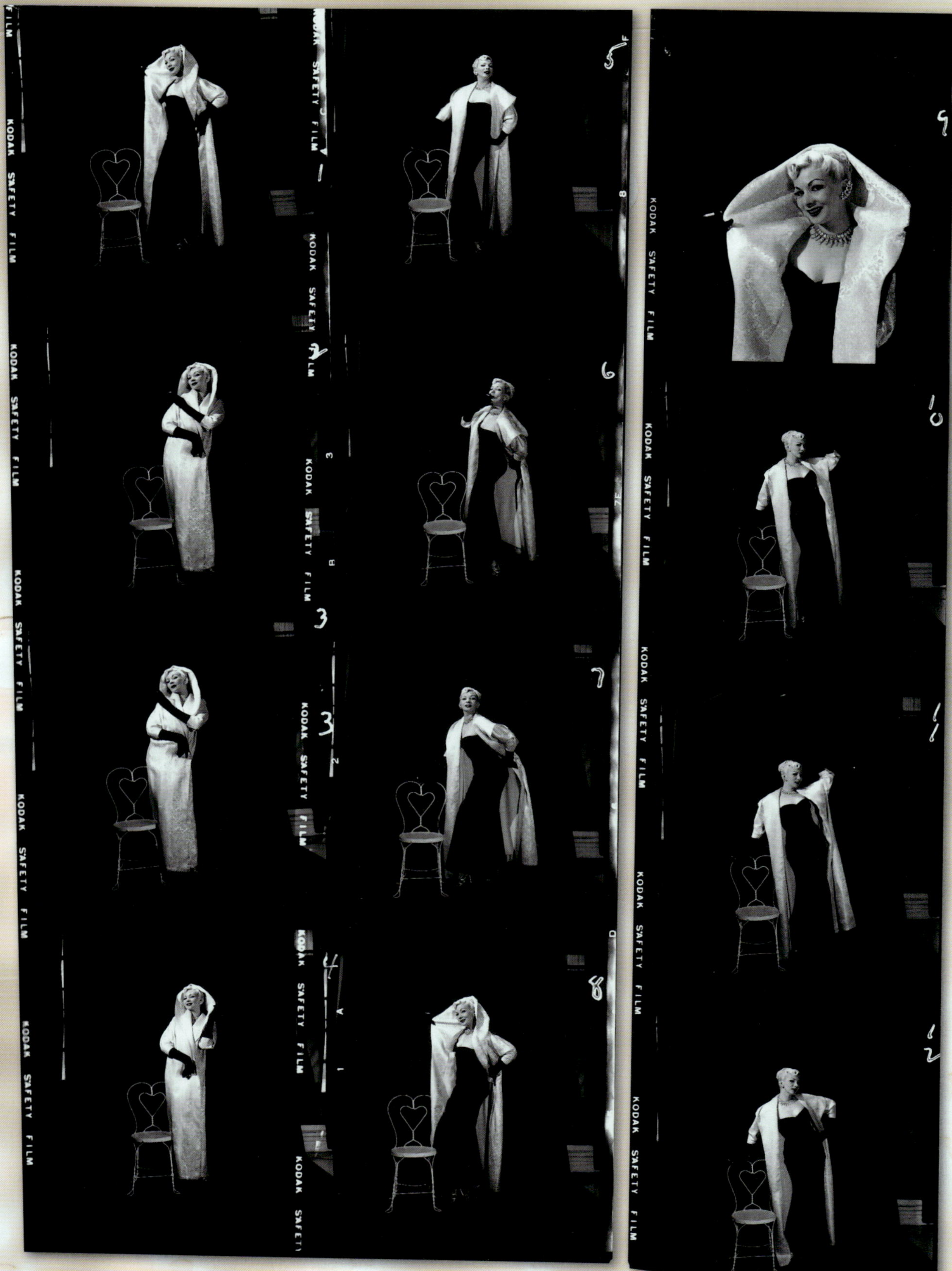
KODAK SAFETY FILM

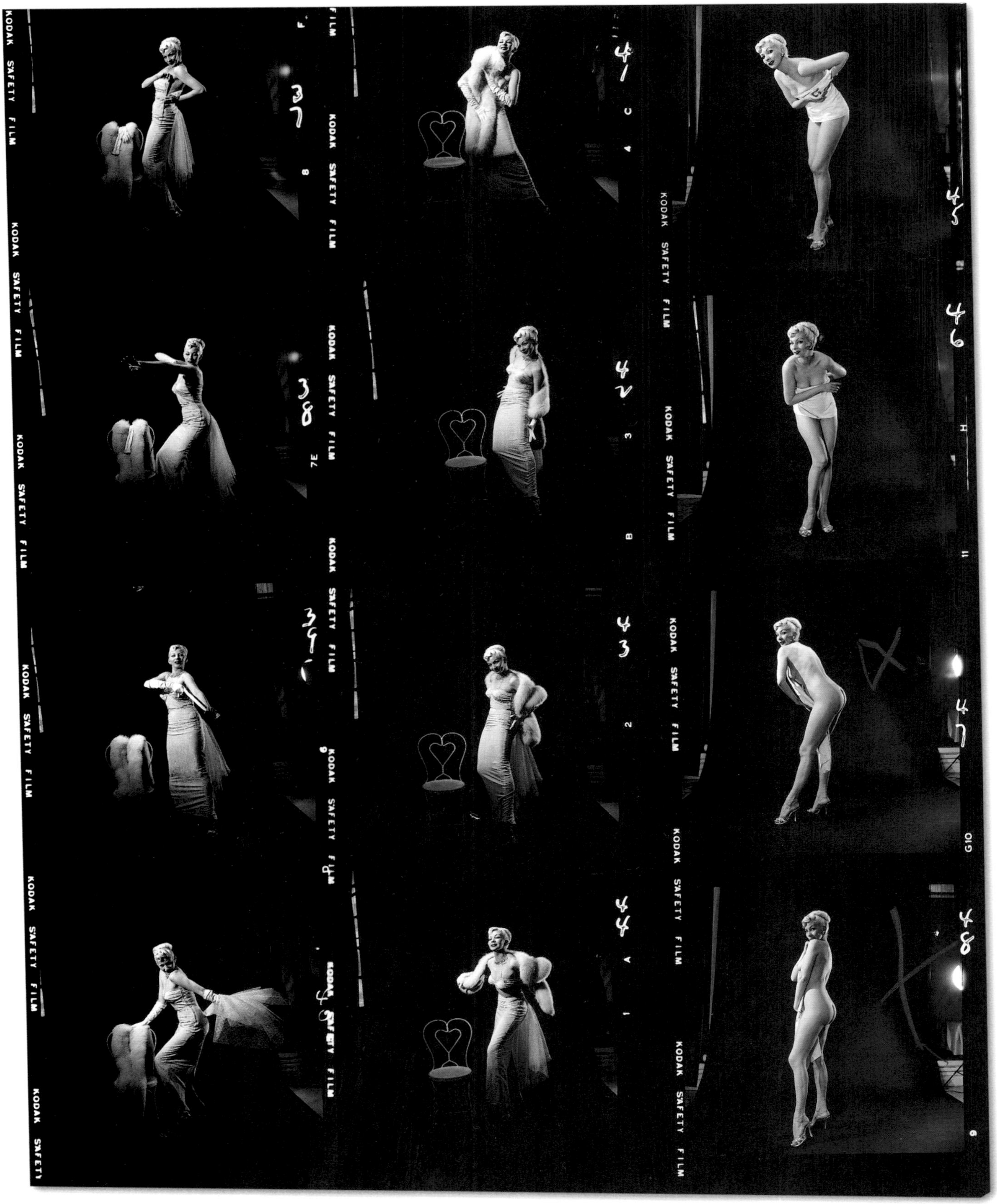

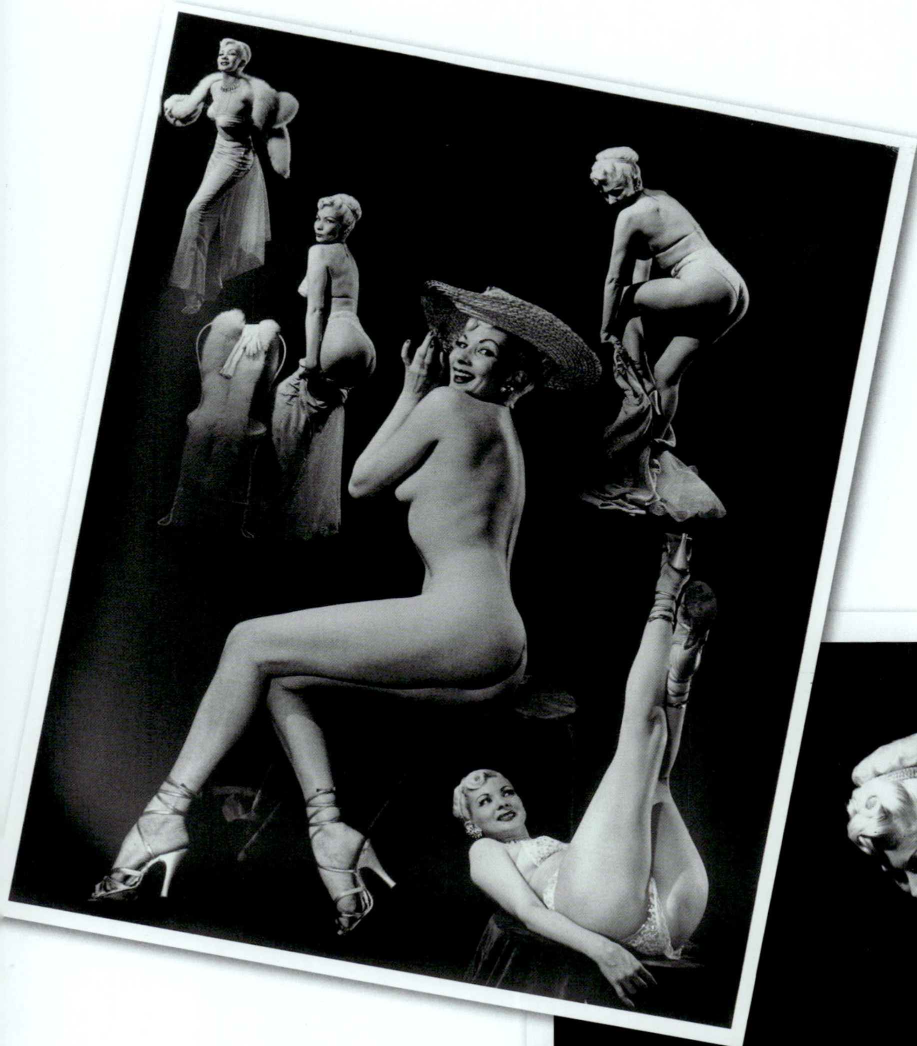

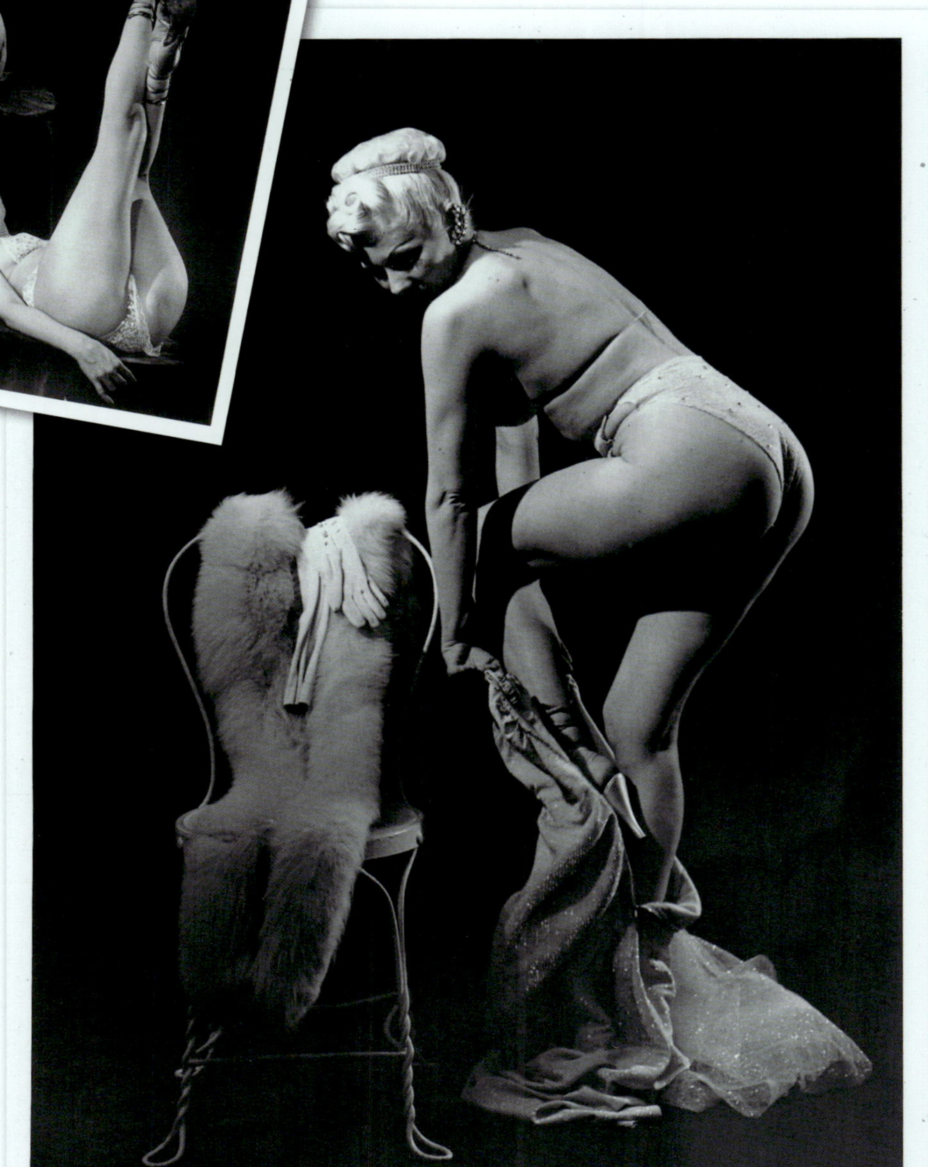

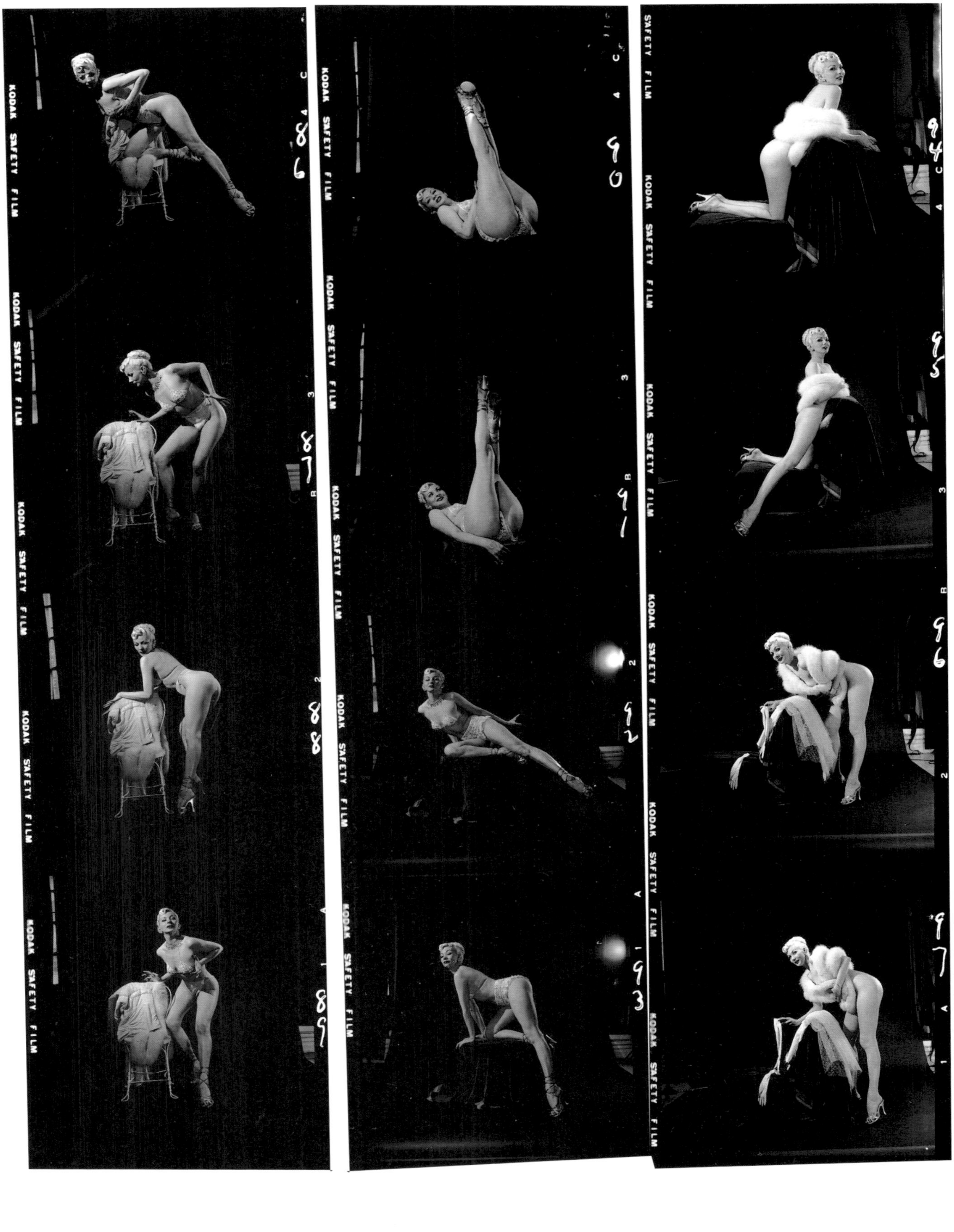

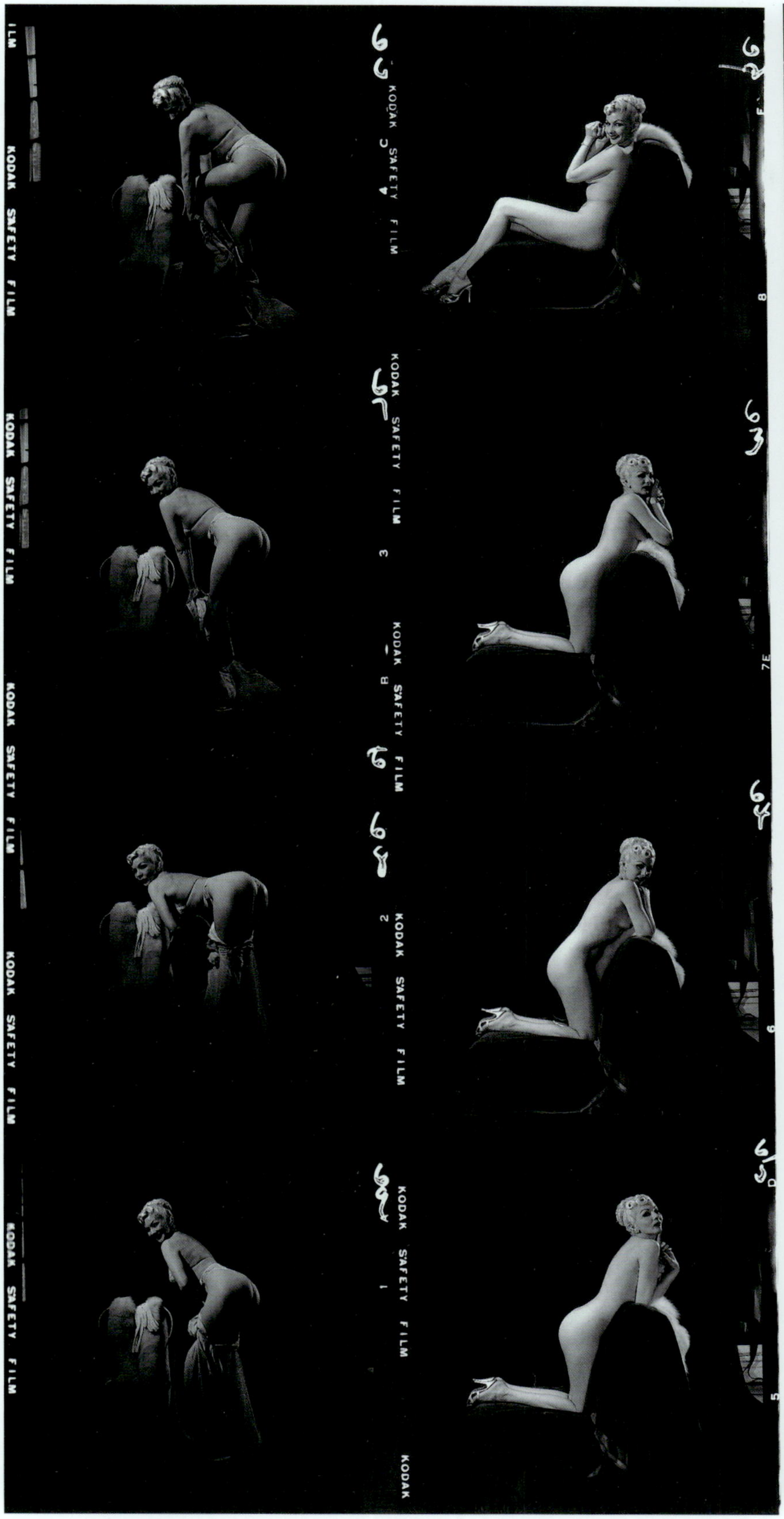

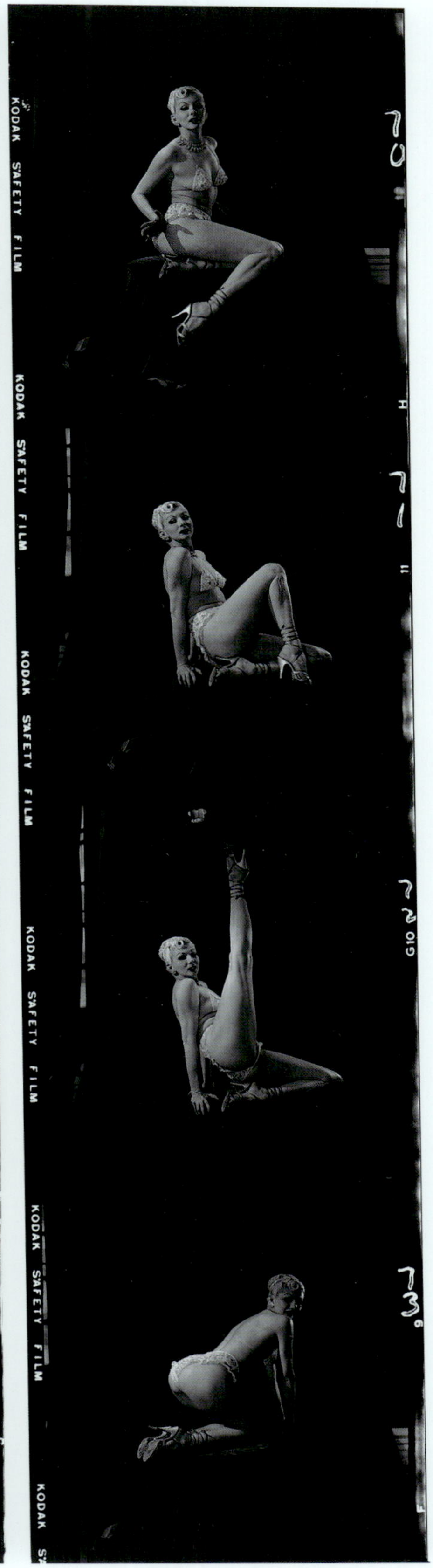

Lisa London

Lisa London

Tall (she's 6'), red-haired Lisa London started out in show business as a cheesecake model. Now she charms audiences in the local bistros of New York. She is an immediate success wherever she plays, believes that a dancer has to (1) like her audience; (2) project, get across to the audience, by showing in face and eyes and in every movement that she loves what she is doing.

Lisa is ambitious, is busy studying modern ballet in off hours. Her ultimate objective is to be a dancer in a Broadway musicale. She is 20 years old now, has been in the business for two years. We predict she'll go far. Measurements: 37-23-40.

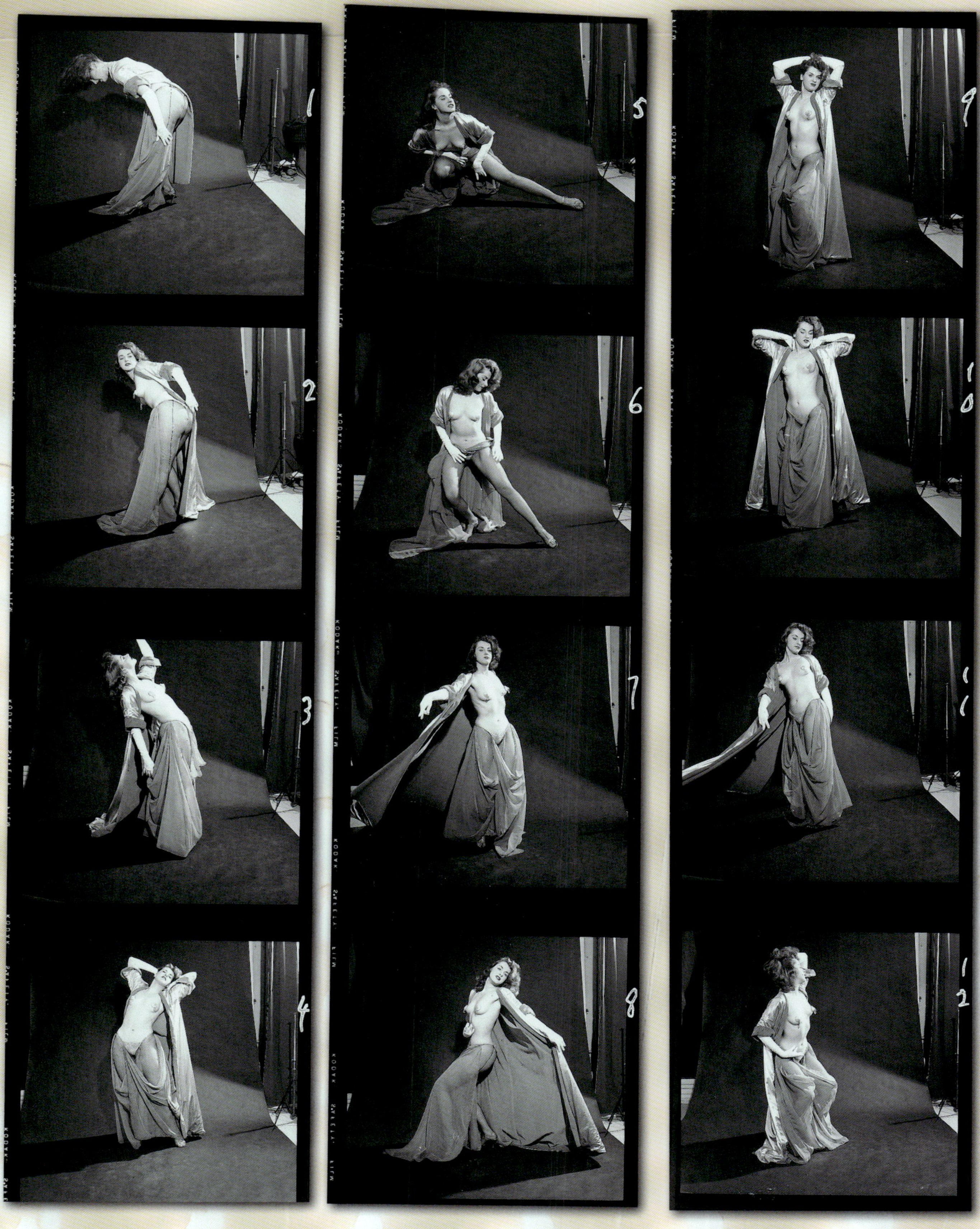

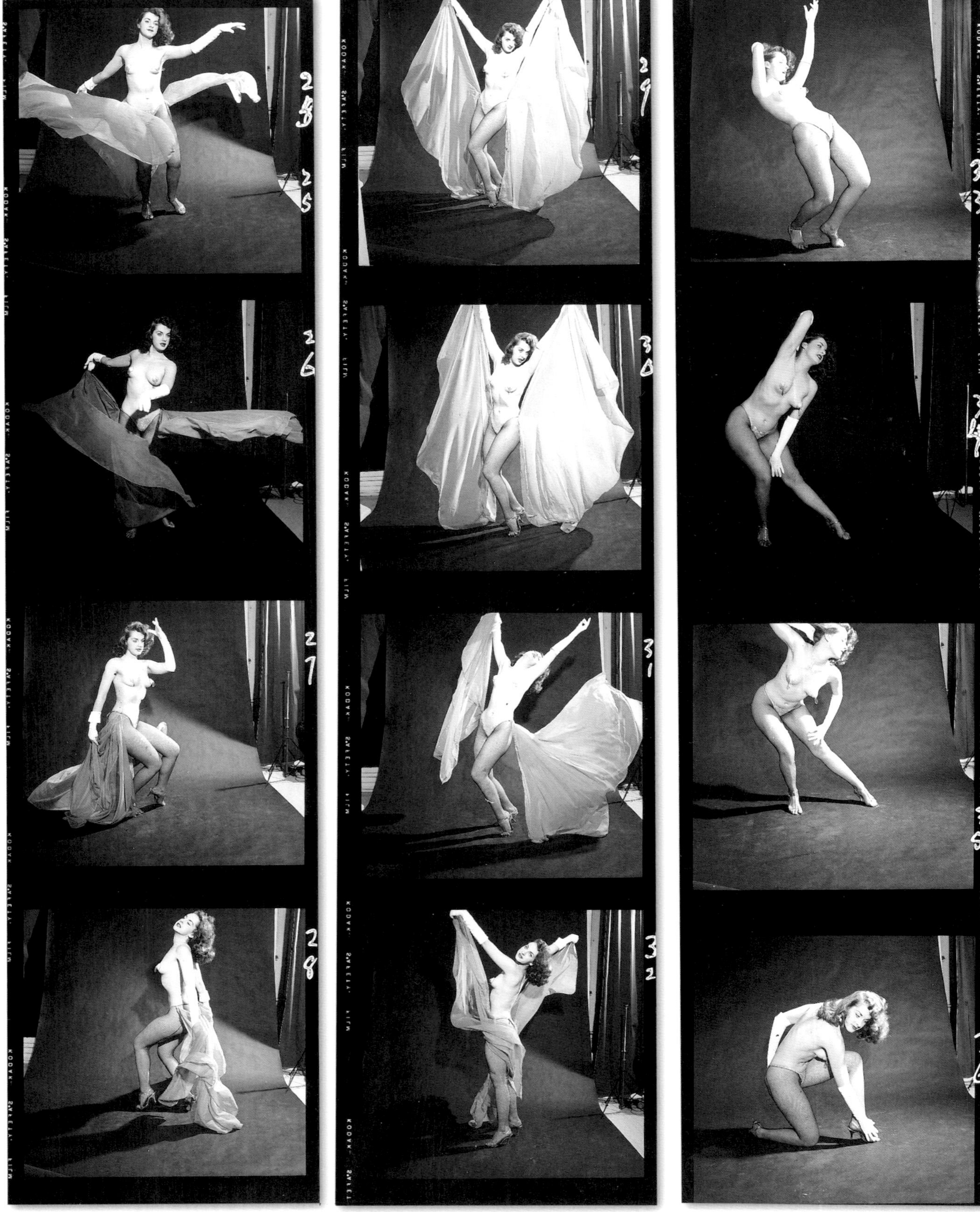

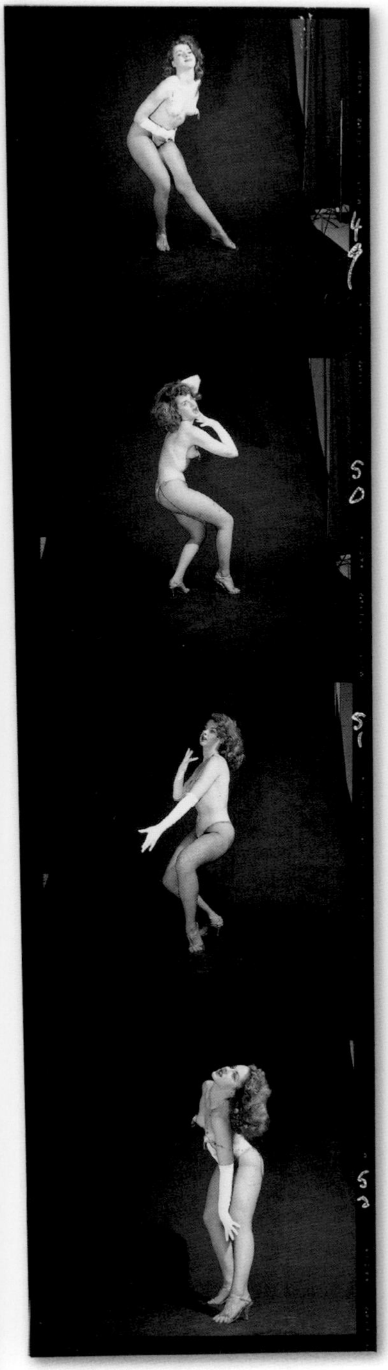

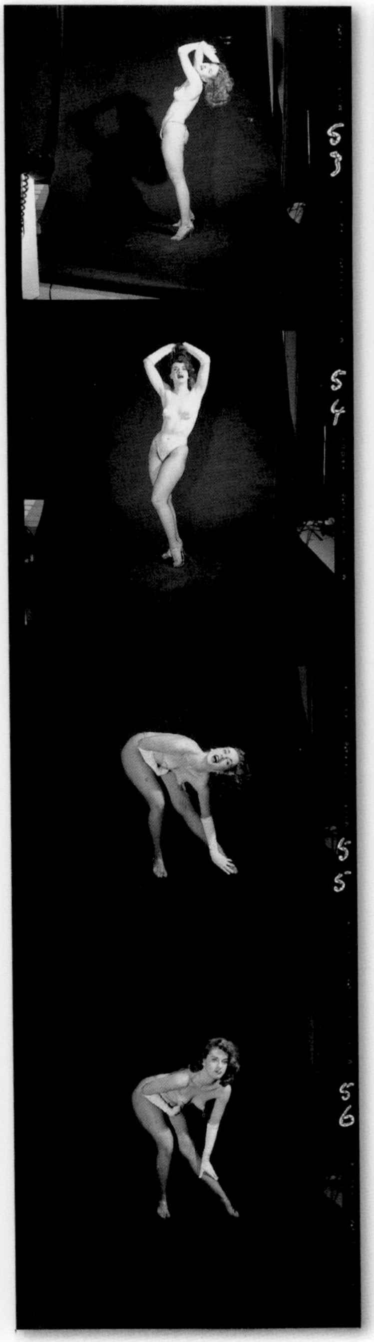

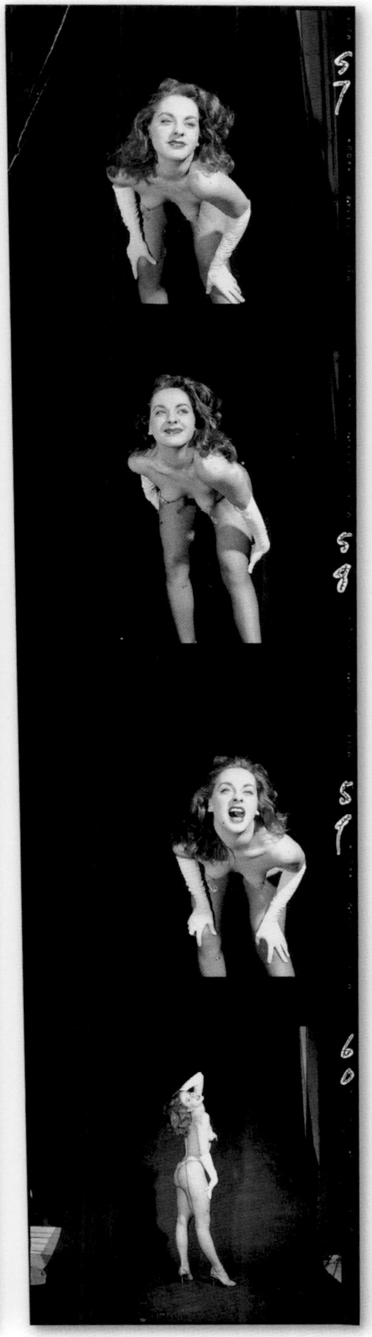

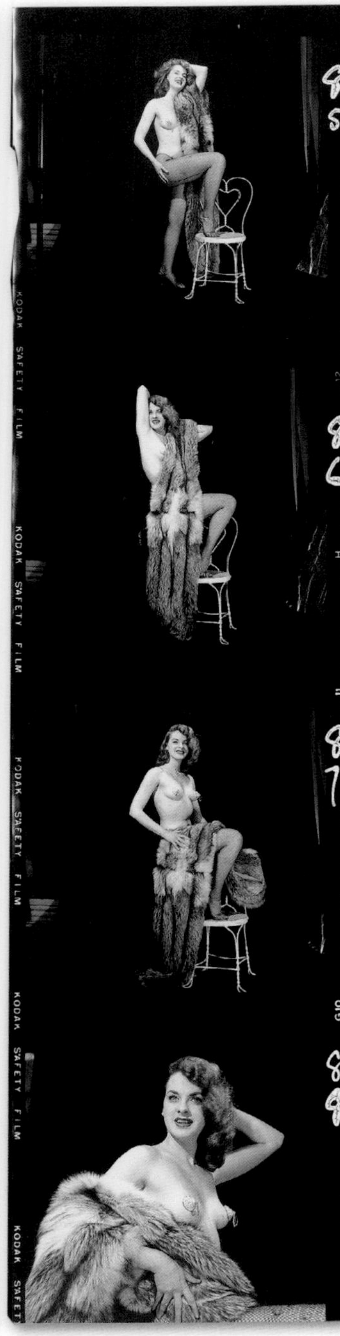
KODAK SAFETY FILM

Liz O'Leyar

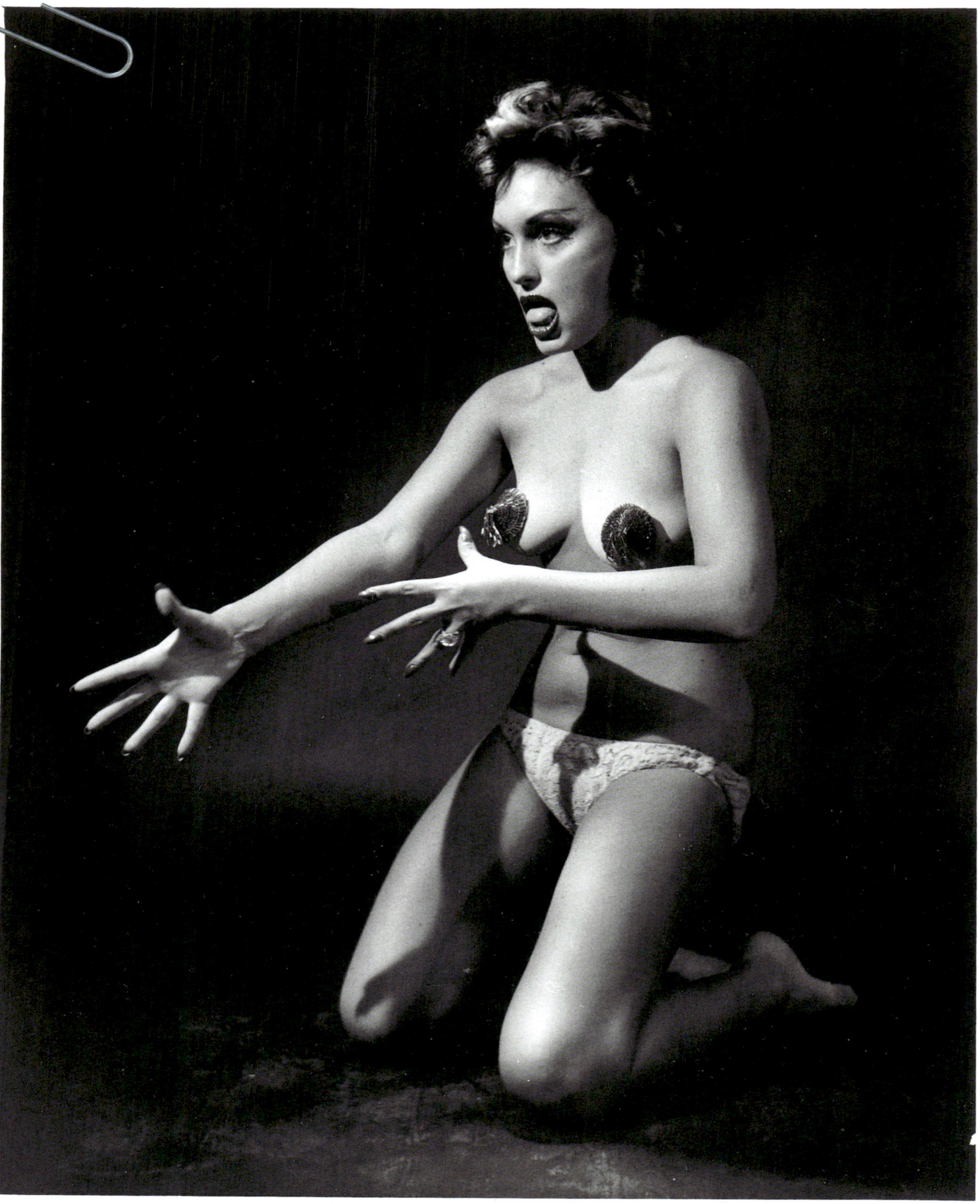

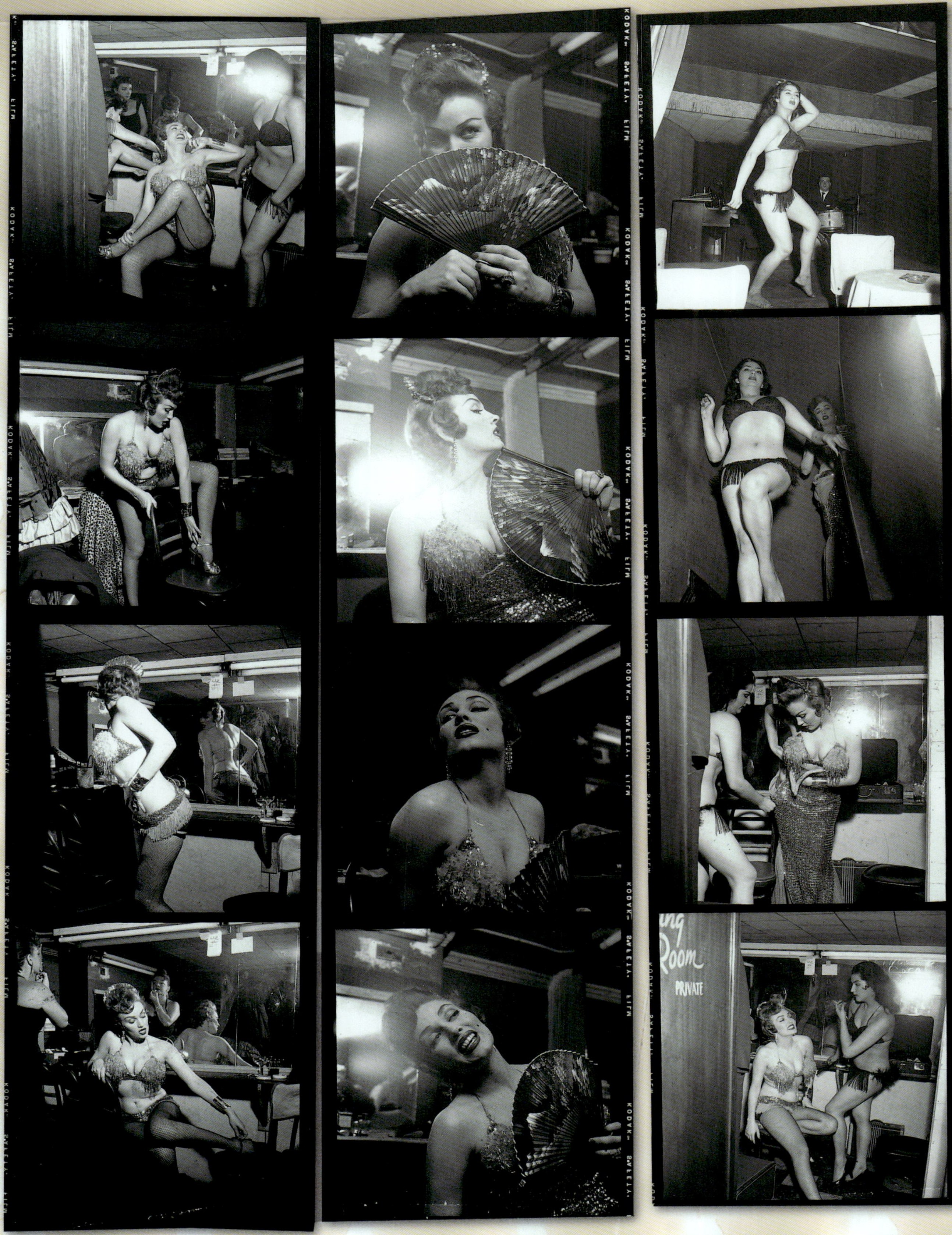
Room
PRIVATE

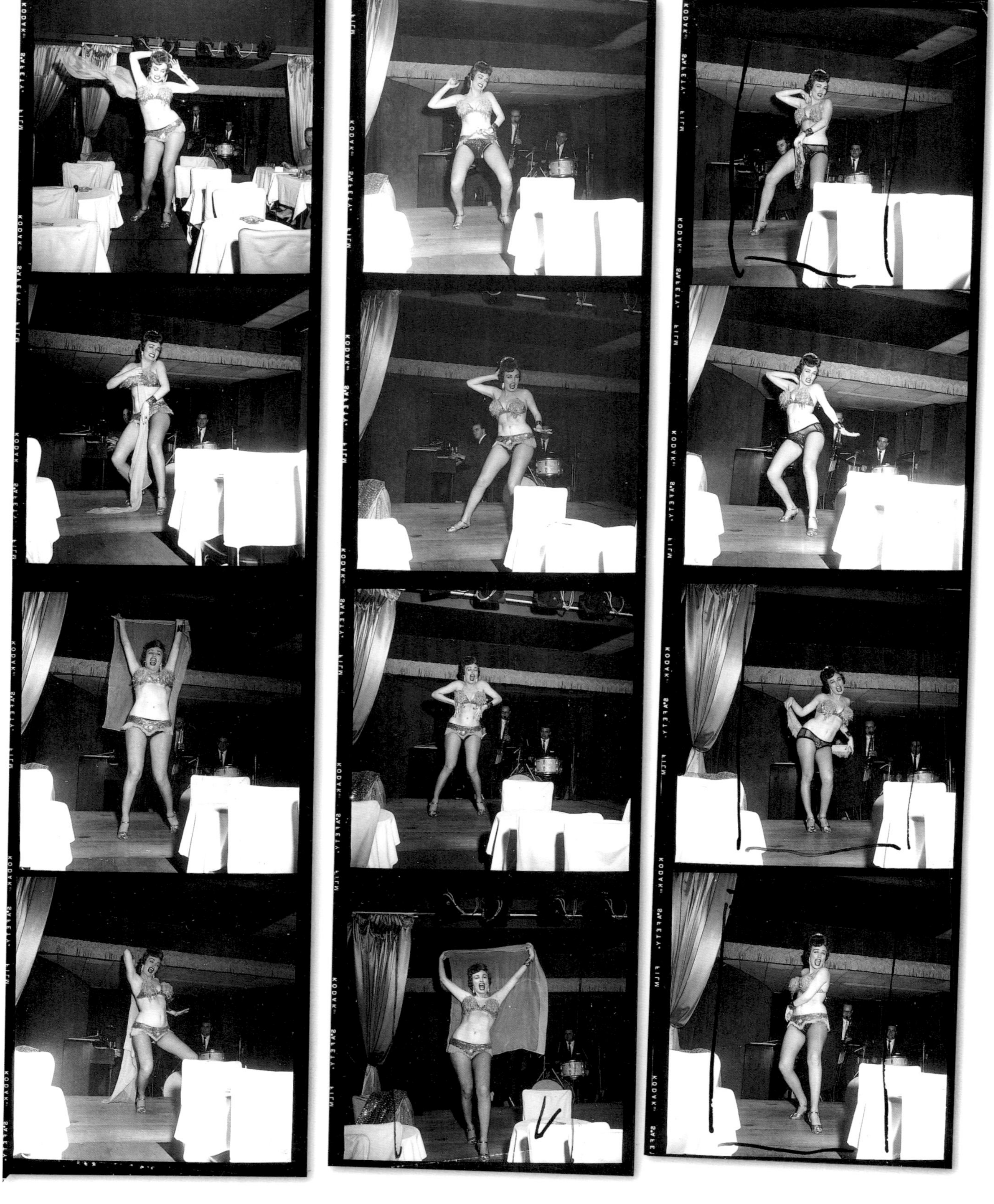

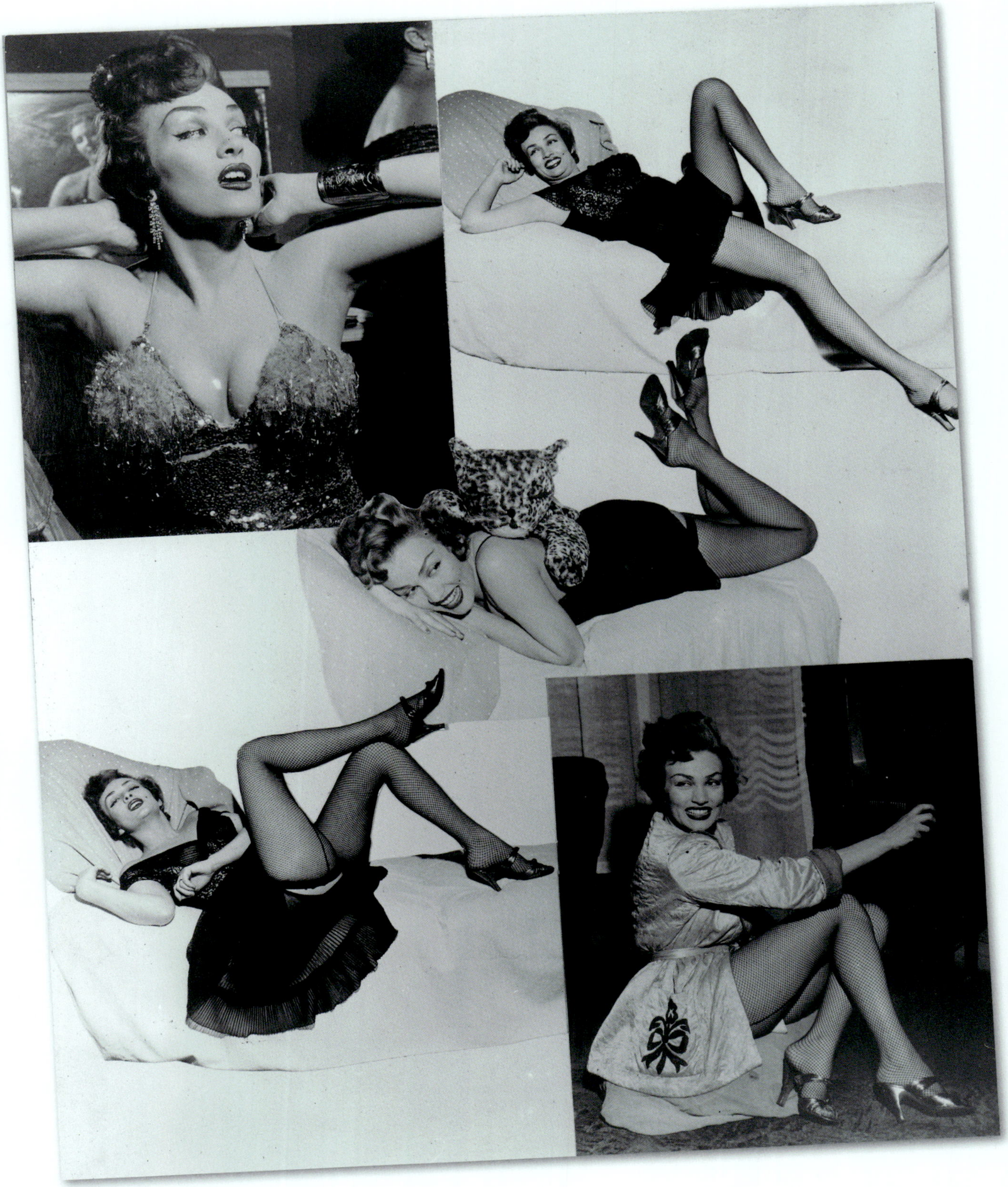

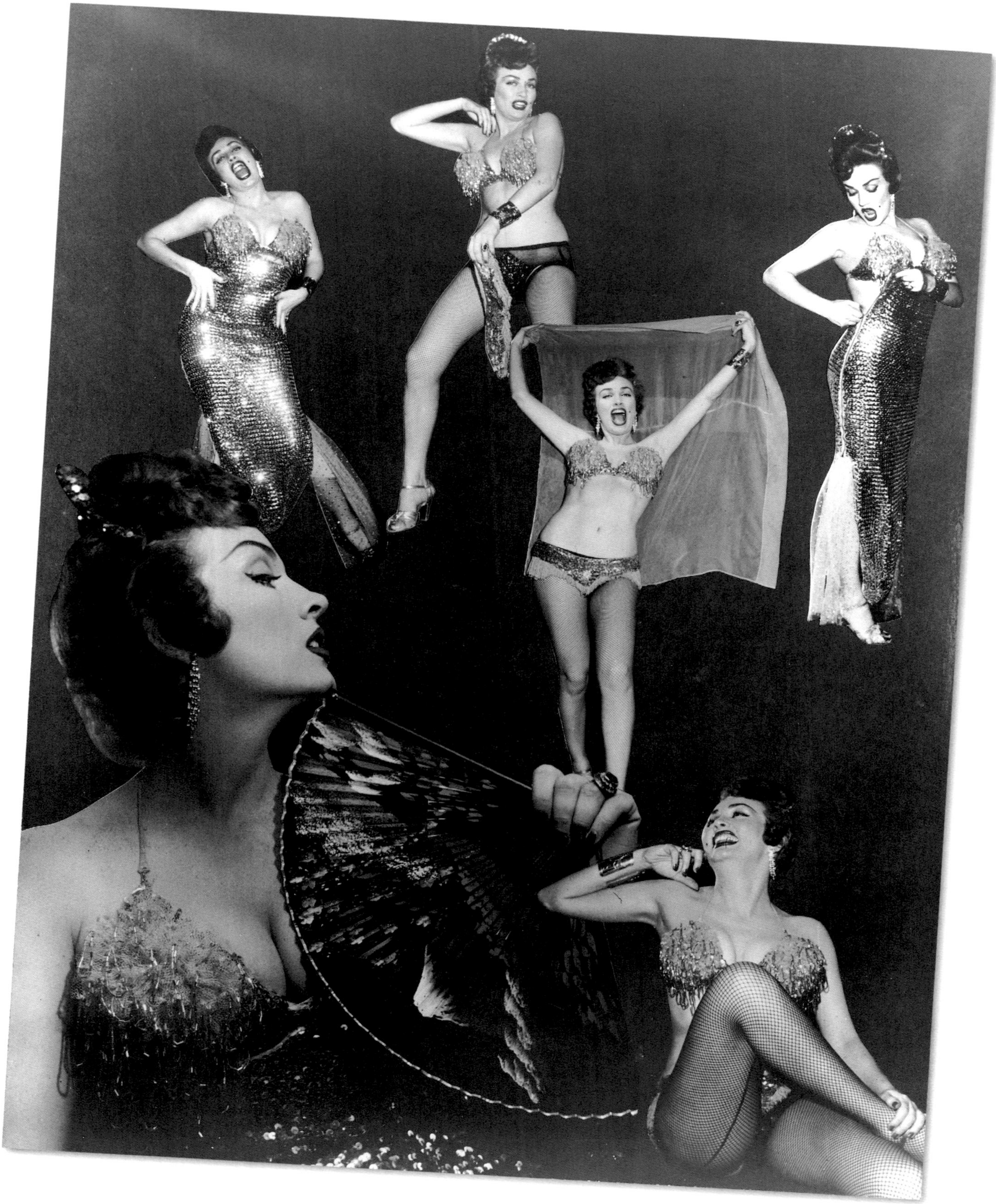

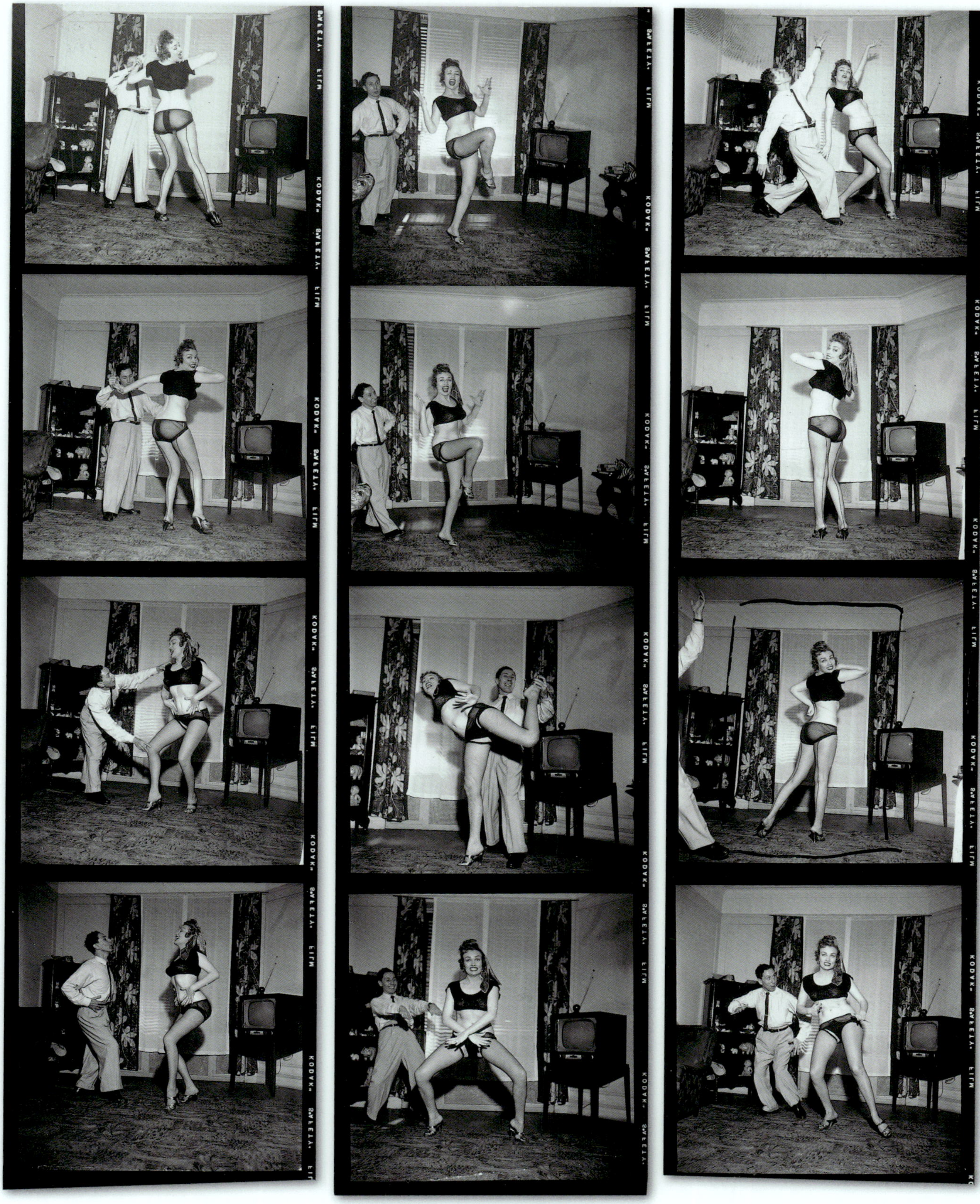

Misty Monaco

MISTY MONACO

Misty Monaco's first fan was a theatrical agent who spotted her slinging hash in a Philadelphia restaurant. After her first club engagement, she showed that her talents were better employed elsewhere. For Misty knows the age-old challenge of a sensuous face and figure to every male. Now Misty travels around in a black convertible with her name spelled out in white letters on the back, so there's no mistaking who the red-haired hazel-eyed celebrity is, up front. She's ambitious, and, like many another night-club star, hopes one day to appear in a Broadway show. She loves to be domestic around the house when not working.

Misty is 5'7", measures 34-24-35.

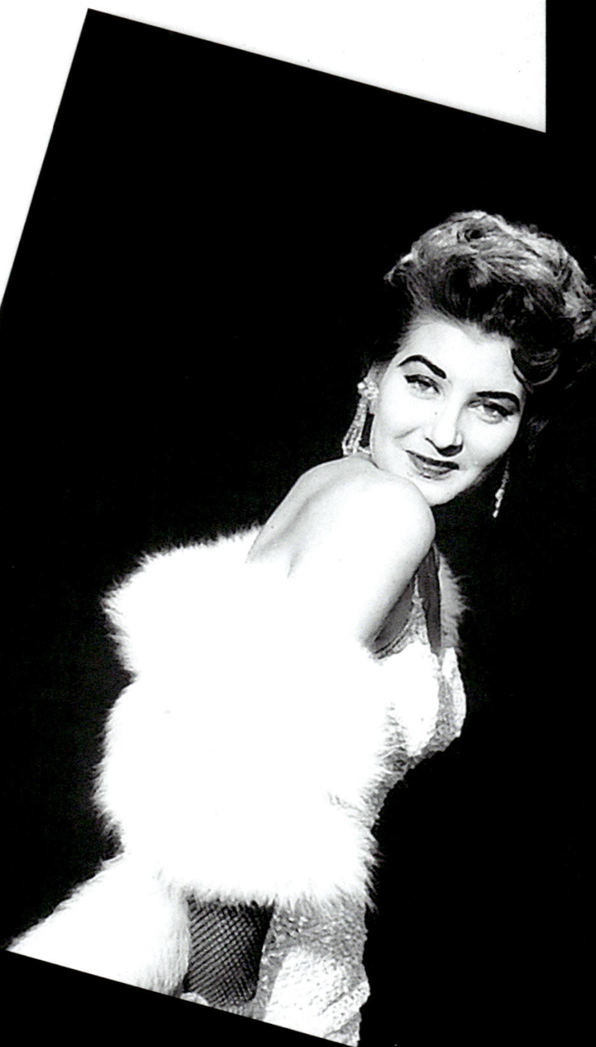

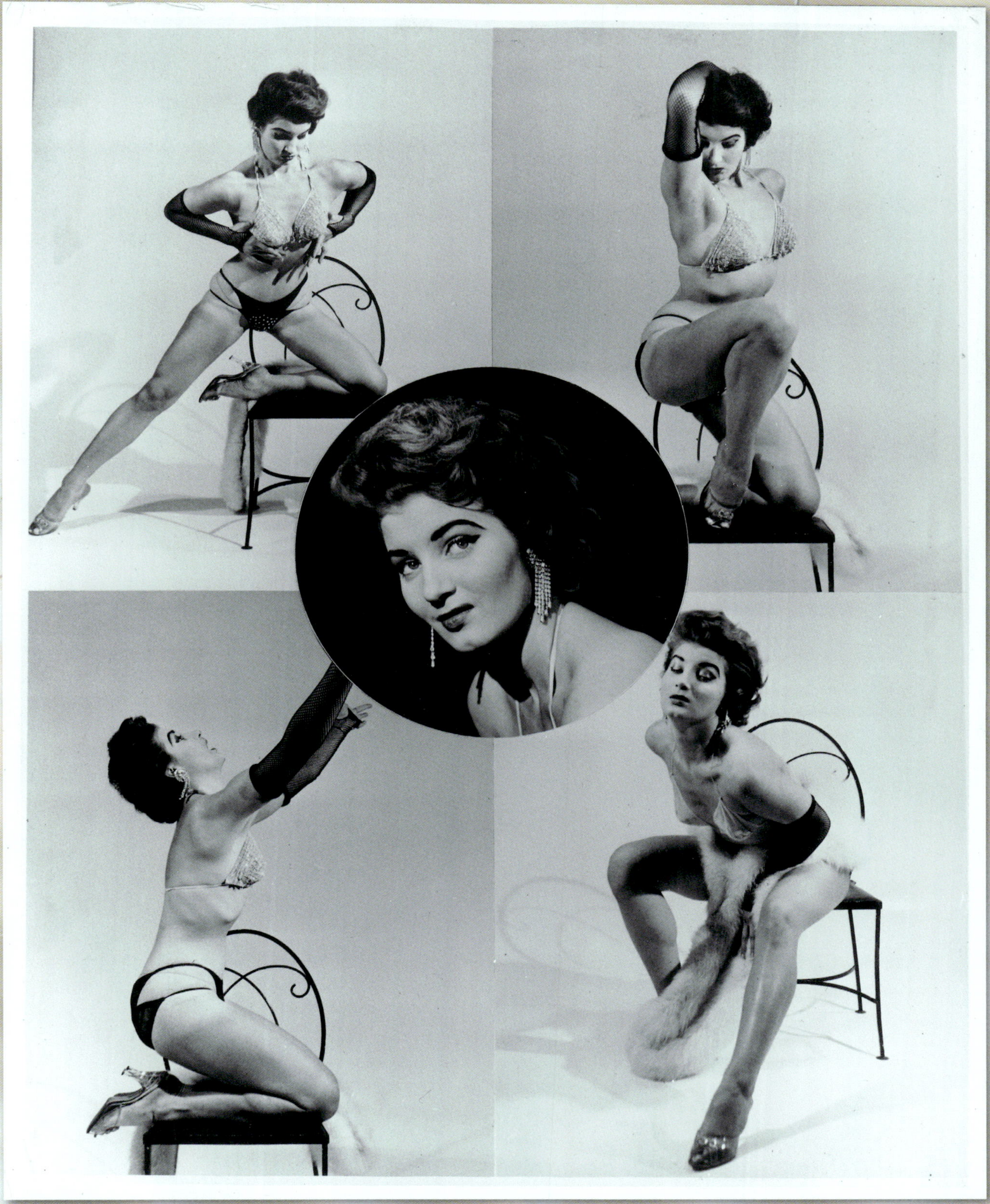

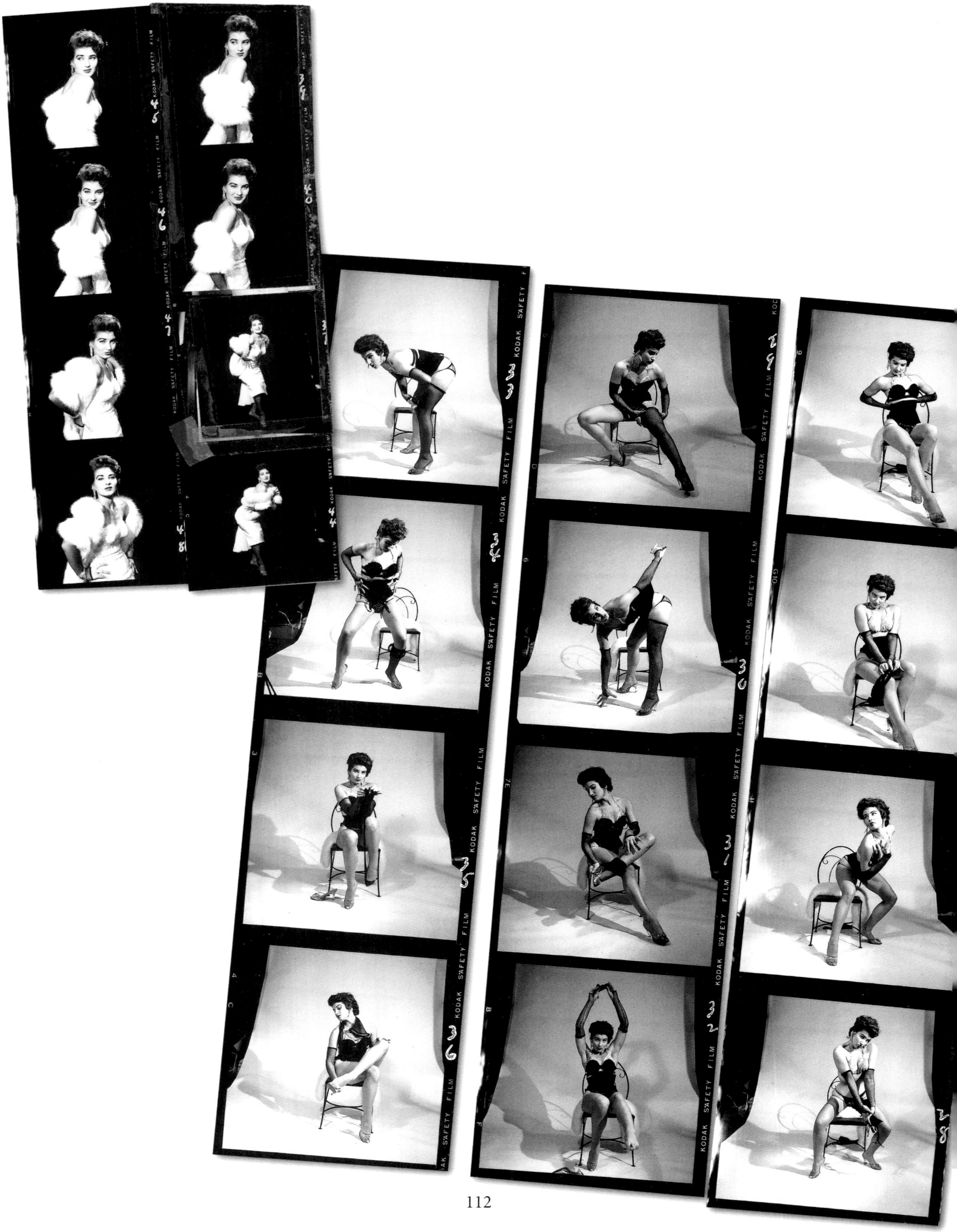
KODAK SAFETY FILM

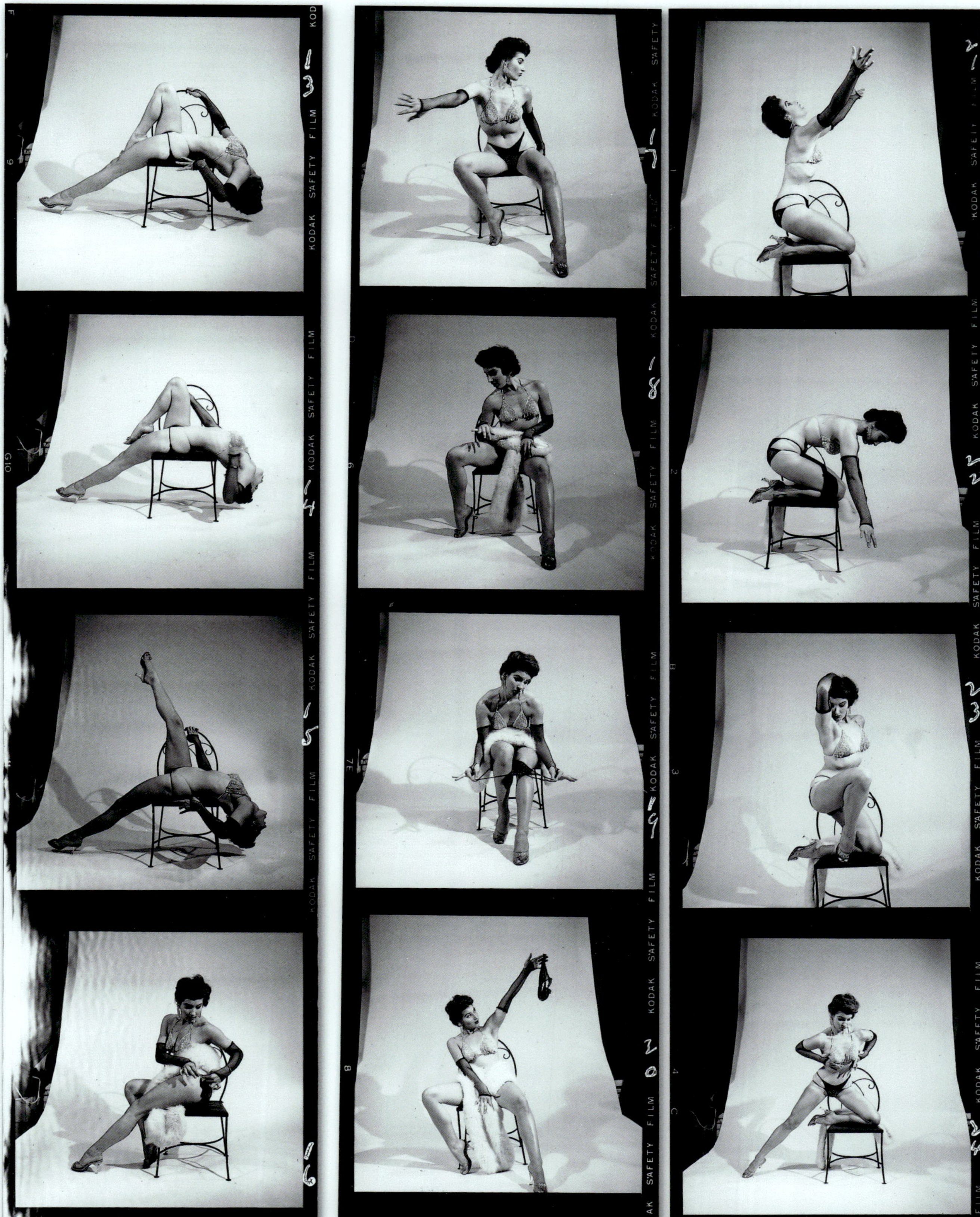
KODAK SAFETY FILM

Murine

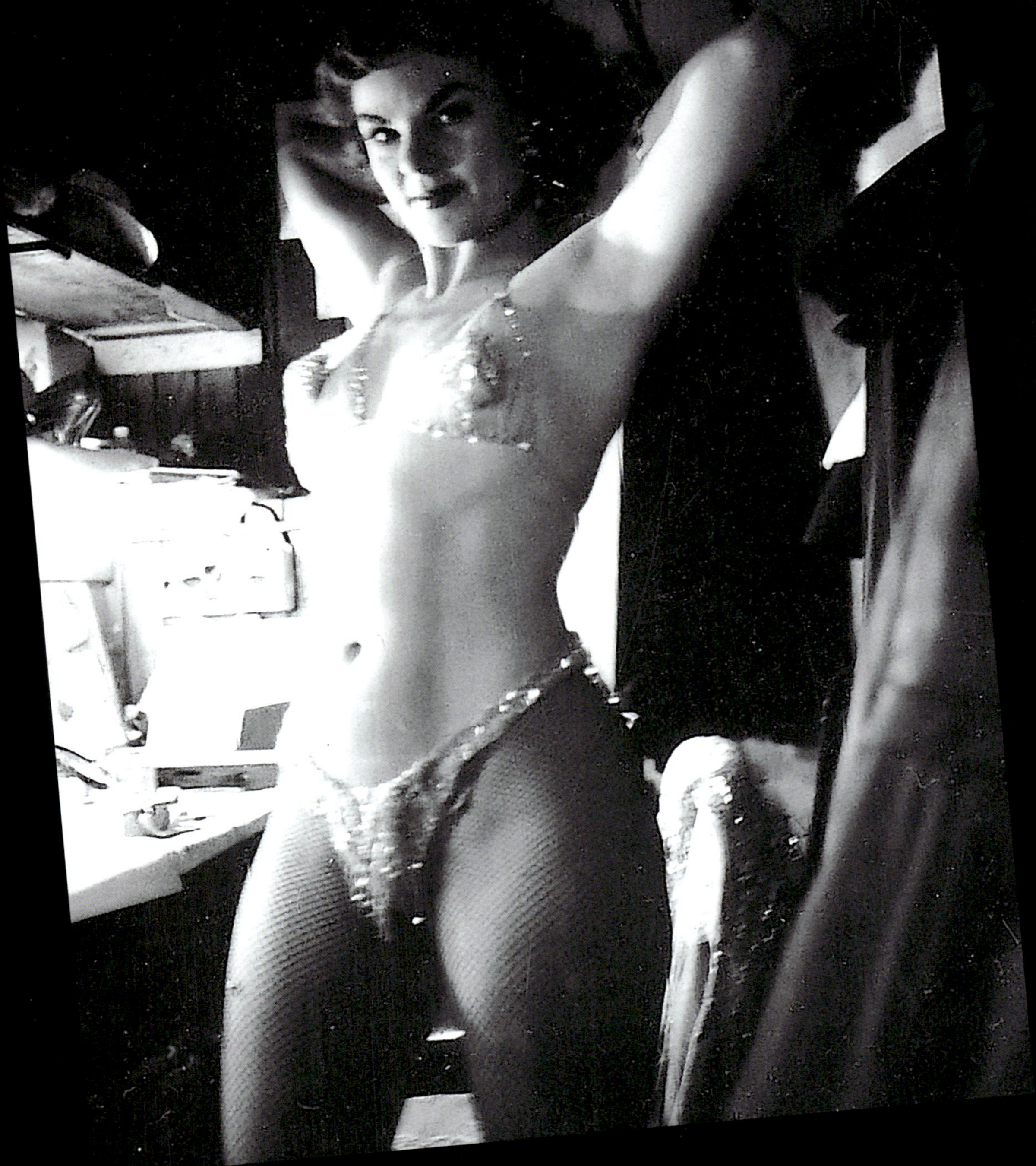

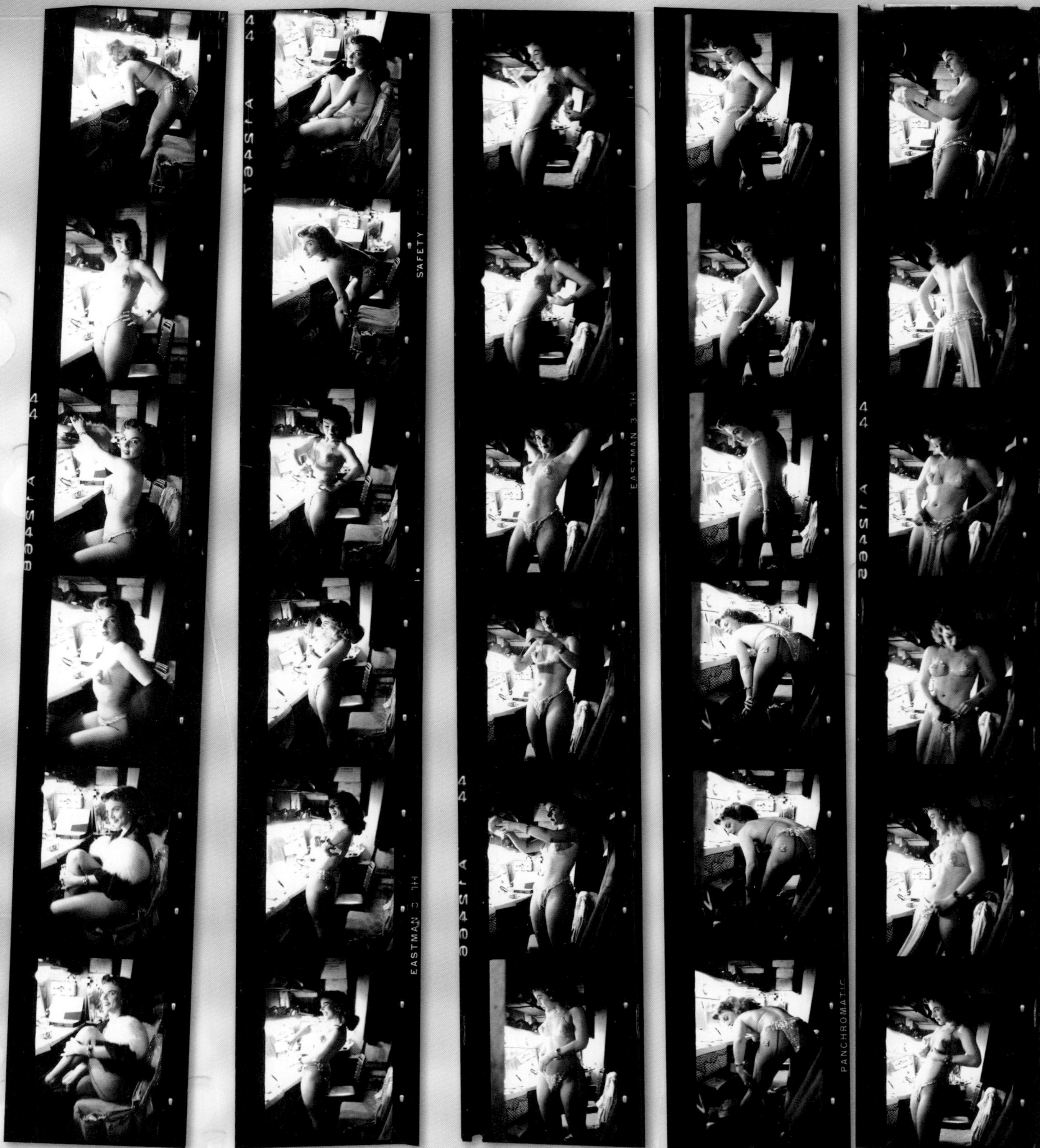
SAFETY
EASTMAN
PANCHROMATIC

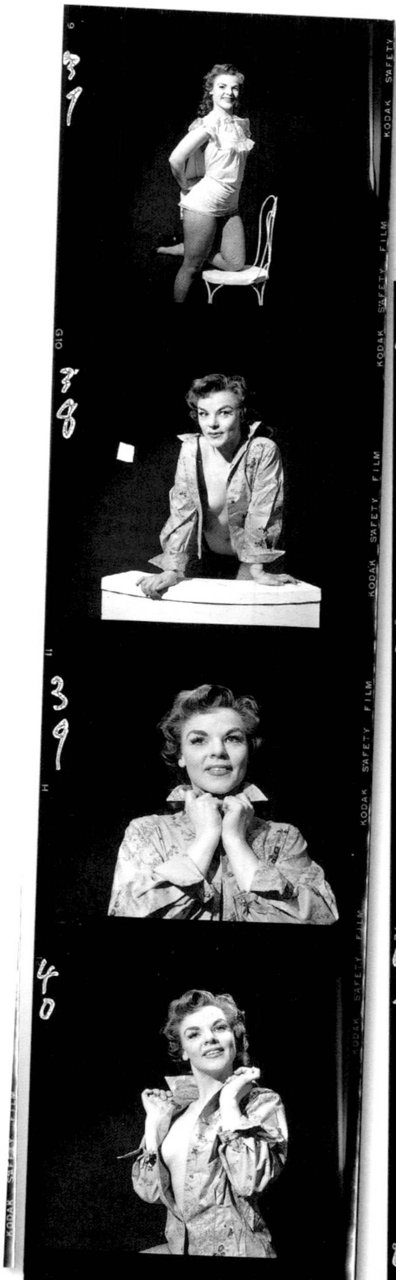
KODAK SAFETY FILM
37
38
39
40

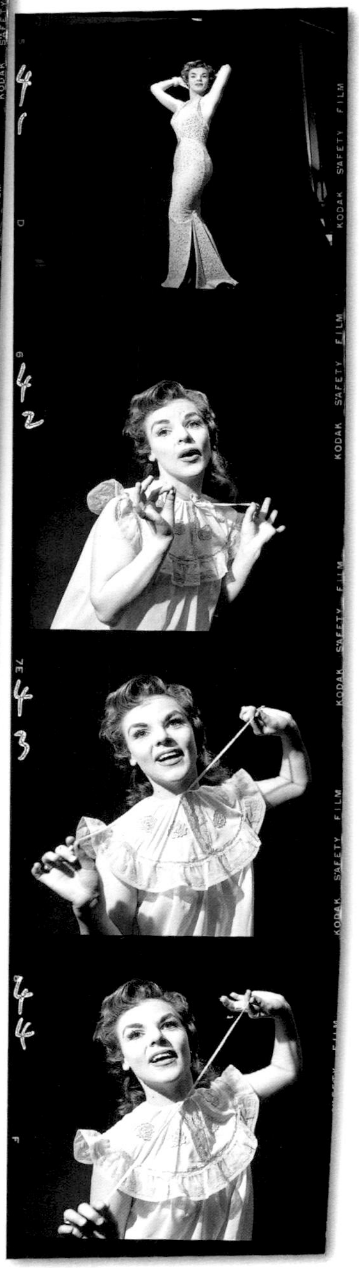
KODAK SAFETY FILM
41
42
43
44

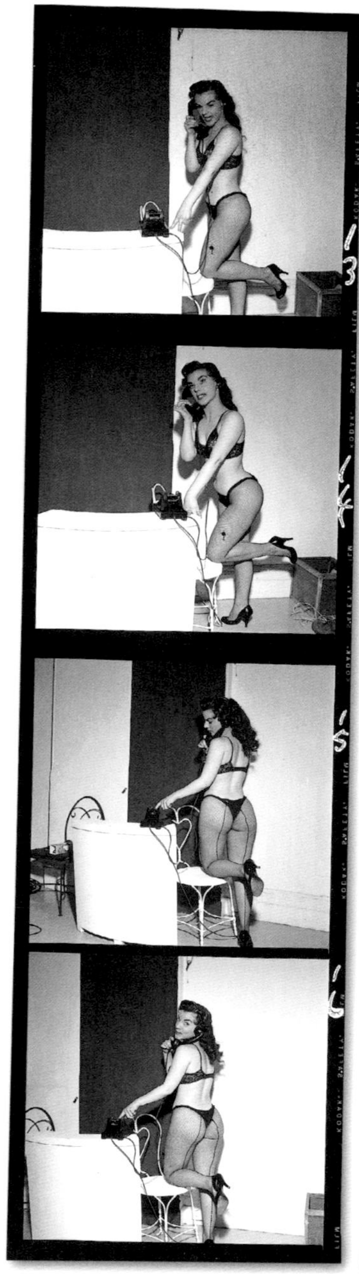
13
14
15
16

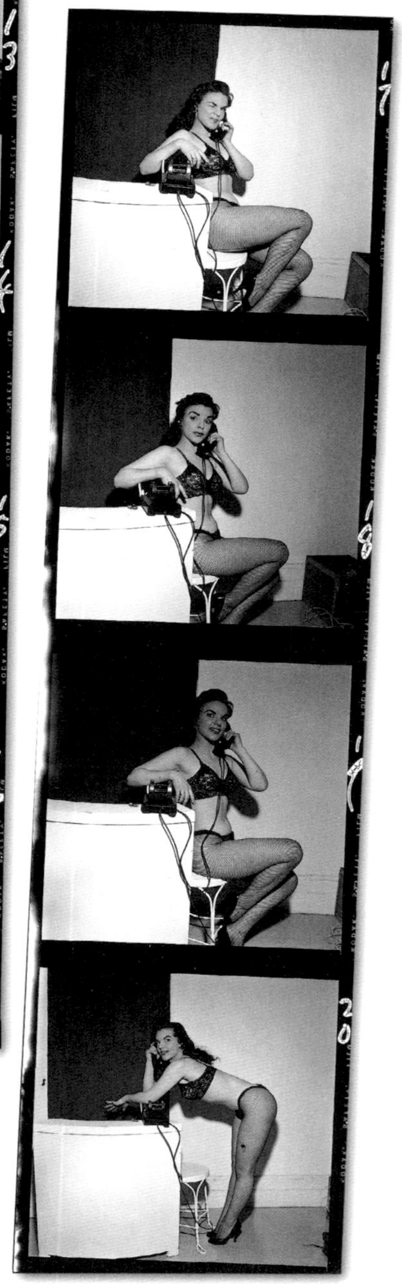
17
18
19
20

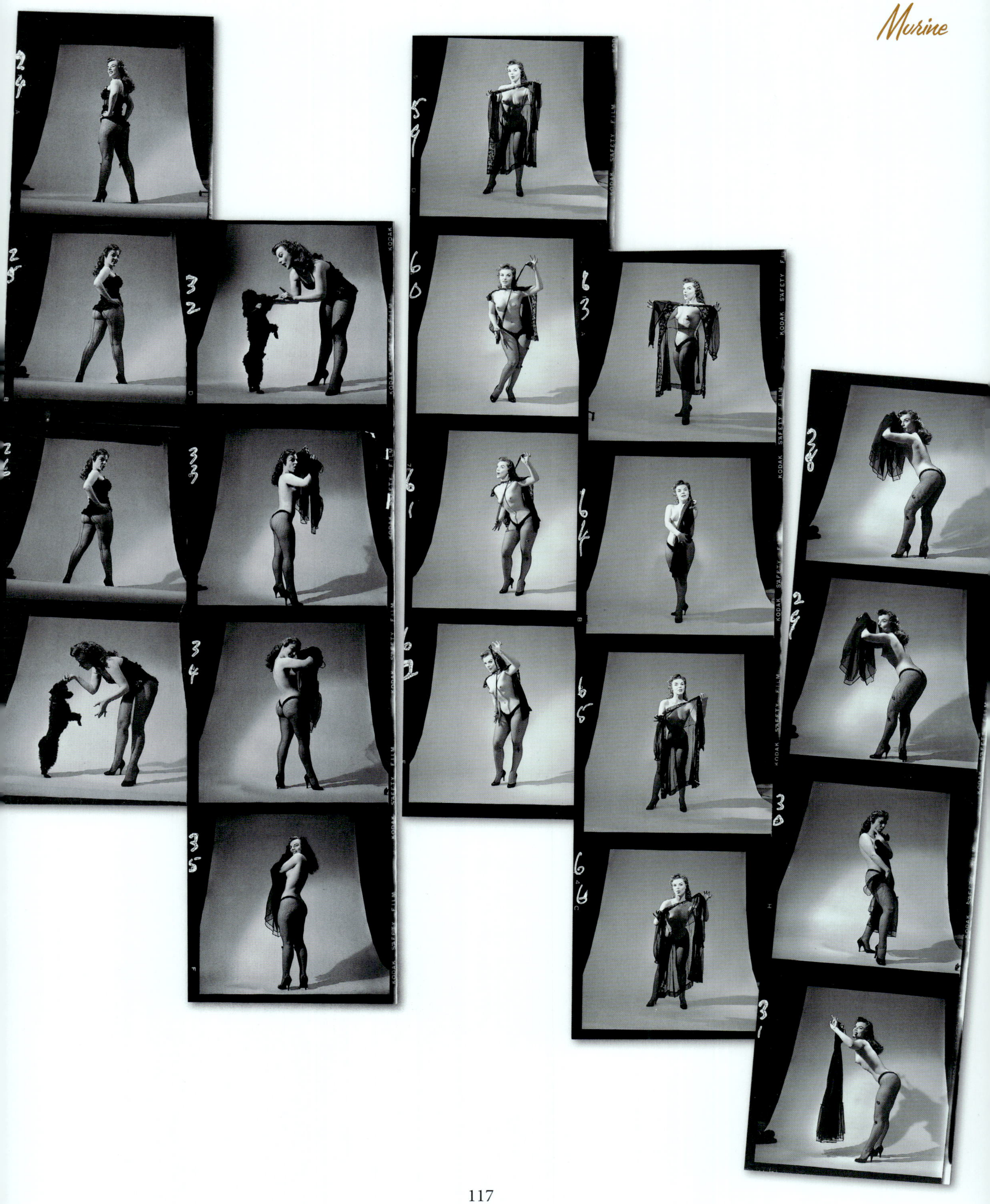

Pat Amber Halladay

SHE STRIPS FOR UNCLE SAM

Pat Amber Halladay owes $14,000 back income tax. The federal boys have an eye on her weekly pay figures as well as her figure. She'll be turning over her earnings to Uncle Sugar for a long time to come.

The flame-haired exotic got into trouble when she signed a 50-50 contract with a manager named Jack A. White , who wasn't very white about the way he handled Pat's ~~XXXXXXX~~ earnings over a 4½ year period. During that time, she said in a court action against against White, her manager drew most of the money and she didn't even know what she made, although her dance act was paid up to $500 a week. Pat said she is dancing now only"to pay off Uncle Sam" because of income-tax assessment due to inadequate returns that White made in her behalf.

Other ~~XXXXXXXXXX~~ shortcomings of White, as testified by Pat in the court action was that her manager beat her and provided her only with "the barest necessities." Needless to say, the judge of the Baltimore Circuit Court, Judge Herman M. Moser, nullified the ten-year contract by which the 28 year-old strip-teaser was "led like a lamb to the slaughter" by her manager. Now the Pay is Hers at last, says Stripper in Suit (Law).

Vital statistics: Pat Amber Halladay is 28 yrs. old, is 5'5" tall, measures 36-26-26.

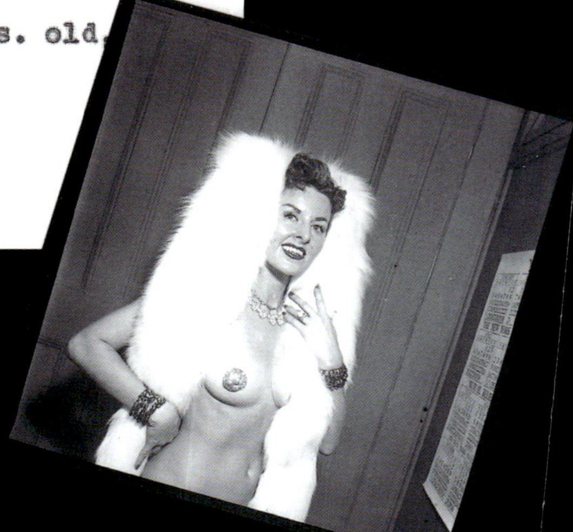

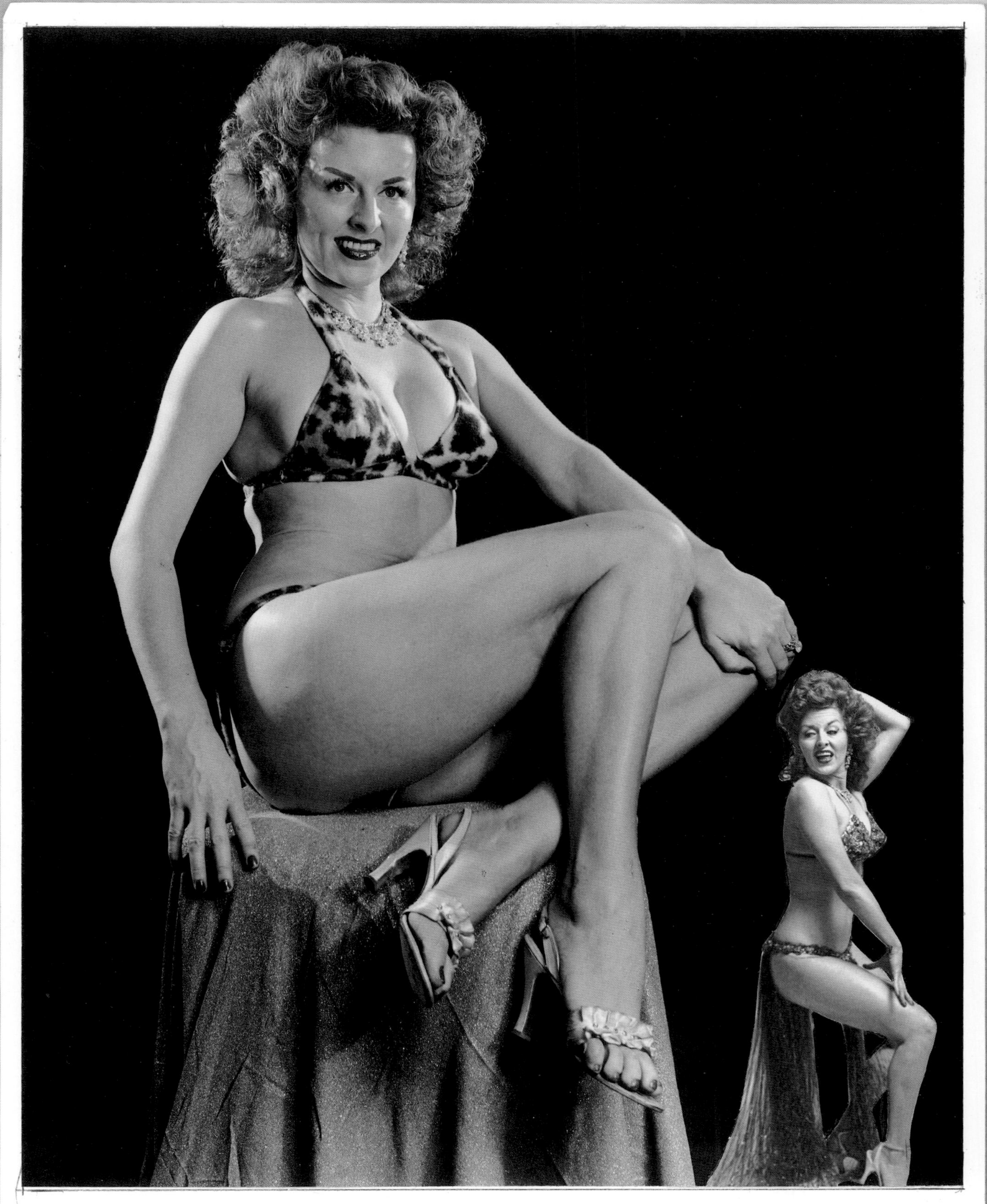

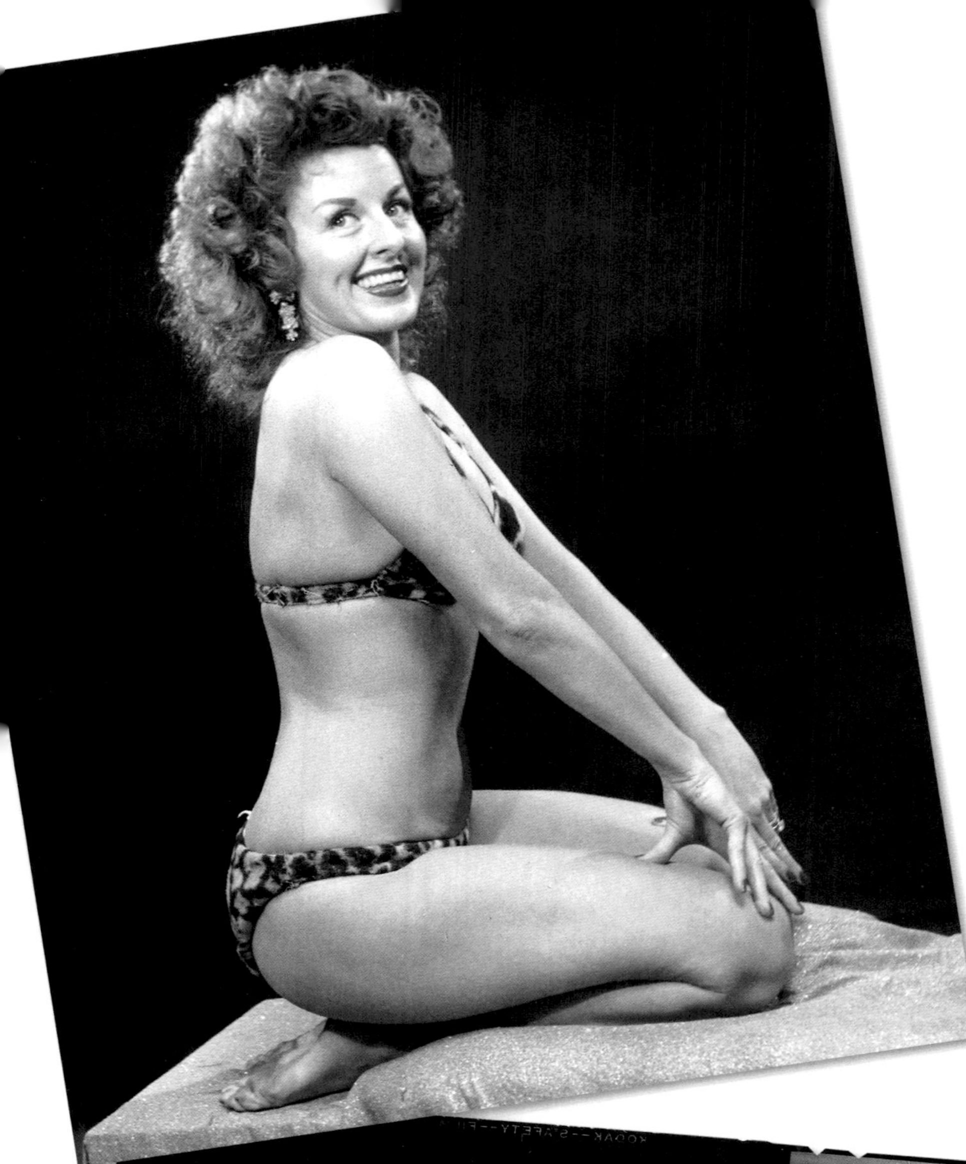

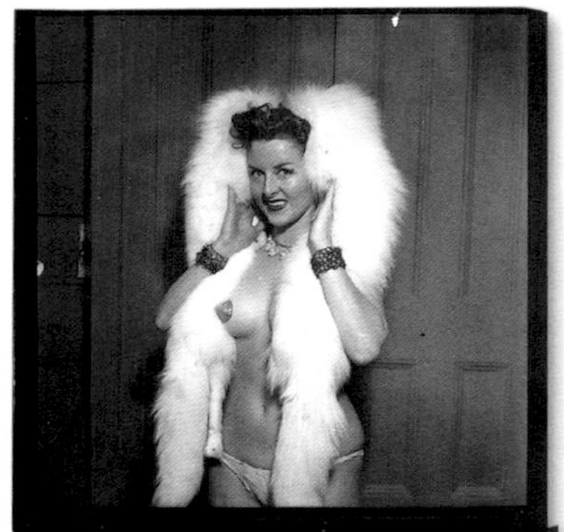

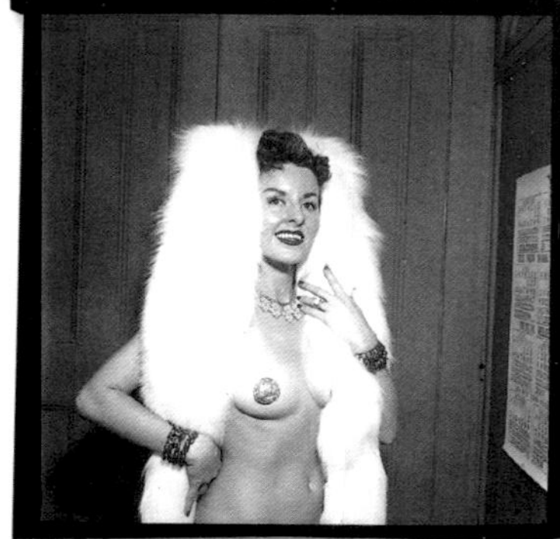

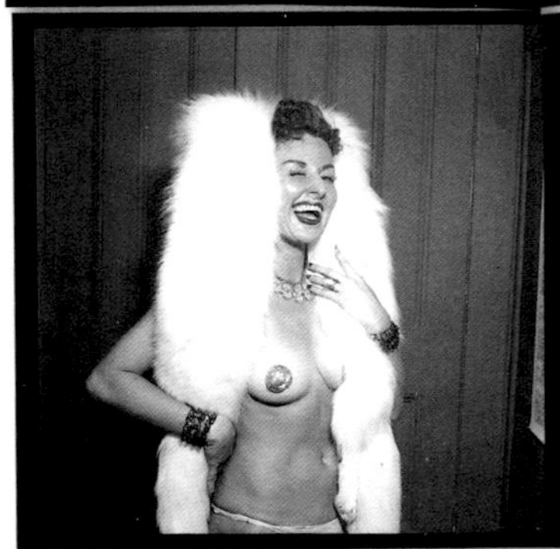

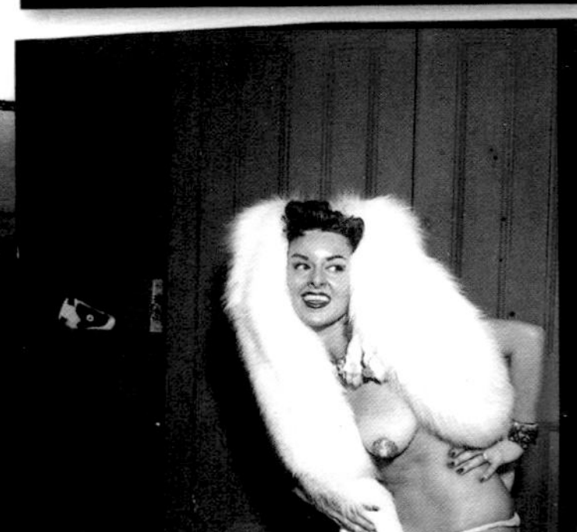

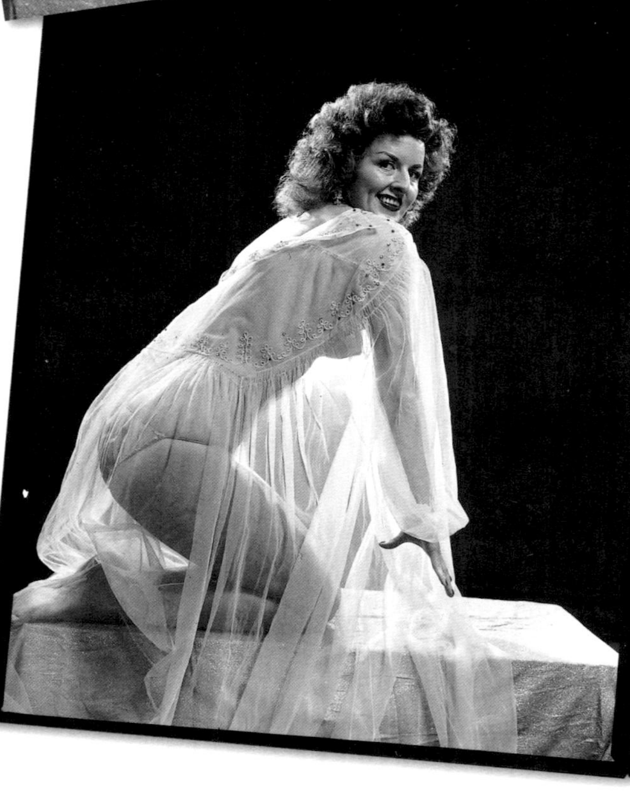

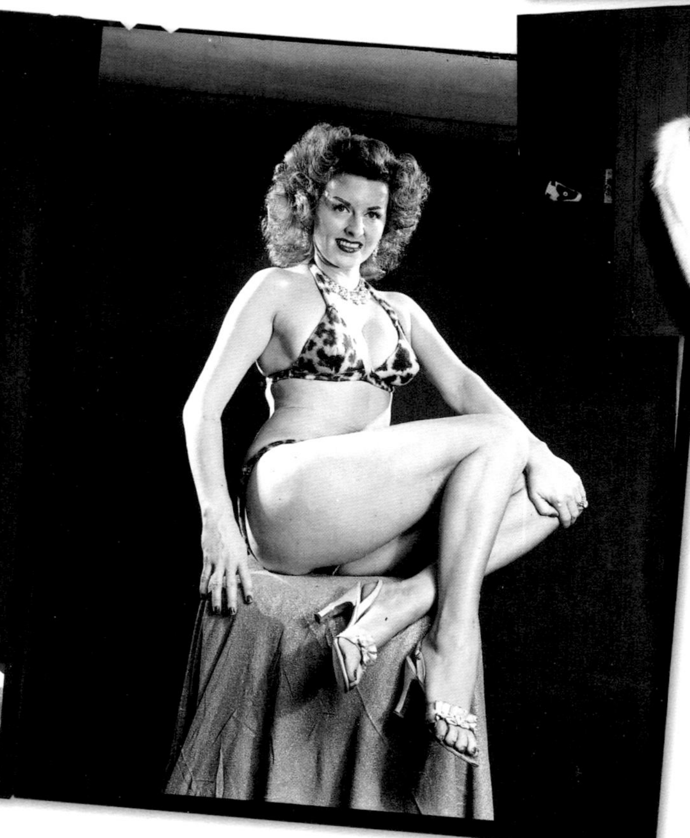

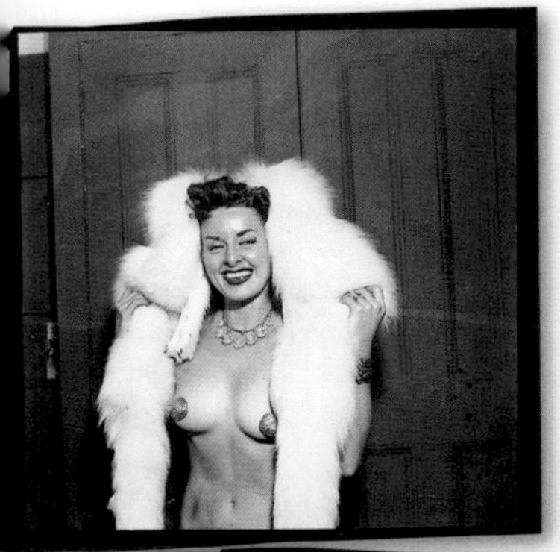
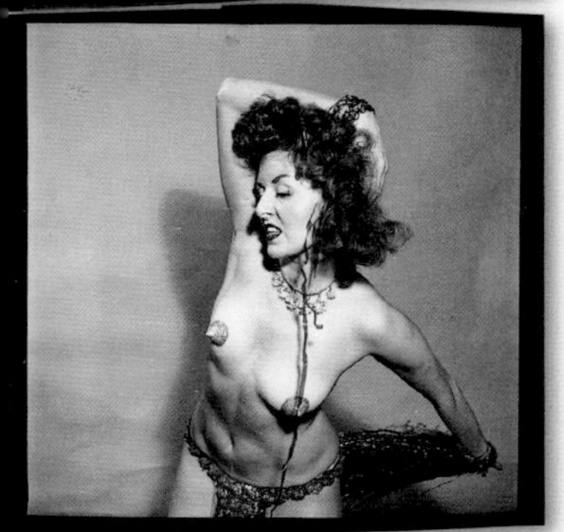
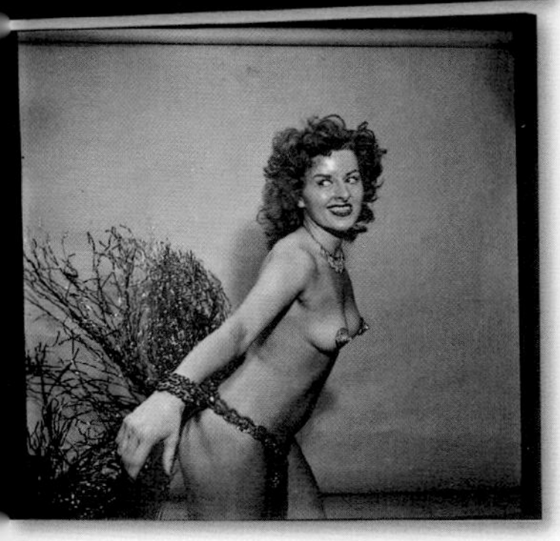
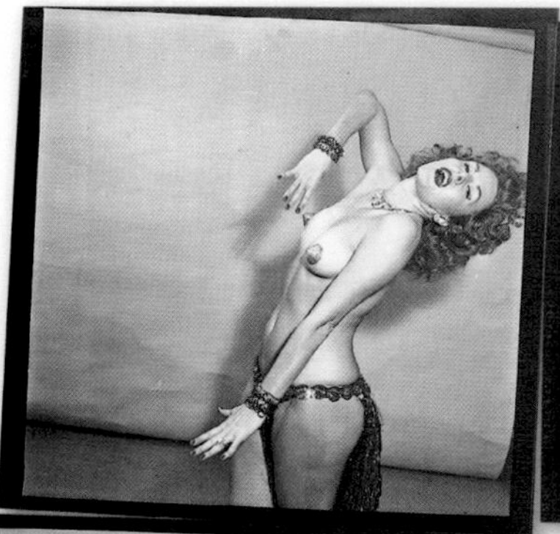
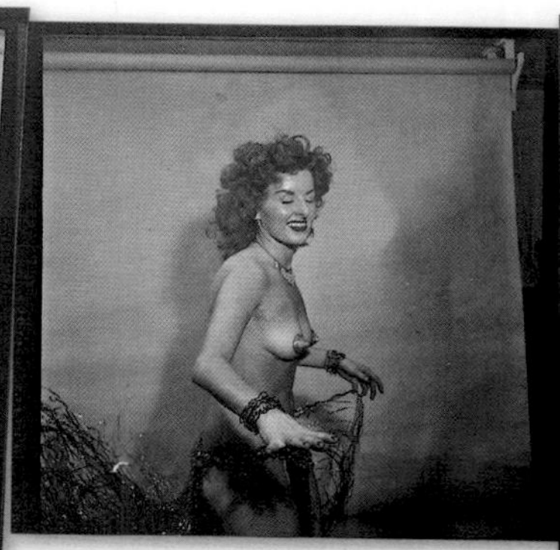
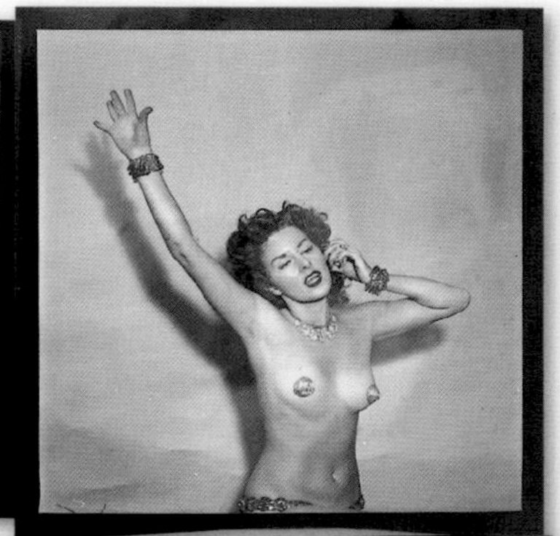
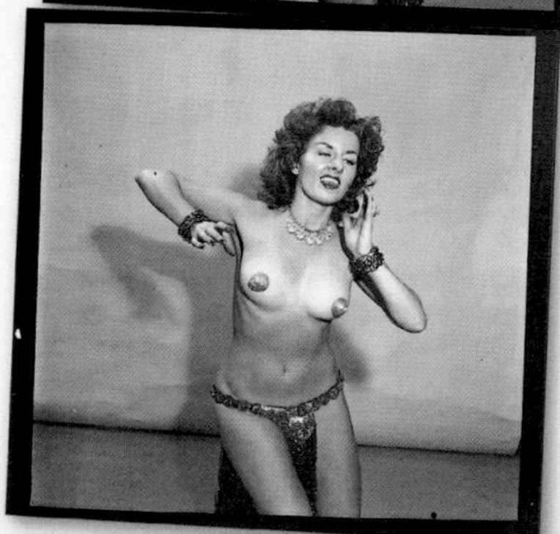
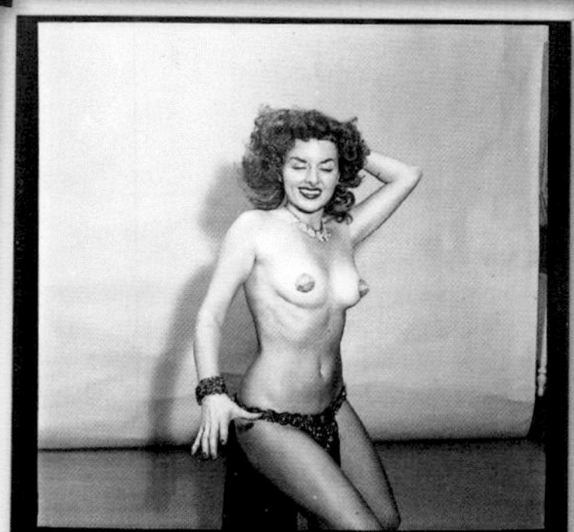
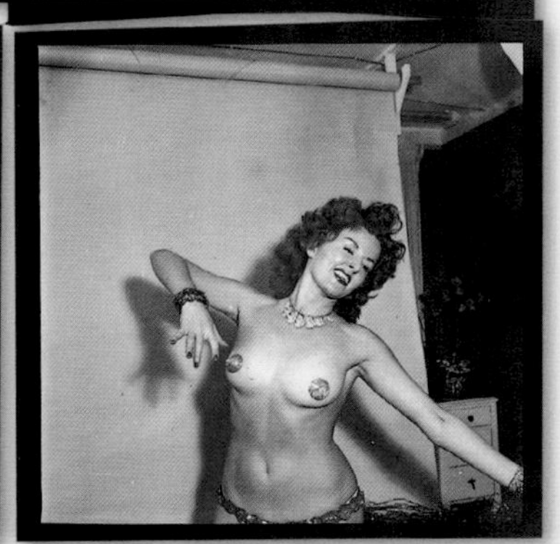
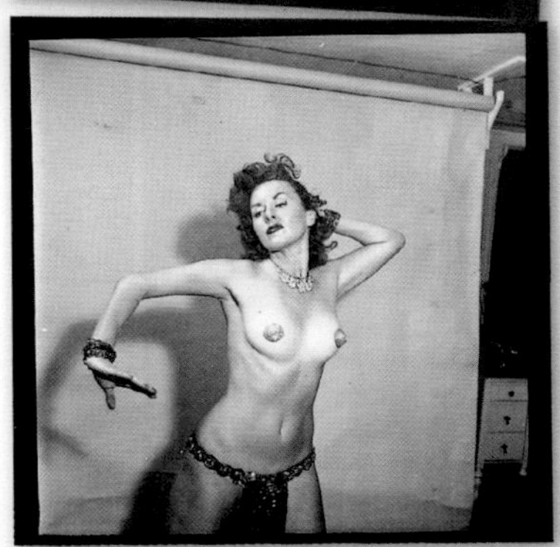
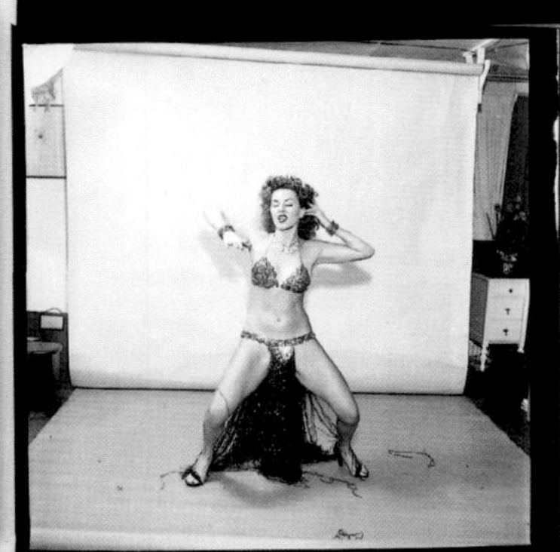
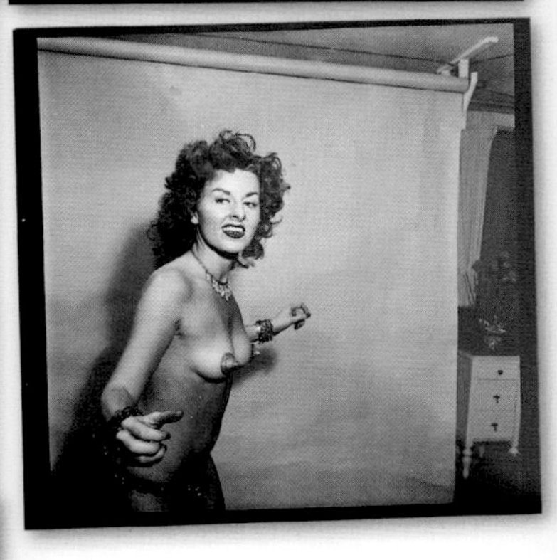
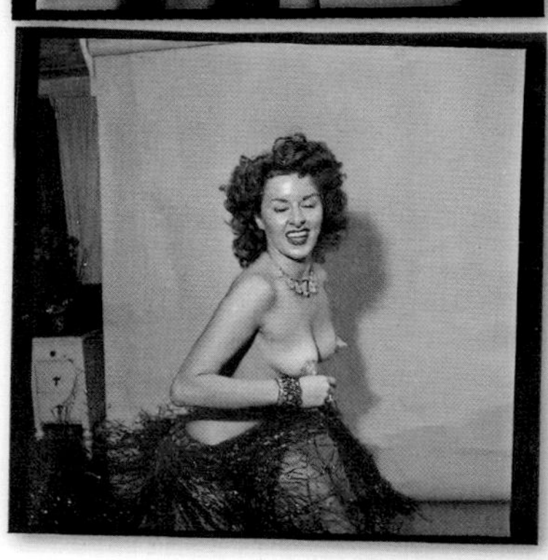
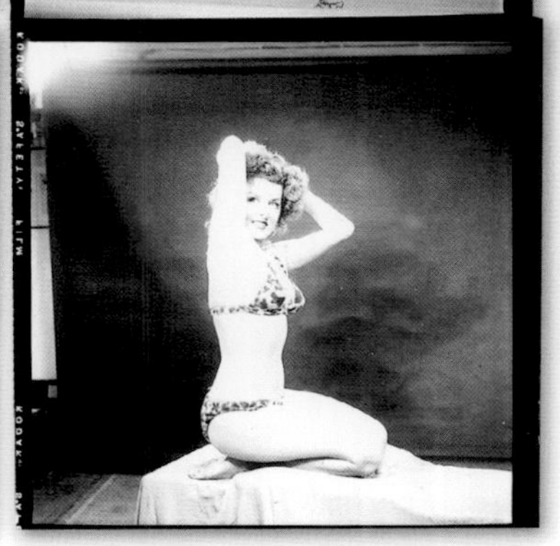

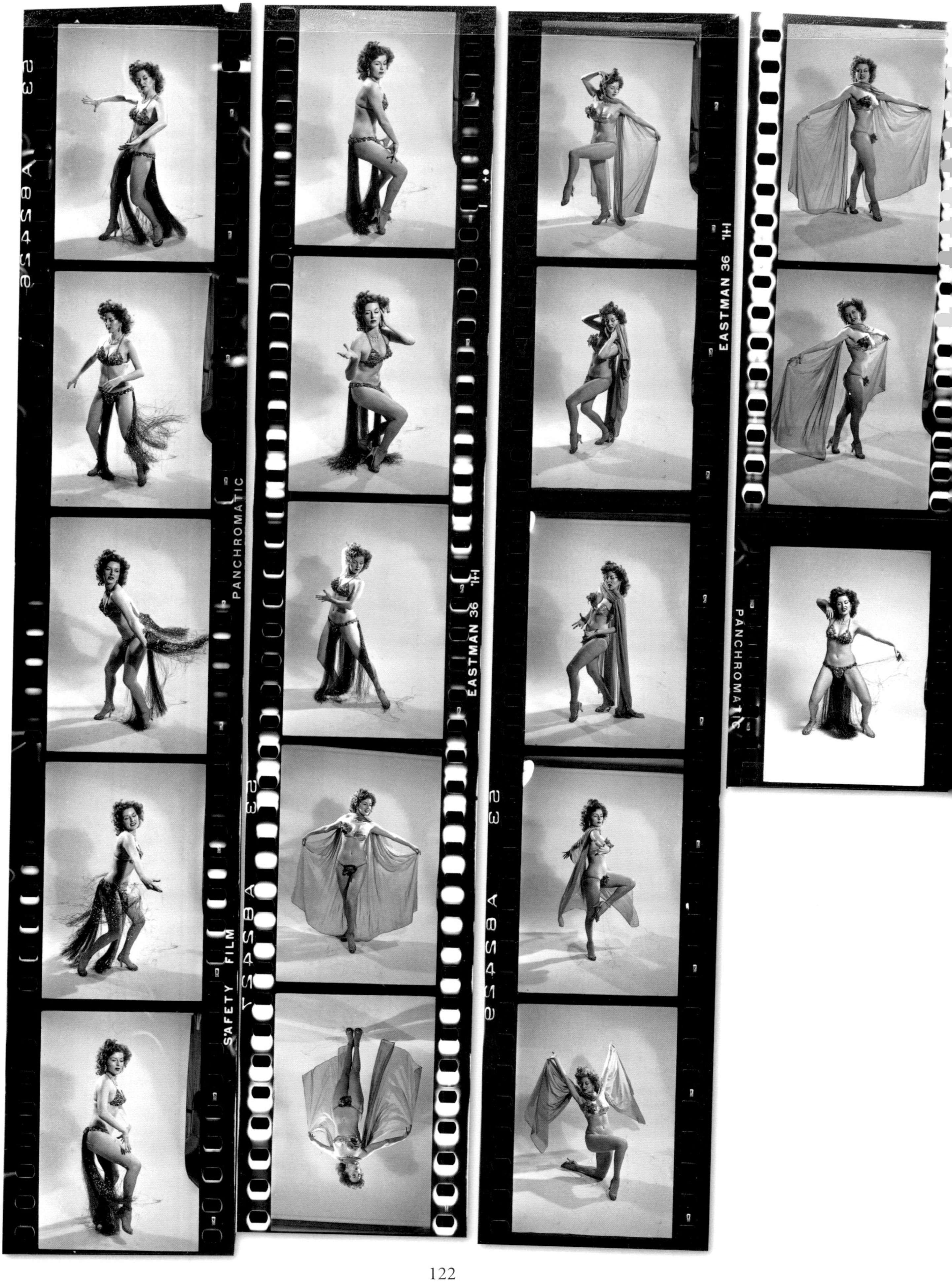

PANCHROMATIC
SAFETY FILM
EASTMAN 36
EASTMAN 36
PANCHROMATIC

Pat Amber Halladay

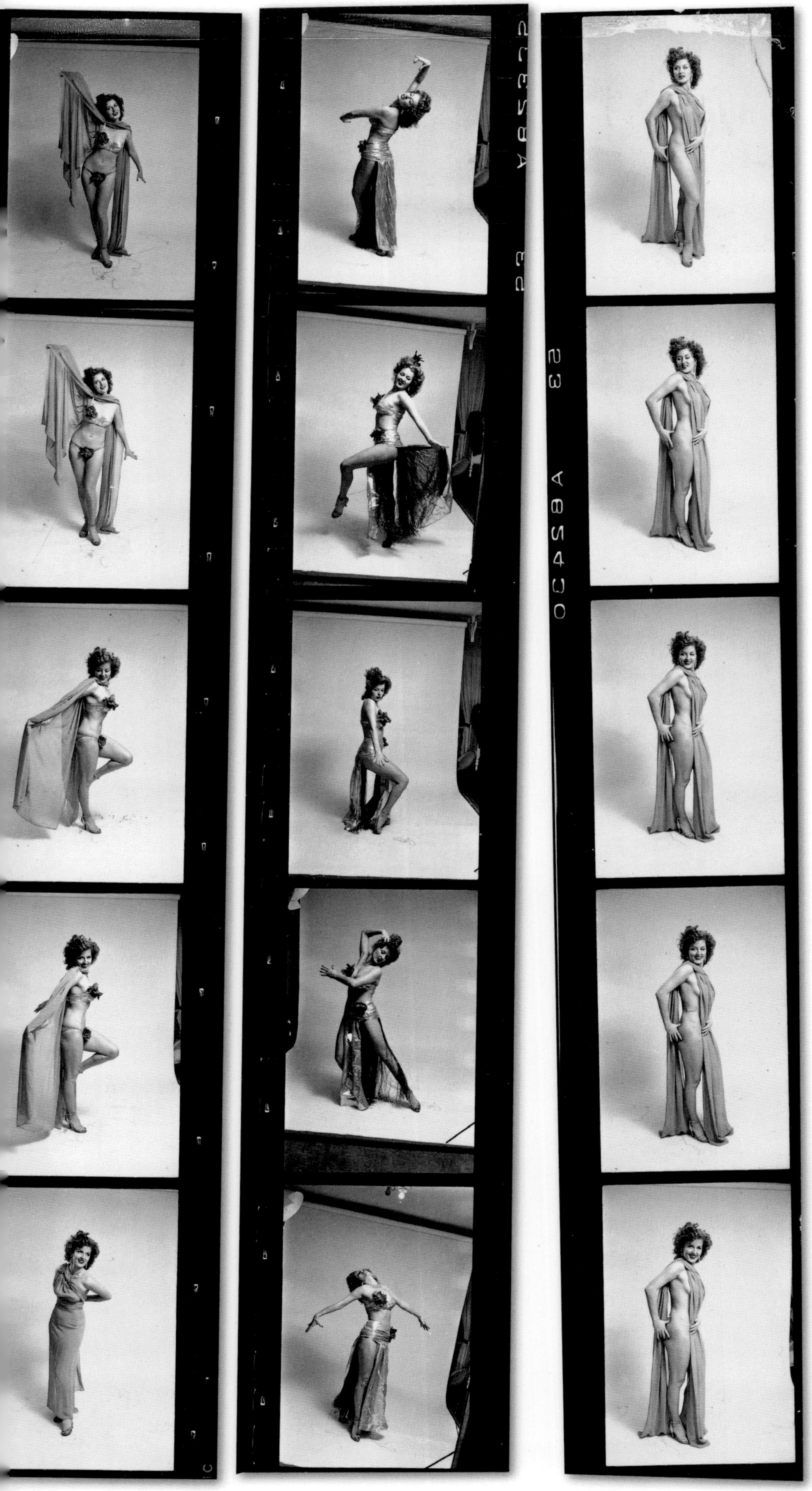

Patricia Lord

PATRICIA LORD

Long-stemmed Patricia Lord wows 'em in the stratOsphere. She's a 5'11" blonde, goes to 6'2" with stage footgear. This 24-year-old willowy wonder has been spreading her charms around the western hemisphere from Cuba to Mexico to Canada and back. Hers is a familiar face and figure at the Hudson Theatre, Union City, the Adams in Newark, the Trocadero in Philadelphia, the Rialto in Chicago.

Here's a career gal who loves to be domestic in her apartment in Union City, cooks, sews, paints for fun. Men in her life ? She lives alone and likes it, but thinks life would be very dull withoutx them.

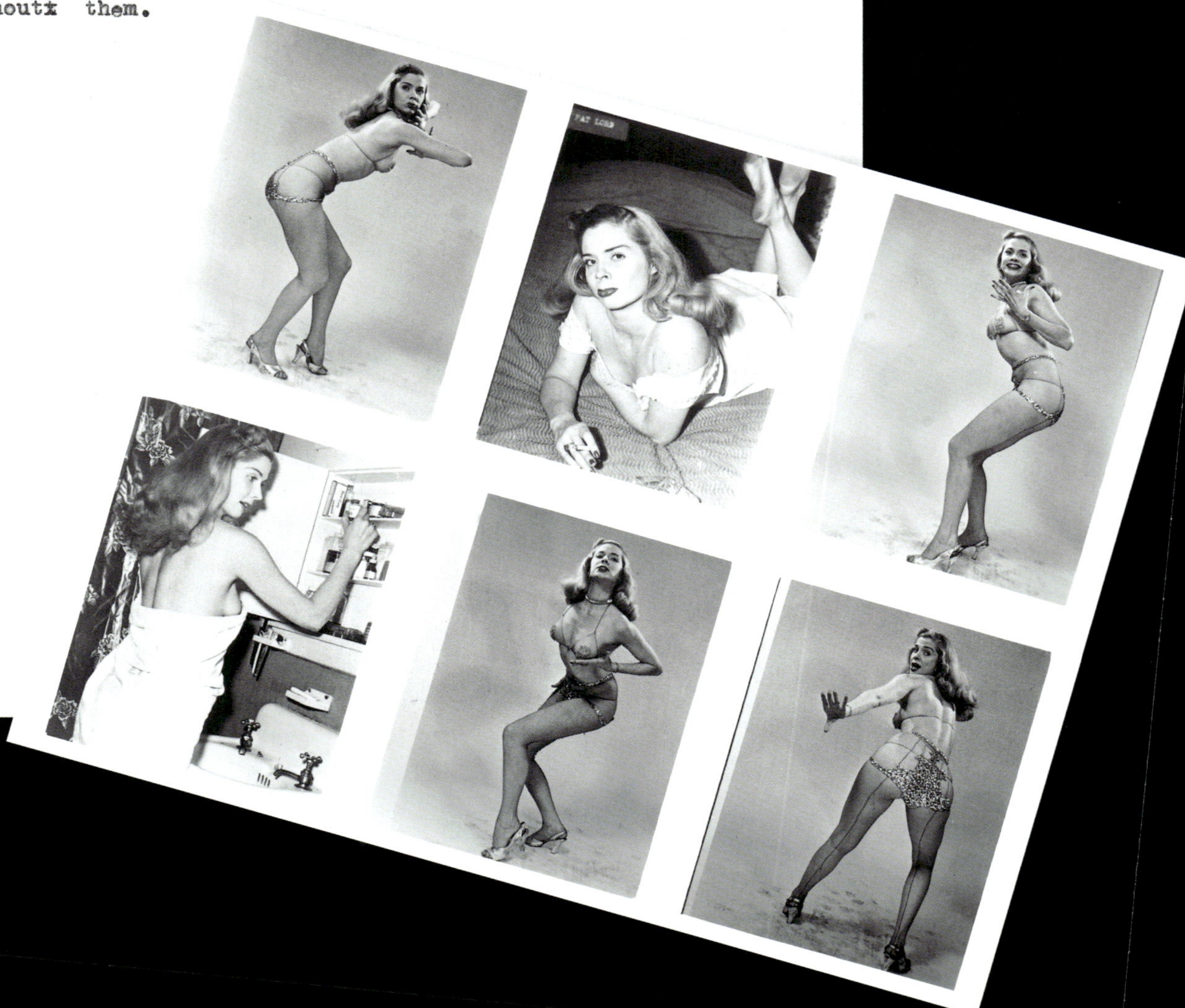

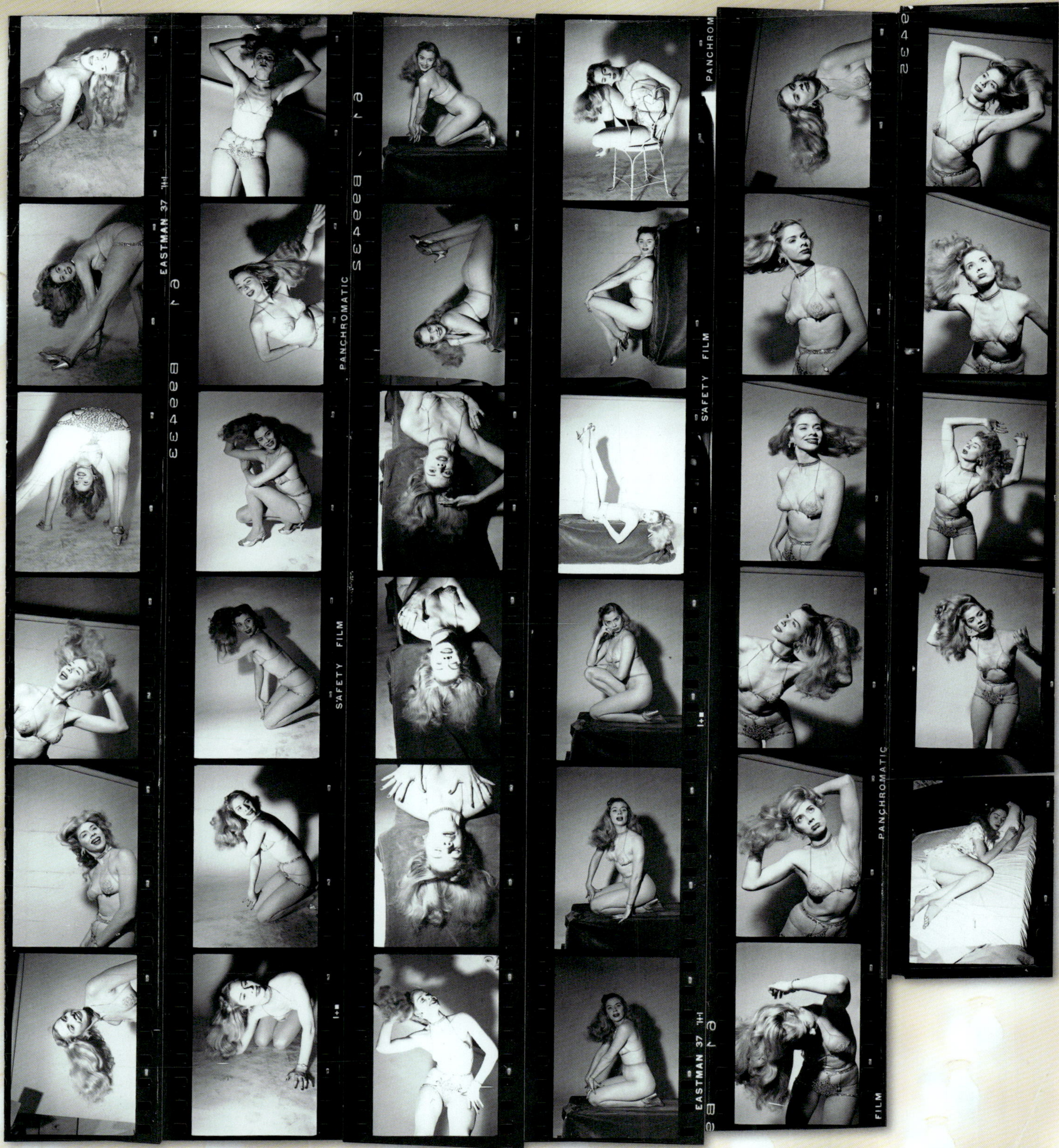
EASTMAN 37
PANCHROMATIC
SAFETY FILM

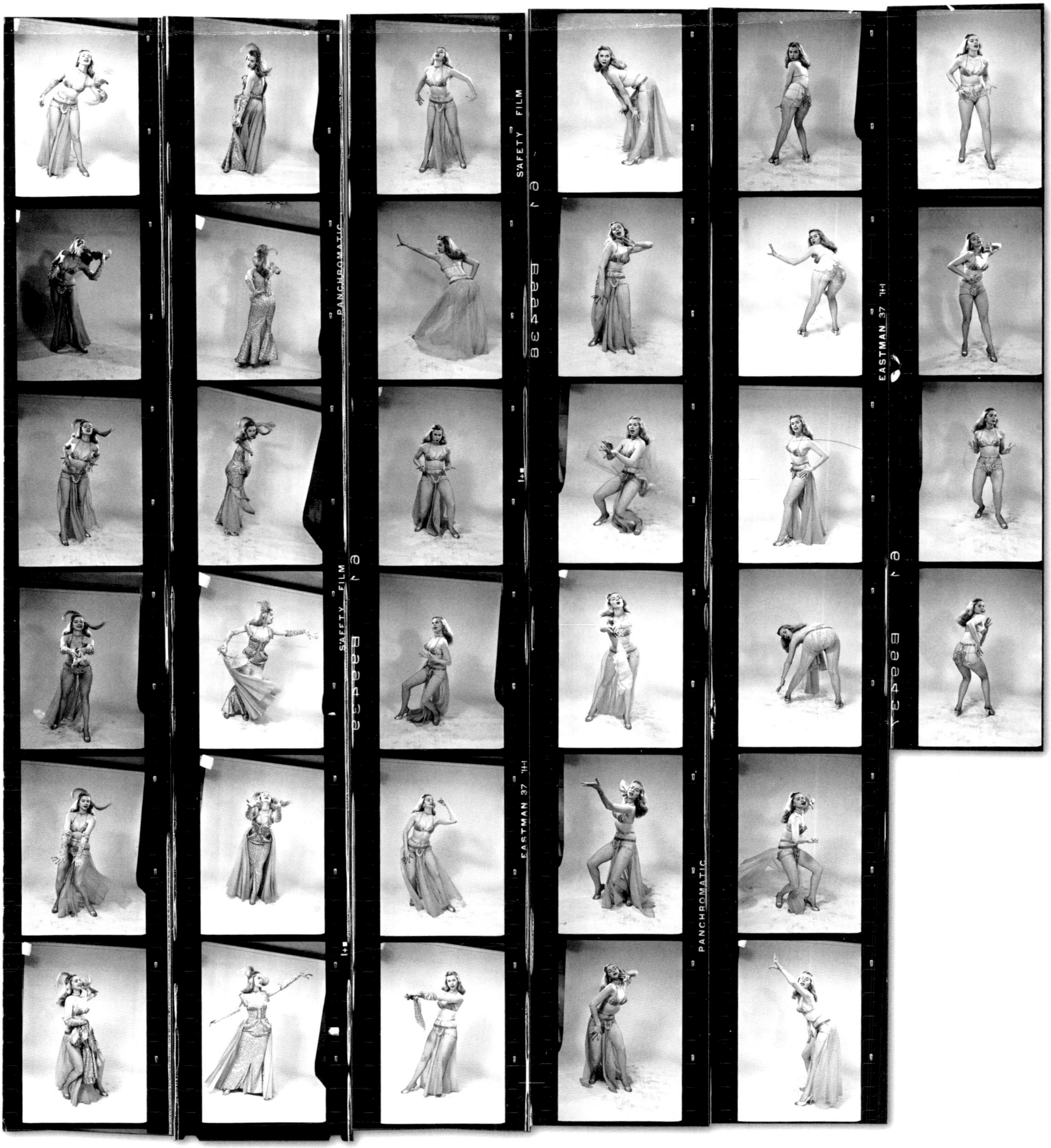
SAFETY FILM
PANCHROMATIC
EASTMAN 37

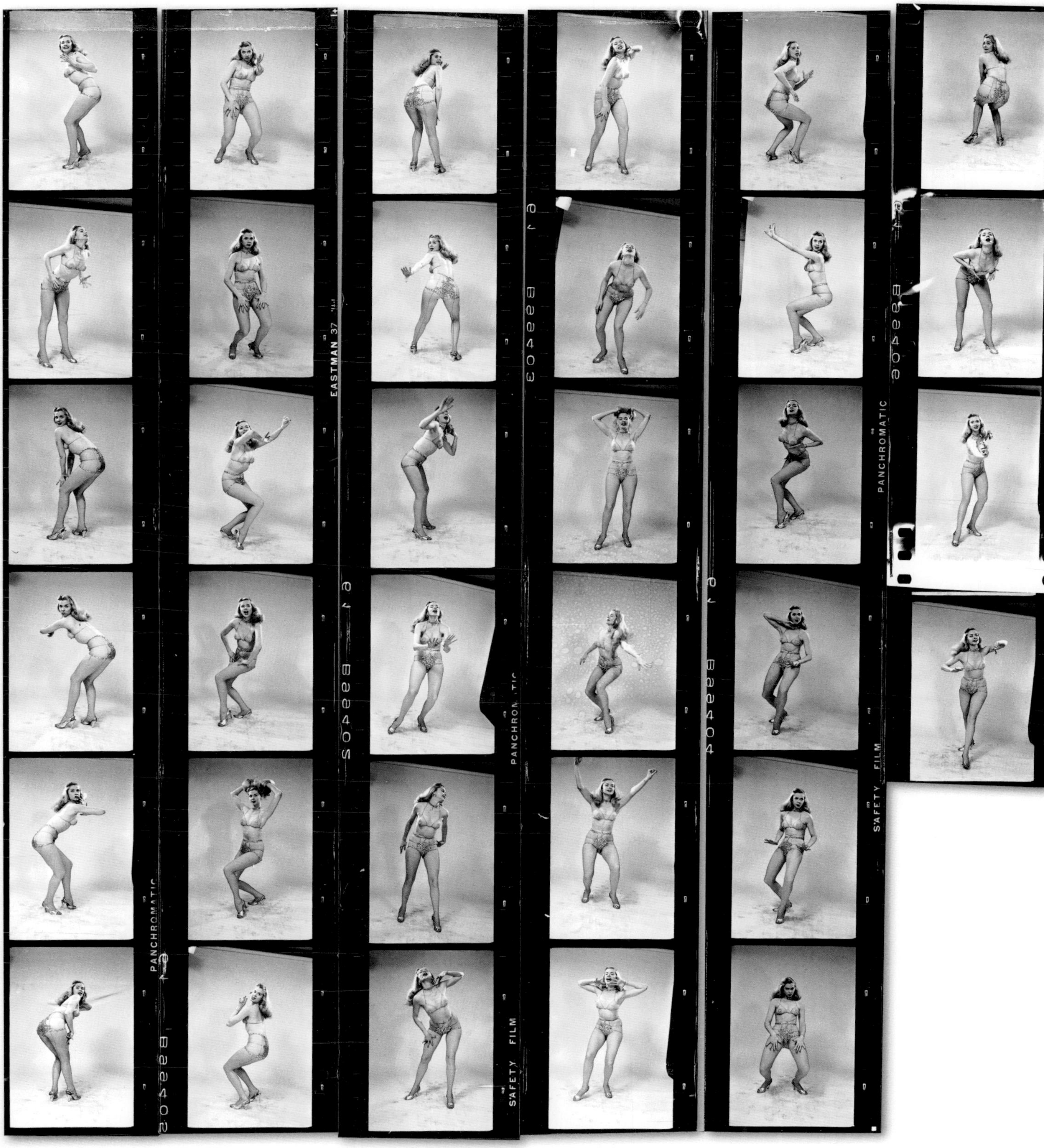
EASTMAN 37
PANCHROMATIC
SAFETY FILM

Paula Uhsan

SHE PLAYS ON TWO G-STRINGS

Tall (she's 6'1"), statuesque Paula Uhsan started out in life as a concert violinist, has a reperteire that would do credit to any virtuoso. Somewhere along the line, however, she became aware of her feminine charms, decided to make use of them in her act. Now she's an exotic dancer who plays fiddle. You've heard of the famous Russian violinists Mischa, Toscha, Jascha ? Now we have Paula and her golden violin. Only she gives the instrument a new twist. Paula is Latvian, not so far from Russia, it says here. Currently booked into a Manhattan night-club, Paula is an immediate success wherever she works. Ask her to play the Air on the G-string. To which we can only add: "Which ?"

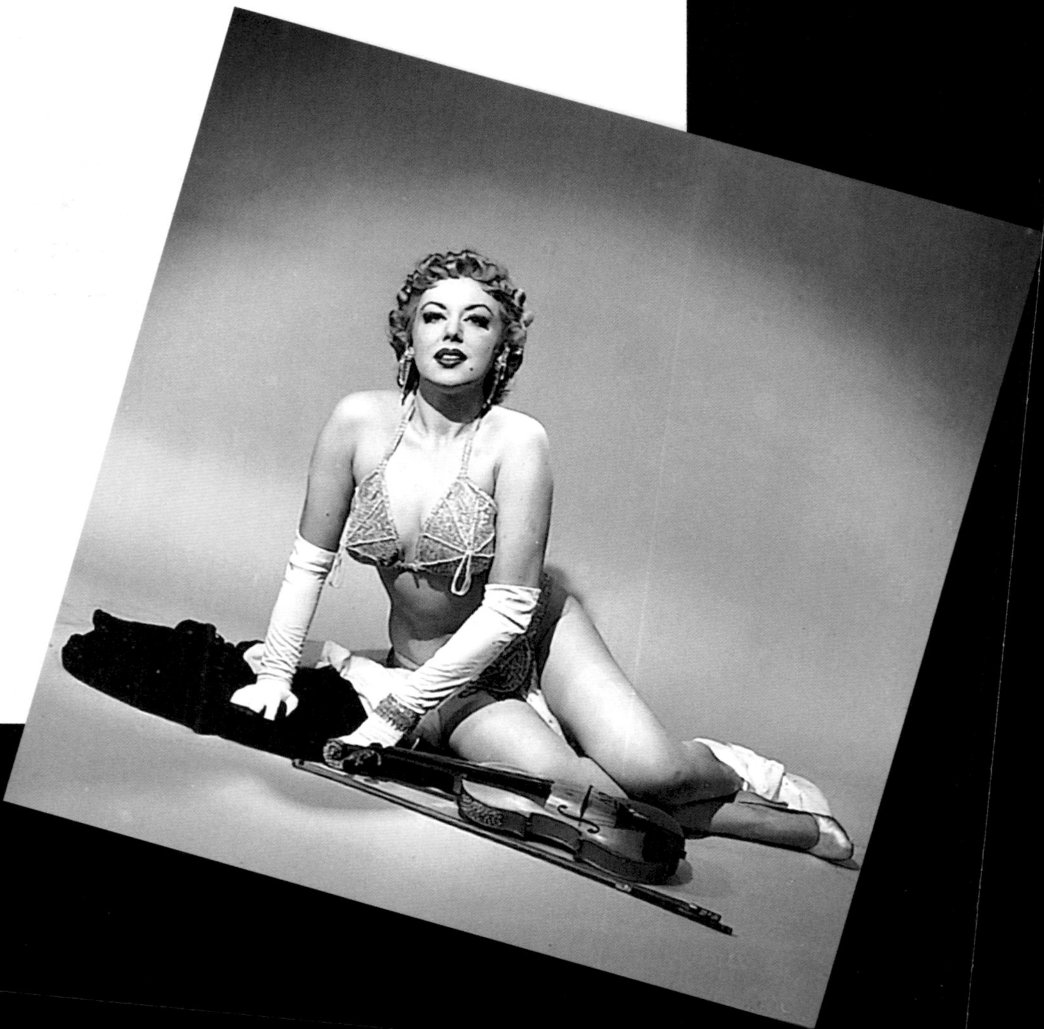

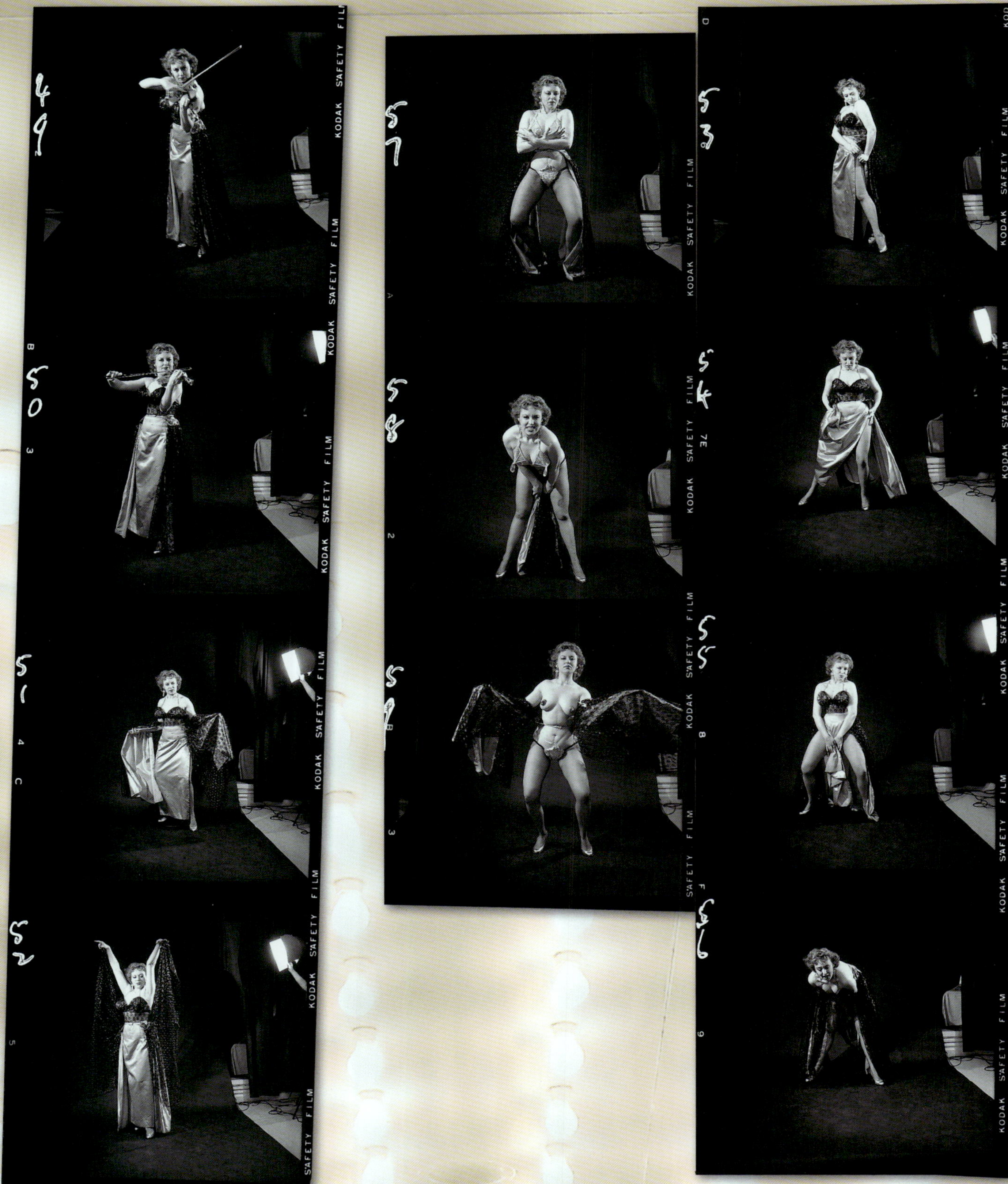
KODAK SAFETY FILM

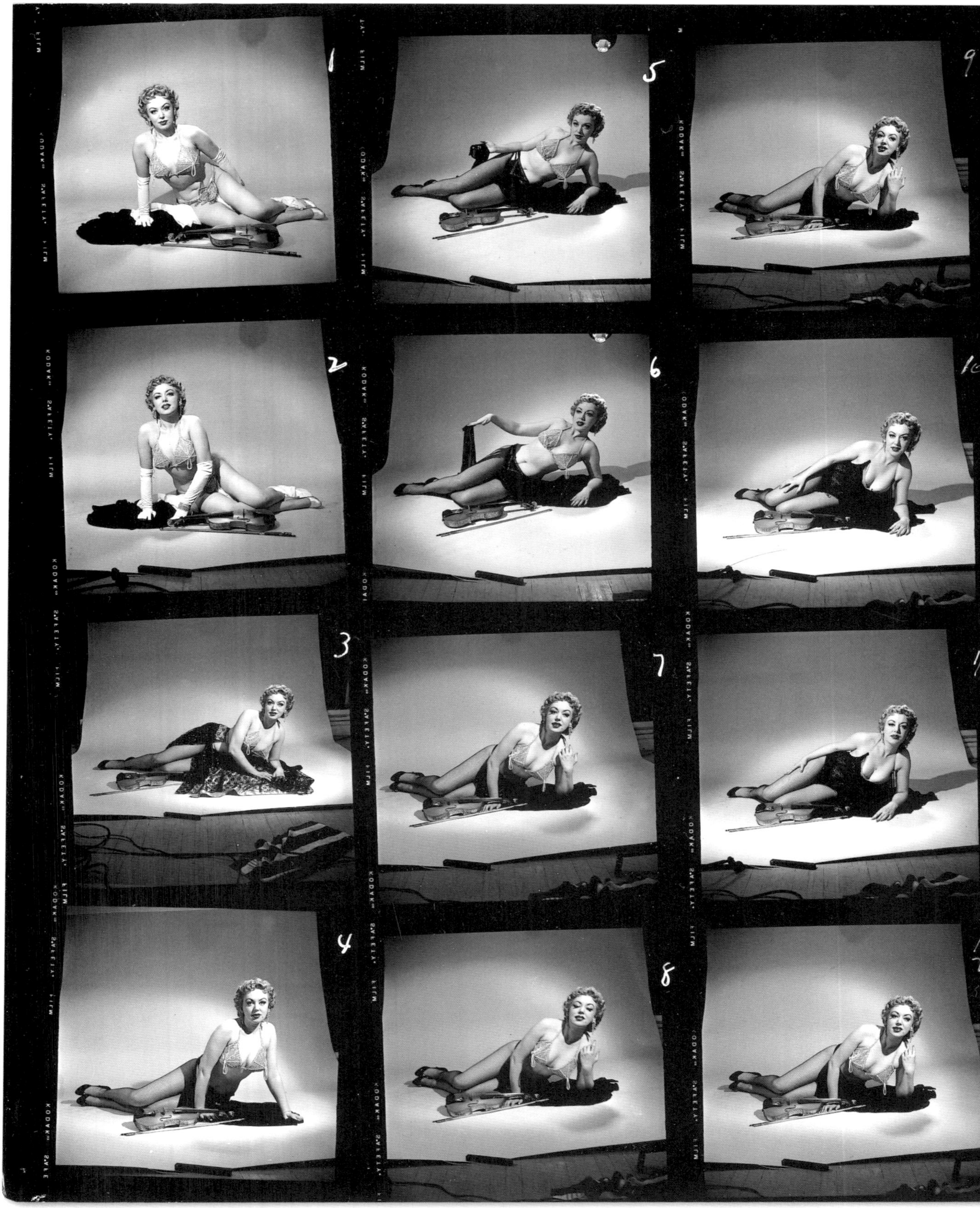

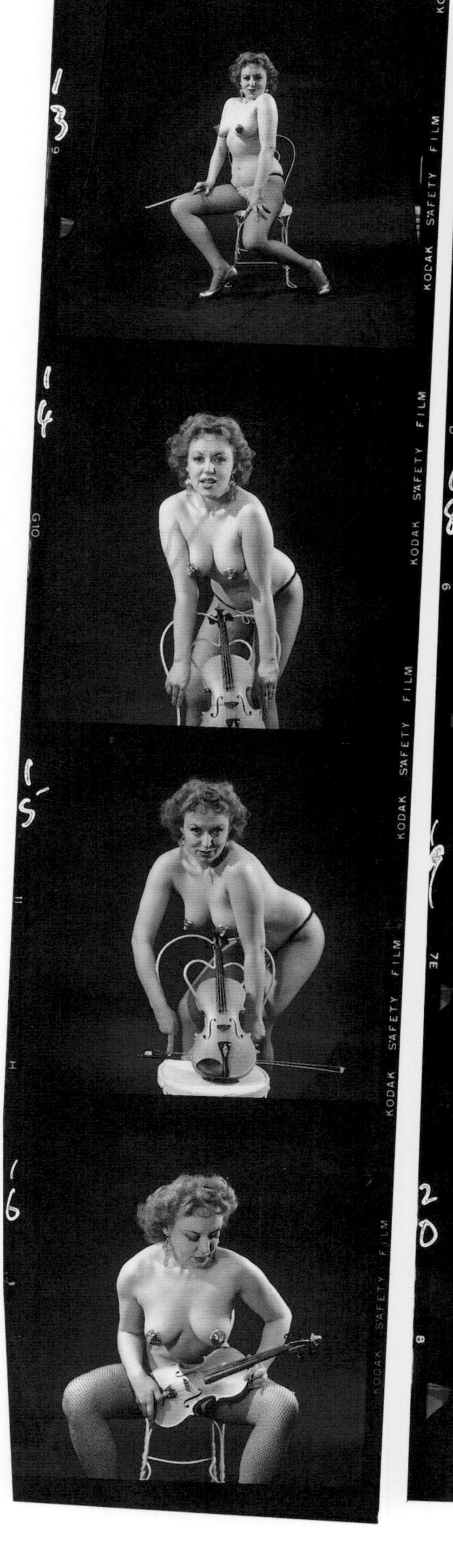
KODAK SAFETY FILM

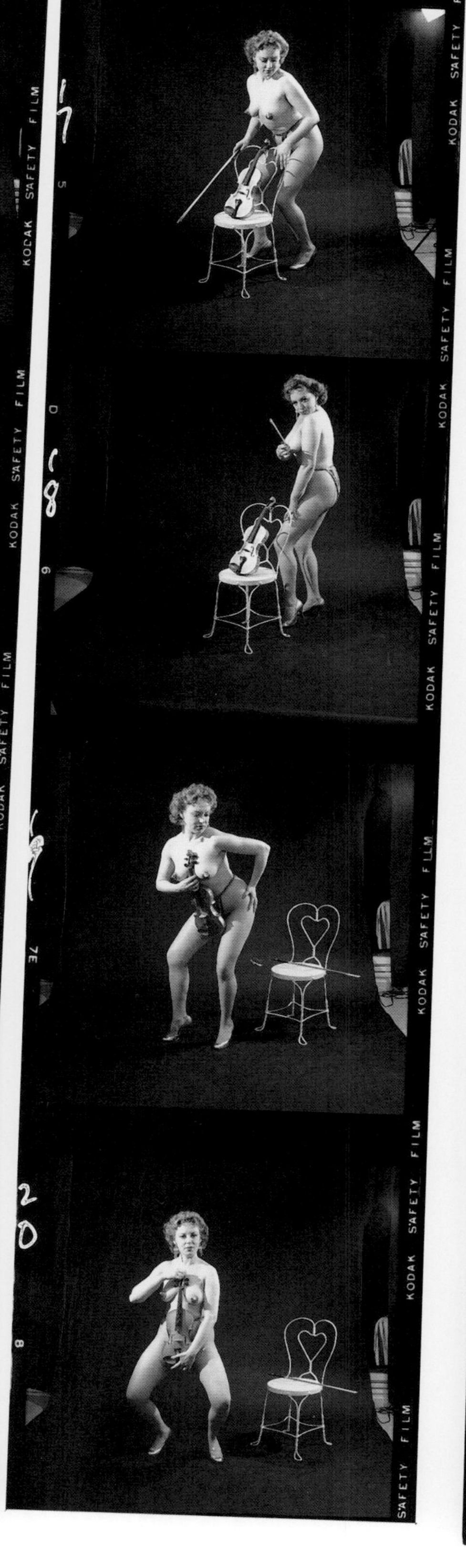
KODAK SAFETY FILM

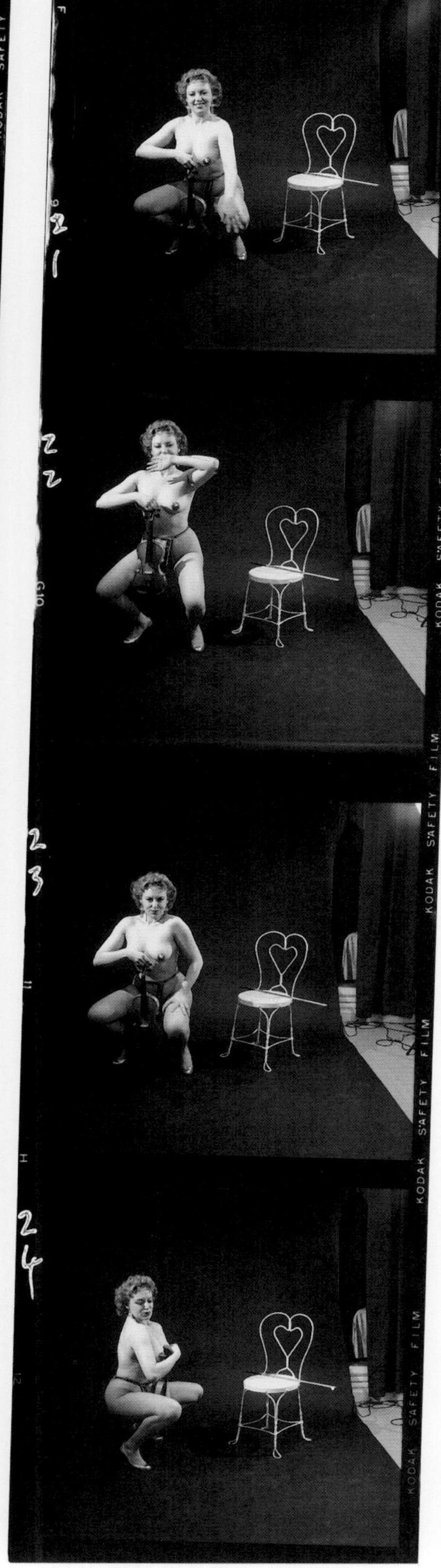
KODAK SAFETY FILM

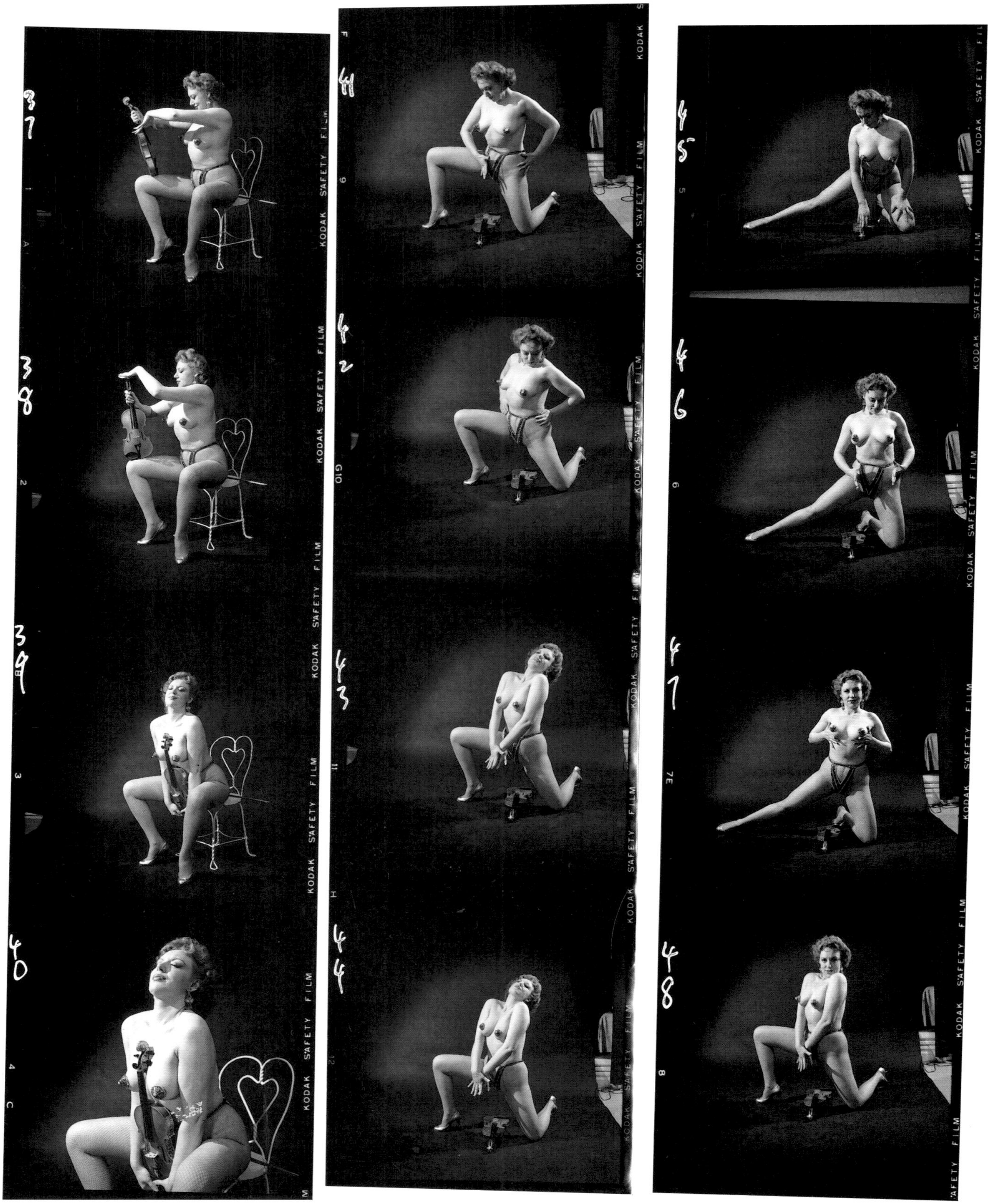
37
38
39
40
41
42
43
44
45
46
47
48
KODAK SAFETY FILM

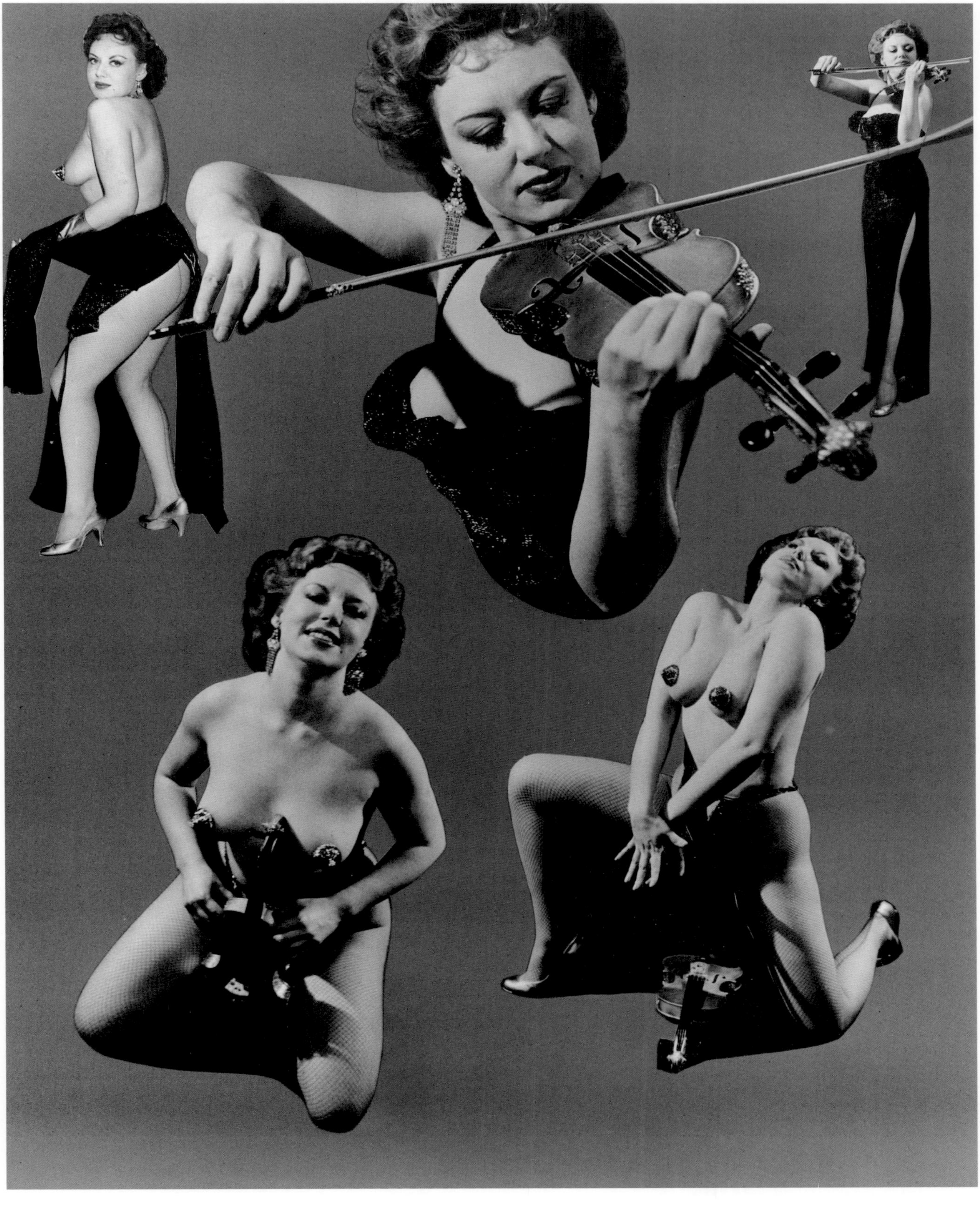

Pepper Powell

PEPPER POWELL

"Men are my favorite pastime," says Pepper. "Take them off this earth and I just don't want to be around." The views of said men toward Pepper are quite mutual, for, Pepper in motion is an unforgettable sight- she brings new life to any audience.

Pepper has adopted the device of using a trick name which at once captures the imagination and makes advertisements more colorful and suggestive in this world of word imagees. There are many others: Blaze Starr, Tempest Storm Brandy Martin, etc. She was one of the three strippers mentioned as top attractions by Harold Minsky in a TV person-to-person interview by Harold Minsky. She is a featured performer wherever she goes- is well known in the east and and the south.

Tall and willowy, with a sublime sense of himor, Pepper measures 5'6" up, 36-23-36 in other directions.

She loves cats and prizefights, likes to hang around Stillman's gym. Of her private life she has this to say: "I am making my own private Kinsey report."

She comes by her trade with a dance background of ballet, and has worked at Afro-Cuban rhythms under Catherine Dunham.

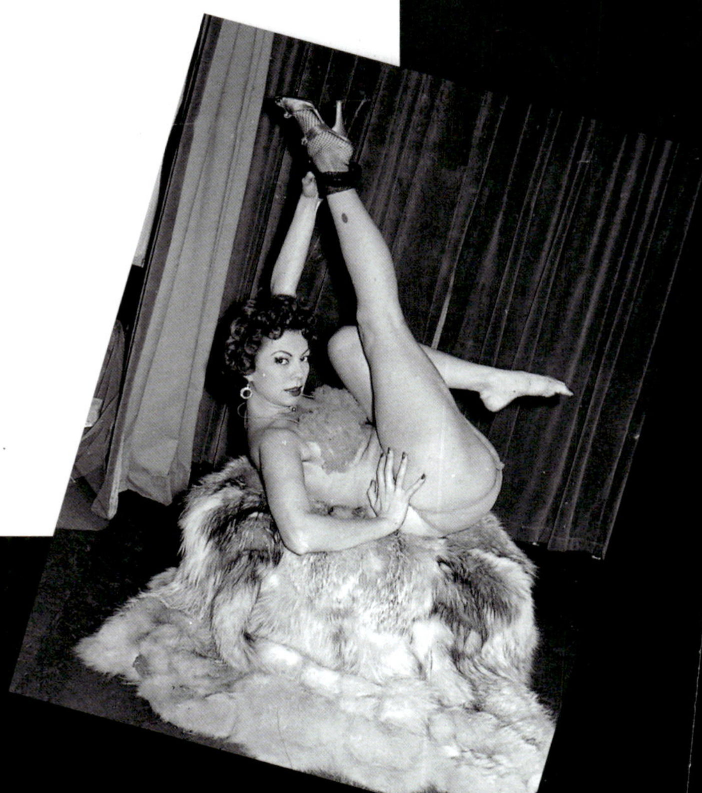

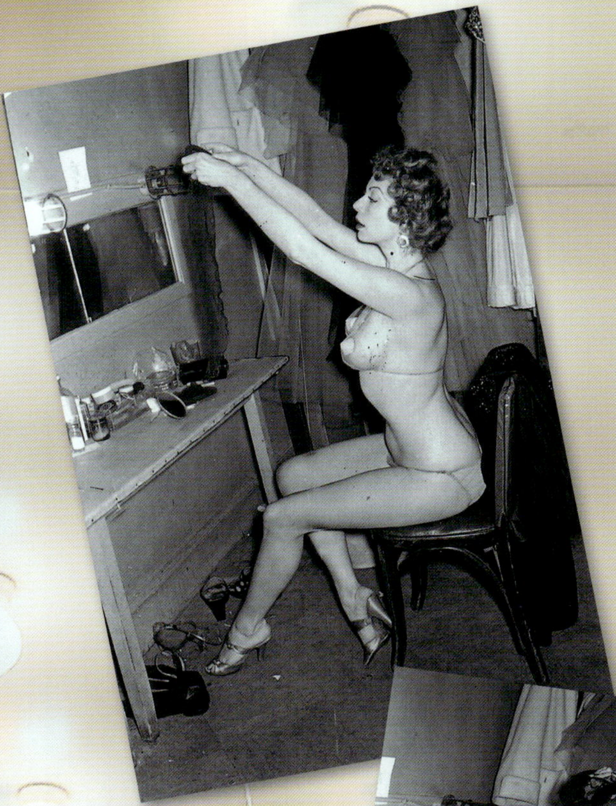

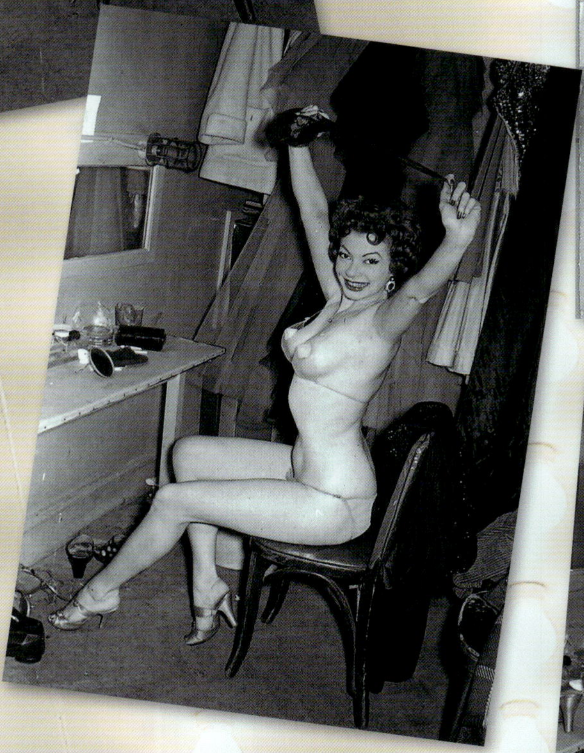

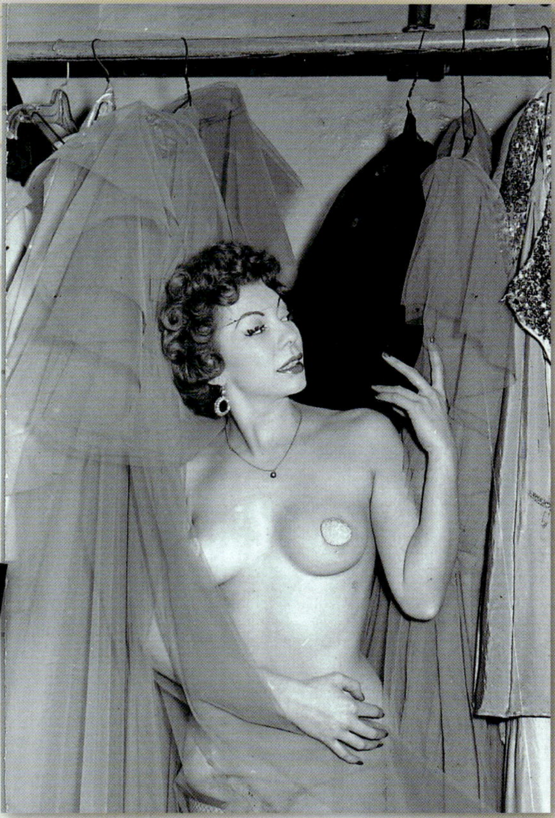

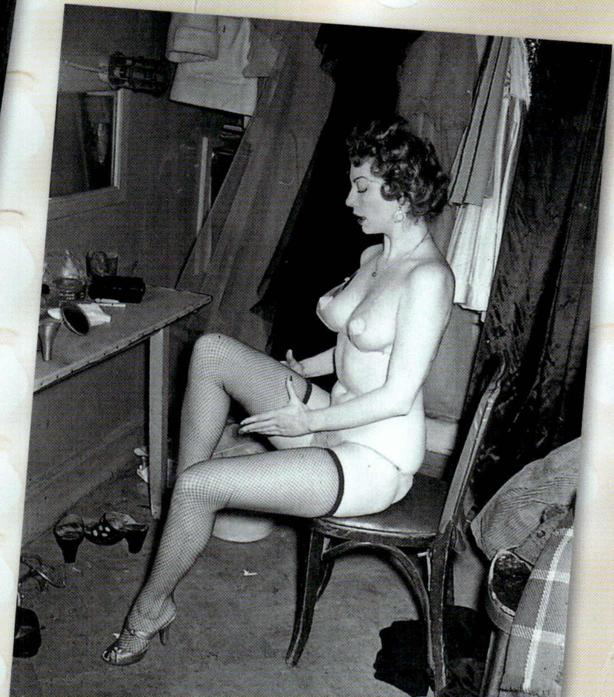

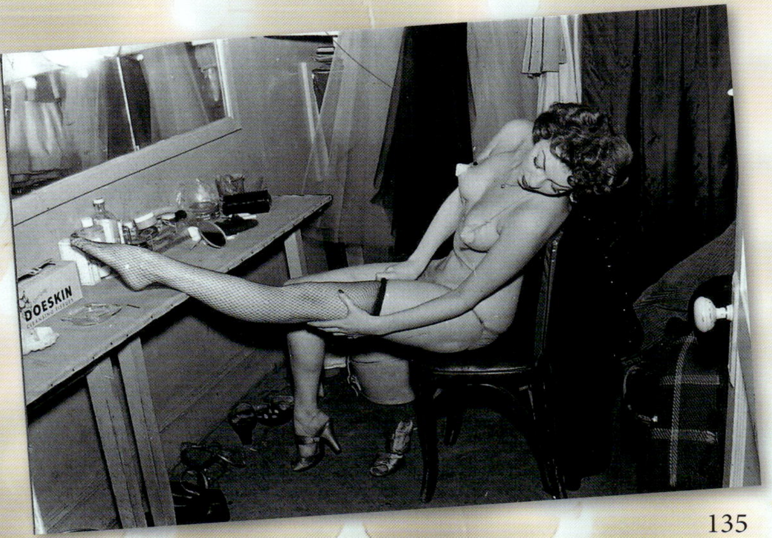
DOESKIN

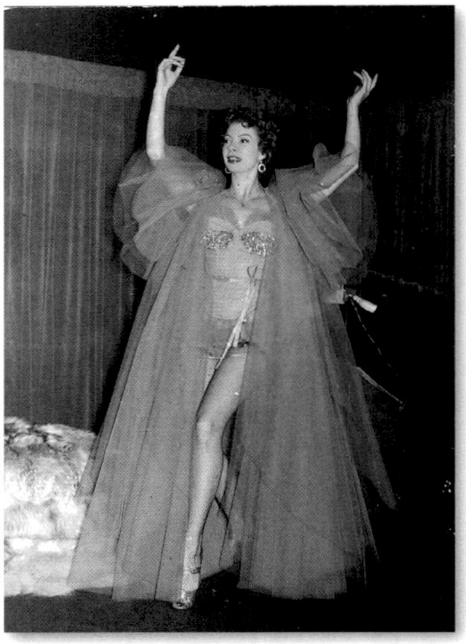
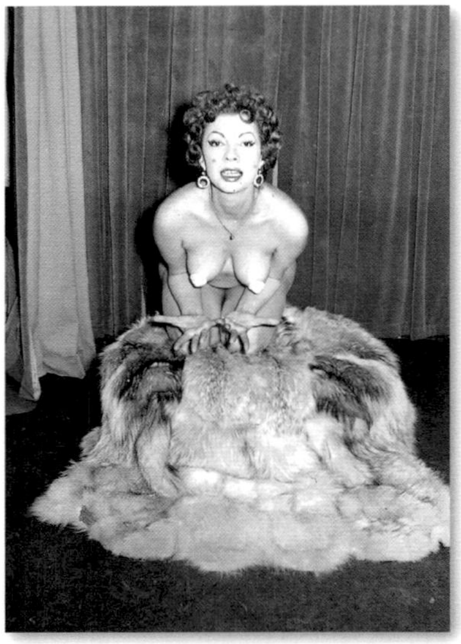
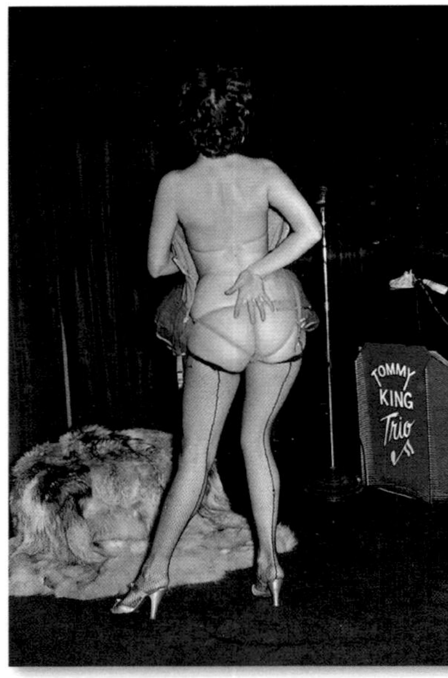
TOMMY
KING
Trio
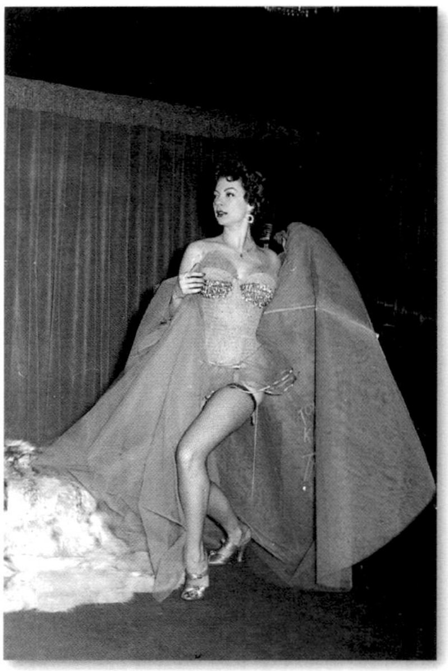
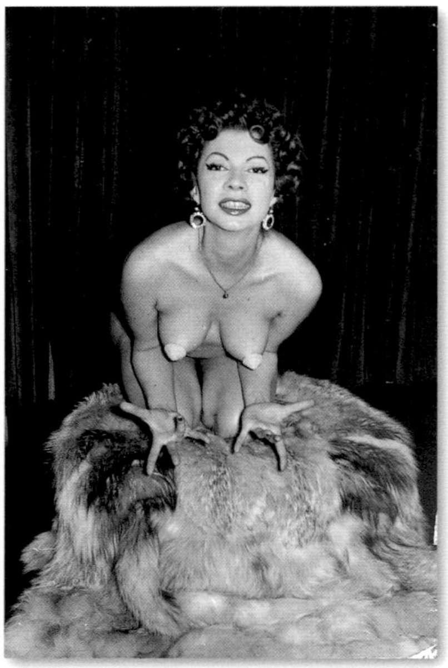
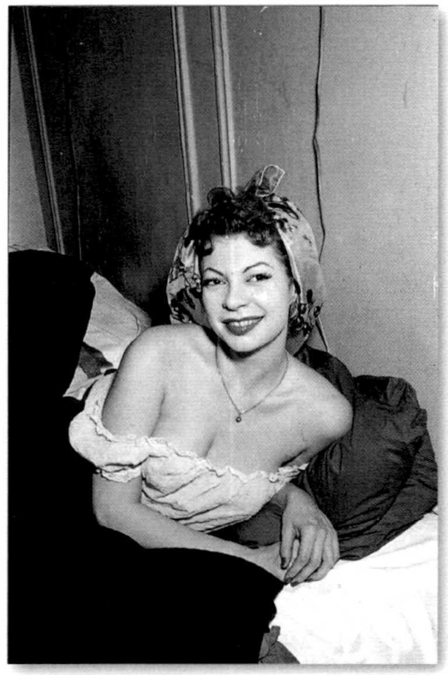
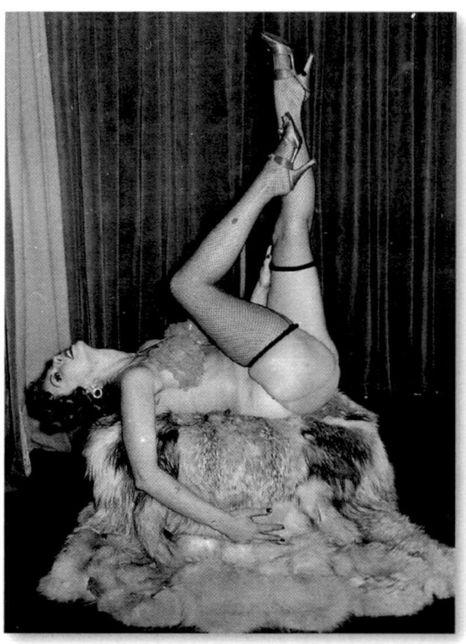
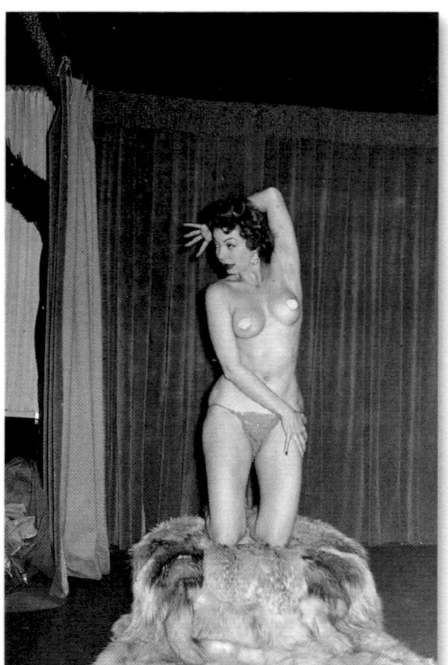
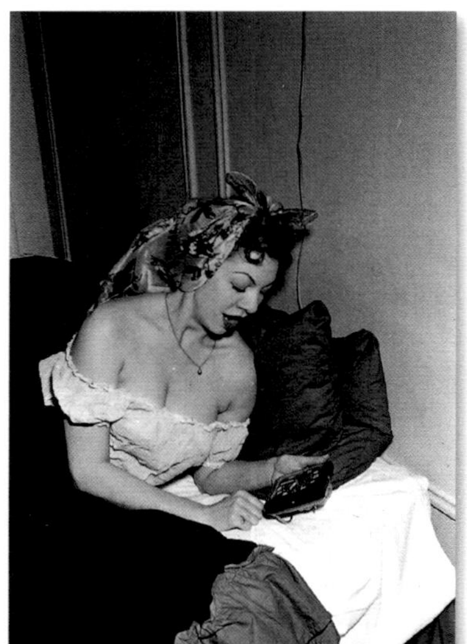

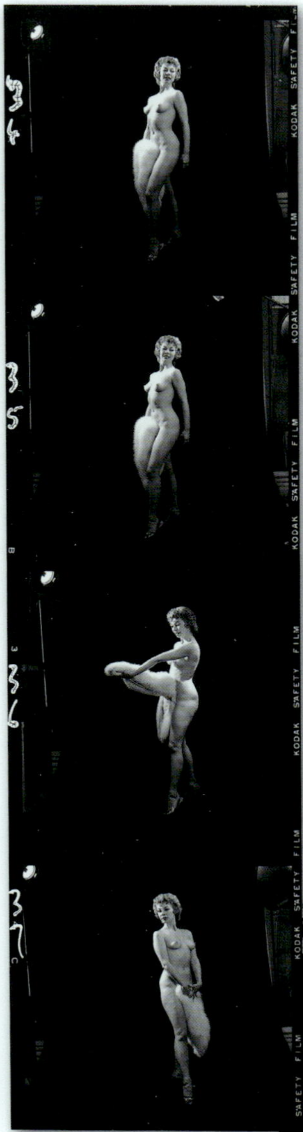

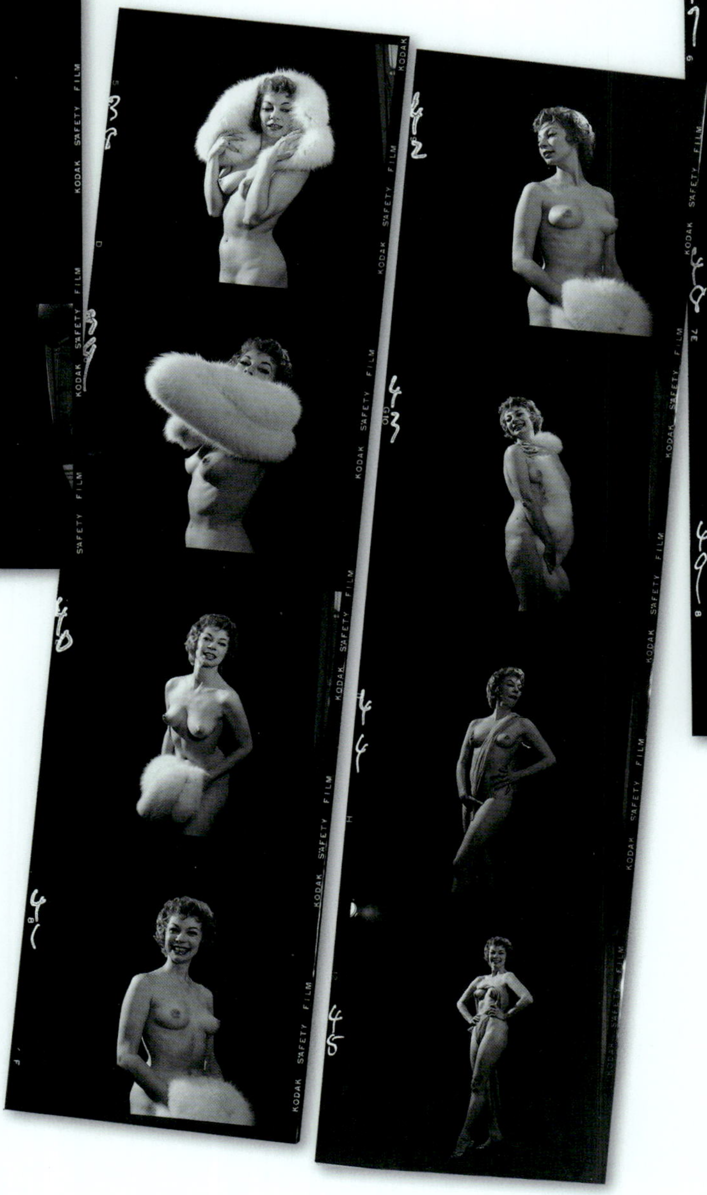

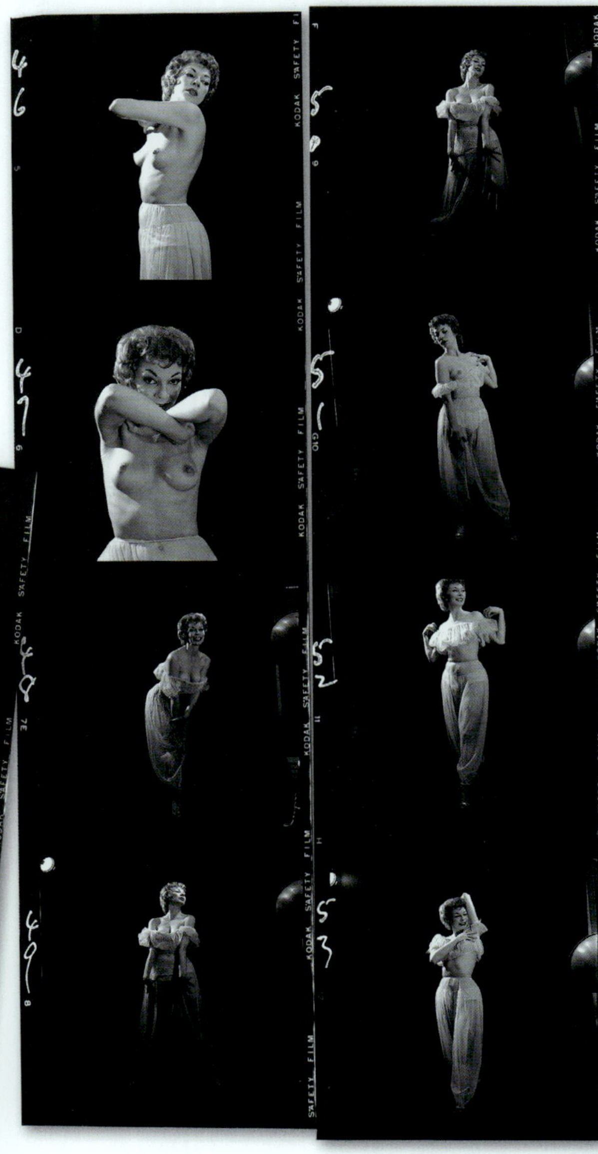

Rita Atlanta

RITA ATLANTA

She's 22-year-old Rita Atlanta who used to be prima ballerina at the Stadt Theatre Ballet in Vienna, her home town, then went on to night club performances in Geneva, Paris, Nice, Lugano, Rome, Brussels and later to North Africa and the Middle East.

She came to America as the wife of an air force colonel, turned to stripping, is now charming audiences on the burlesque circuit. At first, taking off her clothes in front of an audience made her nervous, but the thought of all that extra money acted as a tranquillizer and she got over her nervousness.

Rita has worked in this country for 18 months and is a coming star. She has ability and personality as anyone can plainly see. Characteristic expression: "A gentleman is a wolf with patience...it is better that way."

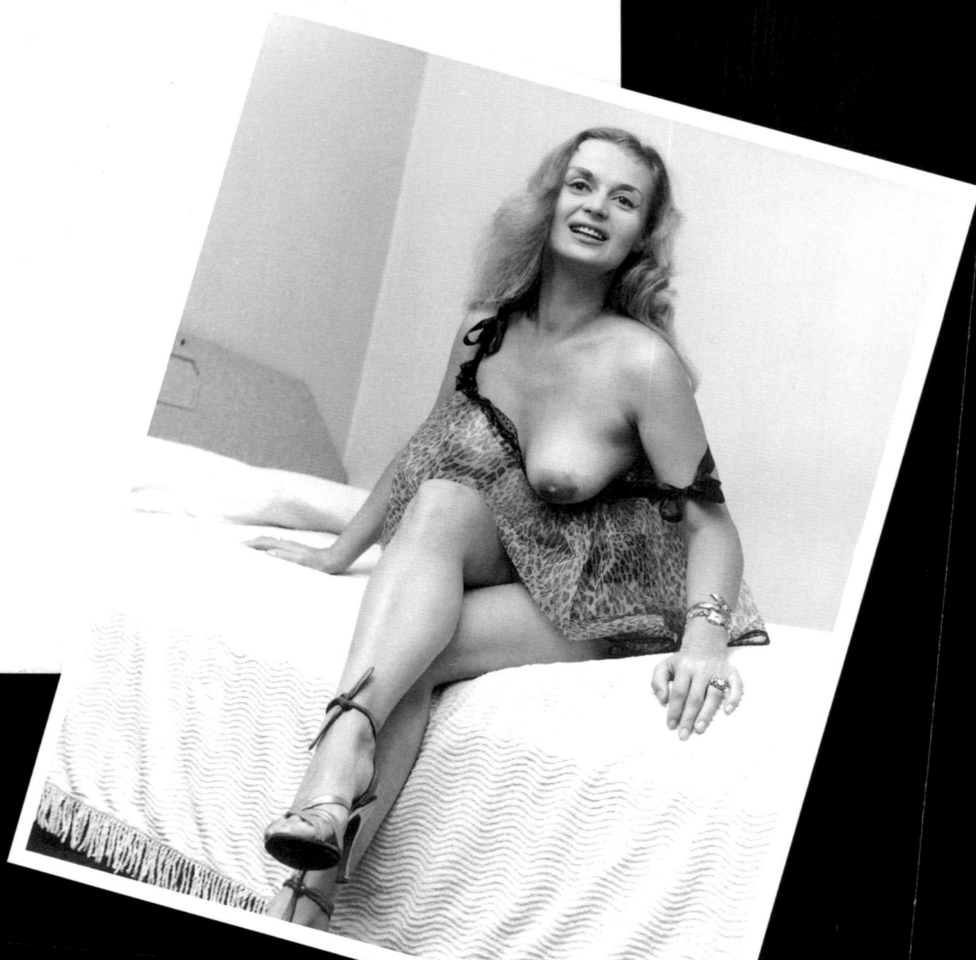

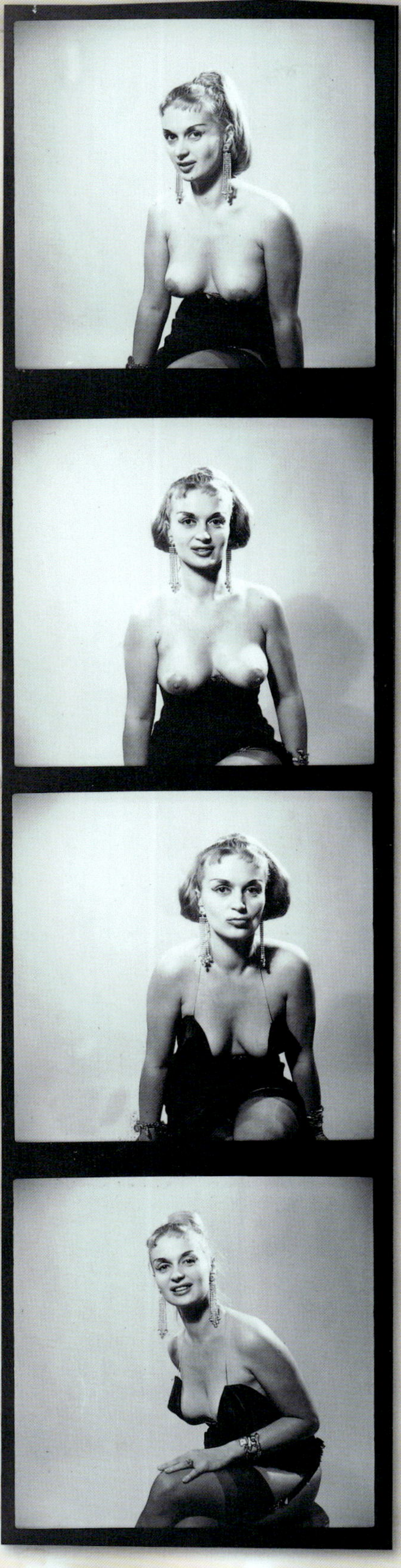

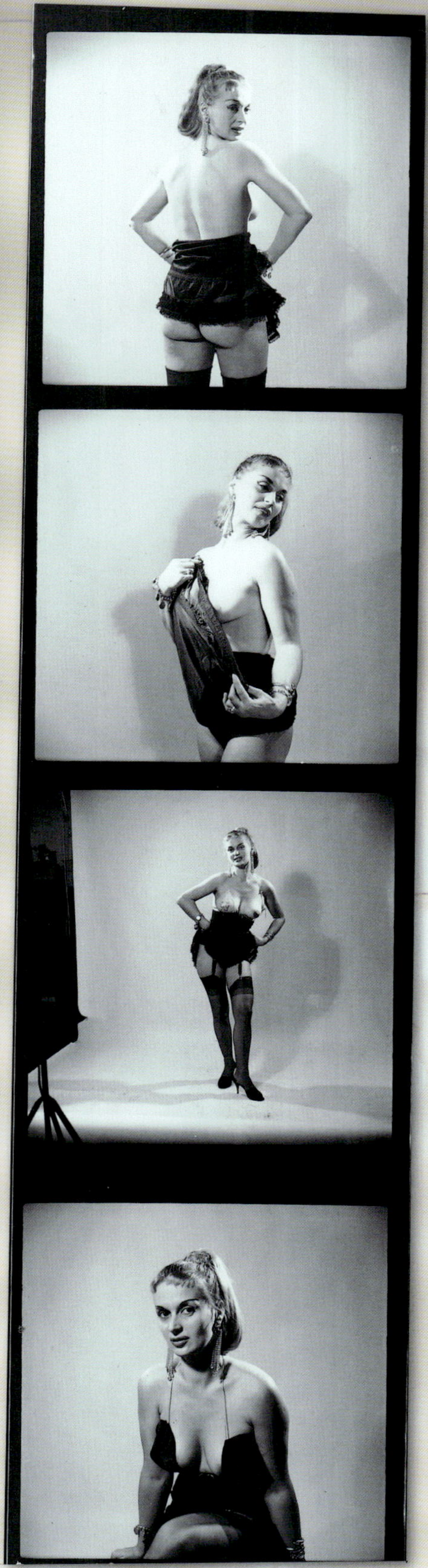

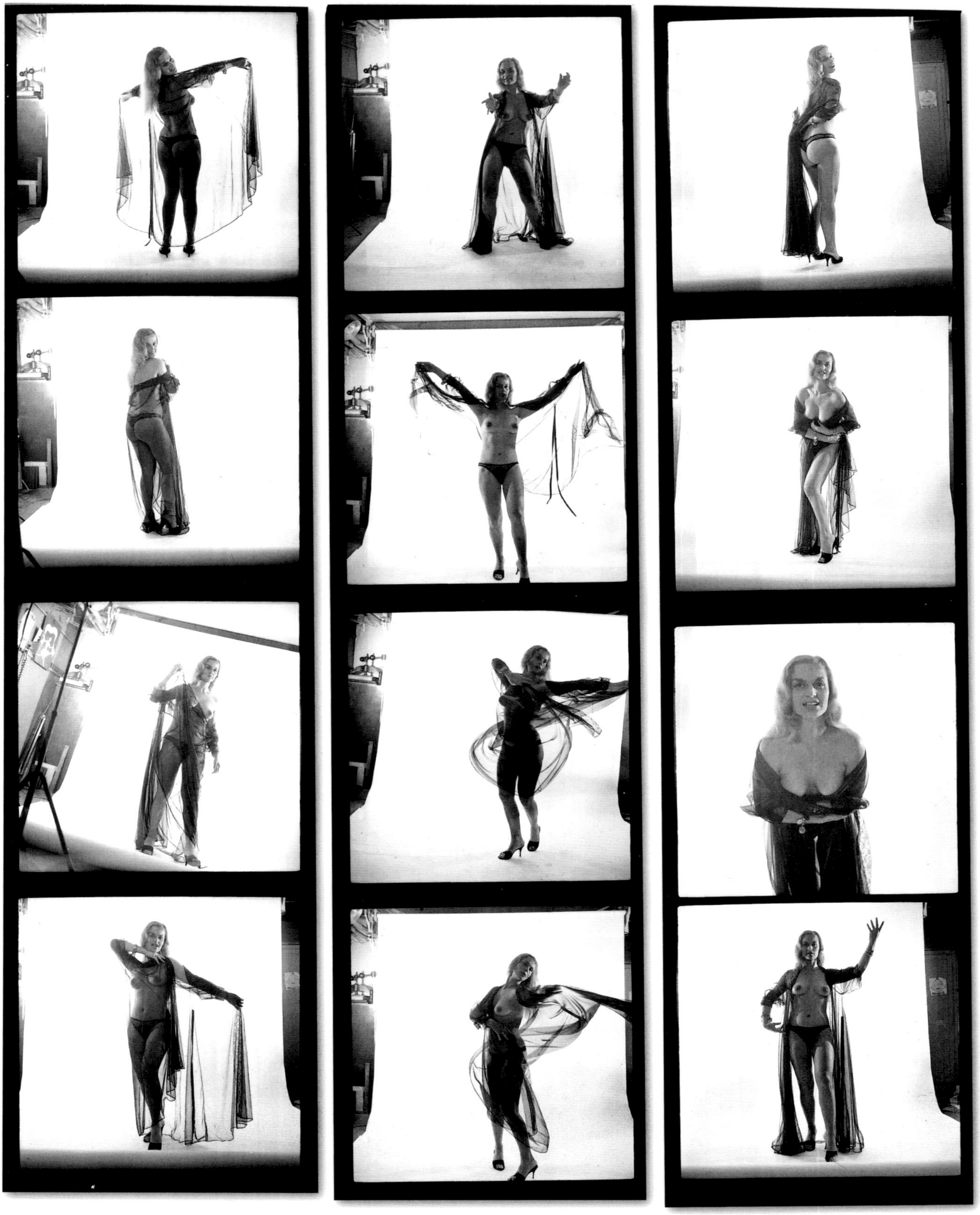

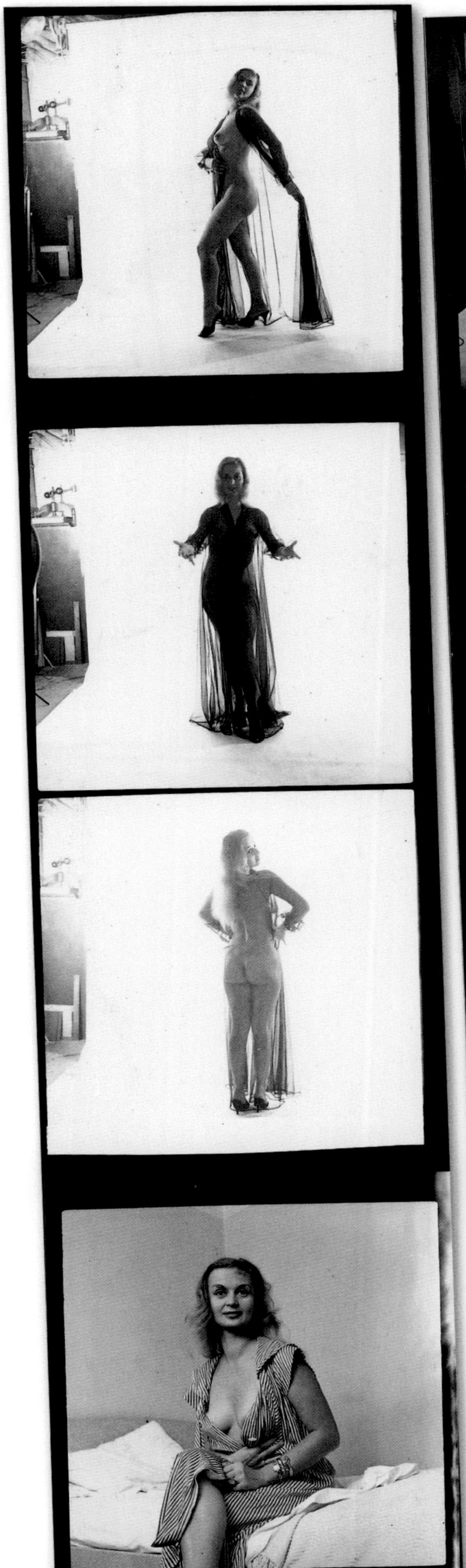

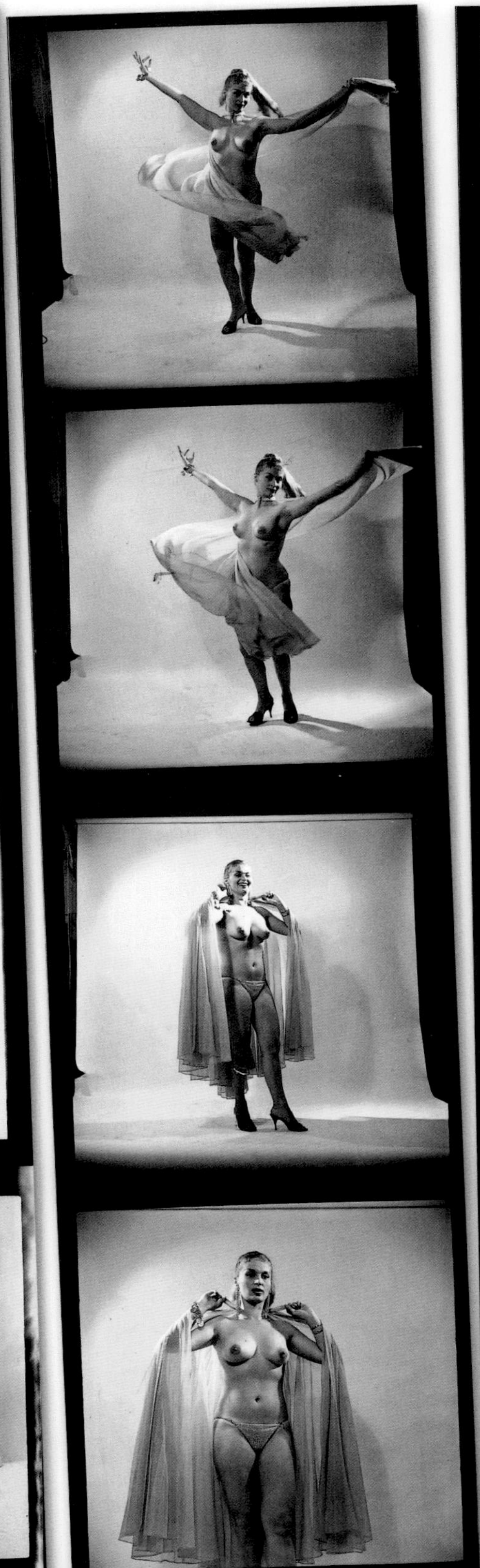

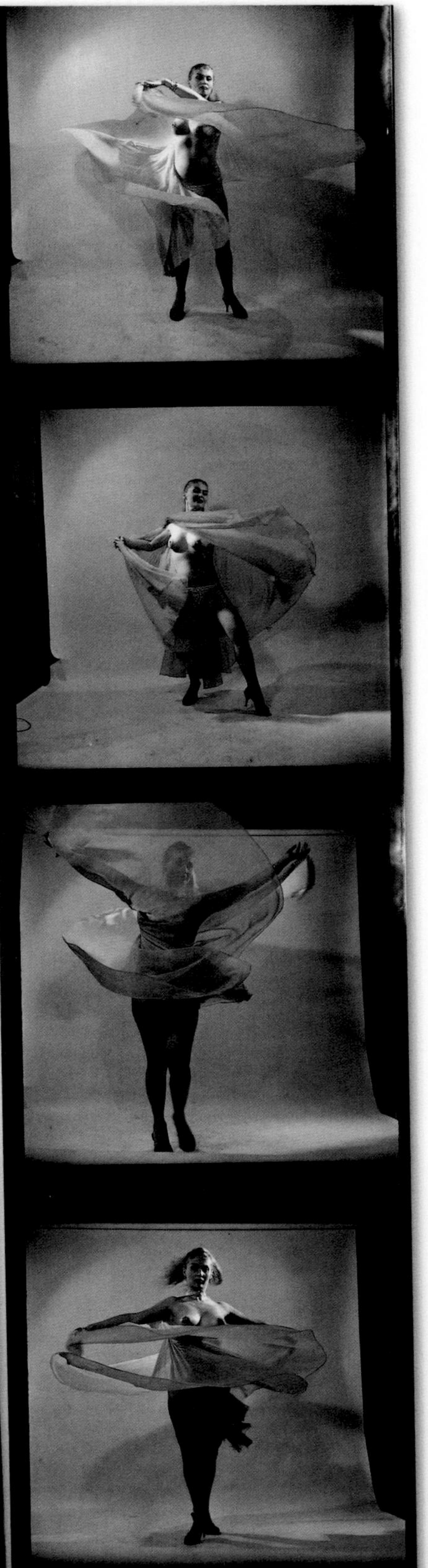

Rita Grable

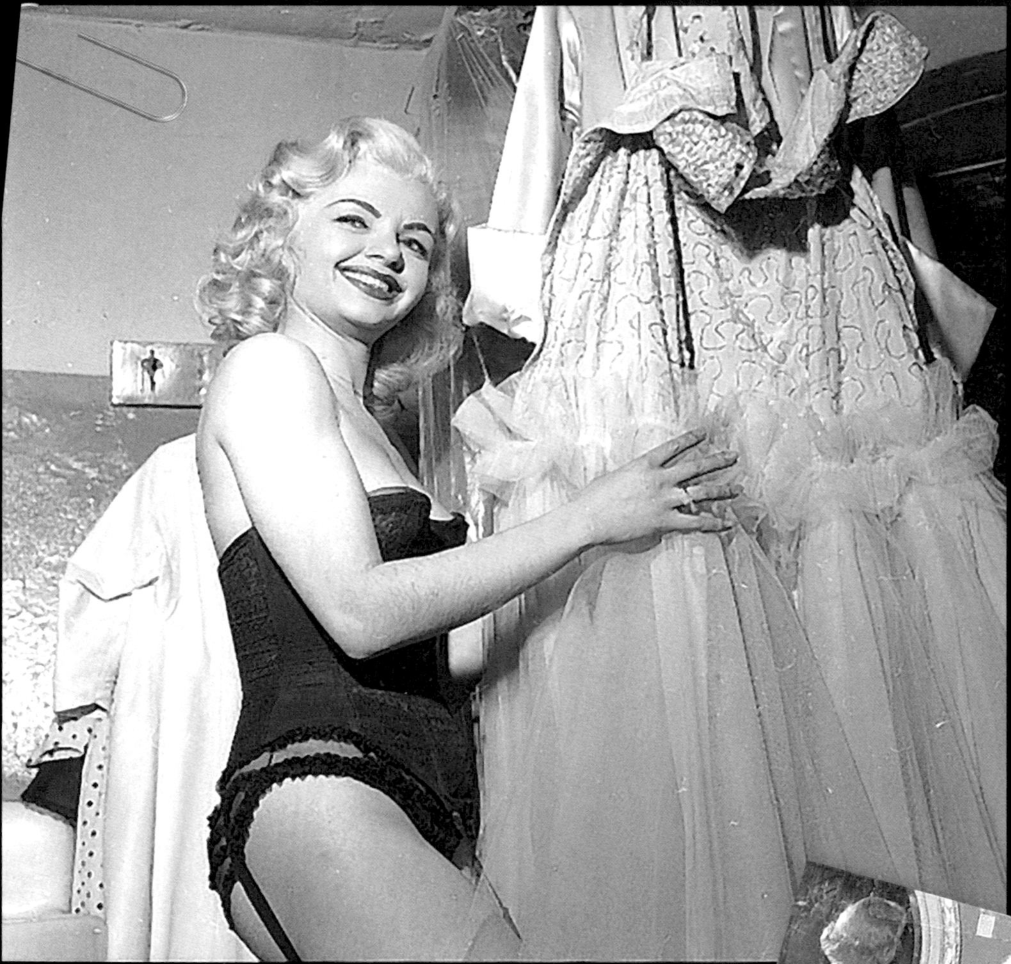

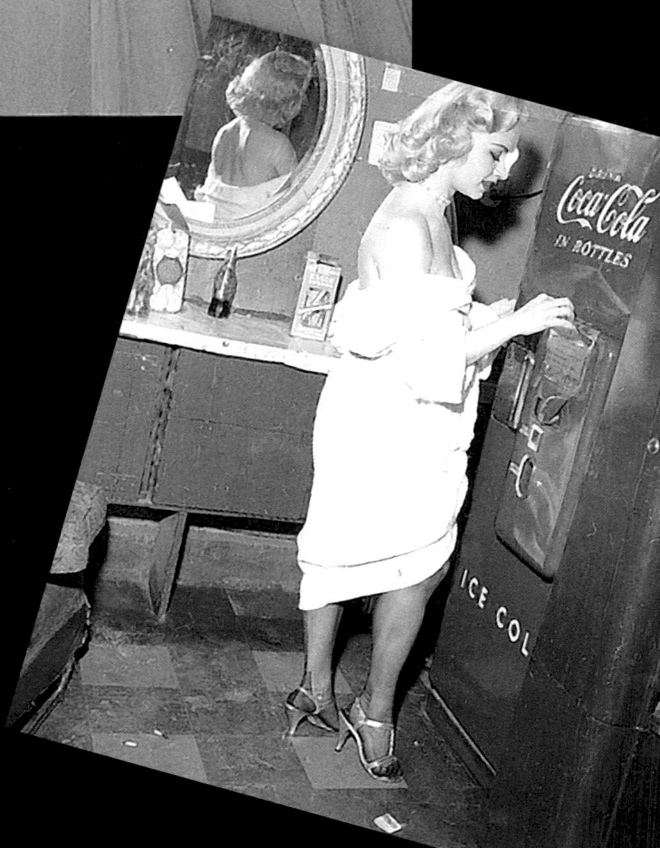

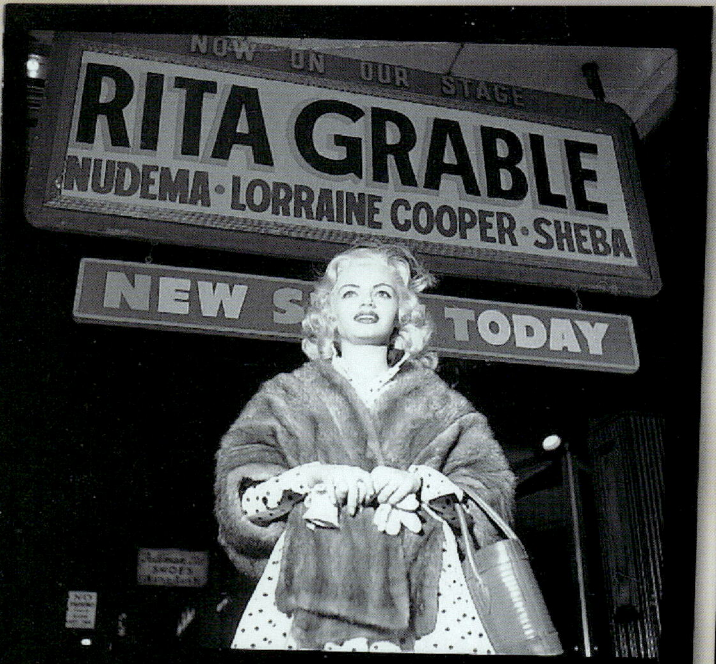
NOW ON OUR STAGE
RITA GRABLE
NUDEMA · LORRAINE COOPER · SHEBA
NEW S TODAY

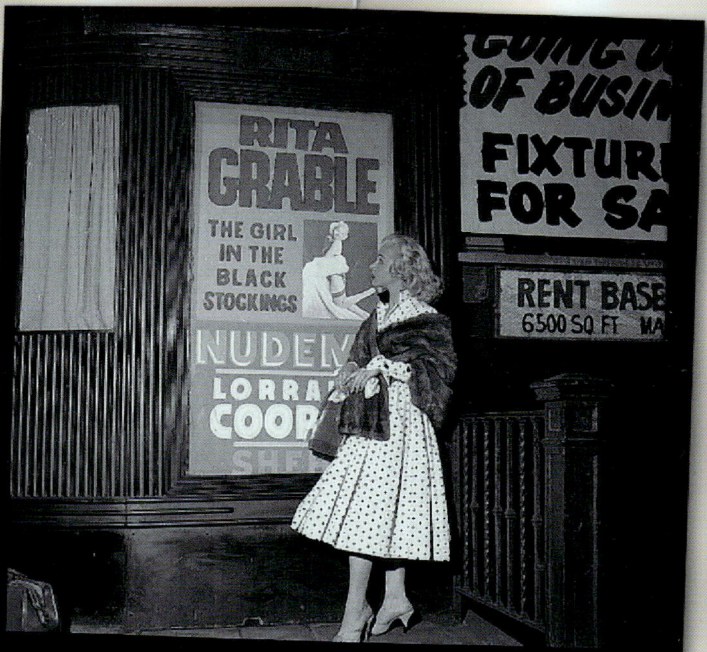
RITA GRABLE
THE GIRL IN THE BLACK STOCKINGS
NUDEM
LORRA
COOP
OF BUSIN
FIXTUR
FOR SA
RENT BASE
6500 SQ FT

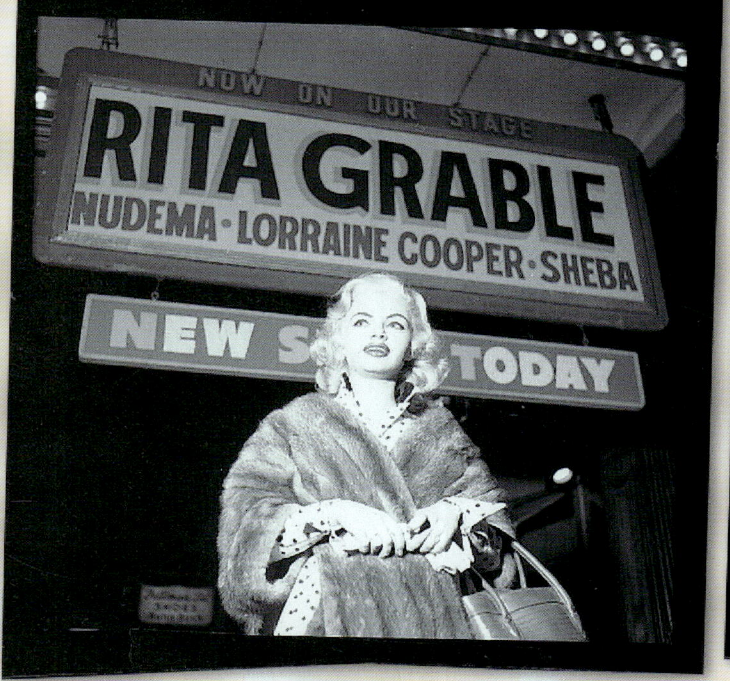
NOW ON OUR STAGE
RITA GRABLE
NUDEMA · LORRAINE COOPER · SHEBA
NEW S TODAY

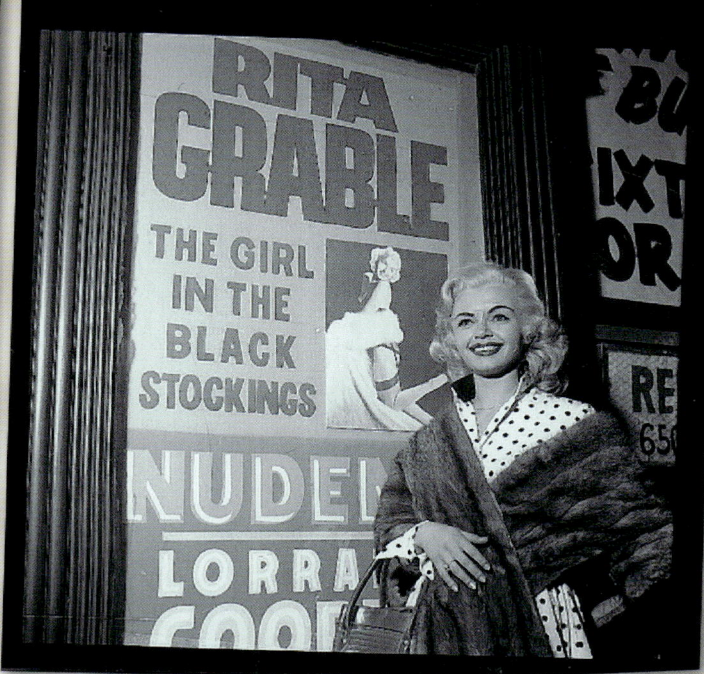
RITA GRABLE
THE GIRL IN THE BLACK STOCKINGS
NUDE
LORRA

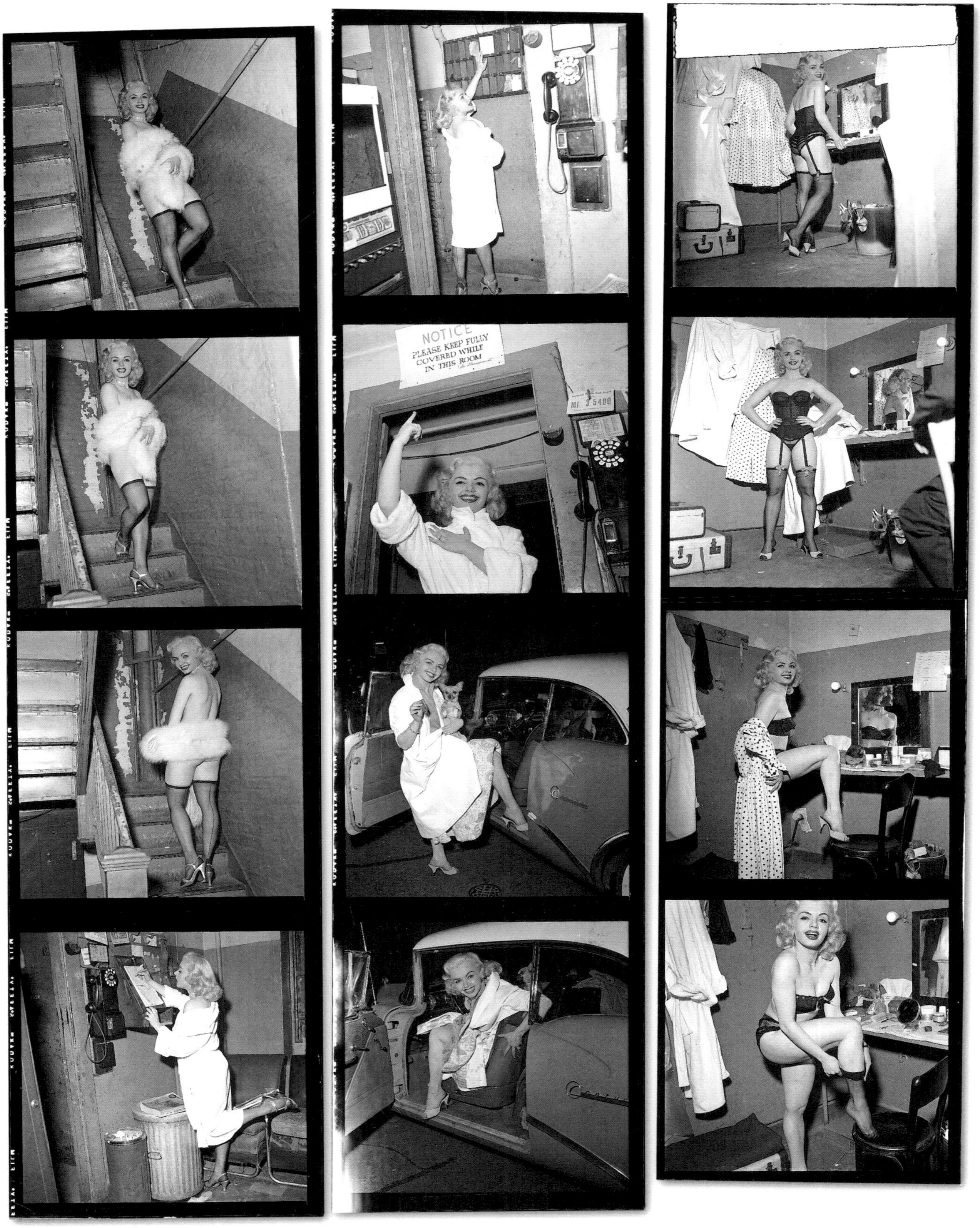
NOTICE
PLEASE KEEP FULLY
COVERED WHILE
IN THIS ROOM
MI. 3-5400

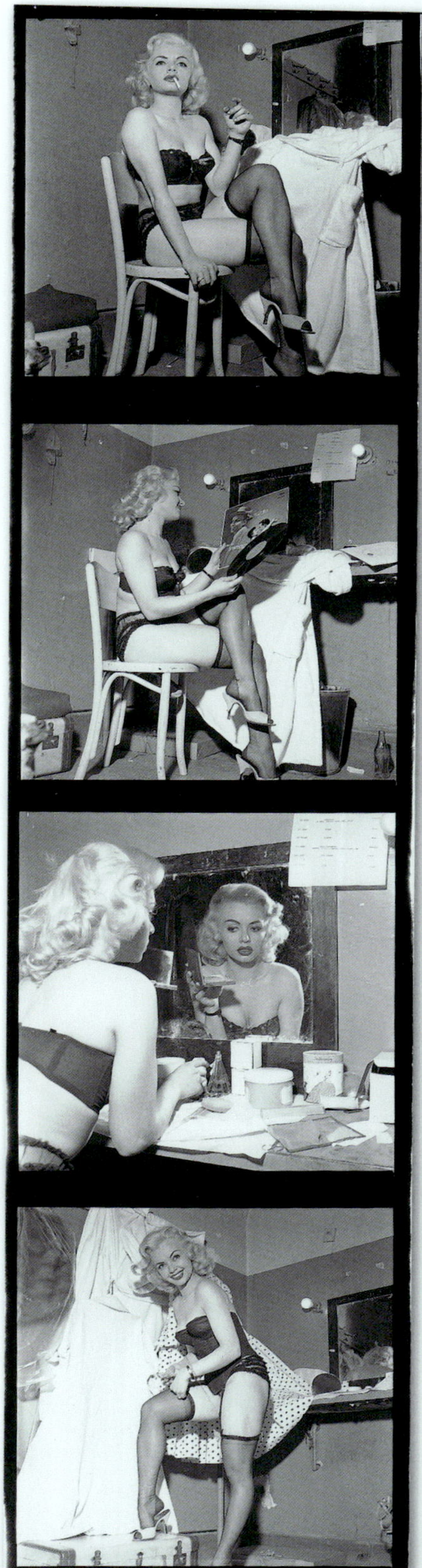

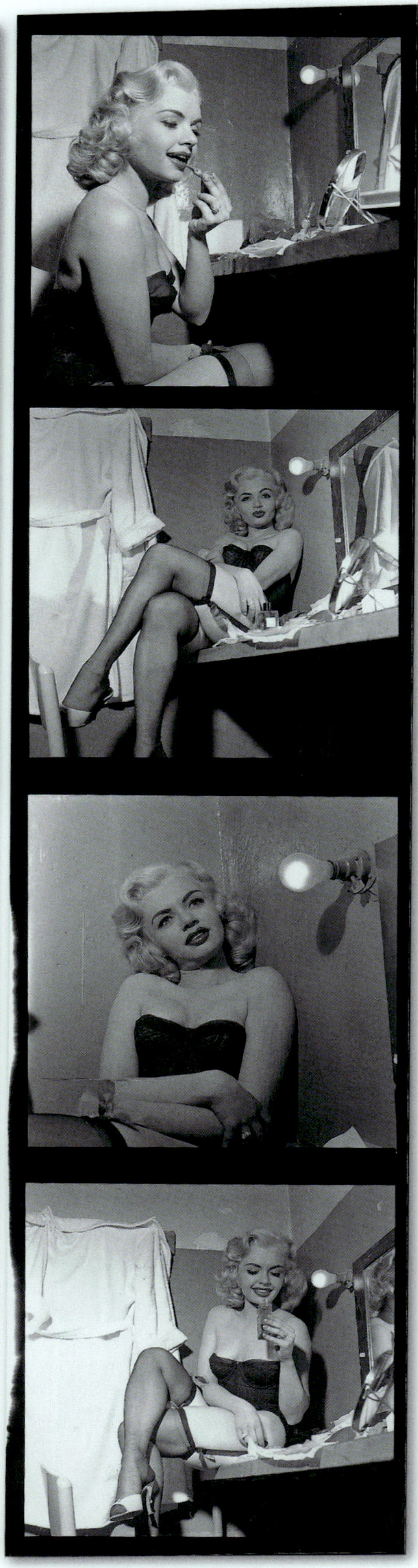

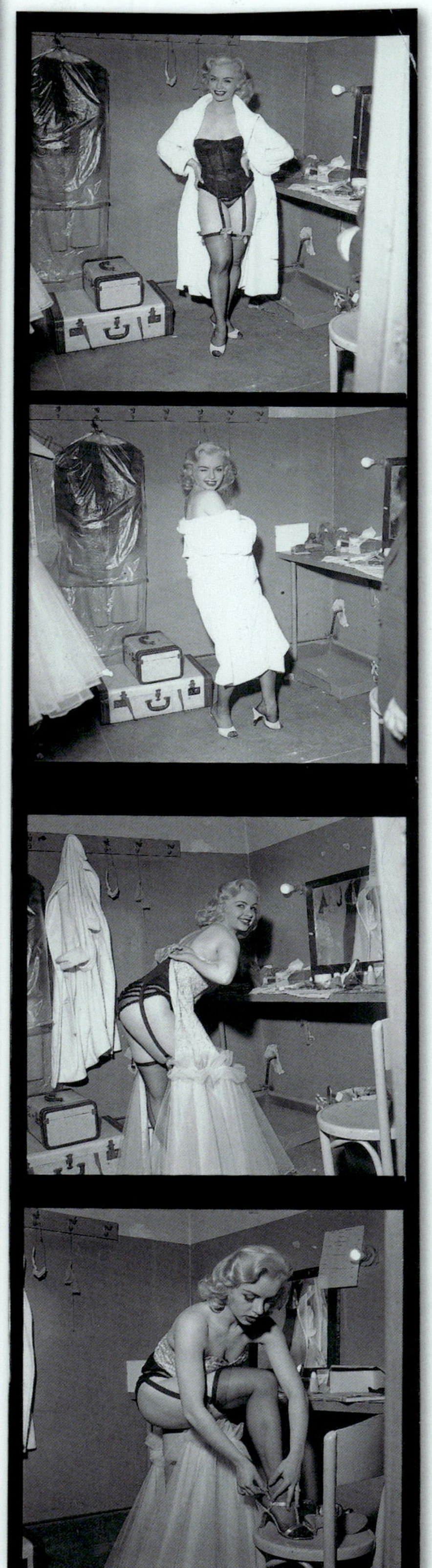

Sharon Knight

SHARON KNIGHT

When scintillating Sharon Knaght made up her mind to
go into the entertainment world, she decided to play it real
smart. Instead of starting right out as a showgirl or chorus
pony
pmy-which she could easily have done without training-she would
study, study and study, until she had a good background in
dancing. And when she finished her training she wouldn't take the
first job that came along. She would wait until she had evoalved
a really different routine.

And that's exactly what bright Miss Knight did. For
three years she studied extensively ballet, along with tap and
acrobatic dancing. At the completion of her studies she worked up
a special dance routine with a top choreographer. This unusual
act so impressed the manager of the El Rancho at Las Vegas that
he signed her up immediately-which is pretty good scoring, con-
sidering it was her first big tryout for a job.

Sharon definitely does not believe in the bump and grind
school of dancing. She takes her clothes off on stage, but the
way she does it is pretty impressive. In her main act she starts
off as a tramp- asleep on a park bench enticingly dressed in rags
and tatters. As she sleeps she dreams of being a rich young woman,
elegantly gowned in furs, silks and jewels-which she dons in a sleep
sequence. At the end she awakes to find she's still a tramp, back
in her rags and tatters. The whole thing is most intriguingly done-
especially when she dances on a large fan, which blows off her clothes.
Her extensive training in the dance isn't wasted here. All of

Sharon's exotic dances are built around a central story theme-each
quite different from the other. In one she might use ballet-such as
The Tramp. In another she might use acrobatics.

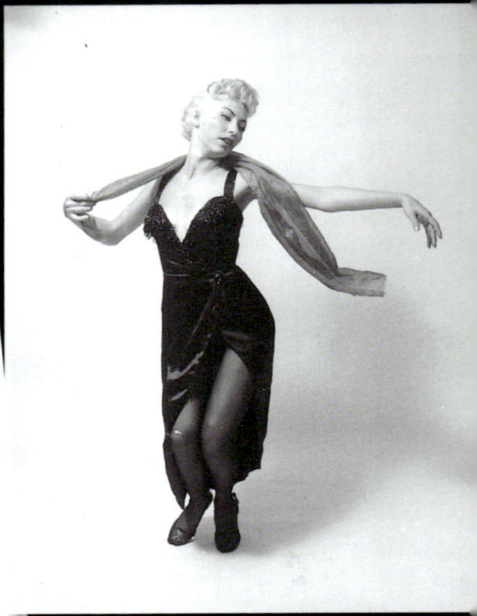

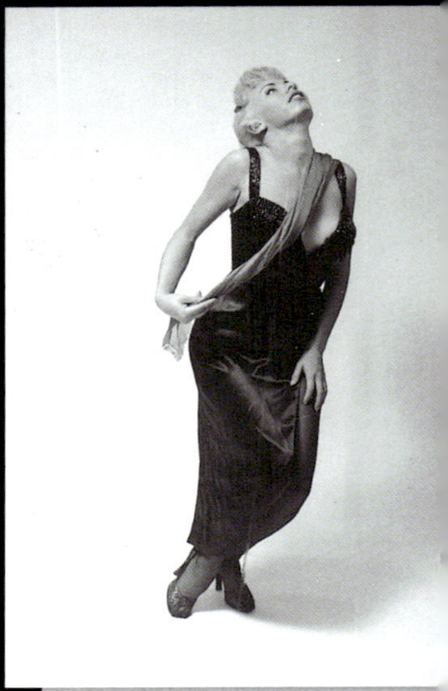

Hard-working Sh
her dancing and it
undrape themselves
sure to stay a long

-Sharon's 24 years o
modelling career. She
calls Washington, D.C.
- she's 5'5" tall, meas
-Sharon, a home girl at
-she has unusual green e

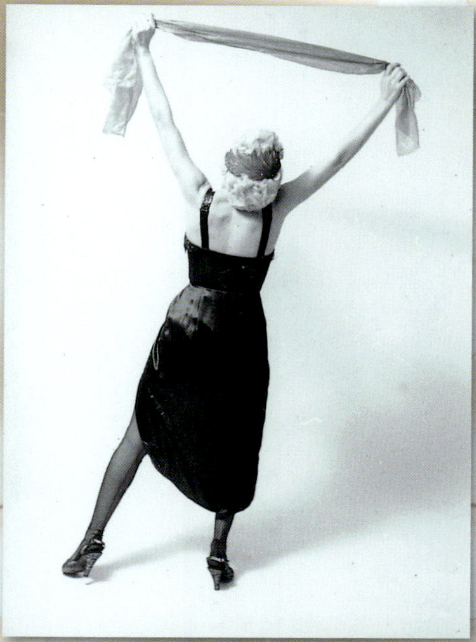

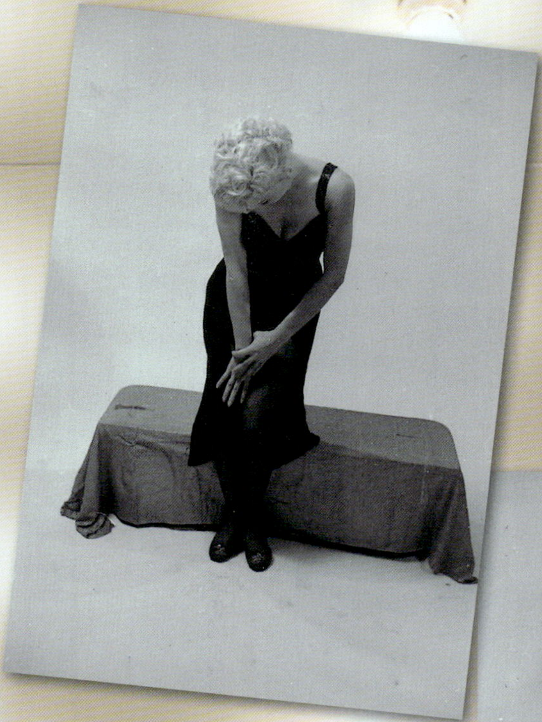

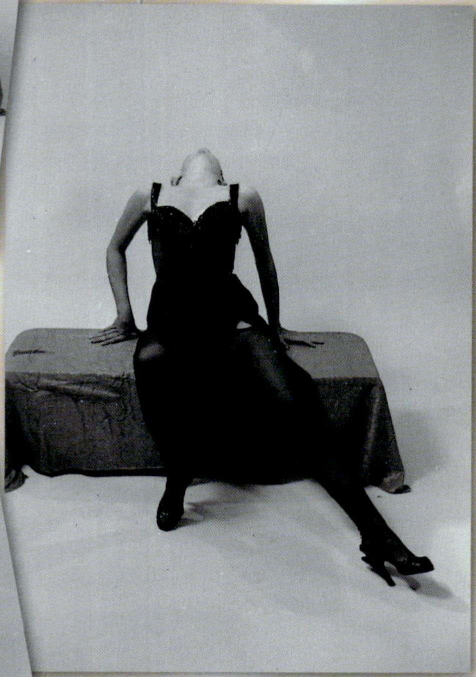

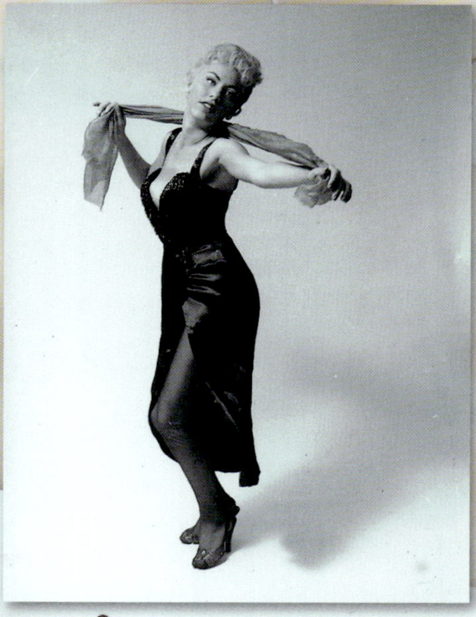

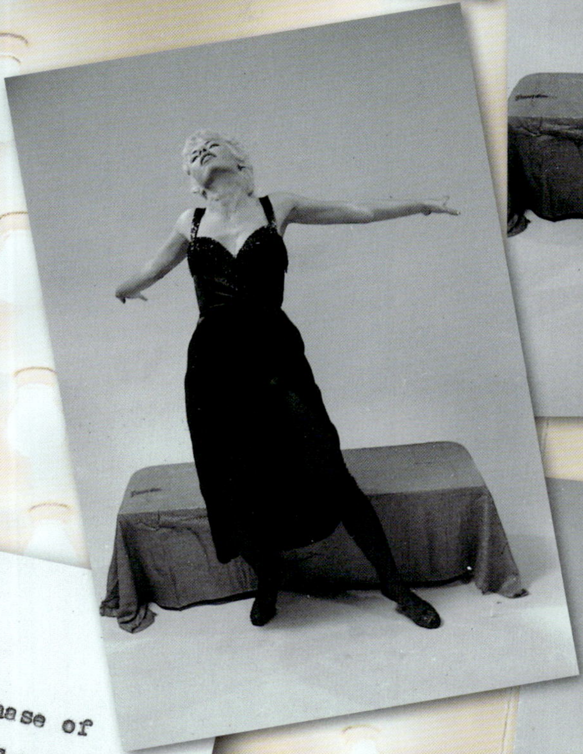

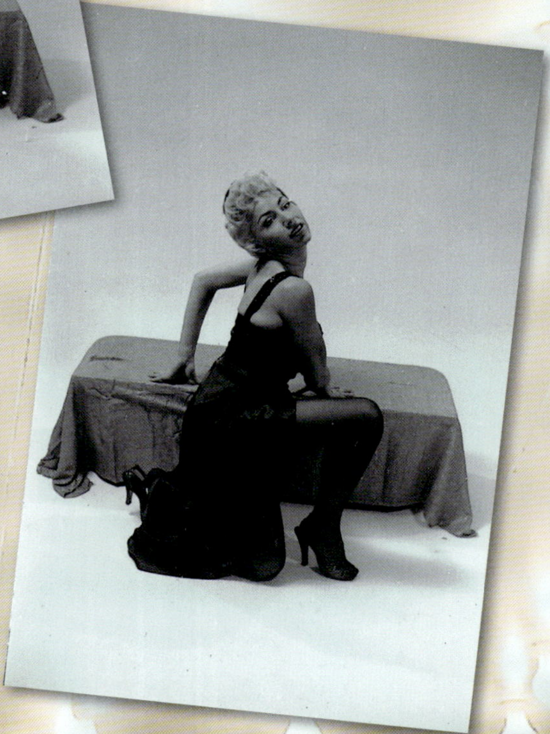

2

s meticulous attention to every phase of
doubtedly continue to pay off. Girls who
tage come and go, but talented Sharon is

in Texas, came to show business via a
ographic modelling in Washington (she
e) New York, Chicago, Los Angeles.
34-35½.

scorns nightclubs once her act is over.

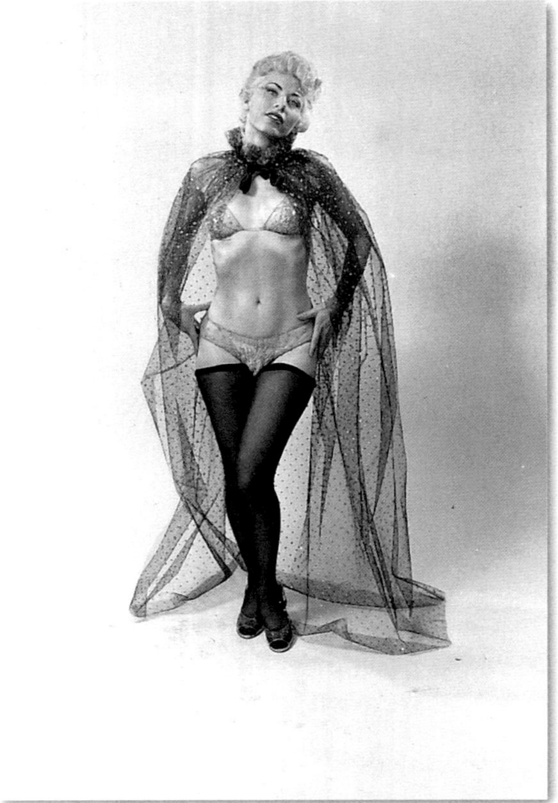

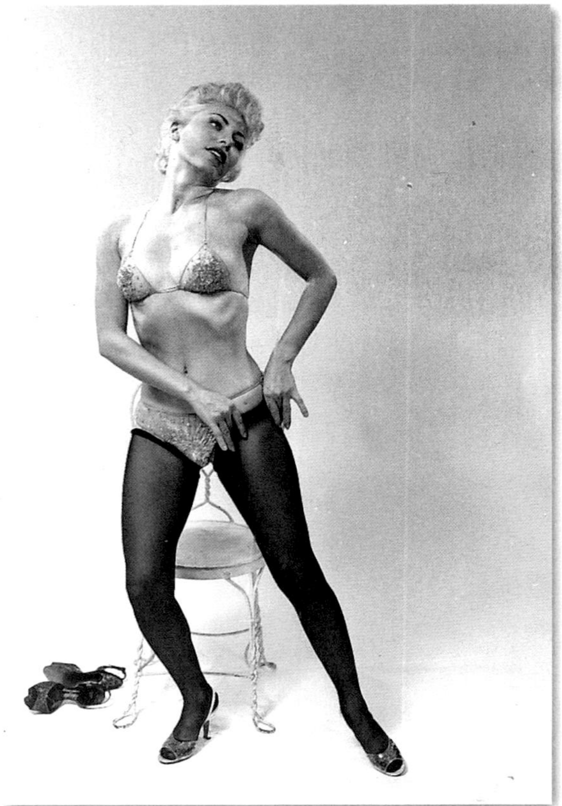

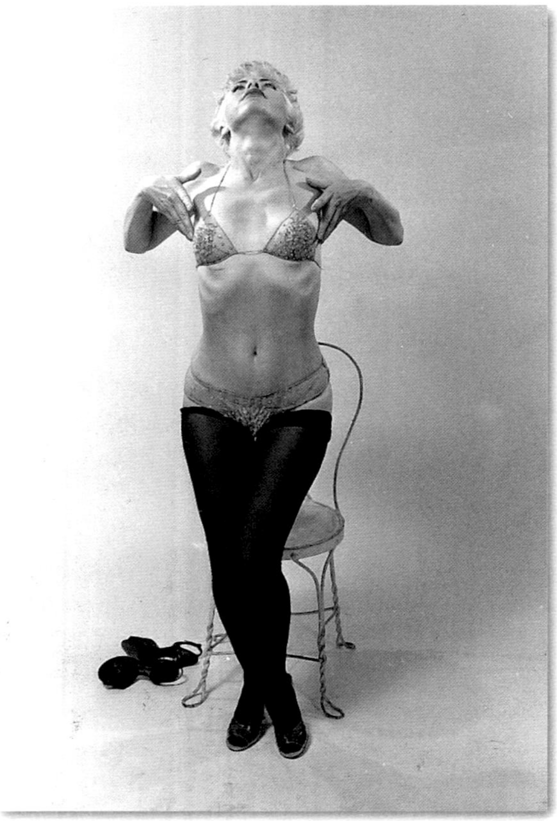

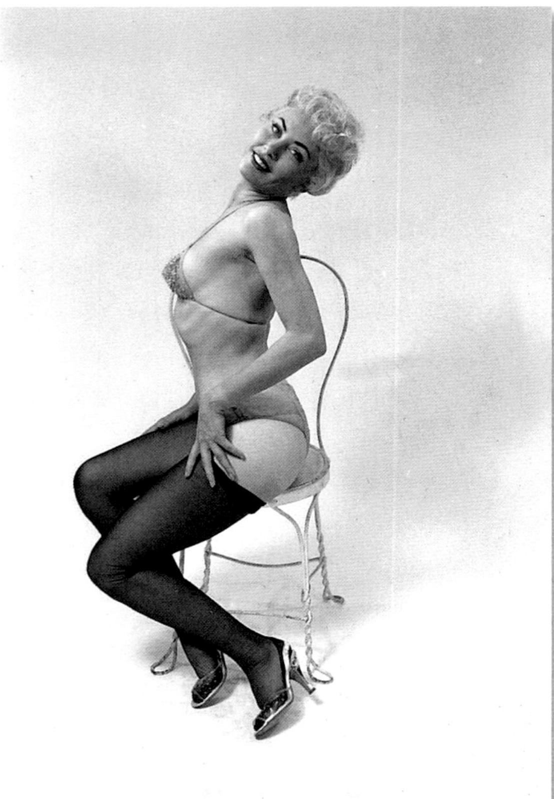

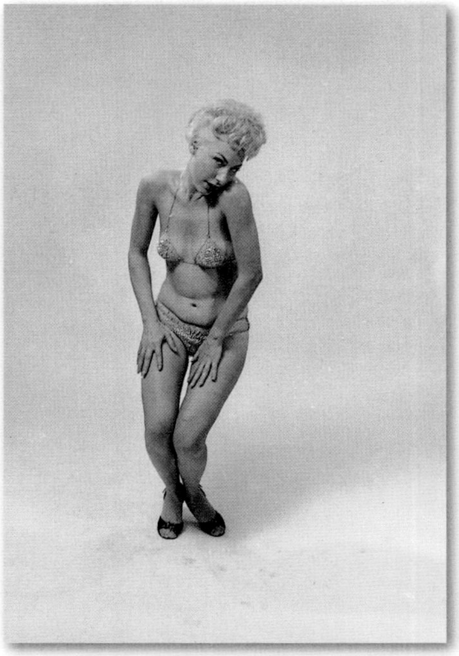
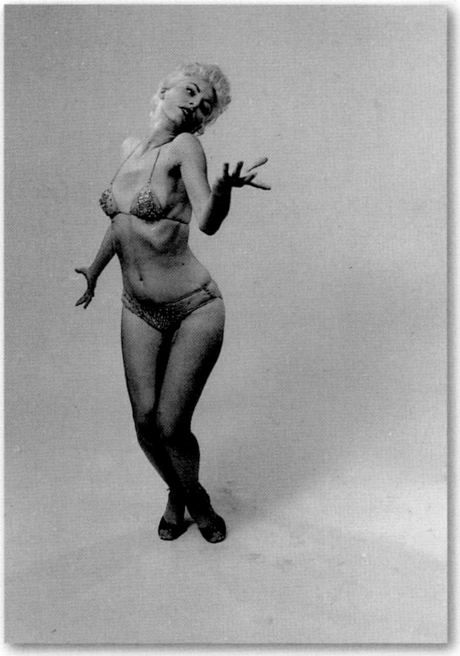
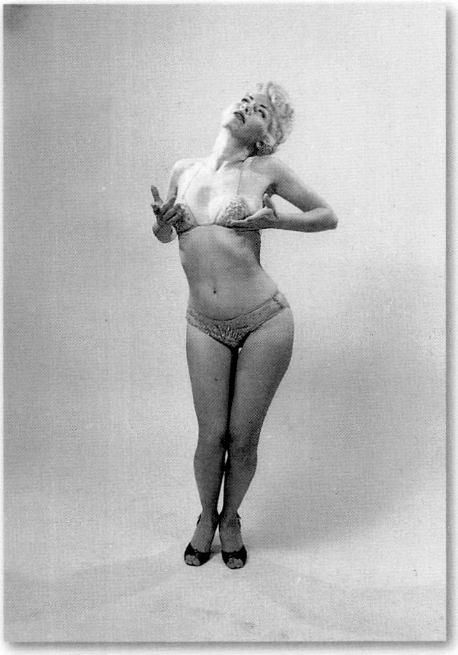
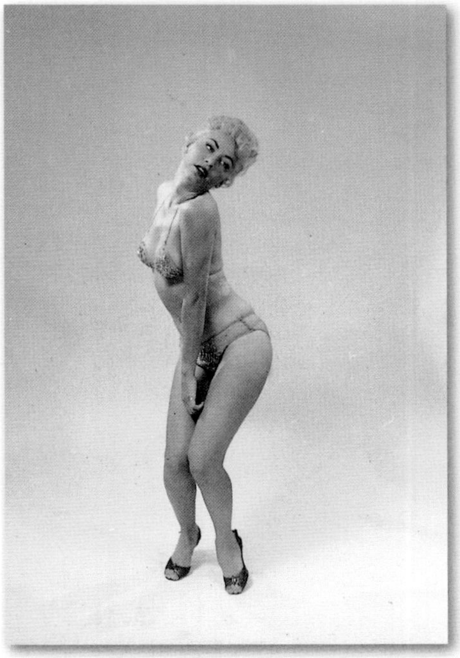
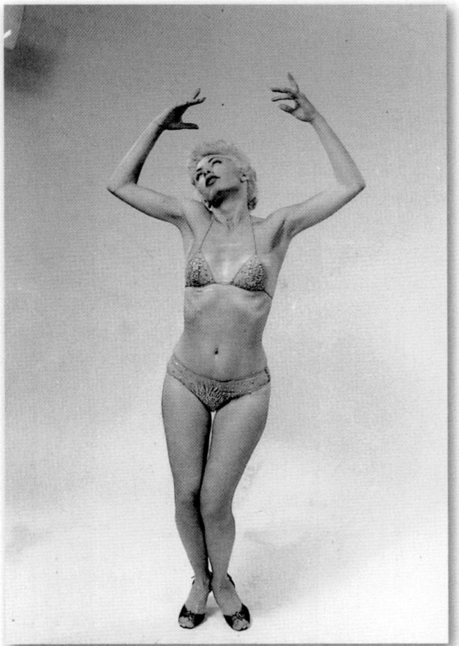
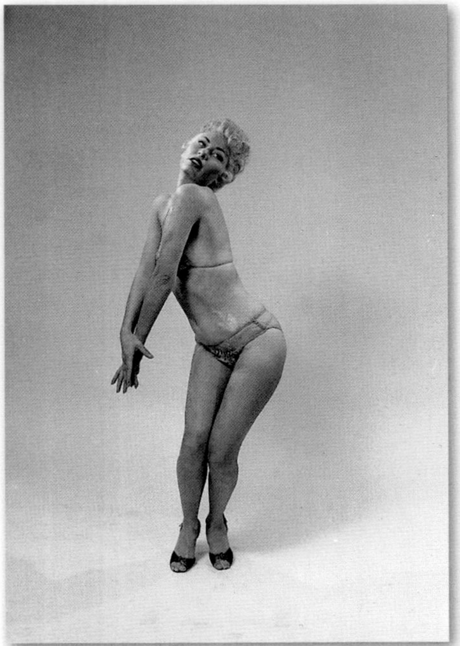

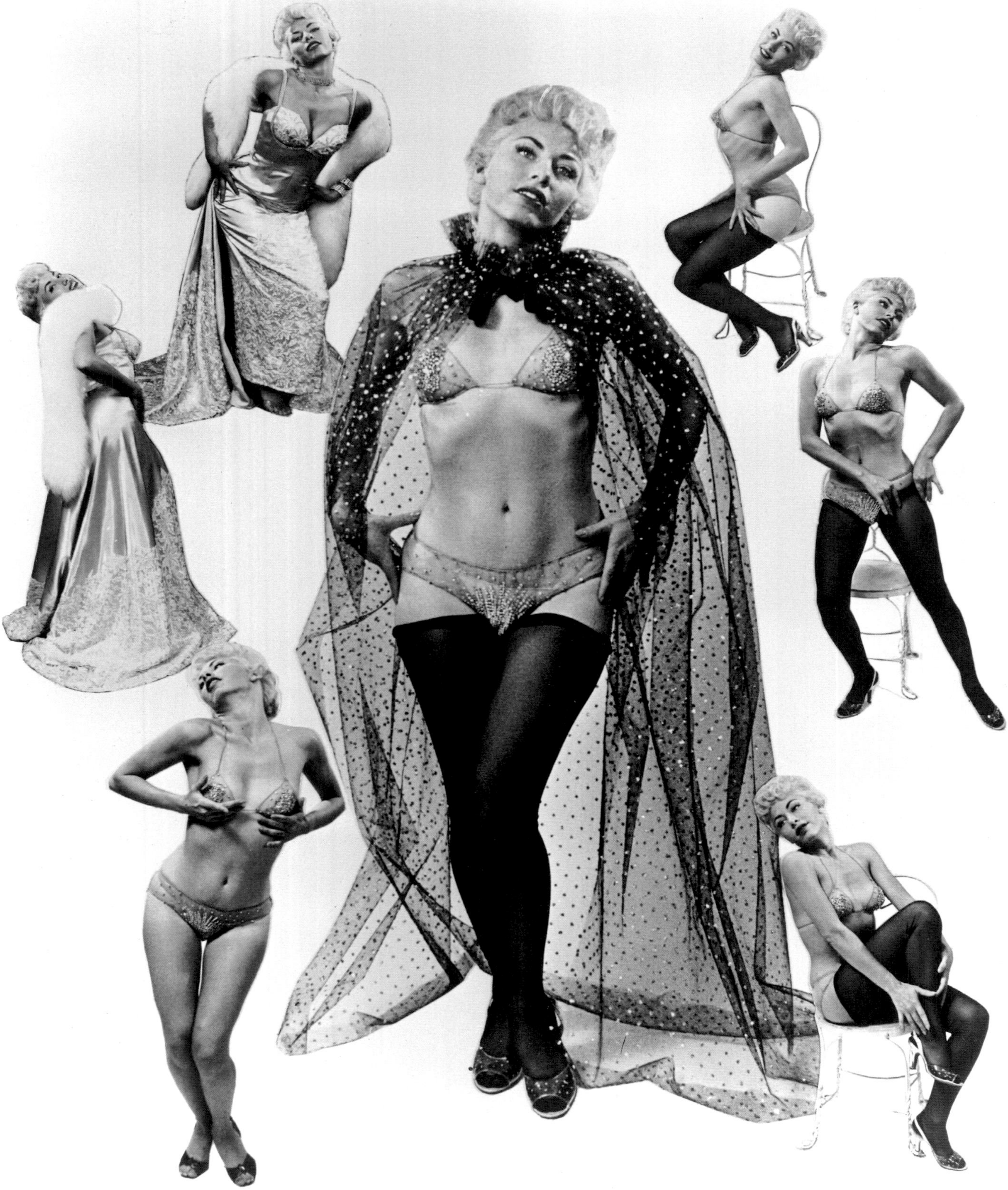

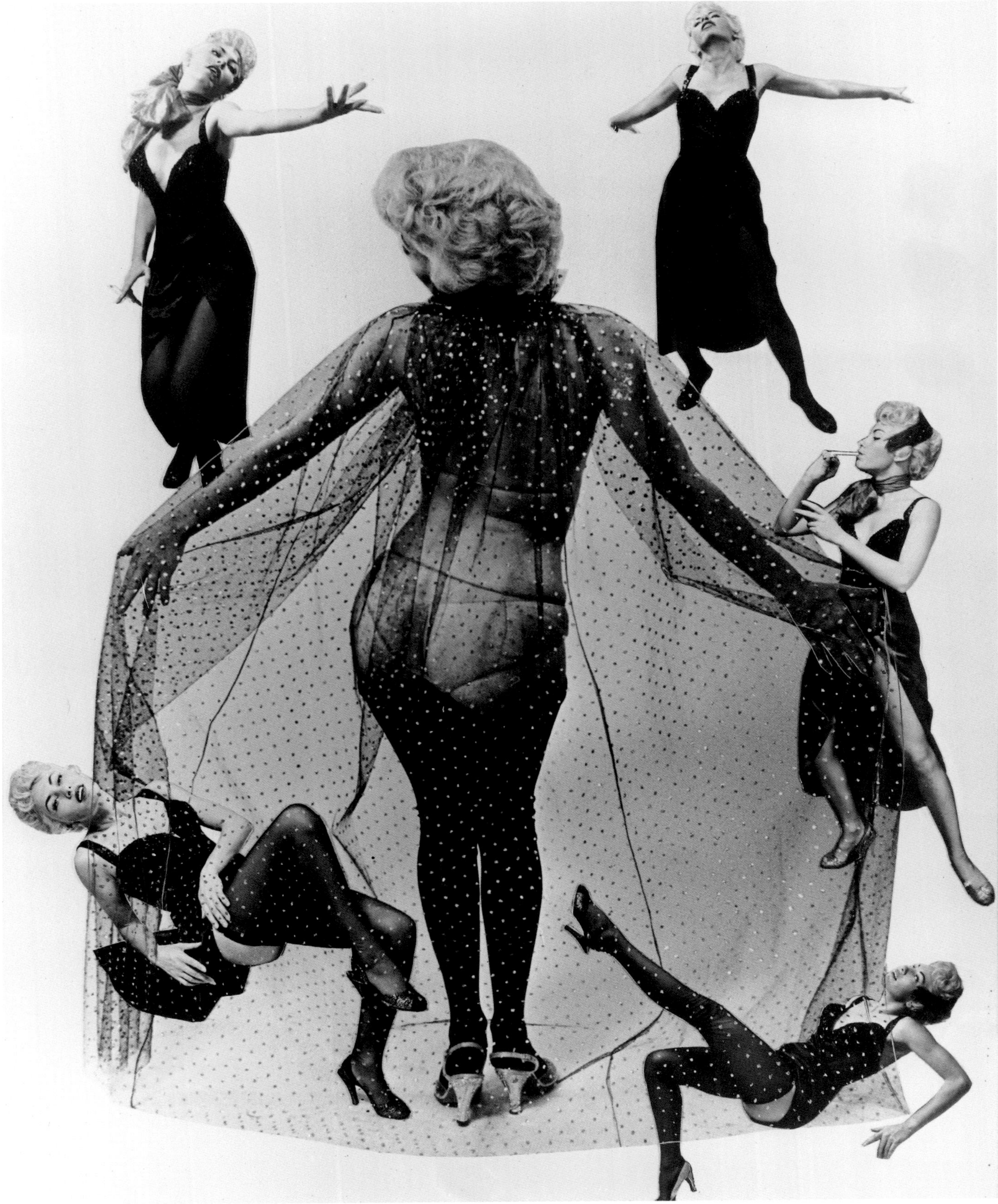

Sonia Sophisticate

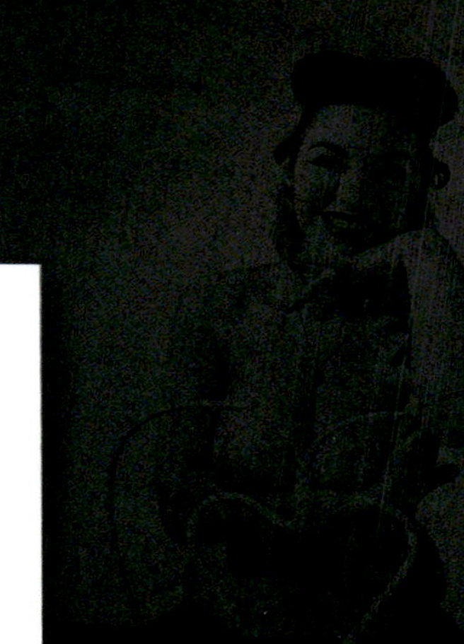

SONIA SOPHISTICATE

"Sonia the Sultry Sophisticate" is a native New Yorker, was a ballet dancer at 15 in the Metropolitan Opera chorus. She was in a number of Broadway shows as a dancer, got tired of starving- decided to take her clothes off and make use of some of her ballet training. Her XXXX watchword is: "If you have a nice body, why hide it ?" She likes to work theatres, loves to get back home in New York between stints. Sonia has worked the major burlesque theatres of the east coast, mid-west, and in Toronto and Montreal. She was a dancing showgirl at the Last Frontier in Las Vegas.

Sonia is 5'6", measures 42-26-36.

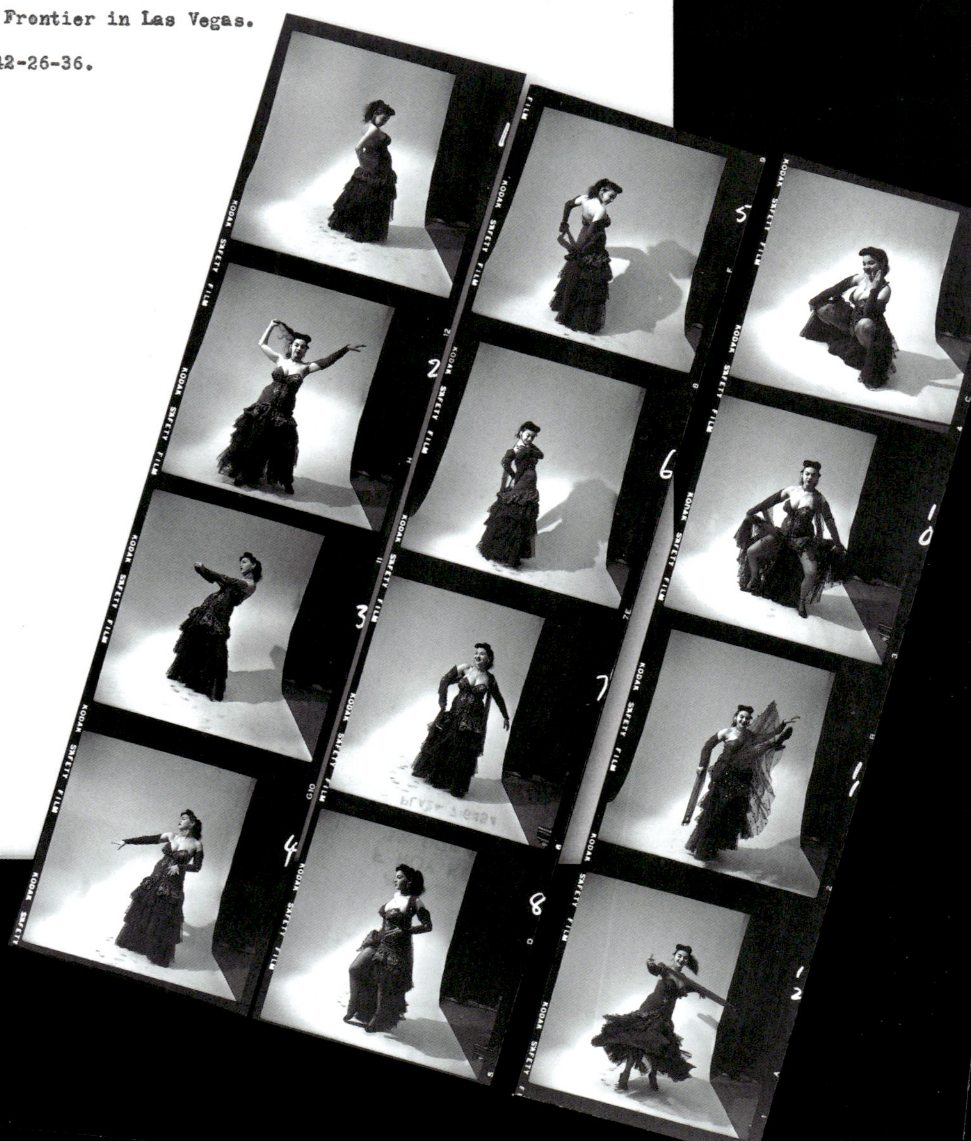

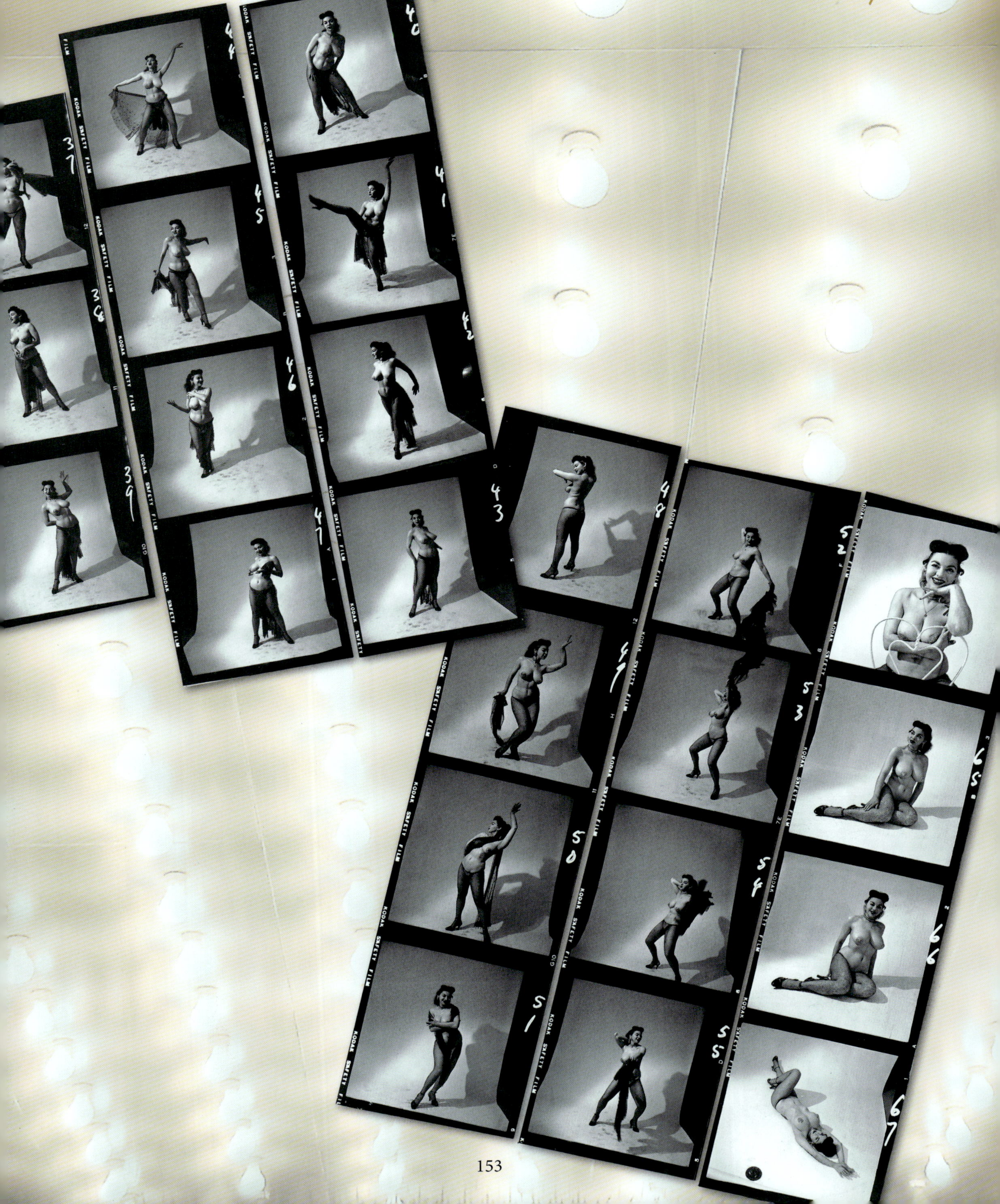
KODAK SAFETY FILM

Suzette

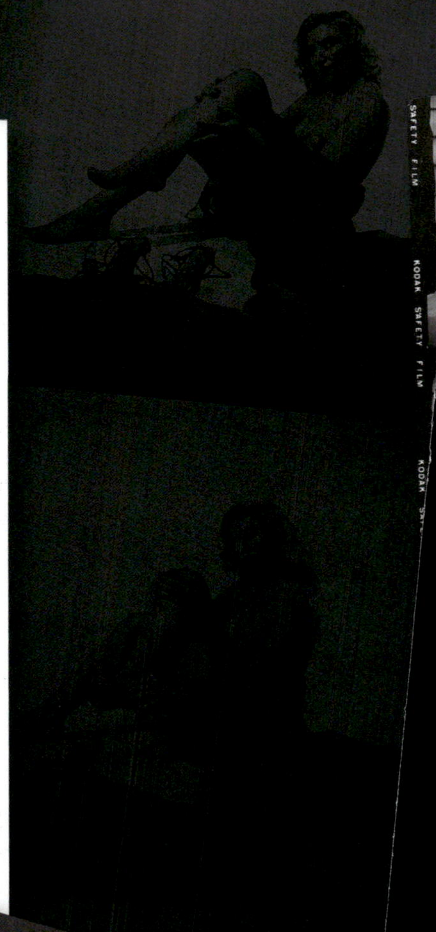

SUZETTE

From Pittsburgh, Pa., comes SUZETTE, tantalizing and notorious, and unpredicatble. Her real name is Corinne Suzette Christine Buinac. Suzette is a natural dancer-she had no formal training, but has that sense of rhythm and natural grace which is just as important. Suzette wanted a life in show business all her life, and, now she's got it she's really happy. One of the group of new faces in the entertainment field, Suzette is ambitious and wants to make a name for herself. She has worked at The Gaiety in Norfolk, the Roxy in Cleveland, the Studio in Washington. Looks like she's well on the way. Suzette is 5'2", measures 34-24-36.

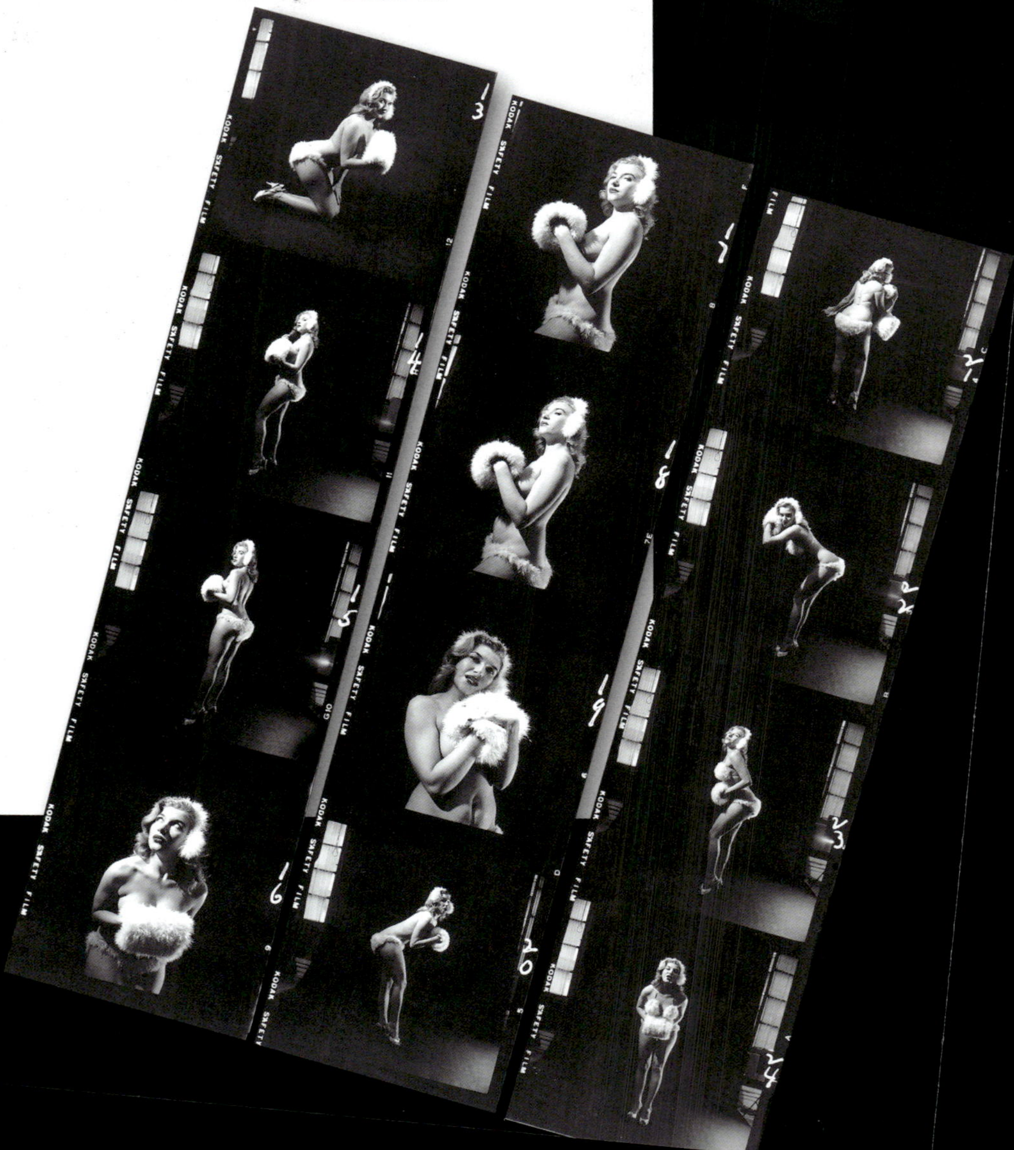

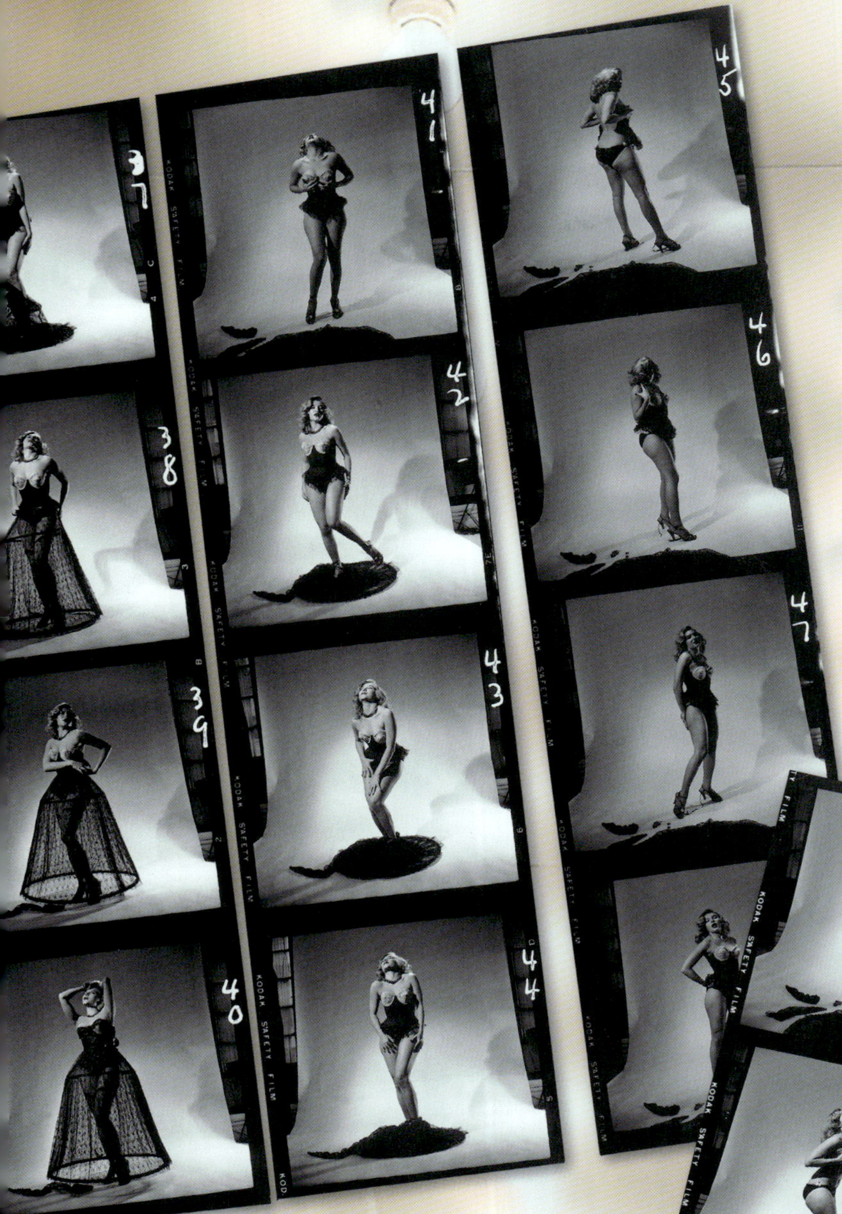

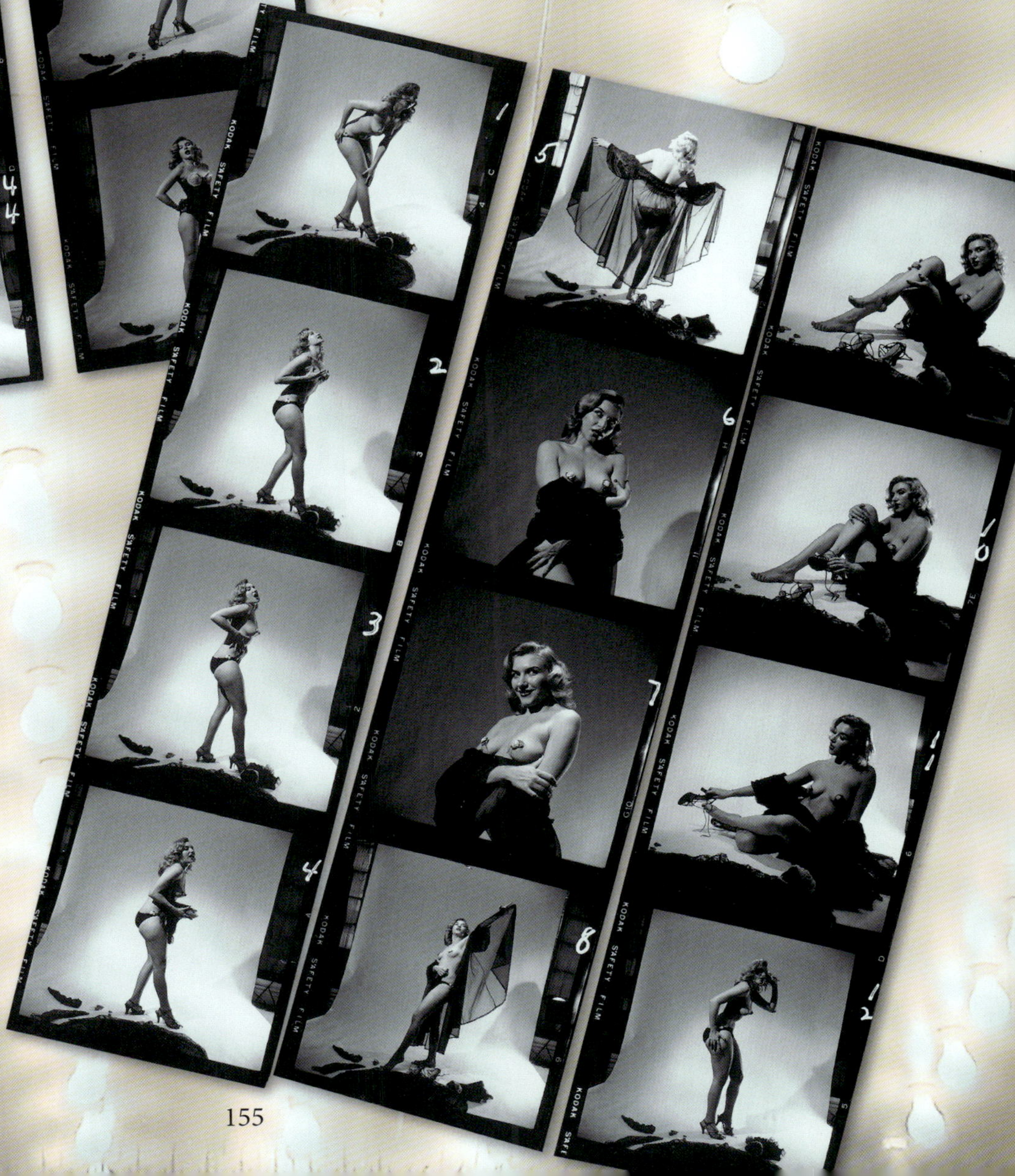

TANA LOUISE,

22-year-old Tana Louise calls Cincinnati her home town. She has been in show business, she says, since she was three years old, has worked the biggest and smallest towns in Florida, California, Canada, has been featured at Minsky's.

Recently she got into Dorothy Kilgallen's column on the charge that she, a peeler, was trying to cash in on the name and reputation of another headliner in show business- Tina Louise, star of the musicale, "L'il Abner". However, there's room for two Louises in the great big world of show business-Tana has a birth certificate to prove that she is working under the name she was born with. She's a mixture of Cherokee, French and Irish. Now who could find a nicer dish ?

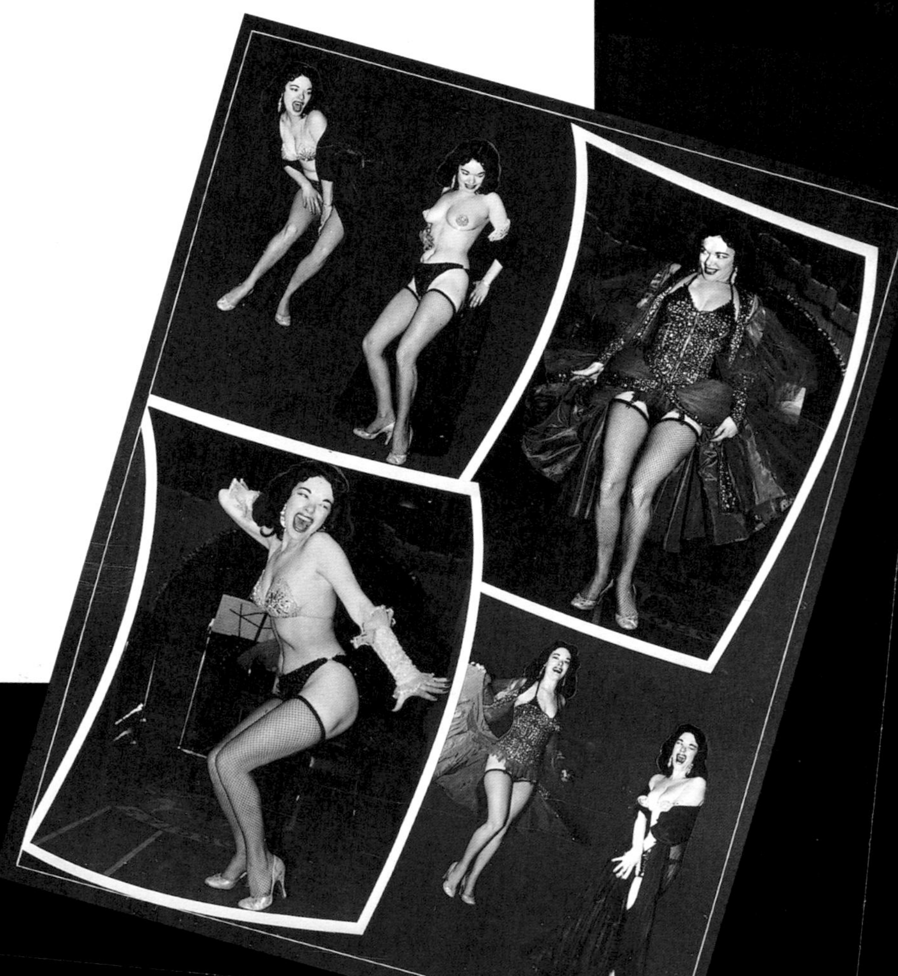

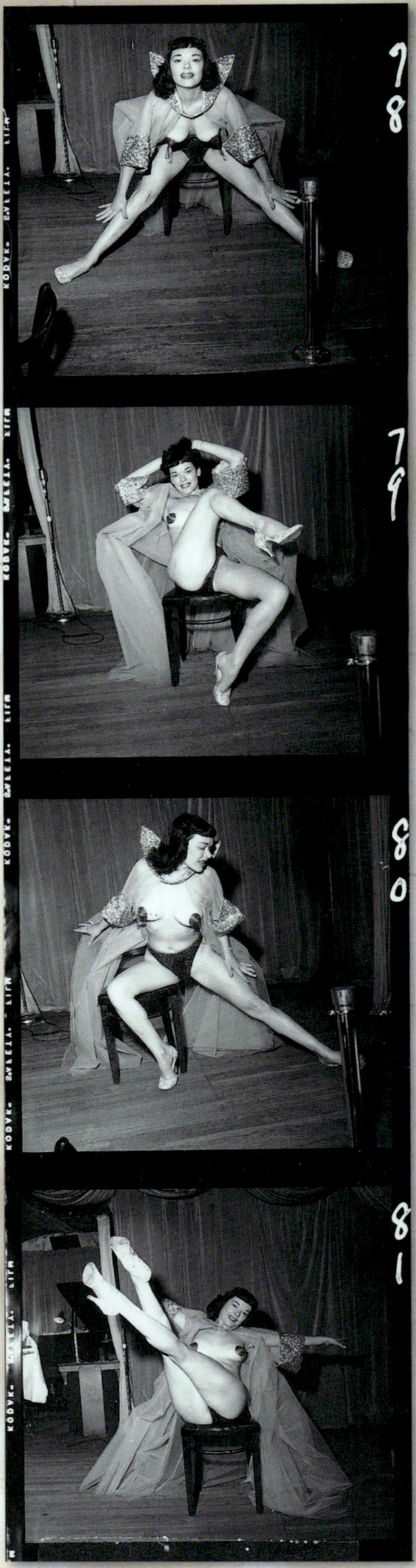

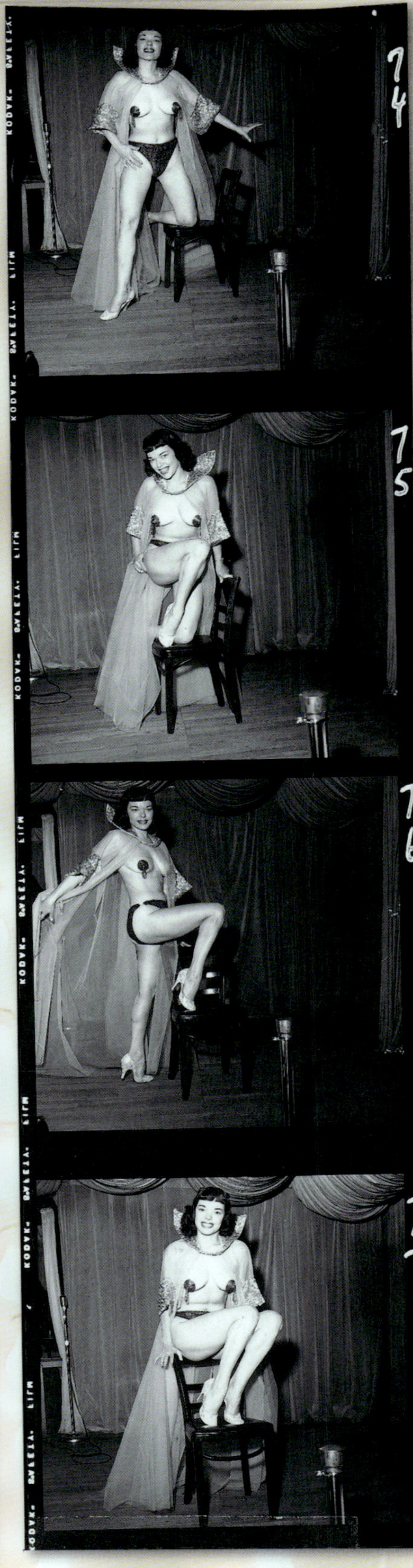

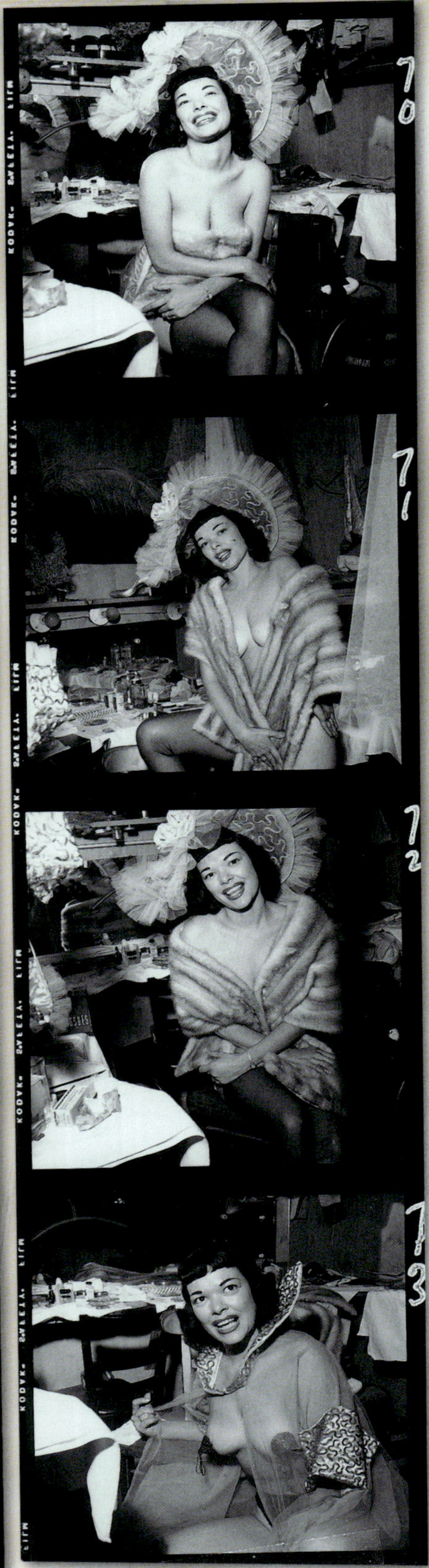

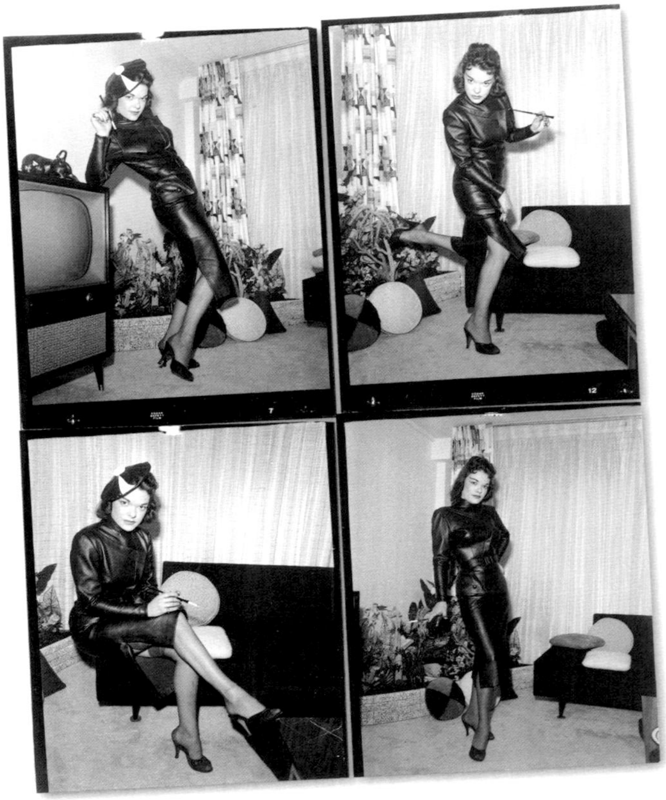
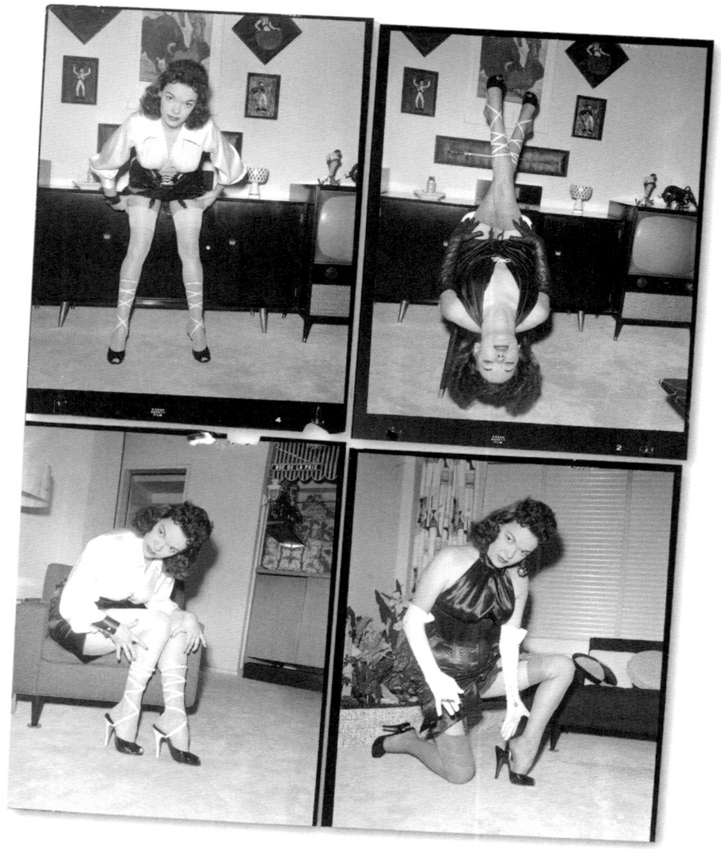
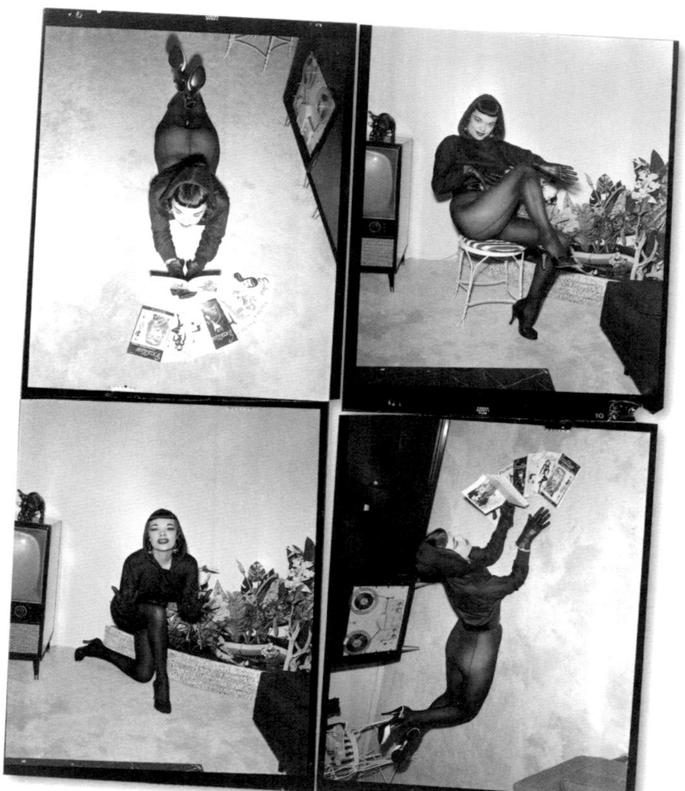
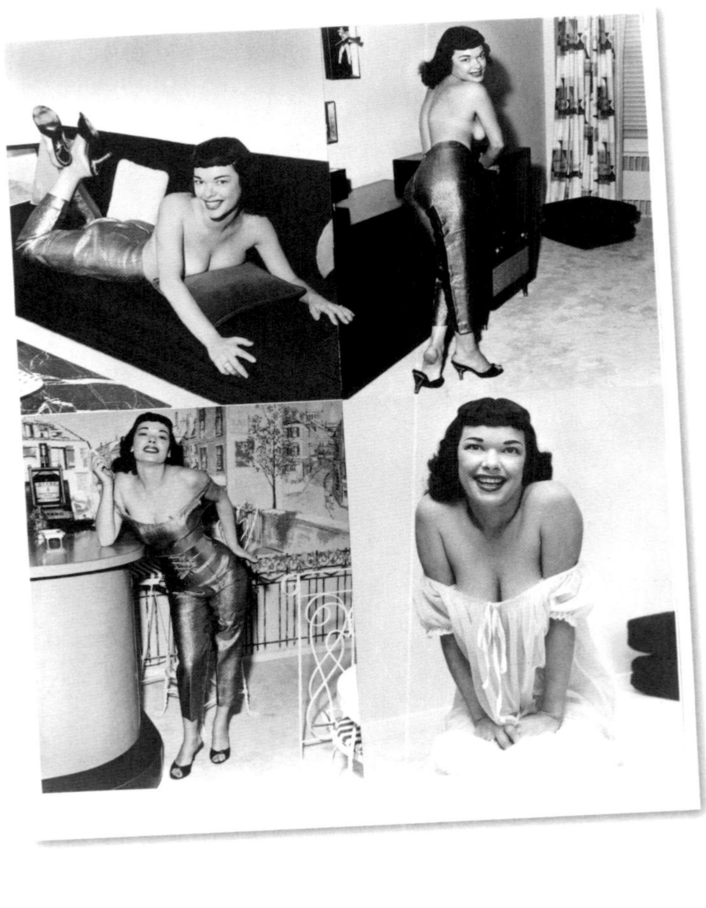

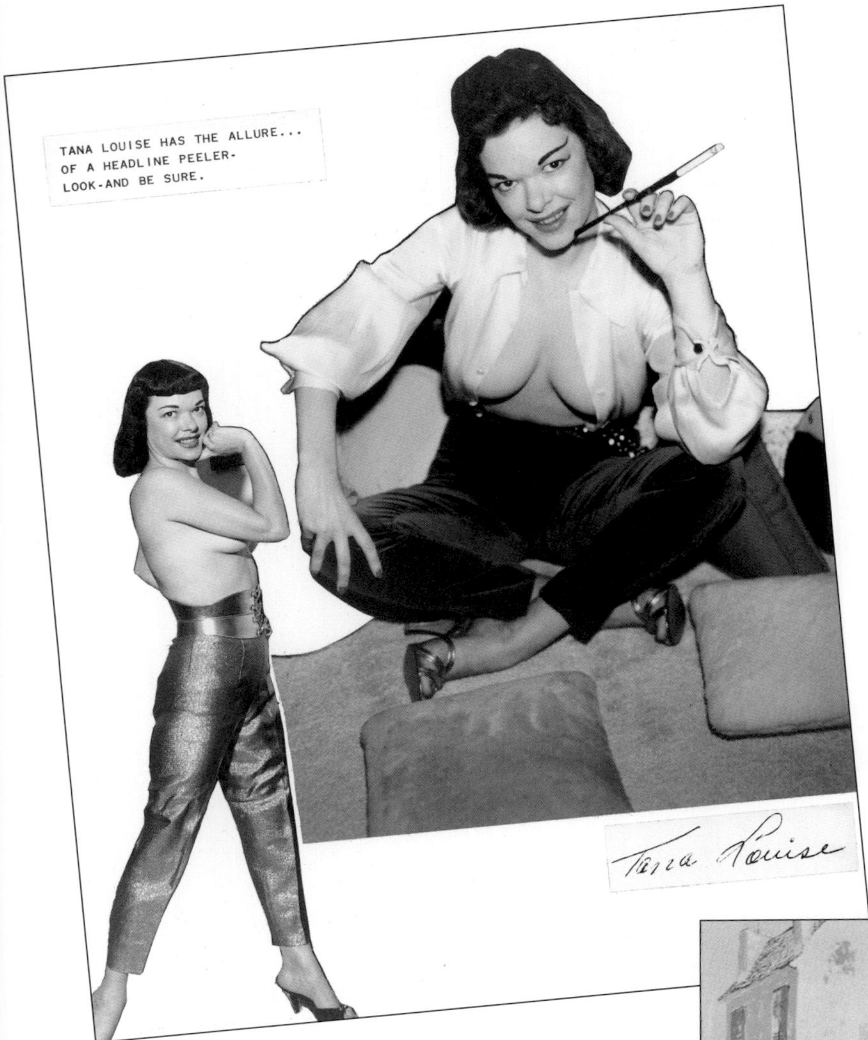
TANA LOUISE HAS THE ALLURE...
OF A HEADLINE PEELER-
LOOK-AND BE SURE.
Tana Louise

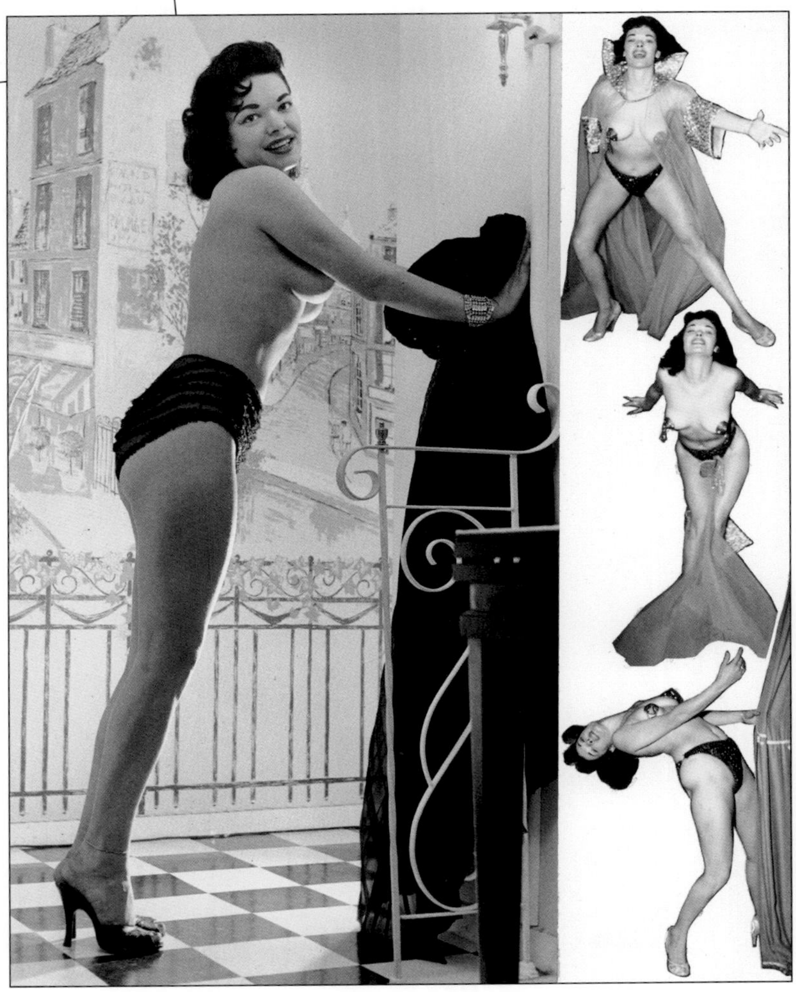

Tempest Storm

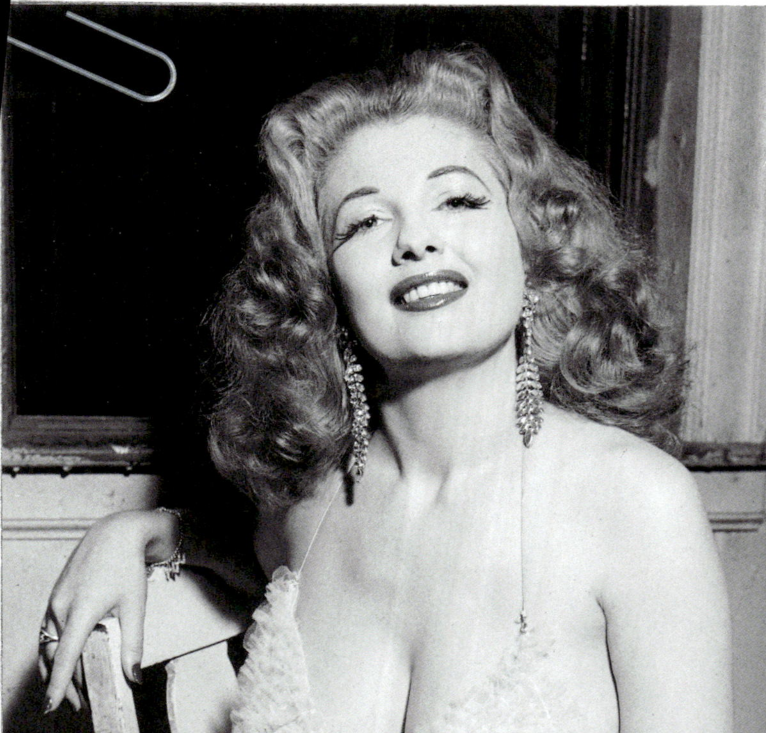

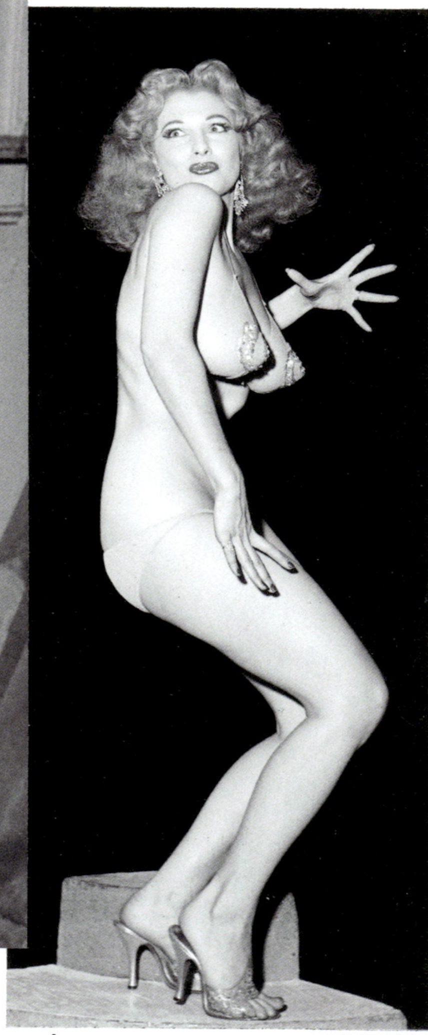

TEMPEST STORM, 'TIS EASY TO SEE...
SPECIALIZES IN
3-D.

Tempest Storm

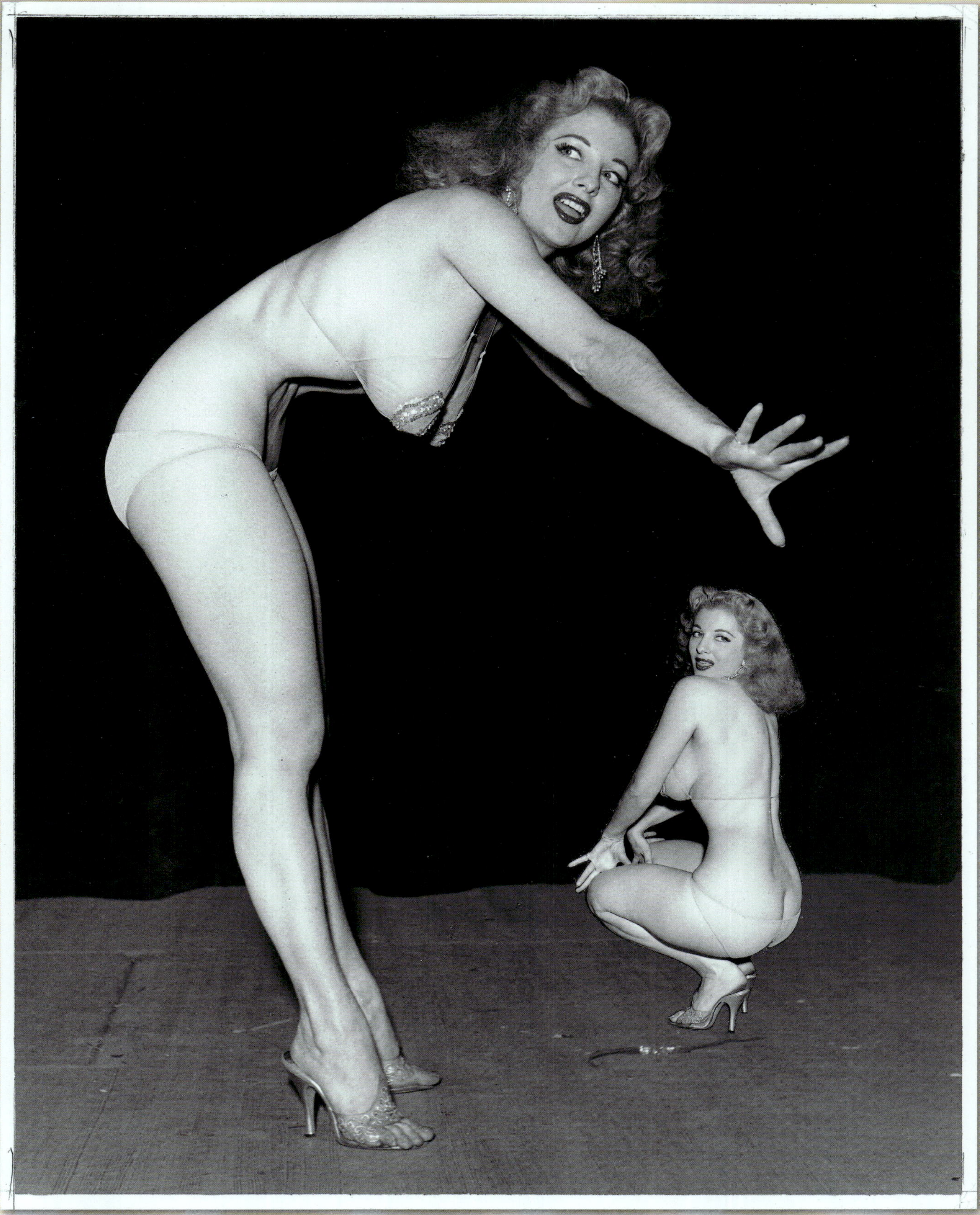

Tequila

TEQUILA

In Spanish Tequila means teapot, in Mexico, the name is associated with a potent drink. The real-life Tequila is potent, sure-nuff. This south-of-the-border citizen currently resides in Philadelphia, andis working the east coast circuit. She is a picture of smoldering beauty with dark, dark eyes and long dark hair, measures 37-24-36, combines in her act American Striptease with Latin innovations. Whether it's "Hooray" or "Ole", one thing is sure- Tequila is hot stuff.

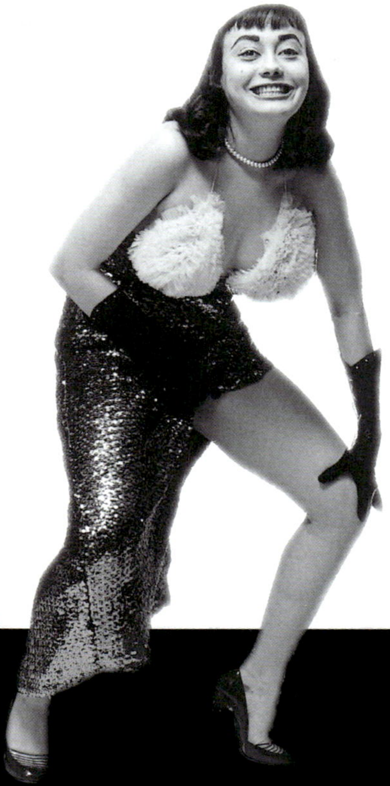

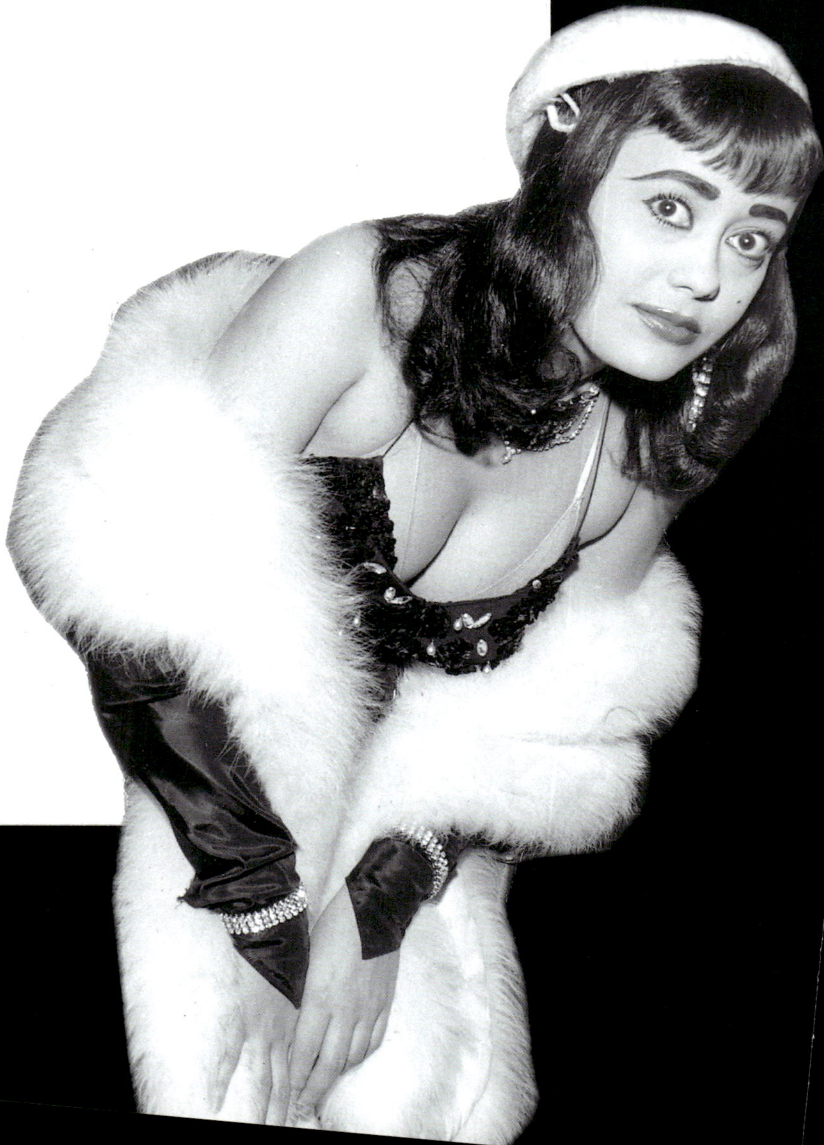

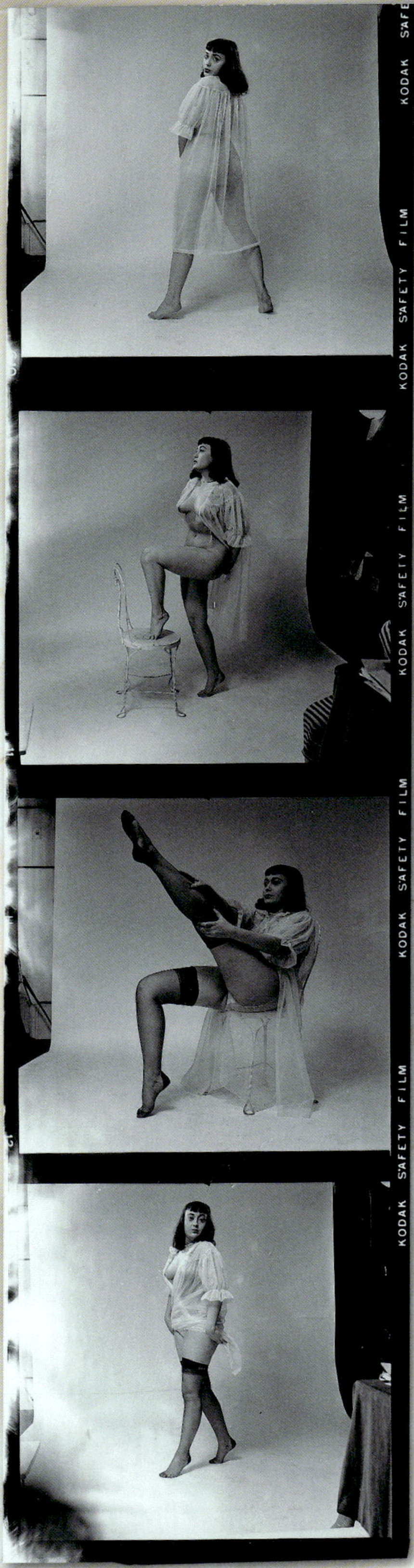

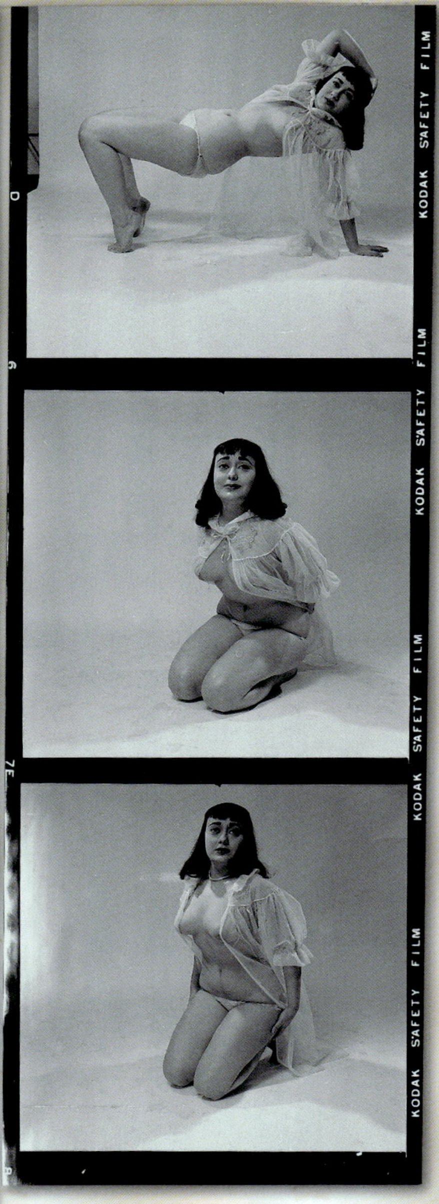

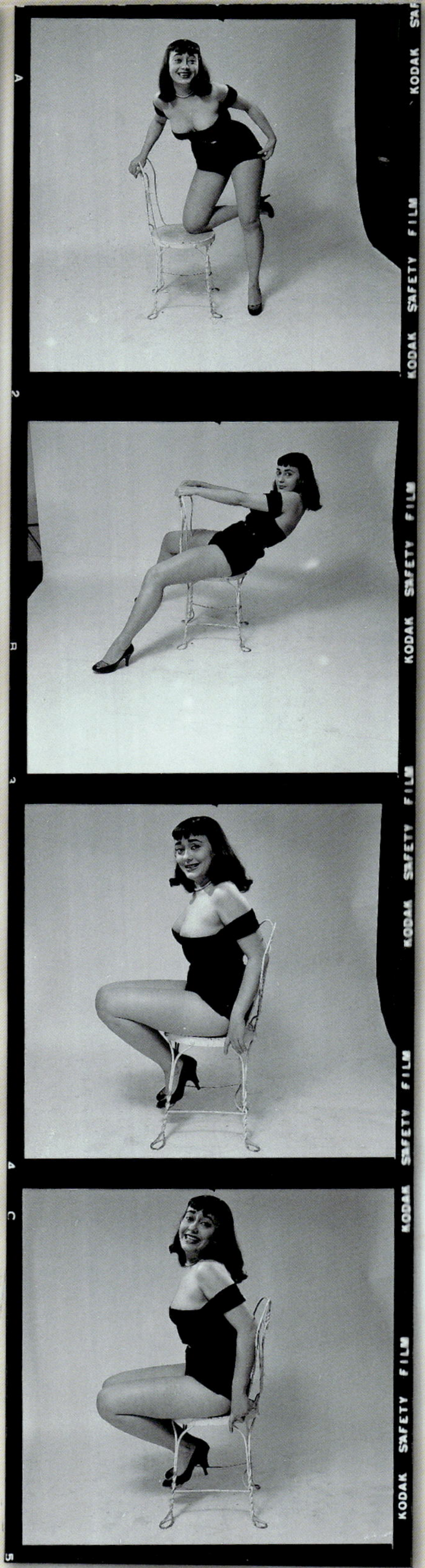

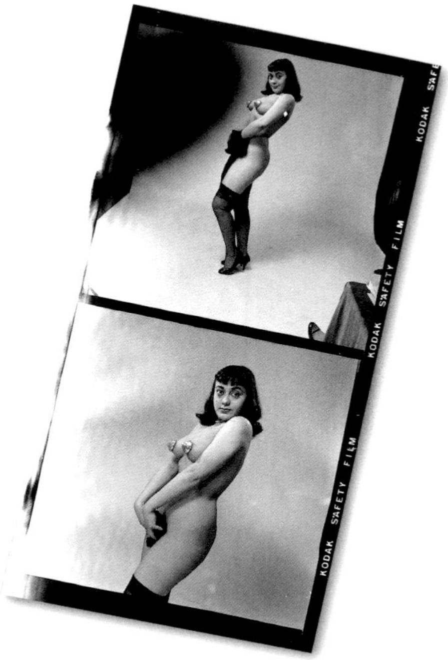

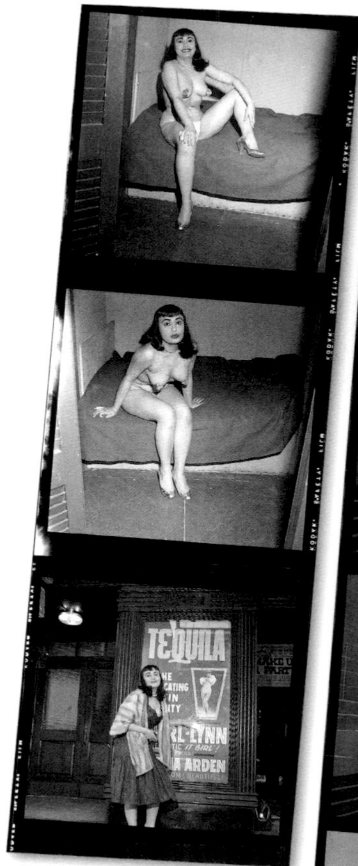

TEQUILA

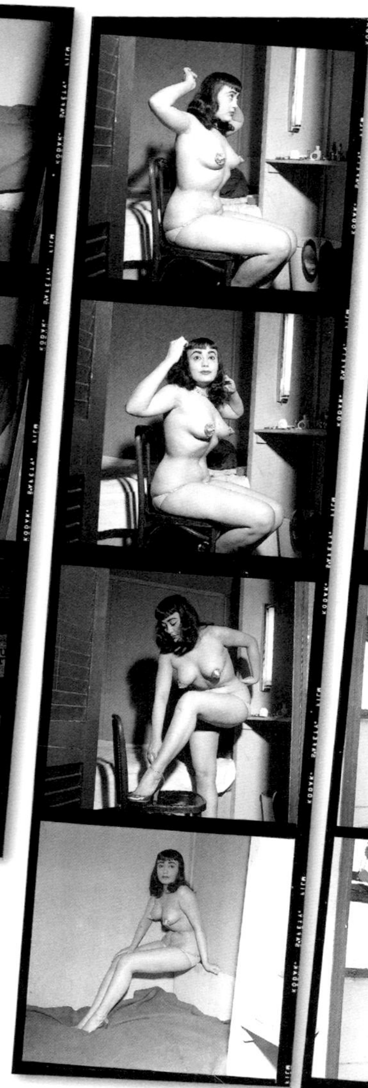

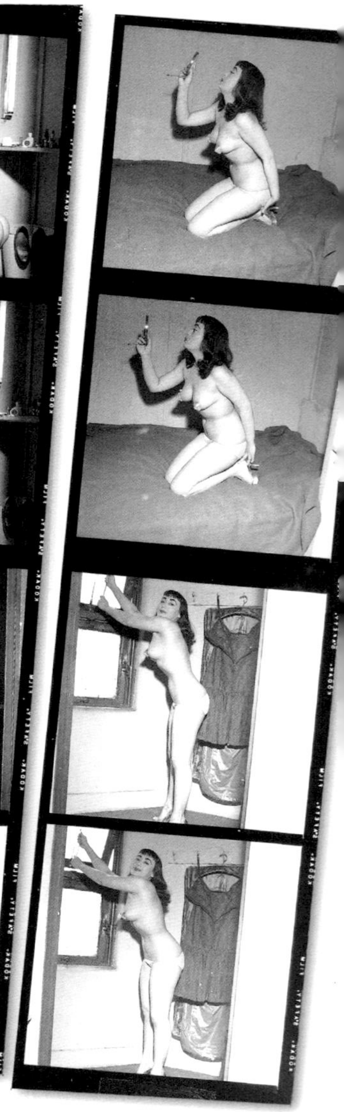

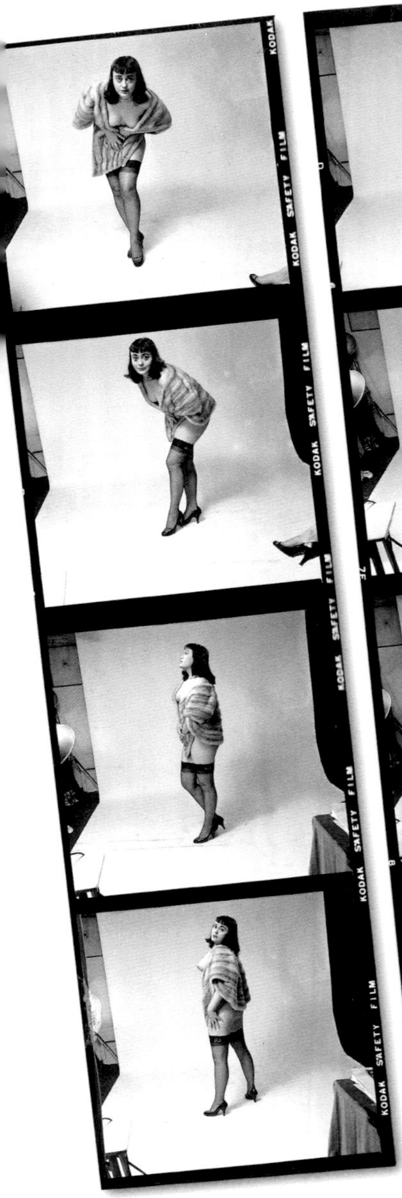

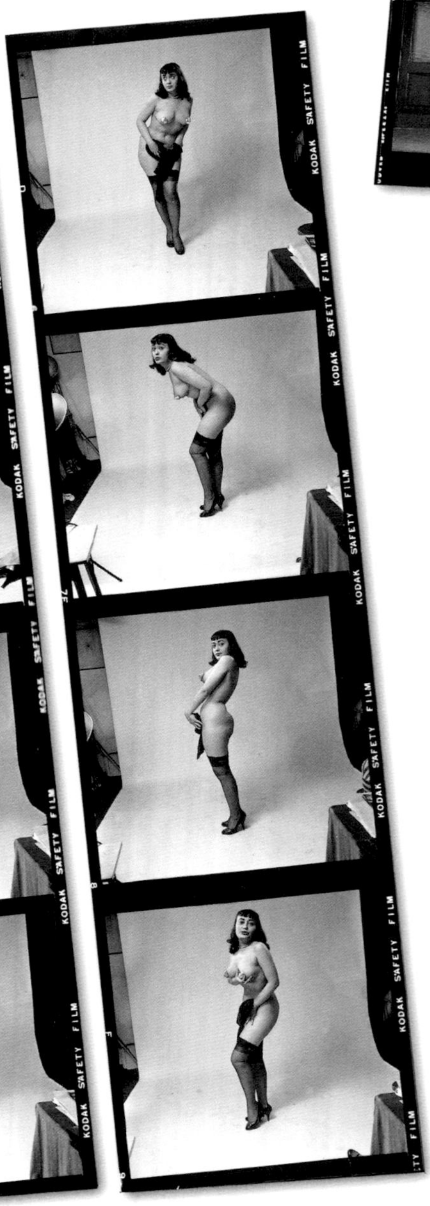

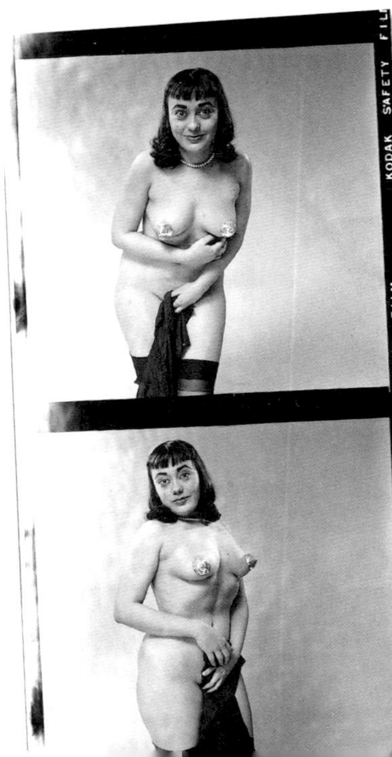

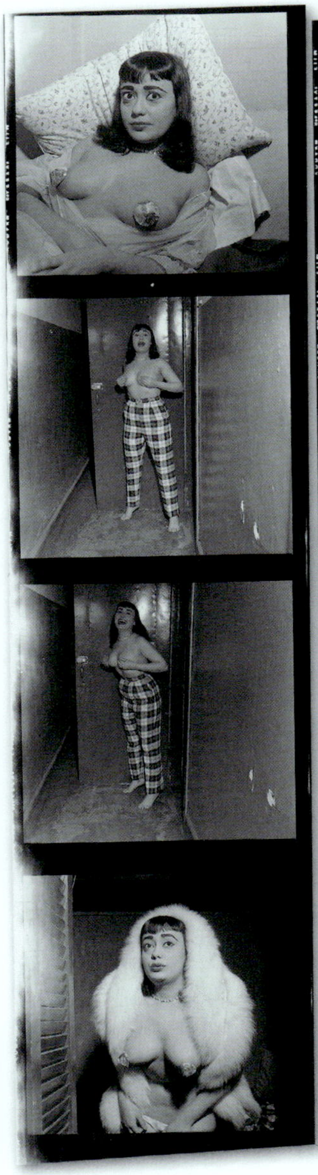

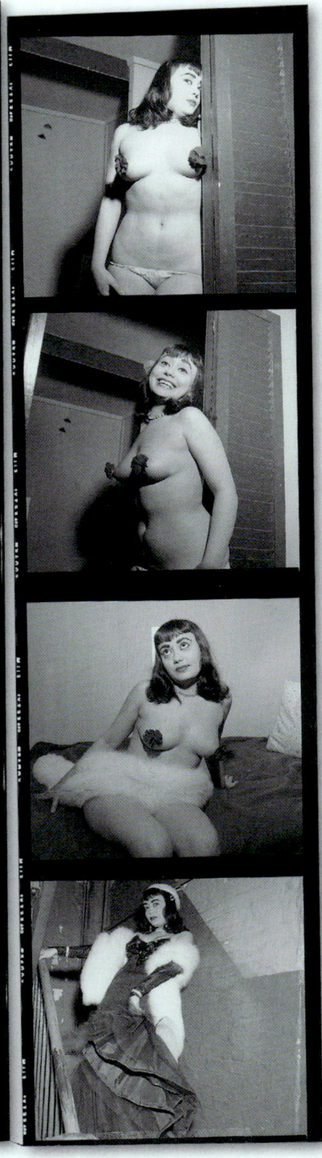

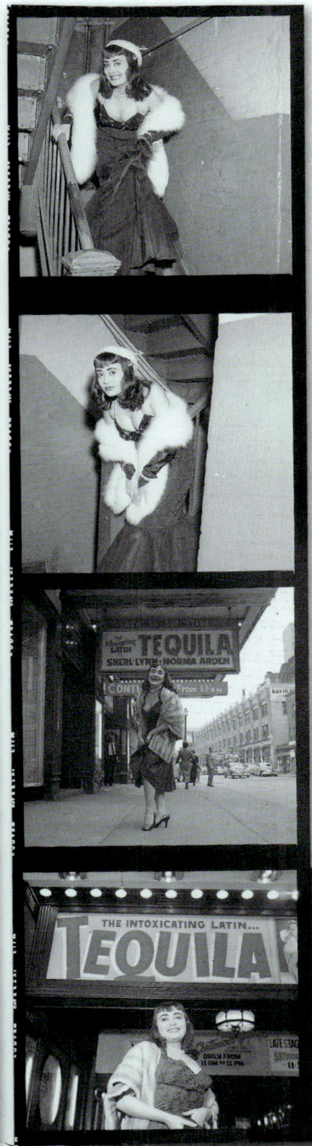
TEQUILA
THE INTOXICATING LATIN...
TEQUILA

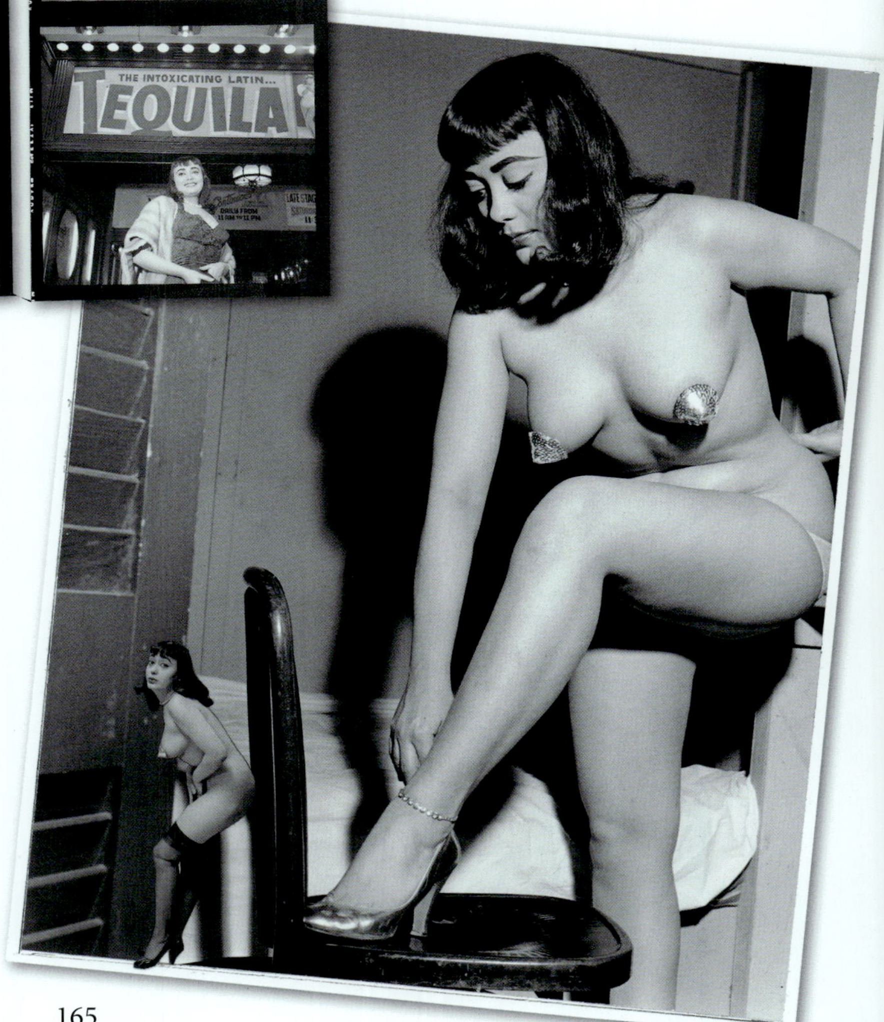

Texas Sheridan

TEXAS SHERIDAN

When Texas Sheridan (she comes from Dallas) was a little girl she had a colored nurse who used to chide her with the threat "You gonna end up a no-good chorus girl." Little did this nurse realize that the girl from Dallas would some day be a feature attraction on stages across the nation-everywhere this southern charmer has played- from California to Florida, from the mid-west to Maine, and points south of the border-notably Puerto Rico and Nassau.

She's 23 years old, 5'7" tall, measures 34-24-34½.

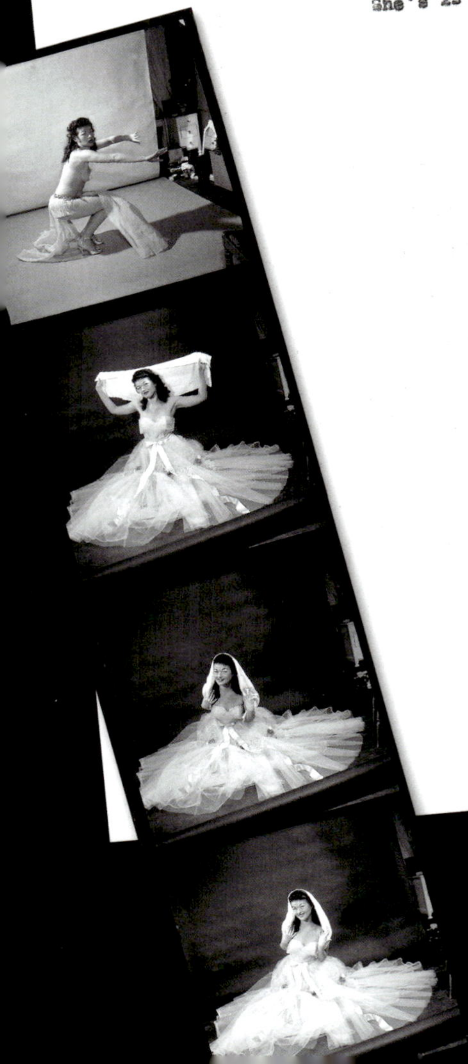

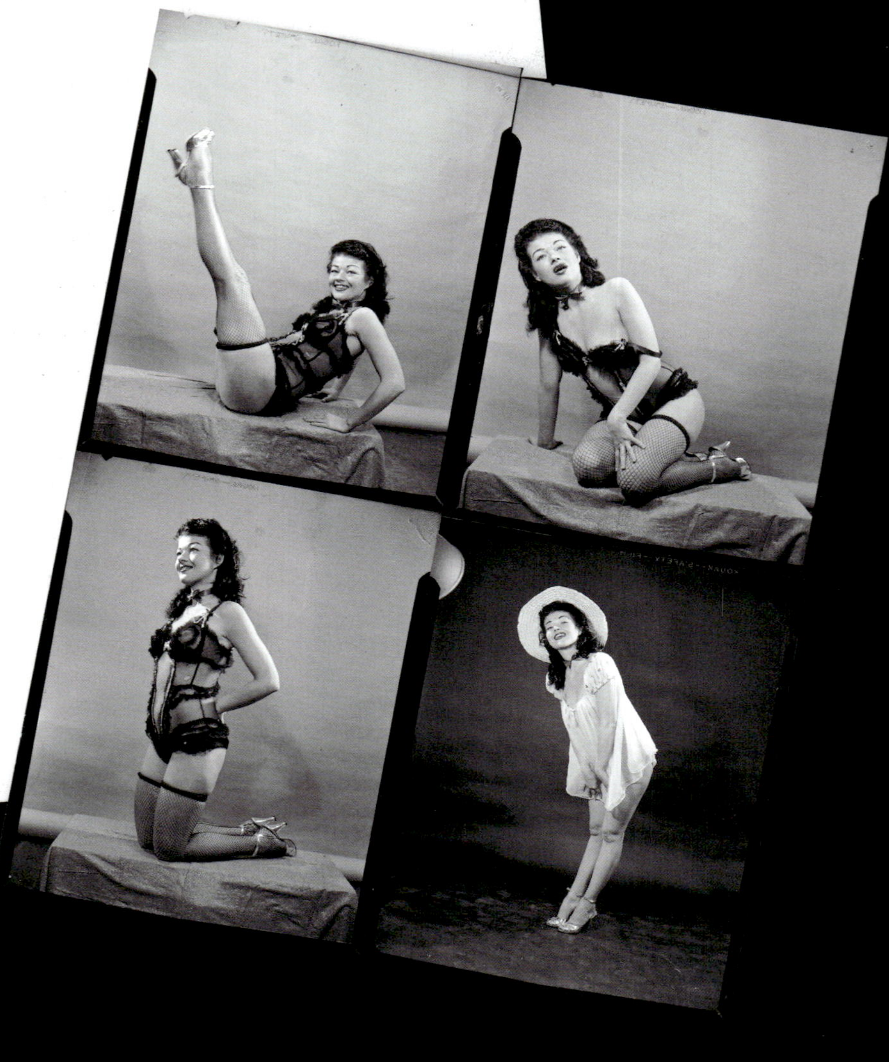

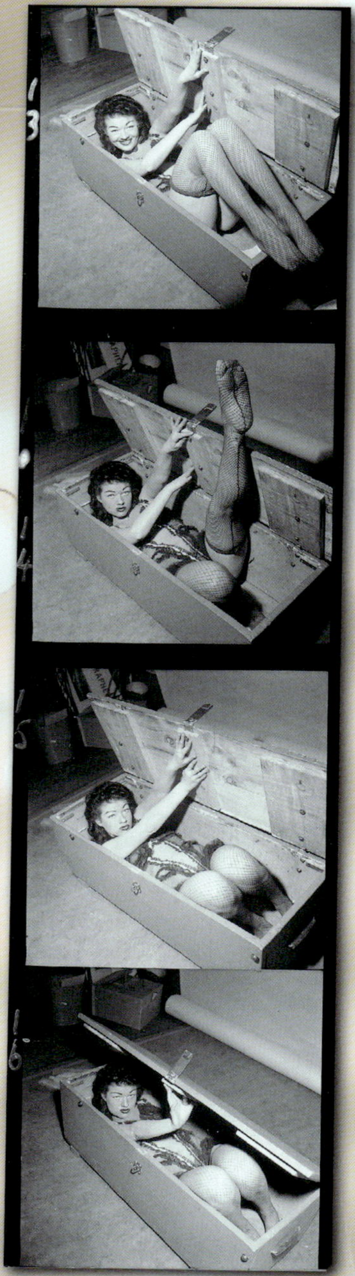

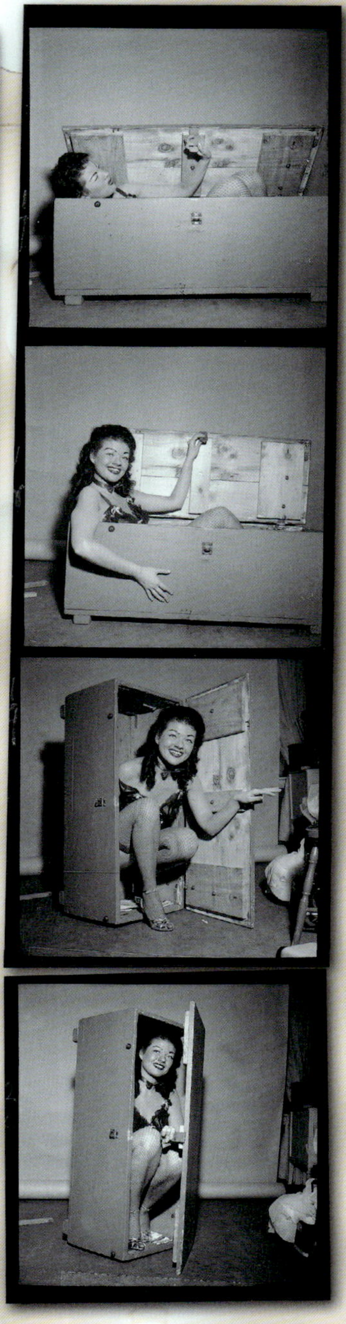

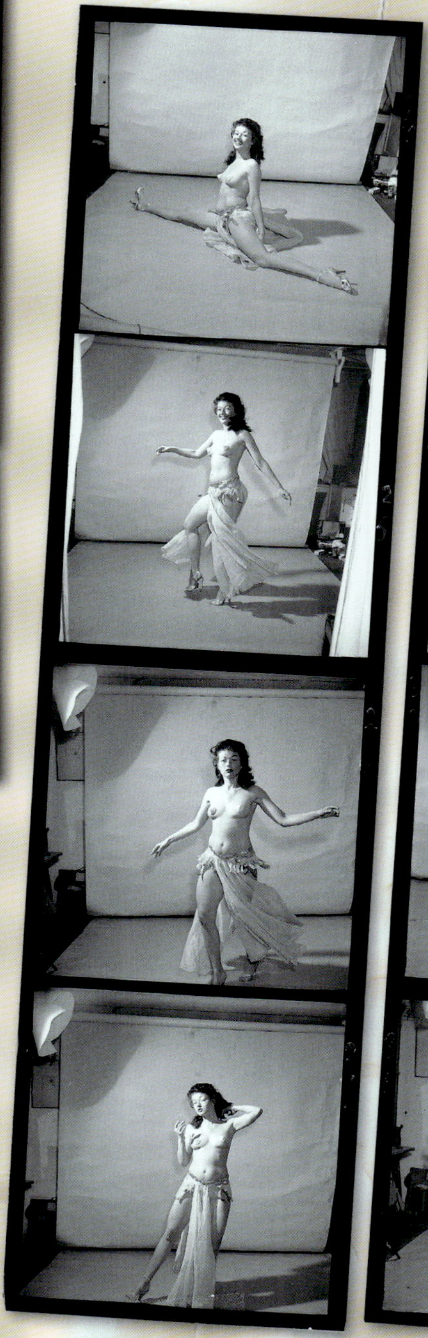

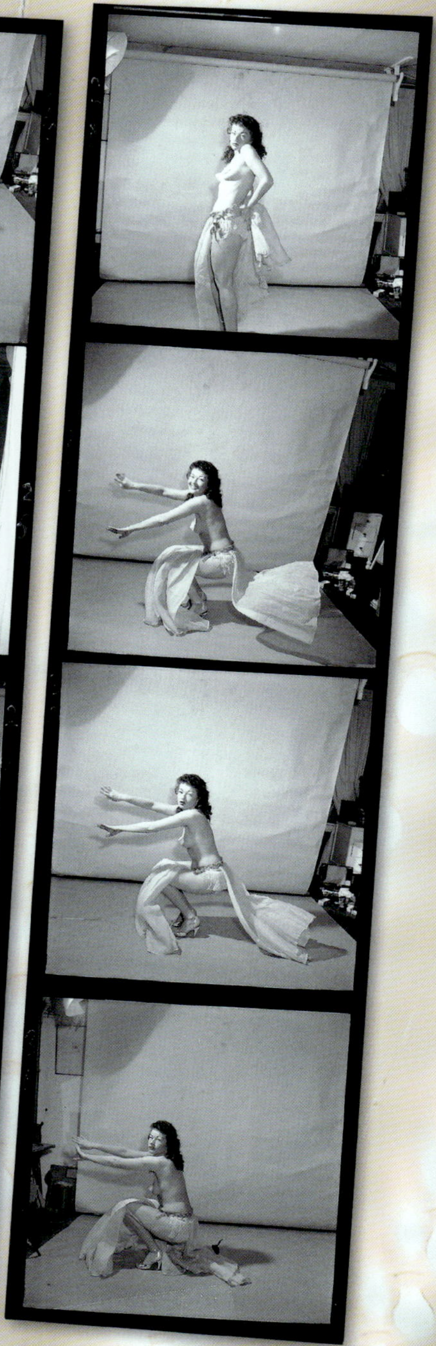

Vicki Palmer

VICKI PALMER

Brooklyn-born Vicki Palmer, newcomer to show business, is a gal to watch- she's going places. The sloe-eyed brunette from Dodger town wows them when she goes through her routine. Fans love to watch her shapely gyrations. Vicki has just come back from a six-months stay in Hollywood where she worked at her dance routines with some of the west coast notables.

She's 20 years old, 5'4" tall, measures ~~37-26-36~~ 36-24-35.

Vicki has her eye on a Broadway musical as her aim in life. She can sing, act, and has danced since she was tiny. Right now Vicki is making a living as a model. Is she a good model ? Ask any photographer who has worked with her.

- hobbies - bringing up her pet Chihuahua
- paint
- has worked in New Orleans _ El Paso L.A. Hollywood.

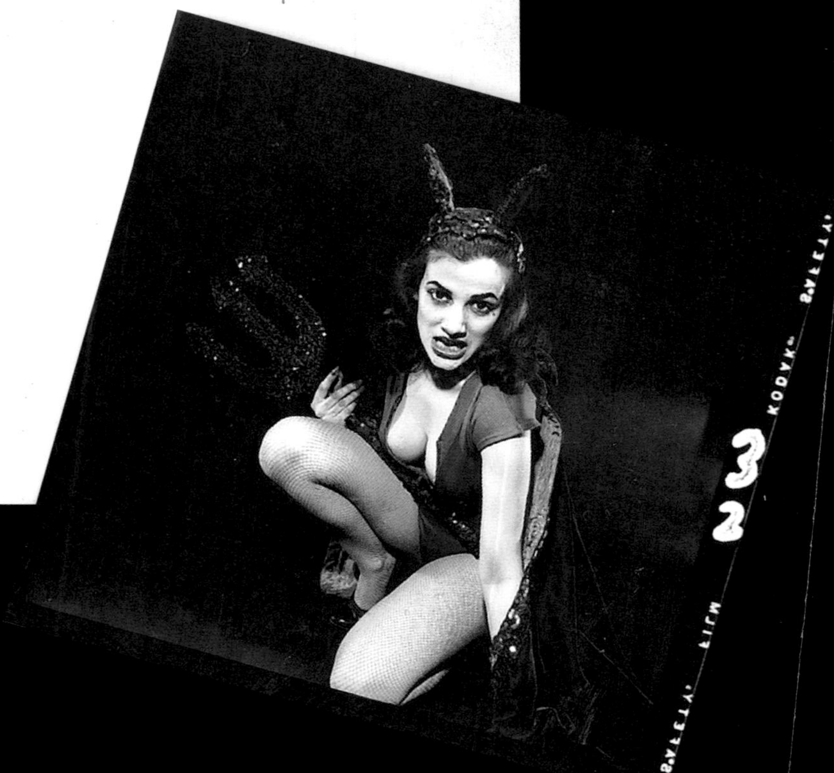

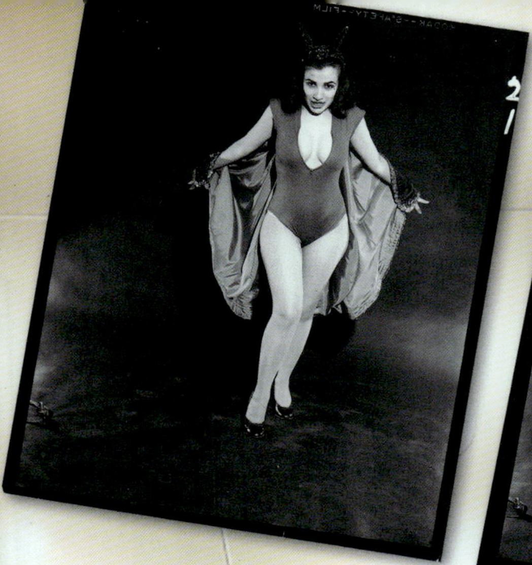

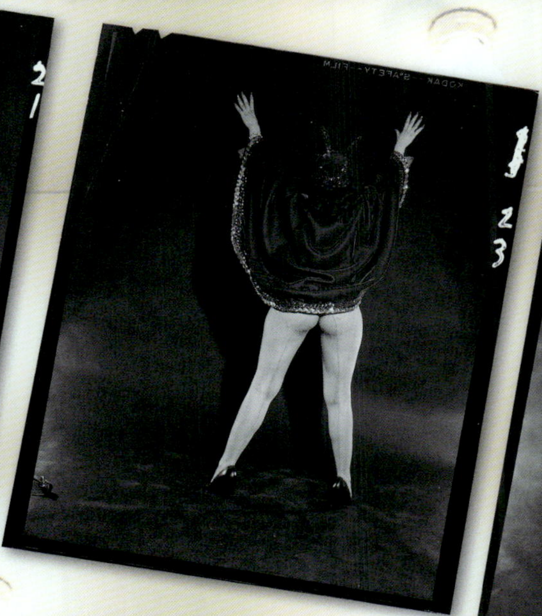

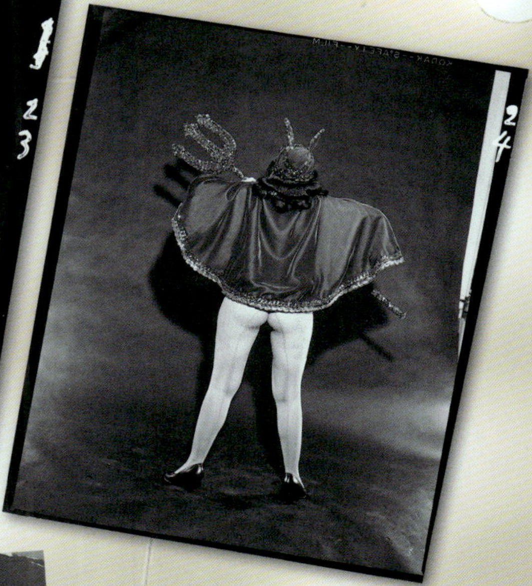

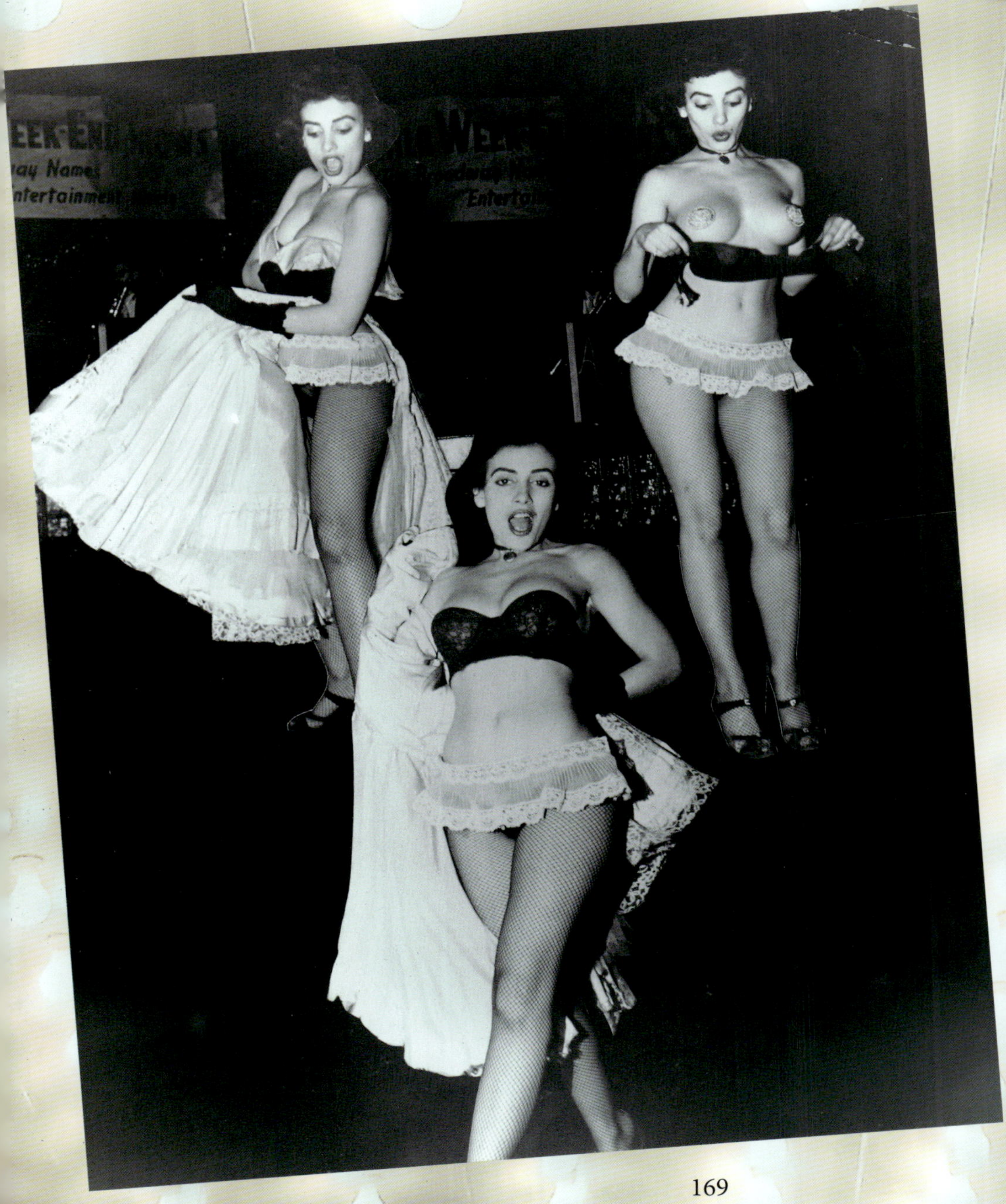

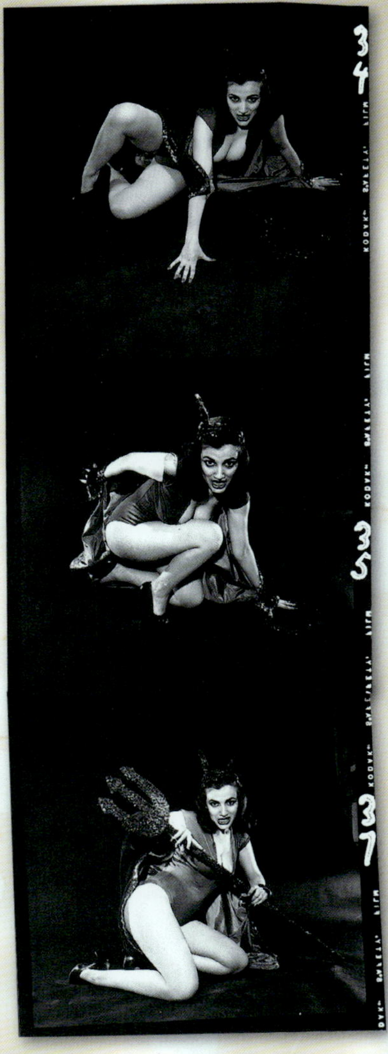

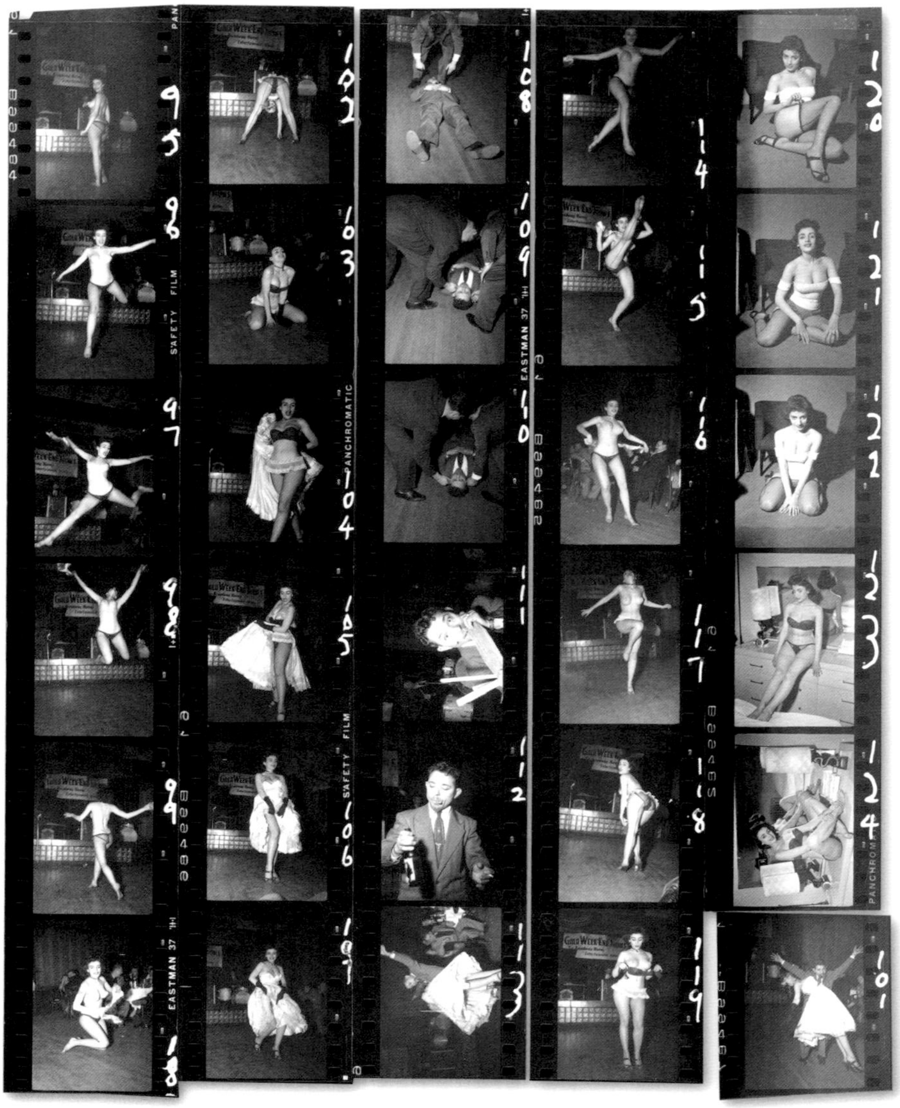

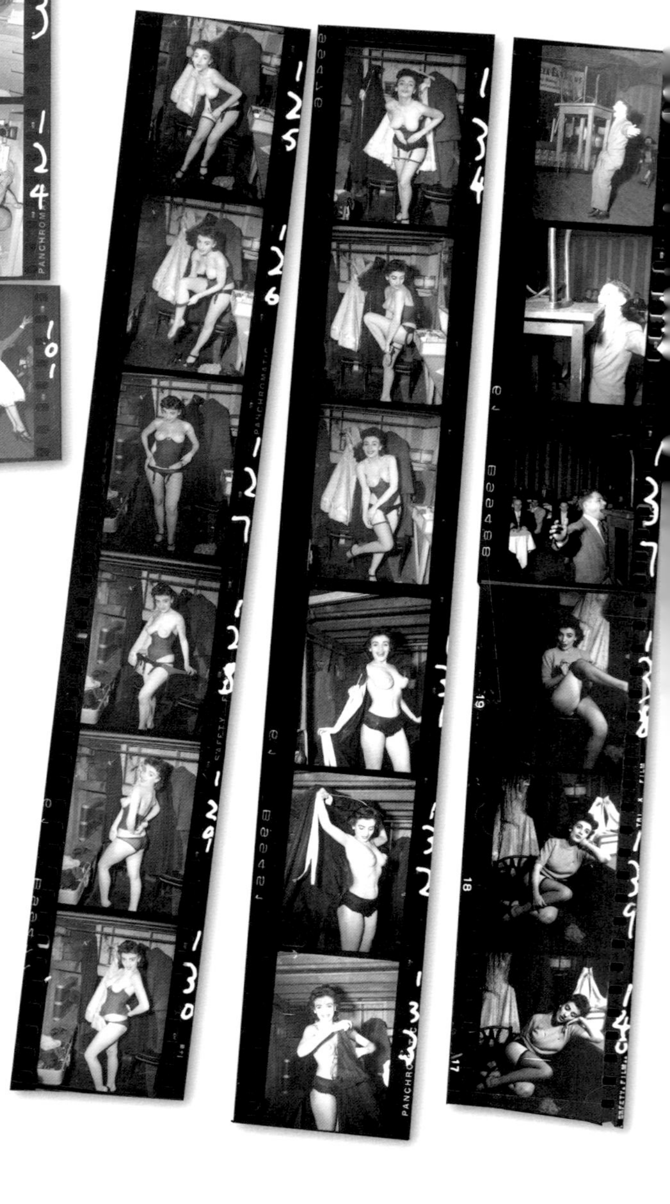

Vicki Palmer

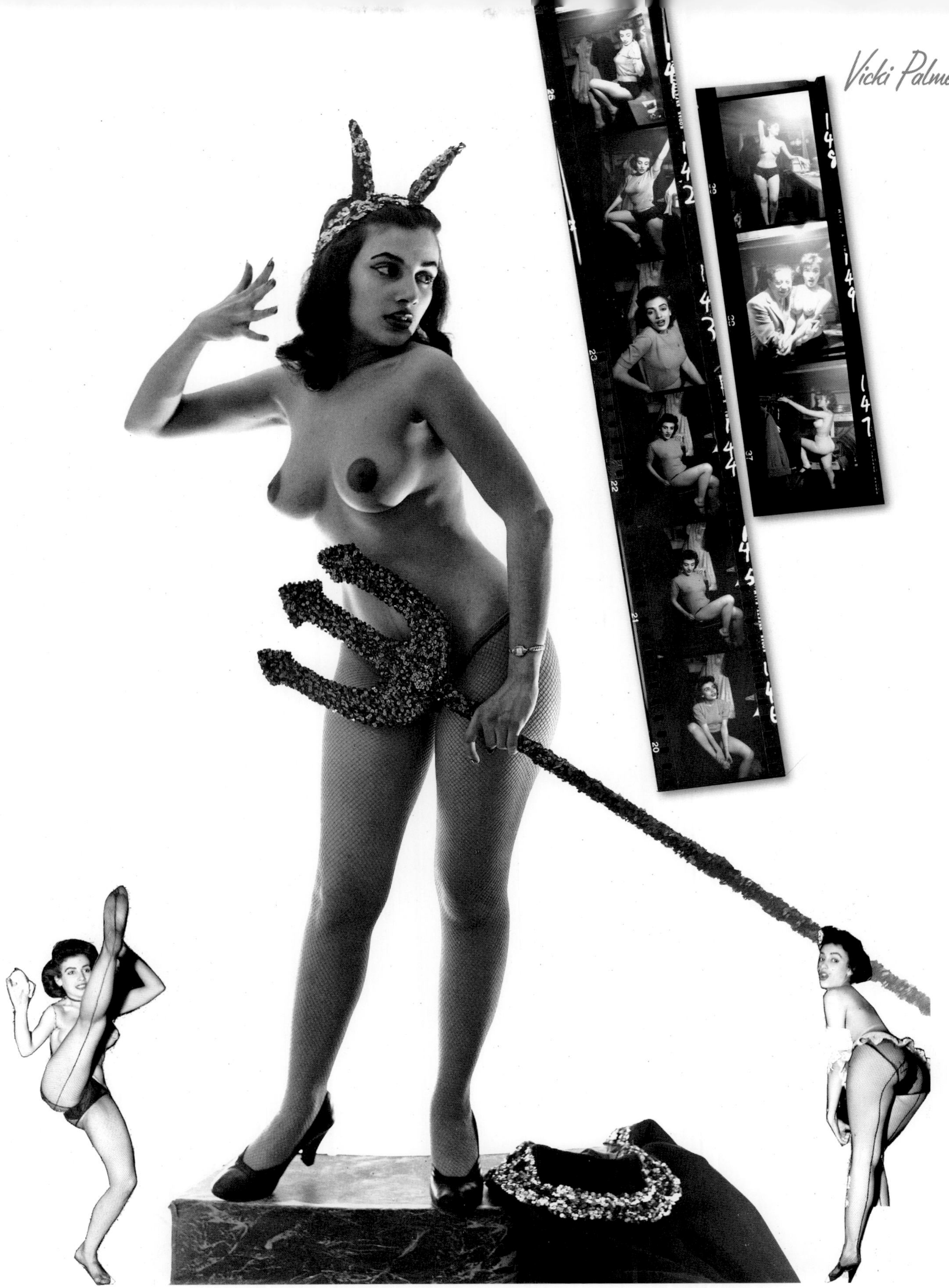

"The Fabulous" Zorita

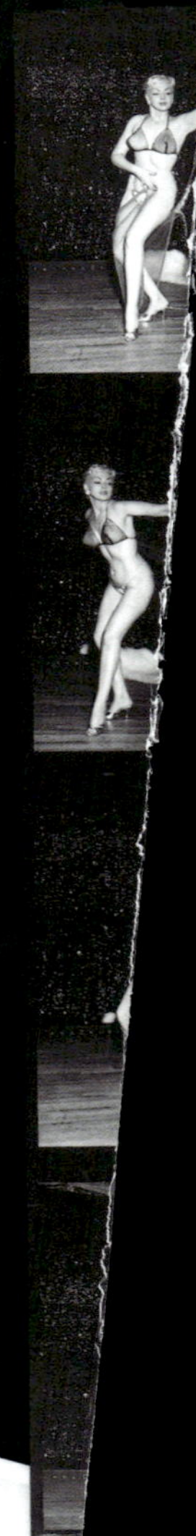

The Fabulous Zorita

Incomparable...Incredible...Unbelievable...Fantastic...
These adjectives...and more, serve to describe the fabulous Zorita.
This amazing personality has delighted male souls from one end of this country to the other with her ummatched brand of subtle sex, exotic allure and just plain femininity. A mistress of the mood, Zorita could be all things to all men. Unquenched fires burn in her slumberous eyes while her moist lips give promise of untold delights yet to come.

This sensuous creature really measures up to all standards. five feet, six inches tall, she XXX tapes in at 39-25-36. She calls Miami Beach her home, but often takes off to tour the night club and theatre circuits around the country.

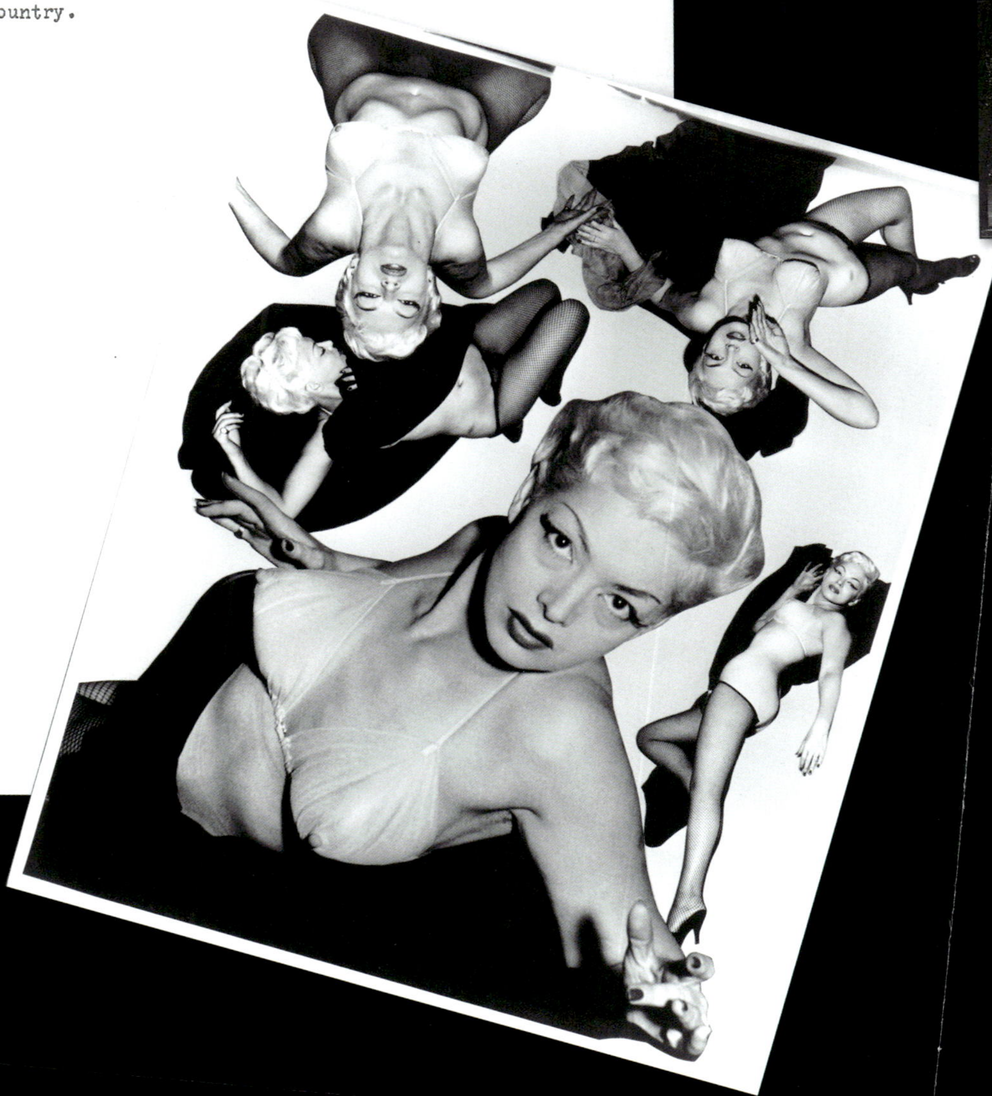

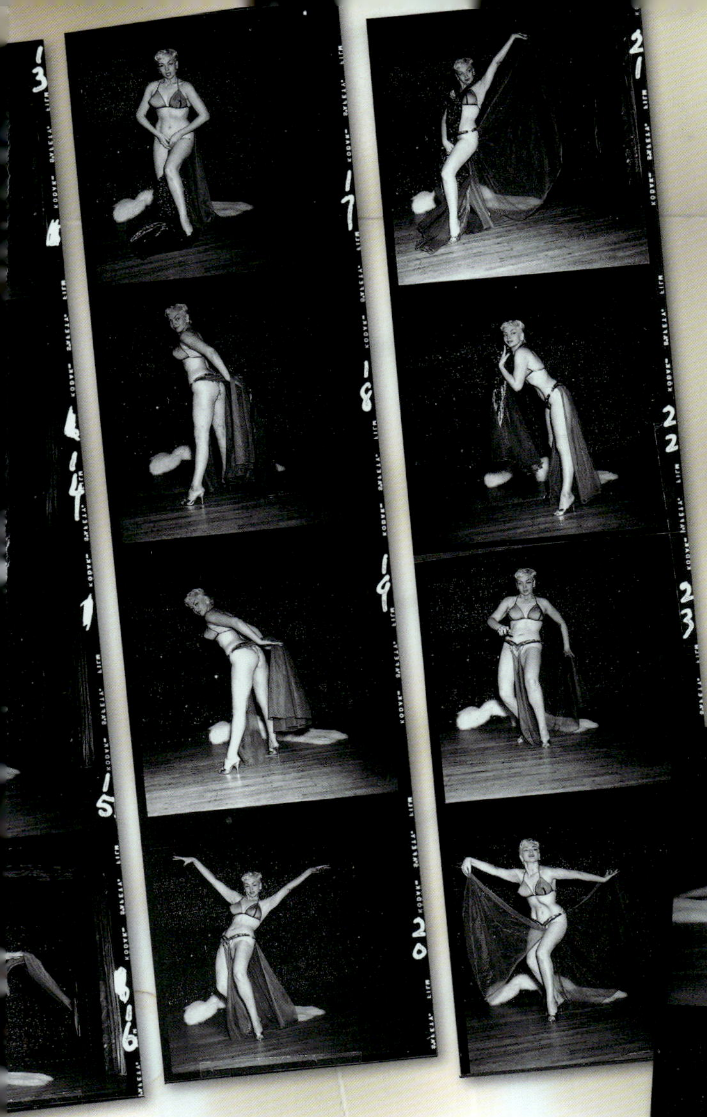
13
17
21
18
22
19
23
15
20
16

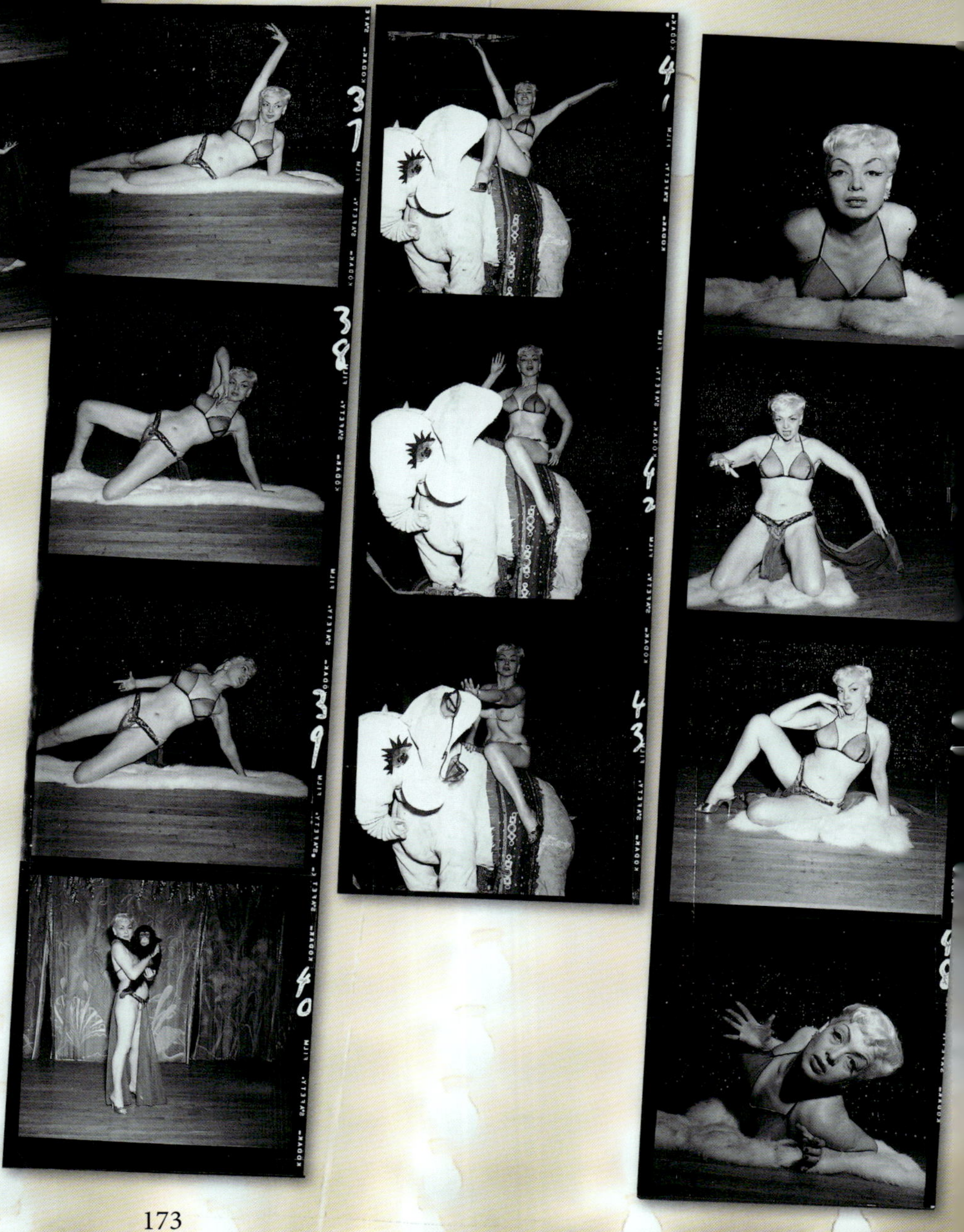
37
41
38
42
39
43
40

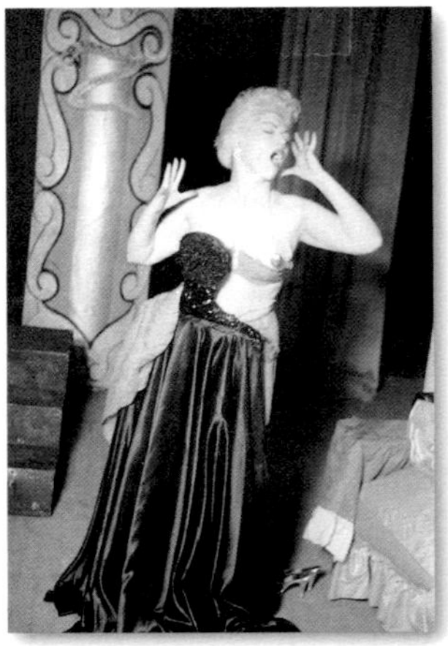
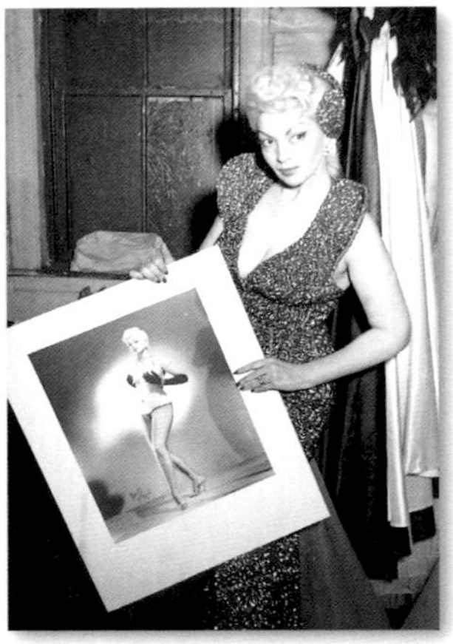
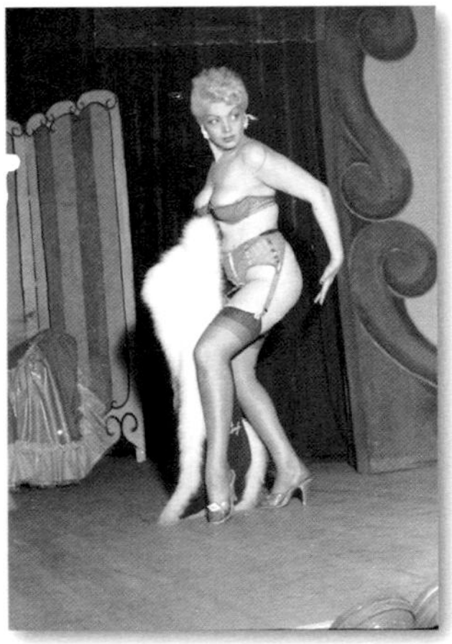
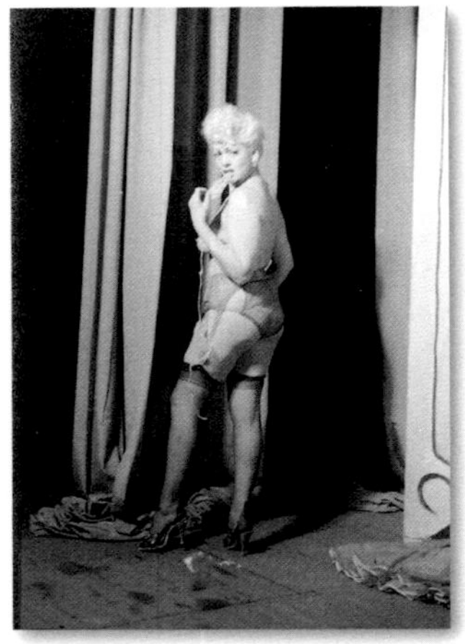
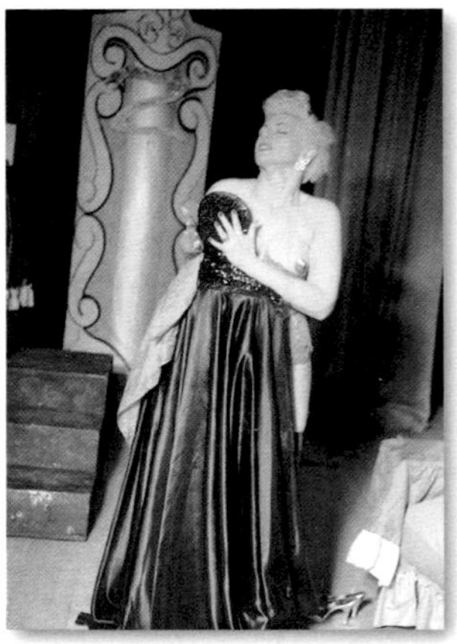
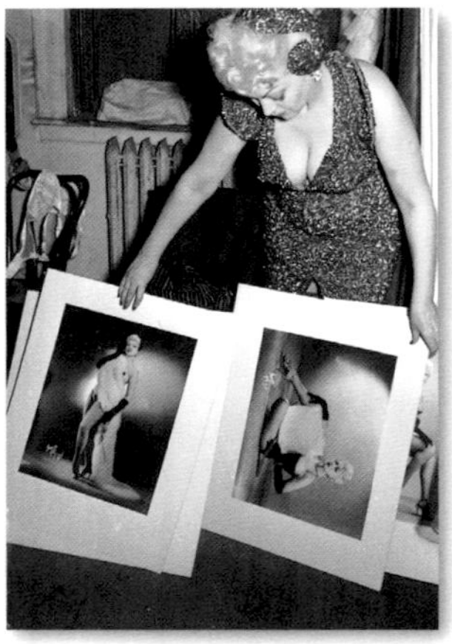
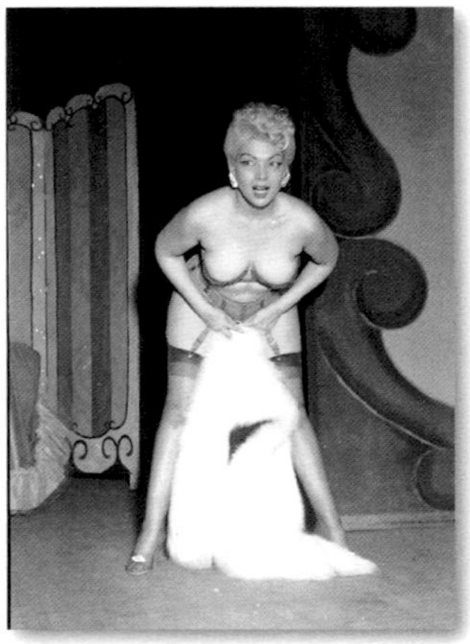
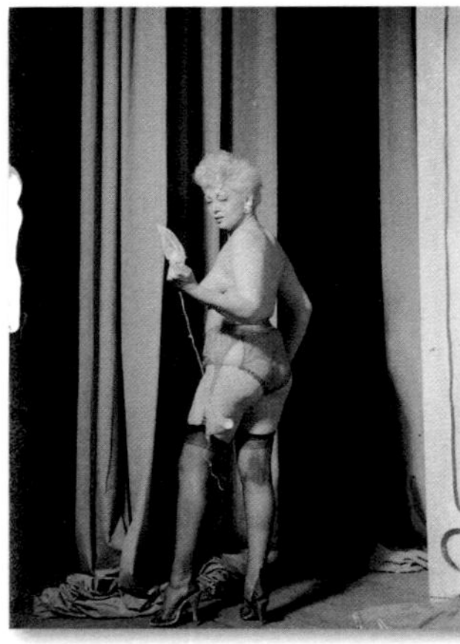
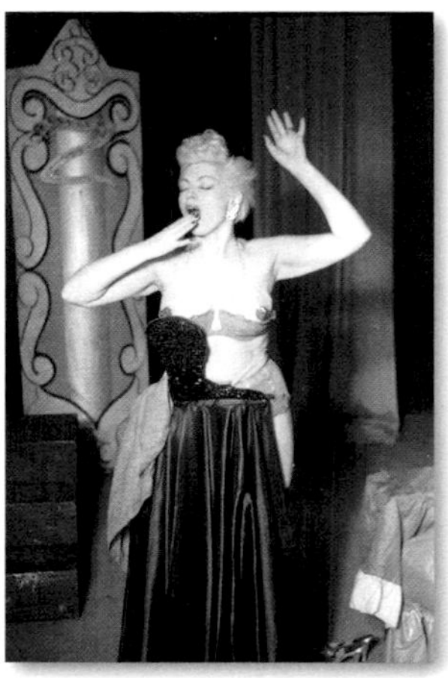
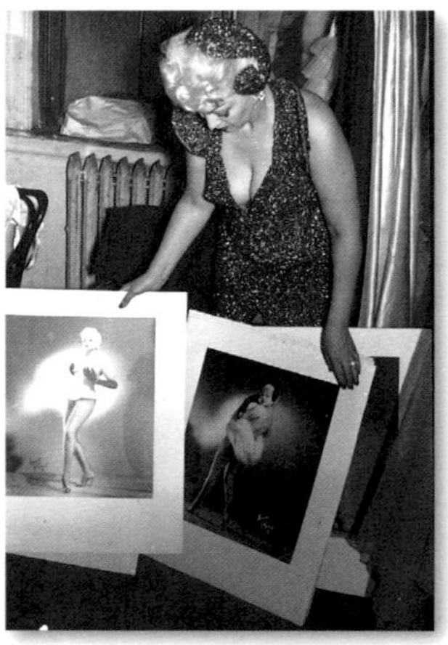
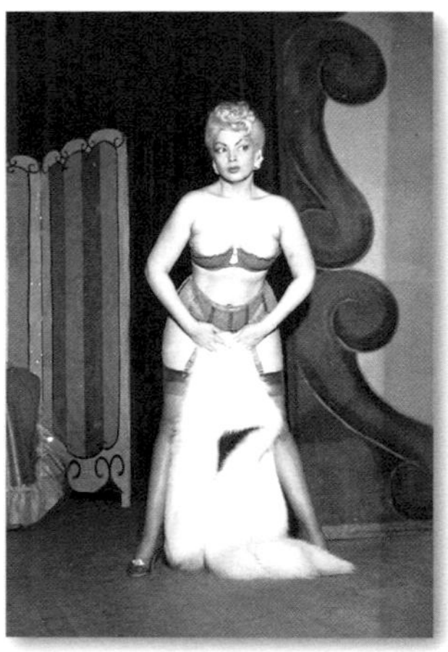
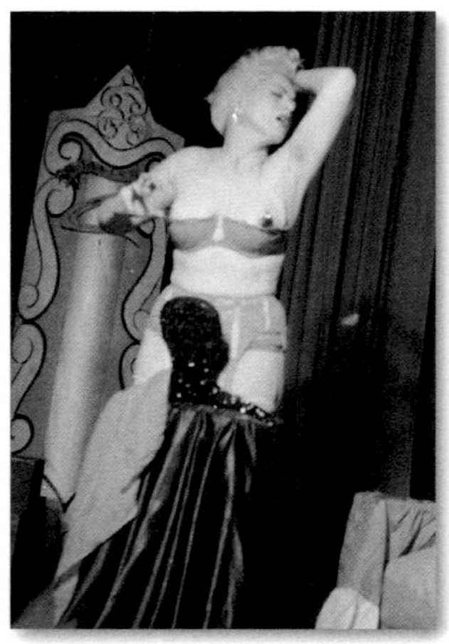
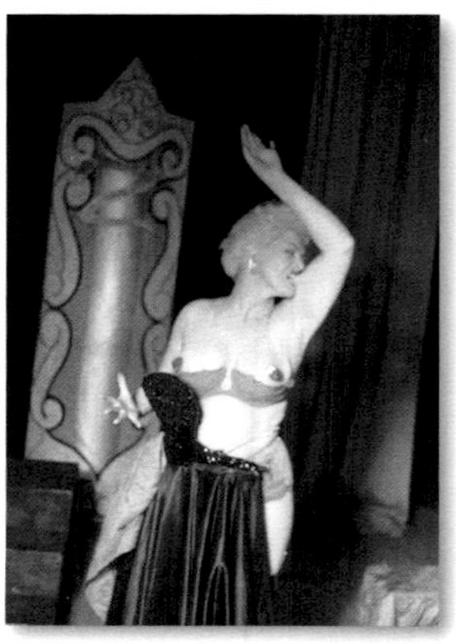
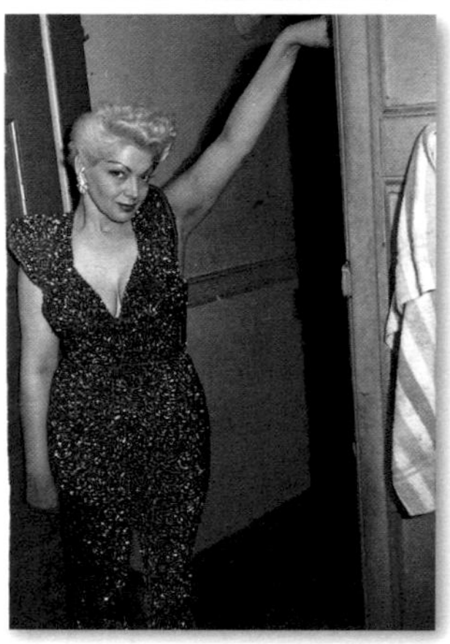
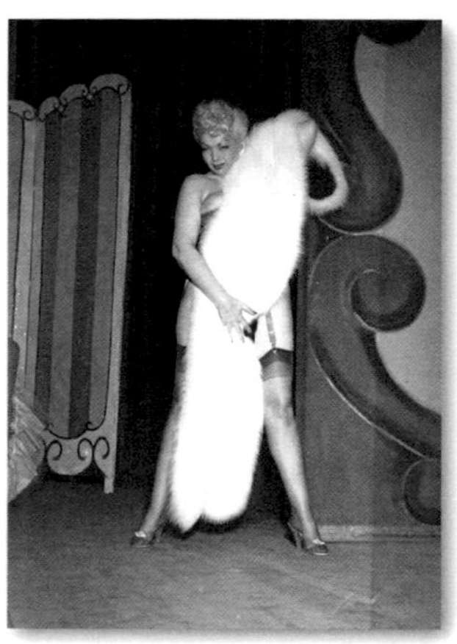
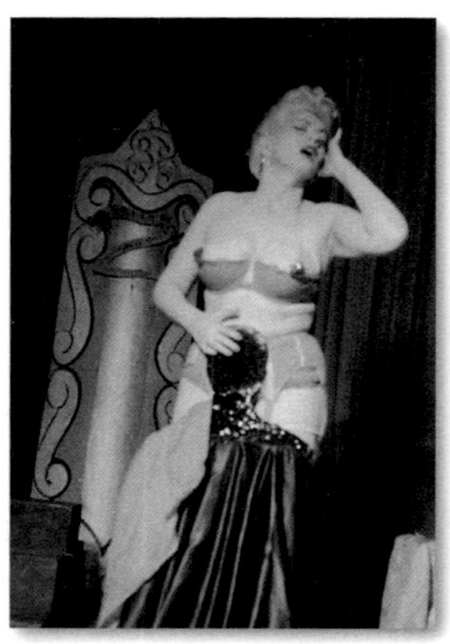

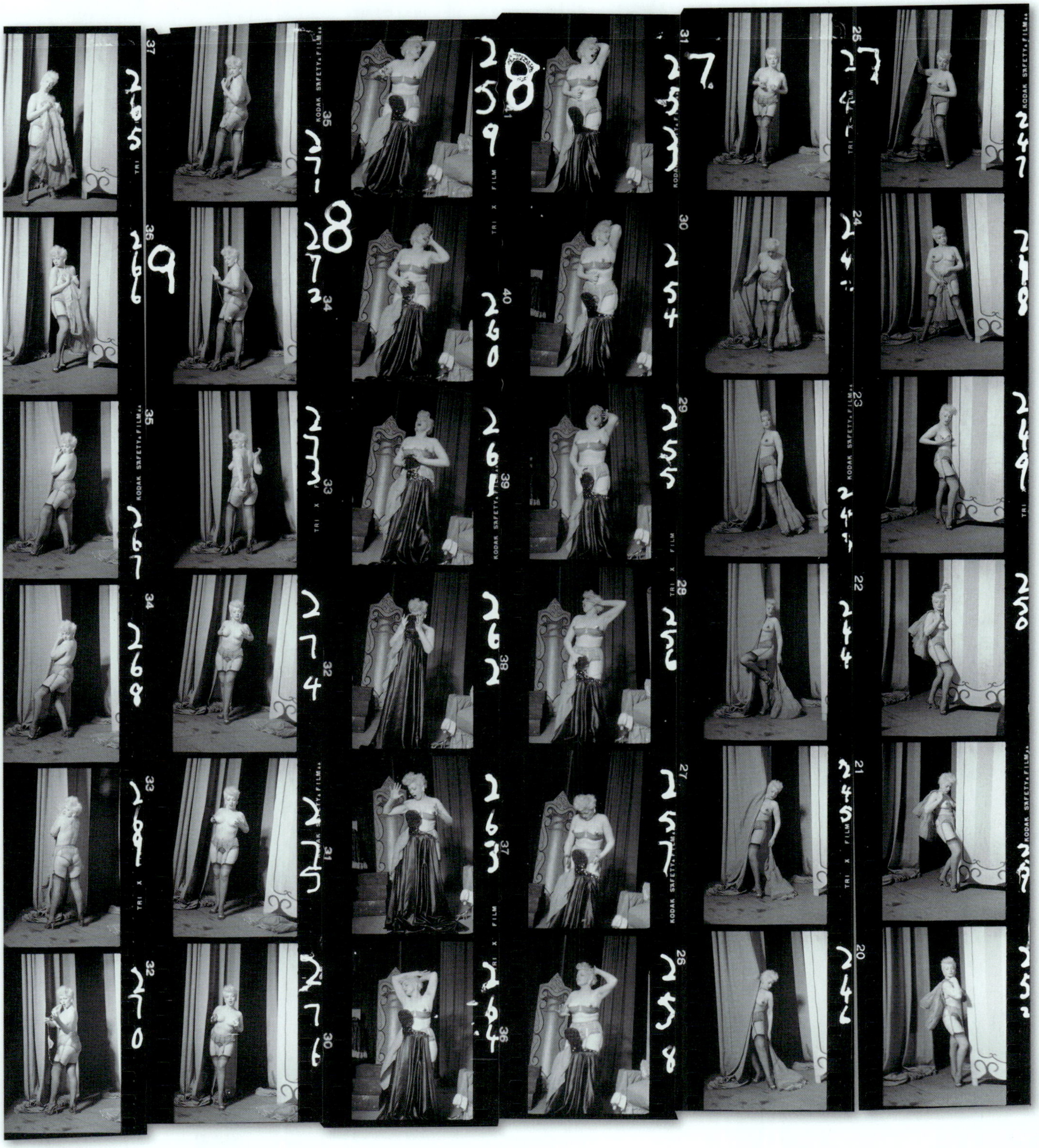

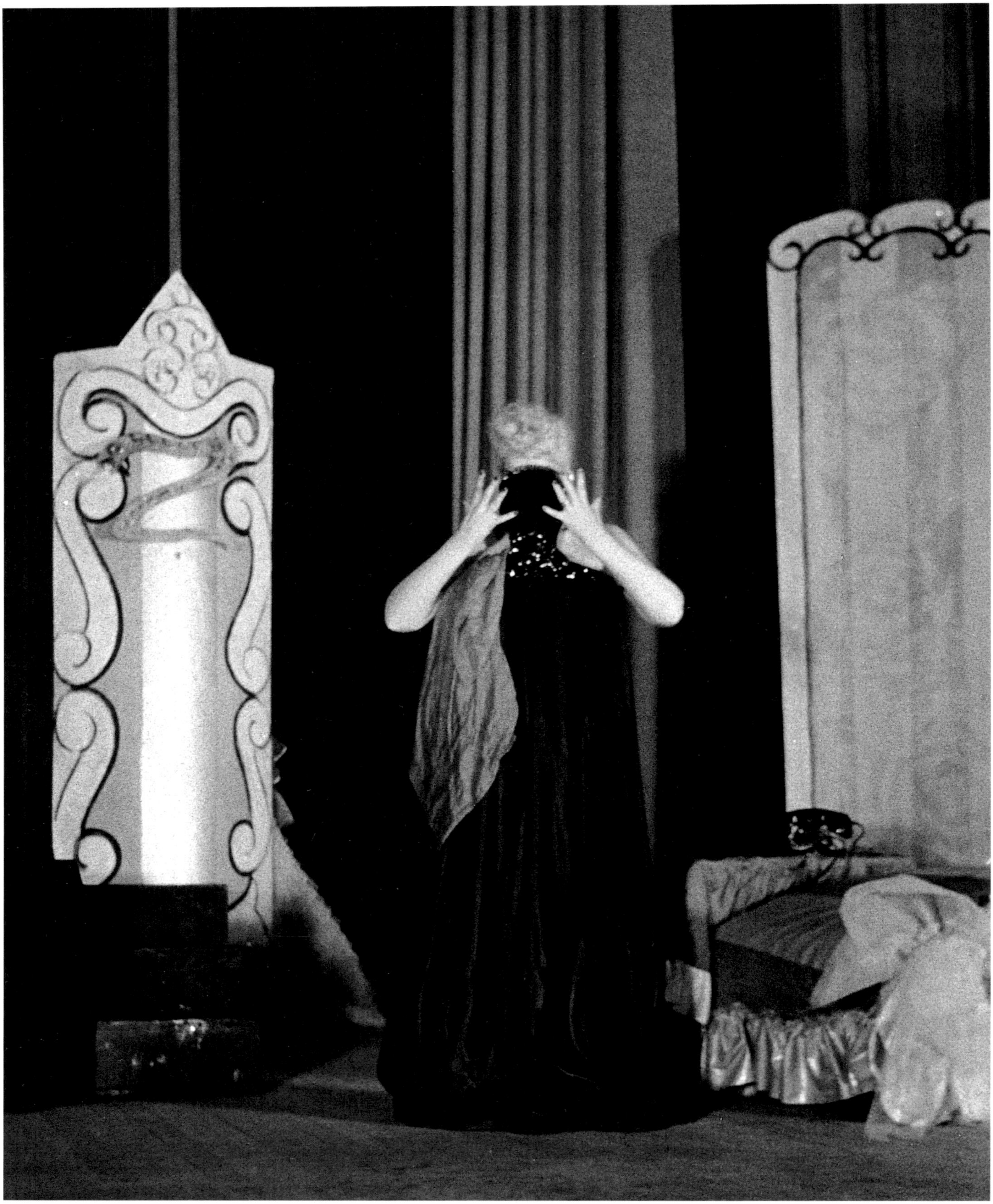

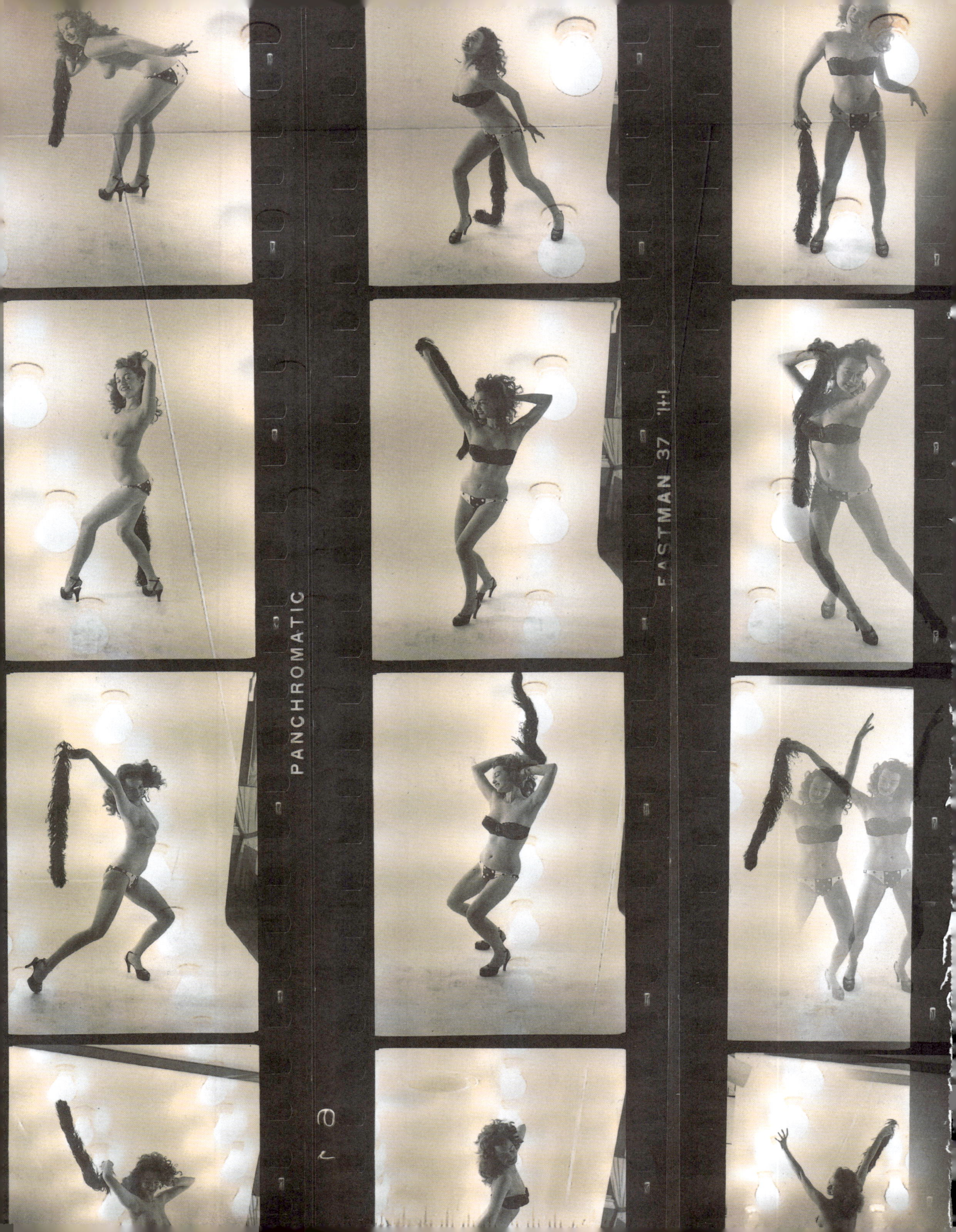
PANCHROMATIC
EASTMAN 37